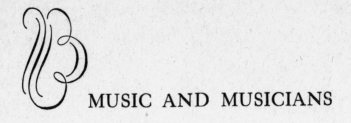

MUSIC AND MUSICIANS

These are Borzoi Books, published in New York by
ALFRED A. KNOPF

LETTERS OF COMPOSERS

AN ANTHOLOGY

1603—1945

Letters

OF

Composers

AN ANTHOLOGY
1603–1945

COMPILED AND EDITED BY
GERTRUDE NORMAN *AND*
MIRIAM LUBELL SHRIFTE

19 46

ALFRED A. KNOPF   *NEW YORK*

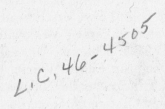

ACKNOWLEDGMENTS

WE WISH to express our appreciation to the following individuals and institutions to whom we are indebted for giving us access to special collections and archives, for making unpublished material available and for their helpful co-operation: Mr. Richard Angell of the Columbia University Music Library; Mr. Arthur V. Berger; Miss Helen Black of the U.S.S.R. Preslit Literary Agency; Miss Suzanne Bloch; Mr. Paul Bowles; Mr. Barnett Byman, Executive Secretary of the National Orchestral Association; Mr. Eric Clarke of the Metropolitan Opera Association; Mrs. Elizabeth Sprague Coolidge; Mrs. Virginia Cunningham; Dr. Walter Damrosch; Miss Helen Dower of the American Music Center; Embassy of the Union of Soviet Socialist Republics; Mr. Lehman Engel; Mr. Lukas Foss; Mrs. Anna Heifetz; Mr. Richard S. Hill; Dr. Jan Lowenbach, Musical Consultant of the Czechoslovak Information Service; Miss Ruza Magloff; Mr. George Middleton; Miss Paula Phillips; Mr. Howland H. Sargeant, Chief of the Division of Patent Administration, Office of Alien Property Custodian; Mrs. Alexandra Shiraeff; Mr. Nicolas Slonimsky; Dr. Harold Spivacke, Chief of the Music Division of the Library of Congress; the Staff of the Music Division of the New York Public Library; Mr. Joseph Szigeti; Dr. Bruno Walter; and Mr. Edward N. Waters.

For permission to print hitherto unpublished material we wish to thank: Mr. George Antheil; Sir Granville Bantock; Mr. Robert Russell Bennett; Mr. Ernest Bloch; Mr. Alfredo Casella; Mr. Mario Castelnuovo-Tedesco; Mr. Carlos Chávez; Mr. Aaron Copland; Mr. Henry Cowell; Mr. Paul Creston; Mr. David Diamond; Mr. Louis Gruenberg; Dr. Roy Harris; Colonel Jean d'Indy; Mr. Charles Ives; Mr. Ernst Krenek; Mr. Ernst Lévy; Mrs. Edward MacDowell; Mr. Douglas Moore; Mrs. Horatio Parker; Mr. Walter Piston; Mr. John Donald Robb; Mr. William Schuman; Mr. Randall Thompson; Mr. Virgil Thomson; and Mr. Edgard Varèse.

We acknowledge with thanks to the following individuals, offices, and companies permission to reprint excerpts from the published works listed below:

The Alien Property Custodian: Max Auer, *A. Bruckner: Gesammelte Briefe;* Else von Hase-Koehler, *Max Reger, Briefe*

[v]

eines deutschen Meisters. Copyright vested in the Alien Property Custodian, 1945, pursuant to law. Published by permission of the Alien Property Custodian in the public interest, under license number A-886.

Miss Emily Anderson, Macmillan & Co., Ltd., London, and The Macmillan Company, New York: Emily Anderson, *The Letters of Mozart and His Family.*

Edward Arnold & Co., London: Berthold Litzmann, *Letters of Clara Schumann and Johannes Brahms.*

Richard G. Badger, Boston, by permission of Chapman & Grimes, Inc., Boston: George Henschel, *Personal Recollections of Johannes Brahms.*

C. C. Birchard & Co., Boston: Rosa Newmarch, *Jean Sibelius.*

J. & W. Chester, Ltd., London: *On Inspiration,* from *The Chesterian* [1928].

J. & M. Dent & Sons, Ltd., London, and E. P. Dutton & Co., Inc., New York: Wilhelm Altmann, *Letters of Richard Wagner,* translated by M. M. Bozman.

Dodd, Mead & Company, Inc., New York: Henry T. Finck, *Grieg and His Music;* Lawrence Gilman, *Edward MacDowell.*

Gerald Duckworth & Co., Ltd., London, and the Liveright Publishing Corporation, New York: Elizabeth Foerster-Nietzsche, *The Nietzsche-Wagner Correspondence,* translated by Caroline V. Kerr.

Durand & Cie., Paris: Jacques Durand, *Lettres de Claude Debussy à son éditeur.*

Faber and Faber, Ltd., London: Otto Erich Deutsch, *Franz Schubert's Letters and Other Writings,* translated by Venetia Savile.

L. B. Fischer Publishing Corp., New York: Franz Werfel and Paul Stefan, *Verdi, the Man in His Letters,* translated by Edward Downes.

Dr. Howard Hanson: *New York Times,* August 11, 1935.

George G. Harrap & Co., Ltd., London, and J. B. Lippincott Co., Philadelphia: Giuseppe Adami, *Letters of Giacomo Puccini,* translated by Ena Makin.

Miss Imogen Holst and the Oxford University Press, London: Imogen Holst, *Gustav Holst.*

Hudební Matice Umelecké Besedy, Prague, by permission of J. & W. Chester, Ltd., London: *Hudební Revue,* Vol. III.

Alfred A. Knopf, Inc., New York: Paul England, *Correspondence between Richard Strauss and Hugo von Hofmannsthal.*

Mrs. Edward MacDowell: *Christian Science Monitor*, January 18, 1919.

Mrs. Alma Mahler-Werfel: Alma Maria Mahler, *Gustav Mahler Briefe*, and *Gustav Mahler, Erinnerungen und Briefe*.

Dr. Daniel Gregory Mason and The Macmillan Company, New York: Daniel Gregory Mason, *Music in My Time*.

New Masses, New York: *New Masses*, Vol. XLI, no. 4 (October 28, 1941).

The New York Public Library, depository of the Beethoven Association: Alexander Wheelock Thayer, *The Life of Ludwig van Beethoven*, edited and revised by Henry Edward Krehbiel.

W. W. Norton & Co., Inc., New York: Nicolas Slonimsky, *Music since 1900*.

The Oxford University Press, London: Charles Sanford Terry, *John Christian Bach*.

Pantheon Books Inc., New York: G. Selden-Goth, *Felix Mendelssohn Letters*. 1945.

M. Marc Pincherle: Marc Pincherle, *Musiciens peints par eux-mêmes*.

Preslit Literary Agency, Moscow: *Novyi Mir*, 1943, No. 4; *Russkaya Mysl*, September 1910; Modest Tchaikovsky, *Zhizn Petra Ilyicha Tchaikovskovo*.

La Revue Musicale, Paris: *La Revue Musicale*, Numéro Spécial "Ernest Chausson," December 1, 1925, and Numéro Spécial "Hommage à Maurice Ravel," December 1938.

G. Schirmer, Inc., New York: Gustave Reese, *A Birthday Offering to Carl Engel*. 1943.

R. N. Smyth, and Chapman & Hall, Ltd., London: Ethel Smyth, *Beecham and Pharaoh*.

Mr. Jean Sibelius, and Alfred A. Knopf, Inc., New York: Karl Ekman, *Jean Sibelius, His Life and Personality*.

Frederick Ungar Publishing Co., New York: Sophie Prombaum, *Richard Wagner and the Seamstress*.

NOTE

OCCASIONAL gaps in the material suitable for this book have made it necessary to omit certain composers who should properly be included here. Letters by earlier composers are extremely rare; those available by later well-known composers were sometimes not interesting enough to warrant their inclusion; and several contemporary composers preferred not to have their letters made public.

In making our selection from the material at hand, we have tried to give adequate representation to the most outstanding figures in the history of music, but our emphasis throughout has been on those composers who happened to write the most readable and informative letters.

To make the letters as complete and authentic as possible, our general practice has been to print letters in their entirety rather than in abridged versions. In the case of letters already existing in English translation, however, we have used the versions of former translators and editors, whether abridged or not. A few deletions were necessary in hitherto unpublished letters and letters translated specially for this book. Such deletions are indicated by the usual three points of omission.

Editorial comment has been limited to essential factual data. An account of the circumstances surrounding the writing of a letter has been provided only when the text required some elucidation.

The symbols S-1 to S-84 in the Contents refer to the "Sources" at the end of the book. Letters in S-81, S-82, S-83, and S-84 are published here for the first time so far as we have been able to ascertain. Approximately half of the letters included were translated specially for this book.

CONTENTS

---

1 See list of Sources, at end of book.
2 Letters thus marked were originally written in English.

LETTERS OF COMPOSERS

AN ANTHOLOGY

1603—1945

JAN PIETERS SWEELINCK

Amsterdam, 1562 — Amsterdam, 1621

❀❀❀❀❀❀❀❀

To the Burgomasters and Aldermen of *Amsterdam*
Amsterdam, March 30, 1603

Your Lordships:

So great is the correspondence between music and the soul that many, seeking out the essence of the latter, have thought it to be full of harmonious accords, to be, indeed, a pure harmony. All nature itself, to speak the truth, is nothing but a perfect music that the Creator causes to resound in the ears of man, to give him pleasure and to draw him gently to Himself. This we recognize at a glance in the excellent arrangement, the splendid proportions, and the orderly movements and revolutions of the celestial bodies. Therefore some have declared that the Firmament is the original Patron of Music and a true image of the elemental region, as can be observed in the number of elements and their four primary qualities and in the wondrous manner in which their opposites are reconciled.

This is the reason why the sages of ancient times, considering that each thing has the property of turning, moving, and inclining toward and in accordance with its like, made use of music not only to bring pleasure to the ear, but principally to move and moderate the emotions of the soul. They appropriated it for their oracles in order to gently instil yet firmly incorporate their doctrine into our minds, and thus, having awakened them, could raise them more easily to the contemplation and admiration of the divine. Orpheus among the pagans and David among the Hebrews made studies of these matters. The latter, truly inspired by the spirit of God, composed psalms, which he gave out to the master singers to be sounded on diverse instruments. His work has been preserved through the unwavering constancy of divine truth, but the work of these singers is unknown to us, owing to the ravages of time.

[3]

Having cast my eye on so excellent a subject, I set myself the task of reclothing these psalms in another music.[1] It is true that others before me have laboured at this, but as with human faces, there being no two that resemble each other in all respects, so is it with the conceptions and creations of the spirit. Therefore I am disposed to hope that my endeavour will not be rejected by those for whose use and delectation I have brought these psalms to light. Should they meet with your pleasure, I shall take occasion in due time, with God's grace, to bring forth the rest.

Meantime I take the liberty of presenting to Your Lordships these first fruits of my labour, not for the value of what they contain, or the merit of him who offers them, still less in the hope or desire of any emolument or advantage that might come to me. My purpose is partly to lend splendour to this my work by gracing it with the names of Your Lordships, and partly in acknowledgment of the close obligation that binds me to those whom I recognize to be the true fathers of my country, who have favoured me in many ways since the time of my youth and who, being students and amateurs of all the polite arts and skills, have placed me in the post that I have occupied for many years in this city.

I beseech Your Lordships to accept my labour in as good part as it is offered you, with a sincere heart, and in humble devotion.

Your Lordships' most humble and obedient servant,
JAN SWEELINCK

---

1 *Cinquante Pseaumes de David*, 1604.

CLAUDIO MONTEVERDI

Cremona, 1567 — Venice, 1643

⊙⥾⊙⥾⊙⥾⊙⥾⊙⥾⊙⥾⊙

To *Alessandro Striggio* [1]

Venice, December 9, 1616

My Most Illustrious Lord and Patron:

I have received from Signor Carlo de Torri your kind letter and the libretto of the sea-fable *Nozze di Tetide.* Your Lordship writes that you are sending it to me for me to peruse carefully and then give you my opinion on how it should be set to music to serve at the future marriage of His Most Serene Highness.[2] I desire nothing but to be of the greatest service to His Most Serene Highness; otherwise I would not say in the first reply that I promptly offer to fulfil his commands without objection and that I shall always most obediently honour and respect his wishes. Consequently, if His Most Serene Highness himself approve this libretto, then I would say that the fable is most beautiful and to my taste.

However, since you request my opinion — I shall obey the commands given me with all respect and promptness — understanding that my opinion is of slight importance coming from one who himself is worth little, and who honours all men of talent, in particular this poet whose name I do not know,[3] and the more so since poetry is not my profession, in respectful observance of your commands, I humbly give you my opinion.

First, in general, I say that the music should be mistress of the air and not only of the water. By this I mean that the melodies described in this fable are all heavy and low and cling close to the earth.

---

1 Librettist for Monteverdi's *Orfeo* and councillor to Duke Ferdinando da Gonzaga of Mantua. Monteverdi had been in the service of the Gonzaga family for over twenty years.

2 Duke Ferdinando da Gonzaga, who was to marry Catherine de' Medici.

3 Scipione Agnelli.

Thus there would be little opportunity for beautiful harmonies, which would be too low, and it would be difficult to hear and to perform them, but I leave this to your most cultivated and discriminating judgment. Because of this defect, instead of one lute there would need to be three, and instead of one harp three, and so on. Instead of a delicate singing voice there would have to be a strong, forced one.

Moreover, in order to express the speech correctly, in my opinion, the melody would have to be supported by brass instruments instead of delicate strings, for it seems to me that the songs of Triton and the other sea gods call for trumpets and cornets, not harps, lutes, and cembali. This is a sea-story and therefore it takes place outside of the city, yet does not Plato write that the lute should be used for the city and the flute for the country (*cithara debet esse in civitate et thibia in agris*)? So either the delicate will not be appropriate or the appropriate will not be delicate.

Then I have studied the list of characters: Winds, Little Loves, Little Zephyrs, Sirens, which would require many soprano voices. Further I note that the Winds — that is, the northern and western Winds — also have to sing. But how, dear sir, can I ever imitate the speech of winds when they do not speak! And in this way how should I ever be able to move the emotions?

Arianna was moving because she was a woman, and Orfeo [4] because he was a man, not a wind. Melodies represent people and not the noises of winds, nor the bleating of sheep, nor the neighing of horses, and they do not imitate the language of winds when this does not exist.

Also the ballets scattered through this libretto lack the proper dance rhythm. The entire fable does not move me at all, and, in accordance with my great ignorance, I do not think it ever will. I do not believe that it proceeds with any naturalness to a suitable ending, and I have great difficulty in understanding it at all. Arianna moved me to a true lament; Orfeo to a prayer; but what kind of music this requires, I cannot possibly imagine. What does Your Lordship wish this music to convey? But I shall always most dutifully and respectfully carry out the commands of His Most Serene Highness, and if it be commanded that I set this libretto to music, I shall do so. Yet considering that there are gods who speak in this piece, I should prefer to hear these gods speak with grace.

Concerning the Sirens, I believe that the three sisters, Signora

4 *Orfeo,* 1607; *Arianna,* 1608.

Adrianna [5] and the others, could sing these roles and compose them as well. Likewise Signor Rasi and Signor D. Francesco their parts. In this we should be following the example of Cardinal Montalto, who wrote a comedy in which each character wrote his own part. Now, if this were a work that developed toward only one ending, as was the case in *Arianna* and *Orfeo*, it would have to be composed by one person; there it was a question of speaking in song, but here it is singing in speech. All the speaking parts are too long, and there are several other considerations.

I beg forgiveness, dear sir, if I have said too much. It is not to find fault, but because I desire to carry out your commands, and if I have to set this to music, Your Lordship will know my way of thinking.

I most humbly and respectfully pay reverence to His Most Serene Highness, and I humbly kiss Your Lordship's hand and pray God for your felicity. I wish you a happy holiday. Your Lordship's most humble and obedient servant,

CLAUDIO MONTEVERDI

To *Alessandro Striggio*

Venice, May 7, 1627

Most Illustrious Lord and Revered Patron:

In accordance with the instructions in your most kind letter, I am sending you *La Finta Pazza Licori* by Signor Strozzi. It has not yet been set to music, or published, or presented on the stage, for as soon as the author had completed it, he gave it to me himself. The copy I am sending you is in his own hand. If the said Giulio [Strozzi] learns that it meets with the approval of His Most Serene Highness,[6] I am certain that he will put it in order with the greatest zeal and celerity, divided into three acts, or in any manner His Most Serene Highness may desire.

He wishes especially that I write the music for this, and I should, indeed, be delighted to see this worthy work adorned by my poor music, for in both beauty of poetry and novelty of invention I have found this work to be very fine and adaptable. Therefore, Your Lordship, if this work is to your pleasure, pay no atten-

5 Adrianna Basile, who had the leading part in his *Arianna*, and her two sisters.
6 Duke Vincenzo da Gonzaga of Mantua.

tion to its present form, since I know that the author will revise it
to your complete satisfaction in a very short time.

The plan and its development are not bad; it is true that the
role of Licori, since it contains a great deal of variety, should be
played by no one but a woman who can appear sometimes as a man,
sometimes as a woman, with lively gestures and varied emotions, for
the portrayal of this woman who feigns madness should have but
one consideration — the present, not the past nor the future. The
characterization of this role should appear in every word she utters,
not only in the general meaning of the phrase. When she speaks of
war, war should be heard in the music; when of peace, then the
music must convey peace; when of death, then death must be expressed. The changes should take place very suddenly, and the person who plays this role, which moves us now to laughter, now to
compassion, will have to relinquish any interpretation other than the
one indicated in the words she has to speak. I believe that no one but
Signora Margherita [7] will be able to interpret this noteworthily. I
am certain that this opera will be one of my most important works.[8]

I am sending you also *Narciso* by Signor Ottavio Rinuccini; [9]
it has not yet been published, or set to music, or presented on the
stage. This gentleman when he was alive — with all my heart I pray
he may now be in heaven — gave me this copy himself. He loved
this work of his and hoped I might set it to music. I have read it many
times and have somewhat digested it, but to confess the truth, Your
Lordship, it seems to me to lack the vigour I wish it had. The large
number of sopranos required to act the nymphs, and the many tenors
to act the shepherds and other characters, would make for little
variety; besides, it is sad and gloomy.

Yet I did not want to fail to send it to Your Lordship for you
to peruse it and pronounce your esteemed opinion. I have no other
copy of these two manuscripts I am sending you, and I should be
most grateful if Your Lordship, after reading them, would return
them so that I can consider them in accordance with my interest and
your opinion of them.

In humble reverence, awaiting the desired commands of Your
Illustrious Lordship, I pray God for your happiness.

Your Lordship's most humble and obedient servant,
CLAUDIO MONTEVERDI

---

7 Margherita Basile.
8 Completed in 1627.
9 Opera librettist for several composers of the period (d. 1621).

To an unknown recipient

Venice, October 22, 1633

Most Illustrious Lord, Your Reverence:

Together with a letter sent me from Padua by the illustrious Signor Vescovo, my esteemed patron, was another one addressed to me by Your Reverence, rich in praise and honour toward my poor person. I was somewhat surprised, but later reflected that from a plant as gentle and virtuous as yourself there could spring no other fruit but of the same nature, and the praise you lavished on me I attributed to those excellent qualities of Your Reverence, who knows me as a growing plant, but not one that gives off any special fragrance. In reply to your most generous and flattering letter, will you accept my gratitude and pleasure and receive me as your most humble servant?

Monsignor the Bishop of San Marco was kind enough to tell me of Your Reverence's noble qualities and rare virtues and he informed me that you were writing a book on music. May I add that I, too, was writing one, but I fear, because of my feeble health, that I may not be able to reach the end. Since I was in the service of the most illustrious Signor Vescovo of Padua, I believe that is the way in which Your Reverence learned of my writing, for I know no other way you may have learned of it. As you have deigned to praise me, I beg you to hear the rest also.

Let it be known, then, that it is true I am writing, but under great strain, because the event that many years ago provoked me to do so was of such a nature as to compel me to continue. At that time I did not perceive that I had promised something to the world that later I should not have the strength to fulfil. Namely, I had promised to make known in print to a certain theorist of the *Prima Pratica* [10] that there existed another method of treating the subject of harmony, which was unknown to him, and which I call the *Seconda Pratica*. The reason was that he took it into his head to publish a criticism of the harmony in some passages of my madrigals. His criticism was founded on the rules of the *Prima Pratica* or the traditional rules. He said this might have been written by a child who was just beginning the study of counterpoint, and that it was not in accordance with our rules of melody. But when he learned of a

---

10 G. M. Artusi (1562–1613), a canon at Bologna and theorist. His *Imperfections of Modern Music* (1600) strongly assailed the new school of madrigalists.

certain refutation published by my brother in my defence,[11] he was silenced to the point where he not only refrained from criticizing me, but even turned his pen in praise of me and began to like and esteem me. However, the great interest aroused as a result of my public promise has compelled me to keep it, and I am obliged to pay my debt. I beg you to excuse my boldness.

The title of the book will be *Melodia, ovvero Seconda Pratica.* By *seconda*, I mean in conformity with current usage; by *prima*, I mean in accordance with the old practice. The book will be divided into three parts corresponding to the three parts of composition. In the first part, I discuss the text; in the second, harmony; and in the third, rhythm. I hope that my work will meet with general approbation.

I put my ideas into practice when I wrote the lament of Arianna. I found no book that showed me the natural way of imitating the emotions; still less, one that could teach me in what imitation should consist, except for Plato, whose meaning was so hidden that I was barely able to see with my poor vision the little that was shown me. I have proved how difficult it is merely to carry out the little imitation I have done, and for this reason I hope that my work will meet with success, for I would sooner be praised little for writing of the new than praised much for writing of the ordinary. I again ask forgiveness for my boldness.

How happy I was to learn that a new instrument has been invented in our time! [12] I pray God for the happiness of its inventor — Your Most Reverend person. In truth, I have thought much and frequently upon the reasons for its discovery, and on the reason why antiquity developed so many different instruments, not only the many in use now, but also those which have been lost and are recorded by theorists of our time and those whose profession it is to have a thorough knowledge of our art. I hope to say something on this subject in my book which perhaps will not displease you.

From my account Your Reverence will be able to understand how pleased I should be to accept the kind offer you have proposed — to honour me with a copy of such worthy matter, containing so much knowledge and discovery. Therefore I beg you to fulfil your

11 Giulio Monteverdi in the preface to Monteverdi's *Scherzi Musicali* (1607).

12 It is not known what instrument is referred to. In the first part of the seventeenth century, the interest in new means of expression and colour stimulated experimentation with and invention of many new instruments, especially of the violin family.

most kind and generous offer, and I beg you to consider me your most humble and obliged servant. I affectionately pay you my humble respects and kiss your honoured hand.

Your Reverence's most devoted and obliged servant,
CLAUDIO MONTEVERDI

HEINRICH SCHÜTZ

Köstritz, 1585 — *Dresden,* 1672

❖❖❖❖❖❖❖❖❖❖

To *Wilhelm Ludwig Moser*

December 30, 1624

Honourable, most learned, and gracious Sir:

Since you desire my personal report and opinions on the music [1] sent you by Samuel Scheidt, Kapellmeister at Halle, I wish to assure you of my constant readiness to serve you. These works (two folio books bound in tawed leather with gilt-edged boards and variegated edges, each book about three fingers thick) are pieces for the organ composed in the Scheidt style and that of the Netherlanders, and they are most pleasing to the ear. The first of these two volumes is dedicated with a special preface to our gracious Lord and Elector.

Further, kind sir, you will probably recall that the said Samuel Scheidt some time ago sent in two other works, the manuscripts of which were nearly lost by one of the boys when I, some time ago, came to pay my respects. But these compositions were not dedicated to our gracious Lord and merely presented to him. They are still in existence, but thus far have not been catalogued since no remuneration has yet been received for them.

In view of this dedication, it is my humble belief that our gracious Lord and Elector should come to terms with him once and for all and grant him some recompense. I venture the opinion since you, dear sir, chose to request it, that 30 to 35 taler would be sufficient. Or, if our gracious Lord so chooses, I believe that 20 taler together with a portrait of His Grace, since part of the work is dedicated to him, would be in keeping with the generous reputation of our gracious Lord.

Of course it remains my most gracious Lord's pleasure and

---

1 The first two volumes of Scheidt's *Tablatura Nova.*

yours, kind sir, to accept my suggestion or to reject it. Commending you to God's protection, I am,

> Your obedient servant,
> HEINRICH SCHÜTZ

❂❂❂❂❂❂❂❂

To the Elector *Johann Georg I of Saxony* [2]

> *Venice*, November 3, 1628

Most gracious and illustrious Elector:

My earnest wish, while offering Your Lordship my humble and obedient services to the utmost of my ability, is that God may grant you the greatest happiness of body and soul.

As is the bounden duty of a subject, most gracious Lord, I do not neglect to notify you hereby that after obtaining your kind permission, I left Dresden on my projected journey to Italy. Because of the blocked passes in Germany and especially along the Venetian border, however, I was unable to reach Venice until a few days ago. I entertain the confident hope, Your Lordship, that with the help of God this journey will widen my experience and help me in various ways in my humble profession.

None the less it is my fervent desire and profound hope that Your Lordship will not regard my absence with disfavour, nor permit anyone to apply for or take the office that I have thus far filled to the best of my humble ability. I hope, on the contrary, that it will remain unfilled until my return, which will be started without delay obedient to my Lord's commands, except for an act of Providence.

Furthermore, my gracious Lord and Elector, I have every reason to express to you my humble gratitude for granting permission to continue my regular salary even in my absence. While I was able to start my journey with these means and to continue it thus far, it will be very difficult and arduous to carry this project further at my own expense, considering the fact that the journey at present is in its tenth week and has already been rather costly.

Further resources will be needed also for the purchase of many new and beautiful musical works, for I feel that since I came here the first time,[3] compositions have changed a great deal. The music

---

2 Schütz's patron.
3 Schütz had visited Venice previously during 1608–12.

suitable at court for dinner, ballets, comedies, and the like, has improved and increased a great deal. Consequently I feel justified in humbly begging Your Lordship (blessed as you are by God's bounty, it would seem but a trifle) to permit me, Your Lordship's most humble and faithful servant, to have an additional grant and accordingly order it added to the draft.

May I assure Your Lordship again with due devotion that my task here aims at nothing but an increase in Your Lordship's fame, and to qualify myself the better to render you my most humble service. In future, so long as God grants me life, I shall show my gratitude more by deed and constant attention to your wishes than now by this flow of words. I shall always attest this by applying myself to the best of my ability. Commending myself (especially now, sojourning abroad) in this most important matter to my Lord's gracious and favourable consideration, and begging God's holy protection for Your Lordship and Electoral house, I remain Your Lordship's most humble and obedient servant,

H. S.

❁❁❁❁❁❁❁

To *Christian Reichbrodt* [4]

Dresden, May 28, 1652

Esteemed Sir:

For three weeks now I have been unable to leave the house because of a bad cold that first bothered my head and finally, if you will pardon the reference, has gone to my legs and developed into erysipelas. Otherwise I would have called on you long ago. But now I can no longer conceal from you that the bass singer who some time ago had to pawn his clothes again, and ever since has been living at his house like a wild beast of the woods, has informed me through his wife that he now must and wishes to leave us.

I do not wish to trouble my gracious Lord with that man's affairs nor presume to influence his decisions, but I leave it to your discretion whether you could procure something for him from our kind patron. In any case, I did not want to neglect notifying him so that if the bass sneaks away on French leave — as I surely think he will — nothing will be held against me, and my gracious Lord and his marshal will have evidence that I have already informed them.

---

4 Privy Secretary to the Elector of Saxony, Schütz's patron.

It is a real pity, though, to lose such an exquisite voice in the choir. What does it matter if in other respects he is a good-for-nothing and that he must cleanse his throat daily with a keg of wine? Naturally such a wide throat needs more moistening than a narrow one. Even if the good fellow were to get his meagre salary right away, it would still not suffice for great banquets. Considering this fellow's housekeeping and management in the proper light, I think one ought to give him his pittance on time. And as long as even that is not done, one surely cannot call him a spendthrift. So far as I am concerned, there the matter ends.

Friedrich Selge and his sons are leaving too, I hear. I should like to talk personally with my most gracious Lord and disclose to him my few ideas about the Electoral *Collegio Musico*, which apparently is almost moribund.

I remain as ever, respected sir,

Your obedient servant,
HEINRICH SCHÜTZ

SAMUEL SCHEIDT

Halle, 1587 — Halle, 1654

✠✠✠✠✠✠✠✠

To Duke *August* of *Brunswick*

Halle, June 19, 1642

Most Serene Highness, Most Esteemed Prince and Lord:

From my
youth until my present age I have composed many motets, concertos for singing, and all sorts of pieces to be played on instruments
alone, such as canzonas, pavans, galliards, courantes, and similar
things, as well as tablatures for the organ.

Now, however, I have taken it upon myself to compose some
spiritual songs for five voices in the manner of a madrigal, a particularly beautiful kind of style, so that when there are five singers present and an organ or instrument of that nature is lacking, these can
be sung without instruments. And when an organ and instrumentalists are at hand, if it is so desired, they can play along very appro-
priately and conveniently. Another beautiful sort of style is to play
a symphony on the instruments, as a sort of prelude, just before the
concerto, motet, or spiritual madrigal. Thus I have composed a considerable number of symphonies in various styles in all the customary keys and clefs, ten in each key, so that when a song is performed
very frequently, it will cause no regret.

Since I do not desire to have these symphonies appear in print,
whereby they would become common, I have made bold to dedicate
them, together with some spiritual madrigals, to Your Lordship for
your court chapel, and I entertain the most humble hope that Your
Serene Highness will accept and receive my poor work and effort
with goodwill, and that you will judge it according to my most
humble intention rather than for the work itself, and that henceforth
you will remain my most gracious Prince and Lord. And should
these new spiritual madrigals meet with your approval and acceptance, in future I shall send more of the same to your Kapellmeister,

[16]

for I am labouring at them daily, and so, if it please God to grant me life, I hope to assemble over a hundred of them very shortly, even before next winter.

I pray Almighty God to grant Your Serene Highness an auspicious reign and all general welfare; commending myself and mine to your kind favour, with utmost devotion,

Your Serene Highness's most humble and obedient servant,

SAMUEL SCHEIDT
Kapellmeister

❀❀❀❀❀❀

To *Heinrich Baryphonus* [1]

Halle, January 26, 1651

I am astonished at the foolish music written in these times. It is false and wrong and no longer does anyone pay attention to what our beloved old masters wrote about composition. It certainly must be a remarkably elevated art when a pile of consonances are thrown together any which way.

I remain faithful to the pure old composition and pure rules. I have often walked out of the church since I could no longer listen to that mountain yodelling. I hope this worthless modern coinage will fall into disuse and that new coins will be forged according to the fine old stamp and standard.

[SAMUEL SCHEIDT]

---

1 Composer and theorist (1581–1655).

JEAN PHILIPPE RAMEAU

Dijon, 1683 — Paris, 1764

❂❂❂❂❂❂❂❂❂

To *Houdart de la Motte* [1]

Paris, October 25, 1727

Sir:

Permit me to refute whatever reasons you may have for not expecting from my theatre music a success as favourable as that of a
composer seemingly more experienced in this branch of composition. At the same time I should like to justify my natural bias in my
own favour without pretending to use my knowledge to greater advantage than you yourself would feel to be legitimate.

A learned musician is generally understood to be a man who
understands everything about the various combinations of sounds.
At the same time, however, he is so engrossed in these combinations
that he sacrifices everything: good sense, feeling, imagination, and
reason. Such a musician is an academician, of a school that is concerned with notes alone and nothing further, so that we are right
to prefer to him a musician who prides himself less on learning than
on taste.

The latter, however, whose taste is limited by the range of his
sensations alone, can excel only in certain types of music that are
natural to his character. If he is naturally tender, he will express
tenderness. If his temperament is witty, lively, playful, his music
will correspond accordingly. Moreover, since he draws on his imagination for everything, without the assistance of art, by this means
of expression he soon burns himself out. In his first fire he was all
brilliance, but this fire consumes itself as he tries to rekindle it, and
nothing remains but banality and repetitions.

---

1 At this time Rameau enjoyed considerable reputation as a theorist and now
wished to compose an opera. He requested a libretto from the poet Houdart
de la Motte, who, however, refused to collaborate. Rameau's reply follows.

Therefore we should like to find for the theatre a musician who would study nature before painting it; not only his taste, then, but his learning and judgment would enable him to select the colouring and shading appropriate to the desired expression. Now, I am far from believing that I am such a musician, but at least I have a better knowledge of colouring and shading than some others who have but a confused idea of these matters and use it in haphazard fashion. They have taste and imagination, but all of this is confined to the reservoir of their sensations, which makes for very limited variety, and beyond this they perceive nothing.

Nature has not completely deprived me of her gifts and I have not surrendered myself to mere combinations of notes so far as to forget their intimate relationship with that beautiful Nature which by itself suffices to give pleaure. But one does not find it in unsown or, worse, barren soil.

Acquaint yourself with the reputation of my two cantatas, which I wrote some dozen years ago; the manuscripts are so well known throughout France that I have not thought it necessary to have them published (especially since I would have to do so at my own expense), unless I could add some other cantatas to go with them. But I cannot do this for lack of texts. One of them is entitled *Enlèvement d'Orithie;* it includes a recitative and the customary arias. The other is *Thétis* where you may remark the gradations in degree of anger I allotted to Neptune and to Jupiter according to whether it seemed right to impart more emotion or more composure to one or the other, and according to the arrangements for carrying out the orders of each.

You need only come and hear how I characterized the singing and dancing of the savages who performed at the Italian Theatre a year or two ago,[2] and also how I have interpreted these titles: *Sighs, Tender Complaints, Cyclops, Whirlpools* (the whirlpools of dust stirred up by strong winds), *Conversation of the Muses, Musette, Tambourine,* and so on.

You will recognize that I am no novice in the art and that it does not appear that I make any great outlay of my knowledge in my productions because I seek to conceal art by art itself. For in this I have in mind only the people of taste and never the academicians, since there are many of the latter and not enough of the former. I could also have you hear some motets for large chorus in which you

---

2 Two Indians who had recently come from Louisiana appeared in war dances there in September 1725.

would see whether I really feel what I wish to express. Indeed, there is sufficient for your consideration.

I am, with all possible esteem, your very humble and obedient servant,

RAMEAU

◘▸◖▸◖▸◖▸◖▸◖

To *A. M. Beguillet*

Paris, October 6, 1762

Sir:

The ancient writers and their disciples filled us with idle fancies which we have difficulty in returning to when we attempt, without a thorough examination, to relate them to what has been written. The ear and the emotions were capable of providing these ancients with agreeable and expressive tunes, but their entire practice was based only on effects without knowledge of their causes, which I have finally developed.

They found the relationships between sounds in divinely inspired order; they discoursed a great deal on that subject, and every reason they were able to advance evaporated like a wisp of smoke. Finally the geometricians and the philosophers became disheartened. Can it be true that up to the present time man has always been so enthralled by this single inspiration that it never occurred to anyone to seek the reason why, despite ourselves, we should be compelled to prefer certain intervals to others after certain sounds, especially after the first sound? Allow your natural feelings to operate in yourself with no preconceived expectation and then try to see if you can ever ascend a semitone after a given semitone, and whether you can do the same thing after two successive tones. Why was this suggested to me in this way? Whence this sensation? What could have given rise to this sensation in me, if it was not the moment itself? It was necessary to test the effect of the sound, and from it three sounds would have been distinguished which form that enchanting harmony, and therefrom one would have proceeded with certainty, as I believe I have done.

The principle is inexhaustible and holds true for theology as well as geometry and physics. Anyone more enlightened than myself should be able to draw the most far-reaching conclusions from this and already I can envision the origin of that final knowledge which cannot be denied without denying the phenomenon from which it is derived.

[JEAN PHILIPPE RAMEAU]

GEORGE FRIDERIC HANDEL

Halle, 1685 — London, 1759

✿✿✿✿✿✿✿✿✿

To *Johann Mattheson*

London, February 24, 1719

Sir:

From your letter dated the 21st inst., which I received today, I realize that I am so greatly obliged to satisfy you more particularly than I have done in my preceding letters, on the two points in question, that I can only state that my opinion agrees in general with what you have so well deduced and demonstrated in your book [1] with regard to solmization and the Greek modes.

I believe the question can be reduced to this: whether one should prefer an easy and more perfect method to another which is accompanied by great difficulties capable not only of disgusting pupils with music, but also of wasting precious time that could be better utilized in probing more deeply into this art and in developing one's talent.

It is not that I should like to declare that one can draw no benefit from solmization, but since one can acquire the same knowledge in much less time by the method used so successfully at present, I do not see why one should not take the road that leads more rapidly and easily to the desired end.

As regards the Greek modes, I find, sir, that you have said all there is to say on this subject. No doubt knowledge of them is necessary to those who would study and play ancient music which was composed according to these modes, but since we have freed ourselves from the narrow limits of ancient music, I do not see what use can be made of the Greek modes in modern music. These, sir, are my opinions, and you would oblige me if you would let me know whether they correspond to what you wished me to give you.

As for the second point, you can judge for yourself that it re-

---

1 *Das beschützte Orchestre* (Hamburg, 1717).

quires a great deal of concentration, which I cannot give to it at present, having some urgent business to take care of. As soon as I have more time I shall go over the principal periods in my professional life, to show you the esteem and particular consideration with which I have the honour to be, sir,

Your most humble and obedient servant,

G. F. HANDEL

❀❀❀❀❀❀❀❀❀

To *Charles Jennens, Jr.*[2]

Dublin, December 29, 1741

Sir,

it was with the greatest Pleasure I saw the continuation of Your kindness by the Lines you was pleased to send me, in order to be prefixed to Your Oratorio *Messiah*,[3] which I set to Musick before I left England. I am emboldened, Sir, by the generous Concern You please to take in relation to my affairs, to give you an account to the Success I have met here. The Nobility did me the Honour to make amongst themselves a Subscription for 6 Nights, which did fill a Room of 600 Persons. so that I needed not sell one single Ticket at the Door. and without Vanity the Performance was received with a general Approbation.

Signora Avolio, which I brought with me from London pleases extraordinary. I have formed an other Tenor Voice which gives great satisfaction, the Basses and Counter Tenors are very good, and the rest of the Chorus Singers (by my Direction) do exceeding well, as for the Instruments they are really excellent. Mr. Dubourgh being at the Head of them, and the Musick sounds delightfully in this charming Room, which puts me in such such spirits (and my Health being so good) that I exert my self on my Organ with more than usual success. I opened with the *Allegro, Penseroso, & Moderato*, and I assure you that the Words of the Moderato are vastly admired. the Audience being composed (besides the Flower of Ladyes of Distinction and other People of the greatest quality) of so many Bishops, Deans, Heads of the Colledge, the most eminent People in the Law as the Chancellor, Auditor General, etc. all which

---

2 Librettist for Handel's *Messiah*, and *L'Allegro, il Penseroso ed il Moderato*.

3 Invited to visit Ireland, Handel wrote *The Messiah*, he declared, to "offer that generous nation something new." First performance, April 13, 1742, in Dublin.

are very much taken with the Poetry. So that I am desired to perform it again the next time.

I cannot sufficiently express the kind treatment I receive here, but the Politeness of this generous Nation can not be unknown to You, so I let you judge of the satisfaction I enjoy, passing my time with Honnour, profit and pleasure.

They propose already to have some more Performances when the 6 Nights of the Subscription are over, and My Lord Duc the Lord Lieutenant (who is allways present with all His Family on those nights) will easily obtain a longer Permission for me by His Majesty, so that I shall be obliged to make my stay here longer than I thought. One request I must make to you, which is that you would insinuate my most devoted Respects to My Lord and My Lady Shaftesbury. You know how much Their kind Protection is precious to me. Sir Windham Knatchbull will find here my respectfull compliments. You will encrease my obligations if by occasion you will present my humble service to some other Patrons and friends of mine. I expect with Impatience the Favour of your news, concerning Your Health and wellfare, of which I take a real share.

as far for the News of your opera's,[4] I need not trouble you for all this Town is full of their ill success, by a number of Letters from your quarters to the People of quality here, an I can't help saying but that it furnishes great Diversion and laughter. The first Opera[5] I heard my self before I left London, and it made me merry all along my journey, and of the second Opera call'd *Penelope*,[6] a certain noble man writes very jocosly, *il faut que je dise avec Harlequin, nôtre Penelôpe n'est qu'une Sallôpe.* but I think I have trespassed too much on your Patience, I beg you to be persuaded of the sincere veneration and esteem with which I have the Honneur to be, Sir,

Your most obliged and most humble servant
GEORGE FRIDERIC HANDEL

---

4 Probably the operas staged by the rival opera company of Niccolo Porpora, Handel's competitor.
5 *Alessandro in Persia*, a potpourri of music by a number of composers.
6 By Baldassare Galuppi (1706-85).

JOHANN SEBASTIAN BACH

Eisenach, 1685 — Leipzig, 1750

❂❂❂❂❂❂❂❂

To Prince *Christian Ludwig,*
 Margrave of *Brandenburg*

Cöthen, March 24, 1721

Your Grace:

Since I had the honour of playing before Your Royal Highness a couple of years ago by virtue of your command, and as I then observed that you took some pleasure in the small talent for music that Heaven has granted me, and upon taking leave of Your Royal Highness you graciously honoured me with a command to send you some pieces of my composition, in accordance with your gracious orders I now take the liberty of presenting my very humble respects to Your Royal Highness with the present concertos which I have written for several instruments.

I humbly pray you not to judge their imperfection by the severity of that fine and delicate taste which everyone knows you have for music, but rather to consider benignly the profound respect and humble obedience to which I have intended them to testify.

For the rest, I humbly beg Your Royal Highness to have the kindness to continue your good graces toward me, and to be persuaded that I have nothing so much at heart as the desire to be employed in matters more worthy of you and your service, and with unequalled zeal, I am, my Lord,

Your Royal Highness's most humble and obedient servant,
JEAN SEBASTIAN BACH

To *Georg Erdmann*[1]

Leipzig, October 28, 1730

Honoured Sir:

    Your Excellency will excuse an old and faithful servant for taking the liberty of inconveniencing you with this letter. It is almost four years since Your Excellency did me the honour of answering the letter I sent you, and as I recall, you graciously requested me to give you some news of my vicissitudes in life, and I hereby proceed to do so.

    My history is familiar to you from my youth until the time of the change that brought me to Cöthen as Kapellmeister. There I found a gracious Prince [2] who both loved and understood music and in whose service I hoped to live out the rest of my days. It turned out, however, that His Serene Highness married a Princess of Berenburg, and then it seemed as if the musical inclinations of the said Prince grew rather lukewarm, especially since the new Princess seemed to be an *amusa*.

    Then it pleased God to summon me here to this town as *Directore Musices* and cantor at the St. Thomas School. At first it was not wholly agreeable to me to become a cantor after having been a Kapellmeister and for this reason I delayed making a decision for three months. However, the position was described to me in such favourable terms (and especially since my sons seemed disposed to study here) that finally I ventured this step in the name of the Most High and I came to Leipzig, passed my examination, and then made the move. Here, as it pleased God, I have remained to this day. But now I find that:

(1) The position is not nearly so advantageous as I had believed.

(2) Many of the incidental fees have been withdrawn.

(3) This town is very expensive to live in.

(4) The authorities are queer folk, little devoted to music, so that I have to endure almost constant annoyance, vexation, and persecution.

    Therefore I feel obliged, with the Almighty's assistance, to seek my fortune elsewhere. Should Your Excellency know of or be

---

1 A schoolmate of Bach's in Ohrdruf and Lüneburg; at this time an agent of the Russian government in Danzig.

2 Prince Leopold von Anhalt-Cöthen.

able to locate a suitable appointment in your town for an old and faithful friend, I humbly beg you to give me the benefit of your valuable recommendation and nothing shall be lacking on my part completely to satisfy and justify your most esteemed recommendation and support, and I shall work with the greatest diligence.

My situation here is worth about 700 taler, and when there are more funerals than usual, the incidental fees increase proportionately. But the air is very healthful here and the past year, for example, the ordinary burial-fees were more than 100 taler less than usual. In Thuringia I could manage nicely on 400 taler and could make that go farther than twice that amount here because of the excessively high cost of living.

Now I must tell you a little about my domestic circumstances. I married again after my first wife died at Cöthen.[3] Of my first marriage three sons and a daughter [4] are still living, whom Your Excellency saw at Weimar and may be pleased to remember. Of my second marriage, one son and two daughters [5] are living. My eldest boy is a *studiosus juris* and the other two attend the first and second class in school. My eldest daughter is still unmarried. The children of my second marriage are still small; the eldest, a boy, is only six years old.

They are all born musicians and I assure you that I can already arrange a concert, vocal and instrumental, with my family, especially since my wife sings a good clear soprano and my eldest daughter is quite competent. I should almost overstep the bounds of courtesy if I were to trouble Your Excellency any longer, so I hasten to close, and with all respect I remain Your Excellency's lifelong most obedient and humble servant.

JOH. SEB. BACH

---

3 His first wife and cousin, Maria Barbara Bach, died on July 9, 1720. He married Anna Magdalena Wilcken on December 3, 1721.

4 In the order of their birth: Catharina Dorothea; Wilhelm Friedemann; Carl Philipp Emanuel; Johann Gottfried Bernhard.

5 Gottfried Heinrich; Elisabeth Juliane Friederica; Regina Johanne.

To *Tobias Rothschieren*, Sr, and other members
   of the *Mühlhausen* Town Council

Leipzig, May 2, 1735

Most Noble and Learned Gentlemen,
and especially Most Esteemed Senior;
Venerated Patrons:

I have been given to understand that Herr Hetze-
henn, the organist to the town of Mühlhausen, died there not very
long ago and that his post has not yet been filled.

Now, my youngest son, Johann Gottfried Bernhard Bach,[6] has
for some time been so proficient in music that I most decidedly consider him competent and able to compete for the recently vacated
post of town organist.

Therefore, most esteemed gentlemen, in all reverence and submission, I request you kindly to grant my son the favour of your
invaluable intercession in helping him obtain the post he applies for,
and thus fulfil my wishes and make my son happy, and so that once
more, as formerly for earlier favours, I may now again find ample
reason to assure you that I remain with unchanging devotion,

Your Honours' and especially the Esteemed *Senior's*
   most devoted servant,

JOHANN SEBASTIAN BACH
Formerly organist at the Church of
St. Blasius in Mühlhausen

⦾⊶⊷⊶⊷⊶⊷⊶⦿

To *Frederick the Great*

Leipzig, July 7, 1747

Most Gracious King:

I hereby dedicate to Your Majesty with the
most humble reverence a musical offering, the noblest part of which
comes from your own exalted hand. I still recall with respectful
pleasure the special royal favour accorded me on my visit to Pots-
dam some time ago, when Your Majesty deigned to play for me on
the clavier a theme for a fugue and most graciously commanded me
to develop it at once in Your Majesty's noble presence. It was my

---

6 Youngest son by Bach's first marriage (1715-39).

most humble duty to obey Your Majesty's command. I soon realized, however, that because of the lack of necessary preparation the development was not as successful as so excellent a theme demanded. Thereupon I determined, and set to work immediately, to develop this truly royal theme in more perfect fashion and then to make it known to the world.

This undertaking has now been carried out to the best of my ability, and it has no other object than the irreproachable one of extolling, if even in small degree, the fame of a sovereign whose power and greatness in all the arts of peace and war, and also especially music, everyone must admire and venerate.

I am emboldened to add the most humble request that Your Majesty will condescend to honour this small work by your gracious acceptance, and further to continue to bestow your most noble favour on Your Majesty's most humble and obedient servant, the composer.

[JOHANN SEBASTIAN BACH]

* * *

To his cousin, *Johann Elias Bach* [7]

Leipzig, November 2, 1748

My dear and honoured Cousin:

Together with your kind letter which arrived yesterday assuring me that you and your dear wife are well, I received the precious keg of new wine, for which I herewith offer you my heartiest thanks. But it is most unfortunate that the keg was damaged, either due to the jolting in course of shipment or for some other reason, since on opening it here for the usual inspection it was found to be almost three-fourths empty, and according to the inspector, it contained only 6 quarts. It is indeed a shame that the smallest drop of this noble gift of God should have been spilled. While I offer you my deepest thanks for this most lavish present, dear cousin, I must confess that *pro nunc* I am in no position to reciprocate. However, *quod differetur non aufferetur* and I hope some time to have the opportunity of acquitting myself of my obligation.

I regret very much that the great distance separating our two cities does not permit us to visit each other. Else I would take the

---

7 Choirmaster at Schweinfurt.

liberty of inviting you to attend the wedding of my daughter Liess-gen to Herr Altnikol, the new organist at Naumberg, which will take place next January. But since the distance I have already mentioned as well as the unseasonable weather does not permit us to have our dear cousin with us in our home, I beg you to help us from afar with your good wishes as a true Christian. With greetings from all of us to you and yours, dear cousin, I remain your most devoted cousin and humble servant,

J. S. BACH

PS. Should you feel disposed again to offer me more of the same liqueur, it would be very expensive because of the exorbitant duty, since it cost me 16 groschen for the freight charges, 2 groschen for delivery, 2 groschen for the inspector, 5 groschen 3 pfennige for the land excise tax, 3 groschen for the general excise tax, so, dear cousin, you yourself can estimate that each quart cost me almost 5 groschen, which makes this present much too expensive.

GIUSEPPE TARTINI

Pirano, 1692 — Padua, 1770

❁❁❁❁❁❁❁

To *Giambattista Martini*

Padua, March 31, 1731

Most Reverend Father:

Your Reverence will be surprised at my not having replied sooner to your very kind letter which I received shortly before Lent. I have not been able to reply since I was engaged in writing, and still am, twelve solo sonatas.[1] I am not publishing these through my own inclination but because I was driven into a mean bargain by a Dutch publisher. But this has nothing to do with our affair and I mention it only to explain my delay so that you will not think I have forgotten my obligation.

Since I do not wish to lose the valuable opportunity afforded by the return of Padre Maestro Appoguidi (having heard him preach, we thank God with all our heart, and if we draw no profit from his sermons, we must strictly account to God), I am writing to you in the greatest haste. To speak very candidly, I was not in the least pleased to hear that you have been discussing my insignificant trash with Maestro Perti [2] and the others you mention. If I were able, I would come to Bologna to study at your school. If — and God knows how this comes from my heart — any observations I have made on the subject of theory seem advanced enough for such a step, which I need so much, and whereby, as a beginner, I would learn so much from these people.

Therefore you cause me to appear utterly ridiculous in discussing me with them, and although I can endure being scoffed at when there is good reason and I deserve it, I do not have the courage to bear being represented as a master, for I am no such thing, and whoever considers me as such is in error. Therefore I beg Your Rever-

---

1 *12 Sonate a violino*, op. 1 (Paris and Amsterdam, 1734).
2 Giacomo Antonio Perti (1661–1756), composer of church music.

[30]

ence to spare me the pain of cutting such a ridiculous figure before these people.

I repeat what I said to you at the beginning. If there is anything in my observations of value to you and your studies, make use of it according to your judgment and pleasure. But if there is nothing of value in them, I hope the proof of my paucity will remain buried in your room and never pass beyond it.

On this condition I am prepared to proceed as I have begun, to oppose all your objections and to show you what our use of two consonant intervals consists in, according to current musical practice. I do not say on this account that there are no more, new intervals but only that they are not known as consonances and, because of the imperfect system of tuning the cembalo, are not known in their true, rightful intonation. Should you desire to present my ideas to the above-mentioned masters as your observations and not mine, you may do so. I should not and cannot prevent you.

But I cannot consent to have such learned men gain the impression of me as someone who is full of pretensions and new improvements and discoveries in the style of the modern school. God preserve me from that! Please regard this as an urgent request and do not allow them to believe that I am something that I am not and shall never be. With the assurance of my humble devotion, ever Your Reverence's most submissive, grateful, and faithful servant,

GIUSEPPE TARTINI

❖❖❖❖❖❖❖❖❖

To *Maddalena Lombardini Syrmen* [3]

Padua, March 5, 1760

My very much esteemed Signora Maddalena:

Finding myself at length disengaged from the weighty business that has so long prevented me from performing my promise to you, a promise that was made with too much sincerity for my want of punctuality not to afflict me, I shall begin the instructions you wish from me, by letter; and if I should not explain myself with sufficient clearness, I entreat you to tell me your doubts and difficulties, in writing, which I shall not fail to remove in a future letter.

---

3 Pupil of Tartini; at this time a student at the Conservatorio dei Mendicanti, Venice.

Your principal practice and study should at present be confined to the use and power of the bow, in order to make yourself entirely mistress in the execution and expression of whatever can be played or sung within the compass and ability of your instrument. Your first study, therefore, should be the true manner of holding, balancing, and pressing the bow lightly but steadily upon the strings; in such a manner that it shall seem to breathe the first tone it gives, which must proceed from the friction of the string, and not from percussion, as by a blow given with a hammer upon it. This depends on laying the bow lightly upon the strings, at the first contact, and on gently pressing it afterwards, which, if done gradually, can scarce have too much force given to it, because if the tone is begun with delicacy, there is little danger of rendering it afterwards either coarse or harsh.

Of this first contact, and delicate manner of beginning a tone, you should make yourself a perfect mistress in every situation and part of the bow, as well in the middle as at the extremities; and in moving it up, as well as in drawing it down. To unite all these laborious particulars in one lesson, my advice is that you first exercise yourself in a swell upon an open string — for example, upon the second or *alamire:* that you begin pianissimo and increase the tone by slow degrees to its fortissimo; and this study should be equally made with the motion of the bow up and down, in which exercise you should spend at least an hour every day, though at different times, a little in the morning and a little in the evening; having constantly in mind that this practice is the most difficult of all and the most essenial to playing well on the violin. When you are a perfect mistress of this part of a good performer, a swell will be very easy to you; beginning with the most minute softness, increasing the tone to its loudest degree, and diminishing it to the same point of softness with which you began, and all this in the same stroke of the bow. Every degree of pressure upon the string, which the expression of a note or passage shall require, will by this means be easy and certain; and you will be able to execute with your bow whatever you please. After this, in order to acquire that light pulsation and play of the wrist from which velocity in bowing arises, it will be best for you to practise every day one of the allegros, of which there are three in Corelli's solos, which entirely move in semiquavers. The first is in D, in playing which you should accelerate the motion a little each time till you arrive at the greatest degree of swiftness possible; but two precautions are necessary in this exercise: the first is that you play the notes staccato — that is, separate and detached, with a little space between every two; for though they are written thus:

they should be played as if there was a rest after every note, in this manner:

The second precaution is that you first play with the point of the bow; and when that becomes easy to you, that you use that part of it which is between the point and the middle; and when you are likewise mistress of this part of the bow, that you practice in the same manner with the middle of the bow; and, above all, you must remember in these studies to begin the allegros or flights sometimes with an up-bow and sometimes with a down-bow, carefully avoiding the habit of constantly practising one way. In order to acquire a greater facility of executing swift passages in a light and neat manner, it will be of great use if you accustom yourself to skip over a string between two quick notes in divisions like these:

Of such divisions you may play extempore as many as you please, and in every key, which will be both useful and necessary.

With regard to the finger-board, or carriage of the left hand, I have one thing strongly to recommend to you, which will suffice for all, and that is the taking a violin part, either the first or second of a concerto, sonata, or song, anything will serve the purpose, and playing it upon the half-shift — that is, with the first finger upon G on the first string, and constantly keeping upon this shift, playing the whole piece without moving the hand from this situation, unless A on the fourth string be wanted or D on the first; but in that case you should afterwards return again to the half-shift, without ever moving the hand down to the natural position. This practice should be continued till you can execute with facility upon the half-shift any violin part, not intended as a solo, at sight. After this, advance the hand on the finger-board to the whole shift, with the first finger upon A on the first string, and accustom yourself to this position till you can execute everything upon the whole shift with as much ease as when the hand is in its natural situation; and when certain of this, advance to the double shift, with the first finger upon B on the first string; and when sure of that likewise, pass to the fourth position of the hand, making C with the first finger upon the first string; and indeed this is a scale in which, when you are firm, you may be said to be mistress of the finger-board. This study is so necessary that I most earnestly recommend it to your attention.

I now pass to the third essential part of a good performer on the violin, which is the making a good shake, and I would have you practise it slow, moderately fast, and quick; that is, with the two notes succeeding each other in these three degrees of adagio, andante, and presto; and in practice you have great occasion for these different kinds of shakes; for the same shake will not serve with equal propriety for a slow movement as for a quick one; but to acquire both at once with the same trouble, begin with an open string, either the first or second, it will be equally useful; sustain the note in a swell, and begin the shake very slow, increasing in quickness, by insensible degrees, till it becomes rapid, in the manner following:

but you must not rigorously move immediately from semiquavers to demisemiquavers, as in this example, or from these to the next in degree; that would be doubling the velocity of the shake all at once, which would be a skip, not a gradation; but you can imagine between a semiquaver and a demisemiquaver intermediate degrees of rapidity, quicker than the one and slower than the other of these characters; you are therefore to increase in velocity by the same degrees in practising the shake as in loudness when you make a swell. You must attentively and assiduously persevere in the practice of this embellishment, and begin at first with an open string, upon which, if you are once able to make a good shake with the first finger, you will with the greater facility acquire one with the second, the third, and the fourth or little finger, with which you must practise in a particular manner, as more feeble than the rest of its brethren. I shall at present propose no other studies to your application; what I have already said is more than sufficient if your zeal is equal to my wishes for your improvement. I hope you will sincerely inform me whether I have explained myself clearly thus far; that you will accept my respects, which I likewise beg of you to present to the Prioress, to Signora Teresa, and to Signora Chiara, for all of whom I have a sincere regard; and believe me to be, with great affection,

Your obedient and most humble servant,
GIUSEPPE TARTINI

JOHANN ADOLF HASSE

Bergedorf, 1699 — *Venice,* 1783

To the Abbé *Giovanni Maria Ortes*

Vienna, September 30, 1769

I have made the acquaintance here of a certain Herr Mozart,[1] Kapellmeister to the Archbishop of Salzburg, a clever man, charming and cultivated, who, I believe, knows his business in music as well as other matters. He has a daughter and a son. The former plays the cembalo proficiently, and the latter, who cannot be more than twelve or thirteen years old, already holds forth as a composer and teacher of music.

I have seen the compositions he is supposed to have written. They are not at all bad and I should not have recognized in them a twelve-year-old author. I dare not question his having written them, for after giving me proof of various styles on the cembalo, he showed me some things which were incredible for that age and admirable even for a grown man.

Since his father wishes to take him to Italy to make him known and wrote me requesting some letters of recommendation, I am taking the liberty of sending you one. I am depending on your kindness. The sole purpose of this letter is to have him meet you and to have him obtain some useful advice which may prove necessary in that country. But if you could also introduce him to some lady of your acquaintance, that would be more than I had hoped for. The father says he will leave Salzburg on October 24 and should arrive by the end of the month.

This Herr Mozart is an extremely courteous and gracious man, and his children are very well bred. The boy, moreover, is handsome, lively, charming, and has excellent manners. I am certain that if he continues to progress as he grows older, he will be a prodigy —

---

1 Leopold Mozart, father of Wolfgang Amadeus.

provided the father does not push him too much and spoil him with undue and exaggerated praise, which is the one thing I dread.

What a long letter! Accept my greetings and forgive me for having written at such length. Believe me, with the most faithful and lifelong devotion, my very dear Monsieur Abbé. The ladies send their respects.

Your most humble and obliged servant and friend,

J. A. HASSE

GIAMBATTISTA MARTINI

Bologna, 1706 — Bologna, 1784

To *Andrea Basili* [1]

> *Bologna*, January 28, 1750

M. Rameau establishes a completely modern system, very different from our best Italian school of the past, and to give you my own insignificant opinion, I believe that we Italians would cause our Italian school great harm in wishing to follow him, considering that our school has laid down the laws for all non-Italians in the past but has never taken any laws from any other school.

It is true that M. Rameau's system may be able to shed great light on the massive, many-voiced style and on church music; however (according to my feeble comprehension), I not only am of the opposite opinion but consider this quite harmful. And if I have to make the comparison, I flatter myself in thinking that my assertion will easily find general concurrence.

I beg your pardon and indulgence if I have flattered myself too audaciously with the kind forbearance of a celebrated man like your illustrious self, who to a profound understanding of the musical profession, unites a noble nature, which commands the respect and love of him who has the good fortune to be, and is proud to sign himself

> [Your humble and obedient servant]
> [GIAMBATTISTA MARTINI]

---

1 Author of a book on counterpoint and other works.

To *Pietro Morandi*[2]

Bologna, August 10, 1776

Dear Friend:

From your very kind letter dated August 2 I have just learned that the symphony[3] you composed and had printed in Venice has been censured, and that the entire reason for this censure arises from the Grave, whose beginning does not suit the taste of your critics. My friend, I do not wish this criticism to disturb you. Remember that whoever publishes cannot avoid such crises. Envy suggests cavilling, and merit has never been left alone, wherefore Seneca wisely remarked that if virtue had a body, envy would be its shadow.

I suppose that your critics dislike the fact that the second violin begins in G *sol-re-ut*, the Grave being in B *fa*. In truth, they thus reveal that they have no knowledge of French music, in which the composers used sometimes to start in one of the chords of the key, whether a third, a fifth, or a sixth, as can easily be seen in the *Journal de musique*, Volume VIII, August 1770, at the bottom of page 4, and in the *Romance* by the editor of that journal,[4] which begins with a sixth. Moreover, I have seen this practised by Monsieur Rameau in the rondo entitled *Tourbillons* on page 27 of his *Pièces de clavecin*, Paris, 1736, and likewise in his drama *Les Fêtes d'Hébé*, performed in May 1739, where the duet "*Non, ne suivez point mes pas,*" etc., on page 4, begins with a sixth. These examples should assure you that when you composed a rondo in the Grave of your symphony and started it in another chord than the fundamental of the key, you did nothing but imitate the French.

And if this does not suffice to calm your mind, look at the masters of the sixteenth century, notably Palestrina, whose works, particularly the hymns, begin indifferently on any chord of the key, taking care only to end on the fundamental chord. Notwithstanding that on pages 70–1 of the first part of my *Esemplare di Contrapunto* I gave a different opinion from what I say here, notice that what you have done in the Grave of your symphony is not subject to the laws I laid down there, since the bass (although it is the cembalo that provides all the accompaniment the fundamental key requires) be-

---

2 Organist (1745–1815), and former pupil of Martini.
3 Symphony in D major for small orchestra.
4 Nicolas Étienne Framéry (1745–1810).

gins only after the fifth beat and in the fundamental chord of the key.

Therefore calm your mind and pay as much attention to the blabbering of your critics as you would to the croaking of frogs. Love me as I love you, and believe me unchangeable. Your dearest friend, your most devoted and obliged servant and true friend,

GIAMBA̅ MARTINI

CARL PHILIPP EMANUEL BACH

Weimar, 1714 — *Hamburg*, 1788

❁❁❁❁❁❁❁❁

To *Johann Joachim Eschenburg* [1]

Hamburg, January 21, 1786

Very dear Professor:

      I am indeed very much obliged to you for your *Handel*. I am in disagreement with Mr. Burney in several places. The same thing happens in Handel's case as in many others, and if people are idolized, they must expect to suffer the basest insults. Here, during Handel's time, Keiser [2] far surpassed him as a song-writer, and Handel never would have become a Hasse or a Graun [3] had he lived to the end of their time. But this was scarcely necessary, for he was great enough, especially in his oratorios.

      But to assert that he excelled my father in organ-playing! No one should say that who comes from England (where the organs are of slight value and lack the pedals) and who consequently has no insight into excellence of organ-playing and perhaps never heard or saw any organ compositions, and, finally, who was certainly not familiar with my father's clavier pieces or especially, his organ pieces. In these the obbligato pedal is used throughout — now the main melody, now the alto, now the tenor is assigned to it — and in the fugues it always happens that a voice is never relinquished and the most difficult passages come out, not to mention the use of the feet with the utmost fire and brilliance — in short, innumerable things about which Burney knows nothing.

      Hasse, Faustina, [4] Quantz, [5] and others who knew Handel well

---

1 German translator of Charles Burney's *An Account of the Musical Performances in Westminster Abbey in Commemoration of Handel* (1785).

2 Reinhard Keiser (1674-1739), a leading composer of the Hamburg opera school.

3 Johann Adolf Hasse (1699-1783) and Karl Heinrich Graun (1701-59), celebrated opera-composers.

4 Faustina Bordoni, Hasse's wife and celebrated prima donna.

5 Johann Joachim Quantz (1697-1773), author of *Versuch einer Anweisung die Flöte traversière zu spielen* (1752).

and heard him play declared in 1728 or 1729, when my father gave a public performance in Dresden, that Bach had brought organ-playing to the peak of perfection. See the Quantz *Anweisung*. In all seriousness, the difference between the two could hardly be greater in this respect. Did Handel ever write trios for two manuals and pedal? Did he ever write five- and six-part fugues for the ordinary clavier? Certainly not. Thus one can hardly permit the comparison, so great is the disparity. Let people examine the clavier and organ compositions of both men.

Forgive my excessive chatter and garrulous scribble. The drollest thing of all is the magnificent foresight of the King, who was bound on preserving Handel's early works at any cost.[6] In no way do I compare myself to Handel, but recently I burned over a ream of old compositions and I am happy they no longer exist.

Continue to love, in spite of this, your most devoted
BACH

---

6 A collection of music belonging to George I included *Six Sonatas for Oboe*, composed in 1694, when Handel was nine years old.

CHRISTOPH WILLIBALD VON GLUCK

Weidenwang, 1714 — Vienna, 1787

❀❀❀❀❀❀❀

To *Gottlieb Friedrich Klopstock*

Vienna, August 14, 1773

Your Excellency:

    I have heard from Père Denis that you would like to have the strophes I composed on your *Battle of Hermann*. I should have seen to this long ago, were it not absolutely certain that you would not care for many of them since they ought to be sung in a certain manner which is not yet *à la mode*. For although you have excellent musicians, it seems to me that music which requires inspiration is still entirely foreign to your country, as was apparent to me by the census taken at Berlin on my *Alceste*.

    So great is my regard for you that if you do not plan to come to Vienna, I promise to make a journey to Hamburg next year in order to make your acquaintance in person, and I promise to sing for you not only much of the *Battle of Hermann* but also some of your sublime Odes [1] to show you how closely I have approximated your greatness — or how much it has been obscured by my music.

    At the moment I am sending you some very simple songs, easy to perform. Three are in German style and three in a more modern Italian style, to which I have added at the same time as a token of appreciation two melodies in the style of the old bards, which you can always cast aside. On their account you will have to find a good clavier-player so as to see them in the most favourable light.

    I have the honour to remain, with profound respect, Your Excellency's very obedient servant,

CHEVALIER GLUCK

---

[1] *Seven Odes of Klopstock for Voice and Clavier* (1780).

To *Le Blanc du Rollet* [2]

[July–August] 1776

I have just received, my dear friend, your letter of January 15, in which you exhort me to continue to work at the opera of *Roland;* this is no longer possible, for when I learned that the administration of the Opéra, who were perfectly well aware that I was occupied with *Roland,* had handed over the work to M. Piccinni, I burned all that I had already written of it, which perhaps was of no great value, in which case the public ought to be obliged to M. Marmontel for having prevented their hearing bad music.[3]

Moreover, I am not the man to enter into rivalry with anyone. M. Piccinni would have too great advantage over me; for in addition to his personal merits, which are assuredly very great, he would also have that of novelty, I having given four works at Paris, whether good or bad, no matter. This must exhaust the imagination; besides, I have shown him the way, and he has only to follow me. Of his patrons I say nothing. Sure am I that a certain politician of my acquaintance [4] will give dinners and suppers to three fourths of Paris for the purpose of gaining proselytes for him; and that Marmontel, who knows so well how to write tales, will relate to the whole kingdom the exclusive merits of M. Piccinni.

I do really pity M. Hebert [5] for having fallen into the hands of such persons; the one an exclusive amateur of Italian music, and the other the dramatic author of operas supposed to be comic. They will make him see the moon at midday. I am sincerely grieved, for this M. Hebert is an excellent man, for which reason I feel inclined to give him my *Armide;* on the conditions, however, that I named in my previous letter. I must repeat that the most essential are that when I come to Paris I am to have at least two months to train my actors and actresses; that I am to be empowered to have as many rehearsals as I shall consider necessary; that no part is to be doubled; and that another opera is to be held in readiness in case any actor or actress should be indisposed. These are my conditions and without their fulfilment I will keep my *Armide* for my own pleasure. I

---

2 Librettist for Gluck's *Iphigénie en Aulide* (1772).

3 Piccinni's *Roland,* with libretto by Marmontel, was first performed on January 17, 1778.

4 The Marchese Carraciolo, Neapolitan Ambassador in Paris.

5 Director of the Opéra, Paris.

have written the music in a manner that will prevent its soon growing old.

You tell me in your letter, my dear friend, that nothing will ever equal *Alceste*,[6] but, for my part, I do not join in your prophecy. *Alceste* is a complete tragedy, and I own I think it very near perfection; but you have no conception of how many shades and different paths music is susceptible. The whole combinations of *Armide* are so different from those of *Alceste* that you will scarcely believe they are by the same composer, and I have also put forth the little strength still left me in order to finish *Armide*. I have striven in it to be rather a poet and a painter than a musician; in short, you will be able to judge for yourself, if they choose to let it be heard. I must confess that I should like to finish my career with this opera. True it is that the public will require at least as much time to comprehend it as was necessary for them to understand *Alceste*. There is a certain delicacy in *Armide* that is not to be found in *Alceste;* for I have discovered the means of making the personages speak so that you know at once, from their mode of expression, when Armide is speaking, when the confidante, etc., etc. I must conclude or you will think that I have become either a charlatan or a lunatic. Nothing has so bad an effect as to praise oneself; it was only admissible in the great Corneille; but when Marmontel or I do so, people ridicule us or laugh in our faces.

You are quite right, however, in saying that French composers have been too much neglected; for, unless I am much mistaken, Gossec and Philidor, who know the requirements of the French opera, would, in my opinion, suit the public infinitely better than the best Italian authors, were it not for the amount of enthusiasm for everything that has the *prestige* of novelty. You also say, my dear friend, that *Orphée*[7] loses when compared with *Alceste*. Good heavens! How can there be any comparison between two works that have nothing in common? The one may please more than the other, but were you to see *Alceste* performed by your inferior actors and any other actress than Mlle Le Vasseur, and on the other hand *Orphée* by the very best you have, you would then admit the balance to be in favour of *Orphée;* the best-composed works, when badly executed, become the most insupportable of all. No comparison can exist between these two works of an opposite nature.

---

6 First performance, Vienna, 1767; presented in Paris in a French version in 1774.
7 *Orfeo ed Eurydice*, first performance, Vienna, 1762. Given at Paris in a French version in 1774.

If, for example, Piccinni and I each composed the opera of *Roland*, then people could judge which of us had succeeded the better, but then any comparison must be a *lame* one. I almost tremble at the idea of people comparing *Armide* and *Alceste*; poems forming such a contrast, the one making you weep, and the other causing solely thrilling sensations. If this should occur, my only resource will be to pray to the Almighty that the worthy city of Paris may recover its good sense. Adieu, my dear friend,

GLUCK

⊙⥼⊙⥼⊙⥼⊙⥼⊙⥼⊙

To *Jean François de la Harpe* [8]

October 12, 1777

It is impossible for me, sir, not to agree to the very judicious observations you have recently made on my operas in your *Journal de Littérature*, October 5; and I find nothing, absolutely nothing, to say in reply.

Hitherto I had the simplicity to believe that in music, as in other arts, all the passions were within its sphere, and that it ought not to please less in expressing rage and fury and the cry of grief than in depicting the sighs of love —

> Neither serpent nor monster is so odious
> As not to please when counterfeited by art.

I thought this axiom true in music as well as in poetry. I was convinced that singing imbued with the colouring of the sentiments to be expressed ought to be modified in accordance with them and assume as many different accents as the poetry had different tints; in short, ought all to tend to one single aim, that of *expression*, and the union between the singing and the words be so close that the poem should not appear to be less composed for the music than the music for the poem.

These were not my only errors: it seemed to me that the French language was not much accentuated and had no determined quantity like the Italian tongue. I was also struck with another discrepancy between the singers of the two nations; if I found in the one voices more soft and flexible, the others seemed to me to put

---

8 Poet and critic (1738–1803); one of Piccinni's strongest defenders in the Gluck-Piccinni controversies.

more force and energy into their action; thence I concluded that Italian singing would not suit the French.

In subsequently looking over the scores of some of your old operas, in spite of the shakes, cadences, and other defects with which these airs are overloaded, I found enough of real beauties in them to make me believe that the French have their own resources within themselves.

These, sir, were my ideas before reading your observations. Instantly light dissipated darkness; I was confounded to find you had learned more of my art in some hours of reflection than I had done after having exercised it for forty years. You prove to me, sir, that it suffices to be a man of letters to entitle you to pronounce on all subjects. I am now fully convinced that the music of the Italian masters is music par excellence, is, in fact, *music;* that singing, in order to please, ought to be regular and methodical, and that even in those moments of excitement when the personage singing, animated by different passions, passes successively from one to another, the composer ought always to preserve the same *motif de chant.*

I agree with you that, of all my compositions, *Orphée* is the only one that is tolerable. I humbly ask pardon from heaven for having *deafened* my auditors by my other operas; the number of times they have been performed and the applause the public has thought fit to bestow on them do not prevent my seeing that they are pitiable; I am so convinced of this that I intend to write them afresh, and as I perceive that you are all for tender music, I propose to put into the mouth of the furious Achilles a song so touching and sweet that the spectators shall be moved by it even to tears.

With respect to *Armide*, I must beware of leaving the poem as it now is, for, as you judiciously observe, "the operas of Quinault, though full of beauties, are composed in a manner unfavourable to music; they are very fine as poems, but very bad as operas." If, therefore, they must become very bad poems (evidently, in your opinion, the only mode to make good operas), I must entreat you to procure me the acquaintances of some *rhymer* who will set to work at *Armide* and insert a couple of arias in every scene. We can together settle the quantity and the measure of the verse, and, provided the number of syllables be complete, I shall not trouble myself further. I, on my side, will work at the music, from which, of course, I must scrupulously banish all noisy instruments such as kettledrums and trumpets; it is now my desire that only oboes, flutes, French horns, and violins (with sordines, of course) should be heard in my orchestra; while my sole object shall be to arrange the words to suit these airs, which will not be difficult, having previously taken their exact dimensions. Then the part of Armide will no longer be a monotonous and tiresome *criaillerie*. She will no longer be a Médée, a sorceress, but an *enchantress*. I intend that in her despair she shall sing an air so *regular* and *methodical*, and at the same time so tender, that the most delicate *petite maîtresse* may listen to it without the smallest shock to her nerves.

If some blockhead should say to me: "Sir, pray remember that Armide in a state of fury should not express herself like Armide enamoured," I should reply to him: "Sir, I do not wish to *offend the ear* of M. de la Harpe; I do not wish to *adhere* to nature, but rather to *embellish* it; instead of making Armide utter cries of anguish, I wish her to *enchant* you." If he were to persist and to declare that Sophocles, in the finest of all his tragedies, did not scruple to present the Athenian Œdipus with bloodshot eyes, and that the recitative or species of declamation introduced, by which the eloquent complaints of that unhappy King were expressed, was no doubt uttered in the liveliest accents of grief, I would again reply that M. de la Harpe objects to hear the cry of a man who *suffers*.

Do I not, sir, thus define the spirit of the doctrine that pervades your remarks? I have procured for several of my friends the pleasure of reading them. One of them said to me on returning your pamphlet: "You ought to be grateful, M. de la Harpe gives you some valuable hints, he makes the confession of his musical faith; do the same in return: send for his poetical and literary works, and through friendship for him note down in them all that does not please you. Many people are of the opinion that criticism produces no other effect on art than that of wounding the artist whom it attacks, and to prove this they say that never have poets had more censors or been more indifferent than in the present day; but consult the journalists on the point and ask them if there is anything more useful to the state than journals. People may object that it does not become you, a musician, to decide about poetry; but is that more startling than a poet, a man of letters, who judges despotically of music?"

Thus spoke my friend; but notwithstanding my gratitude to you, sir, I feel on due consideration that I cannot follow his suggestions without incurring the fate of him who, in the presence of Hannibal, made a long harangue on the art of war.

[Christoph Willibald von Gluck]

To the Comtesse *de Fries*

Paris, November 16, 1777

Madame:

They have plagued me so much about music and I am so sick of it that at present I would not write a single note for so much as a louis. Thus you can judge the degree of my devotion to you since I have brought myself to arrange the two songs for harp that I have the honour of sending you.

No one has ever stirred up a more terrible and fiercely disputed battle than I with my opera *Armide*.[9] By comparison, the intrigues against *Iphigénie*, *Orphée*, and *Alceste* were but little skirmishes between light troops. To ensure a great success for Piccinni's opera,[10] the Ambassador of Naples is indefatigably caballing against me at court and among the nobility. He has won over Marmontel, la Harpe, and some academicians to writing against my system of music and style of composition. The Abbé Arnaud, M. Suard,[11] and several others have risen to my defence, and the quarrel has become heated to the point where, after insults, they would have come to blows had mutual friends not brought them to order.

The *Journal de Paris*, which is issued every day, is full of it. This dispute has made the fortune of the editor, who already has more than 2,500 subscriptions in Paris. Well, here is the revolution in French music with all its pomp and splendour. Enthusiasts say to me: "Sir, you are fortunate to enjoy the honours of persecution; all the greatest geniuses have followed that path." I'd like to send them and all their fine speeches to the devil.

The fact is that the opera, which was said to be a failure, has earned 37,200 livres in seven performances, not including subscriptions or boxes rented by the year. Yesterday, at the eighth performance, they took in 5,767 livres. Never was there such a throng and such unbroken silence. The parterre was so closely packed that one man, when asked by the usher to remove his hat, replied: "You take it off, because I can't move my arms." This aroused laughter.

I saw people leaving with their hair disordered and their clothes as soaked as if they had fallen into a river. You have to be

---

9 First performance, September 23, 1777, Paris.
10 *Roland* (1778).
11 François Arnaud (1721–84), writer on music; J. B. A. Suard (1734–1817), critic.

French to pay this price for entertainment. There are six places in the opera that cause the audience to be carried away and lose self-control. Visit us here, madame, and witness the tumult; it will entertain you as much as the opera itself.

I am in despair at not being able to leave yet because the road is bad. My wife is too afraid. I beg you to present my compliments to the Baron and to M. Gontard.

> I remain, with deepest respect, your very humble
> and obedient servant,
> LE CHEVALIER GLUCK

To *Valentin* [12]

Vienna, April 17, 1782

Sir:

Your kind letter brought me much pleasure and I thank you for it. It is extremely flattering to me and in it I discern the imprint of an ardent mind, eager to learn, as well as the foundations of an excellent character and a good heart, which do you much honour. If my state of health permitted and if I were still able to undertake something in the manner of dramatic art, I should place nothing before acceptance of your offer and I am persuaded that both of us would be satisfied with each other.

For several months I have been ill following an apoplectic stroke that occurred last year. My head is weak, my right arm is paralysed, and I am incapable of doing any sustained work whatever. I am not permitted to do so, and in any case it would be impossible for me. You see, sir, that I am unable to accept your request, which speaks well for you and is an honour for me. This is against my will, but there is nothing to be done.

You are young, sir, and you are full of goodwill. Work, and I have no doubt of your progress, your advancement, and your success. Persistence and courage in your studies, reflection and balance in the total ensemble of your work, and, above all, the pursuit of truth in your expression. This, combined with the rules of art, will carry you far. The simplicity of nature and the strength of sentiment should be your guide more than anything else. Whoever

---

12 Director of music to the Duke d'Aiguillon at Bordeaux.

strays from these generally falls into absurd incongruities that keep one in the class of mediocrity.

These are my masters; they should be yours. In this school, with the necessary natural and acquired qualities, one enters upon the true path. A considerable number lose their way through failure to observe their conduct in pursuing the customary routine. Plumb the depths of these masters, consult them, interrogate them. They are docile toward those who seek them out. They listen to you. They answer you. They lead you on.

Farewell, sir. Accept these few words of advice given you by an invalid who is no longer good for anything but that, and be persuaded of the feelings of esteem which you deserve, which you have inspired in me, and with which I have the honour to be, sir,

Your very humble and obedient servant,
LE CHEVALIER GLUCK

FRANZ JOSEPH HAYDN

Rohrau, 1732 — Vienna, 1809

☙☙☙☙☙☙☙

To *Herr Roth* [1]

[Esterház, Hungary] December 1787

You wish me to write an *opera buffa* for you. Most willingly, if you are inclined to have a vocal composition of mine for yourself alone, but if with a view to produce it on the stage at Prague, I cannot in that case comply with your wish, all my operas being too closely connected with our personal circle,[2] so they could never produce the proper effect, which I calculated in accordance with the locality. It would be very different if I had the invaluable privilege of composing a new opera for your theatre. But even then I should risk a great deal, for scarcely any man could stand beside the great Mozart.

I only wish I could impress on every friend of music, and on great men in particular, the same depth of musical sympathy and profound appreciation of Mozart's inimitable music that I myself feel and enjoy; then nations would vie with each other to possess such a jewel within their frontiers. Prague ought to strive to retain this precious man, but also to remunerate him; for without this the history of a great genius is sad indeed and gives very little encouragement to posterity to further exertions, and it is on this account that so many promising geniuses are ruined. It enrages me to think that the unparalleled Mozart is not yet engaged by some imperial or royal [3] court! Forgive my excitement, but I love the man so dearly!

I am, etc.

JOSEPH HAYDN

---

1 A friend in Prague who asked Haydn to write a comic opera for performance there.

2 Haydn entered the service of the Esterházy family in 1761, becoming Kapellmeister in 1766; he retained this position for over thirty years.

3 On December 15 of that year Mozart succeeded Gluck as chamber composer to Emperor Josef II.

To *Maria Anna von Genzinger*

Estoras, February 9, 1790

Much esteemed and kindest Frau v. Genzinger:

Well, here I sit in my wilderness; forsaken, like some poor orphan, almost without human society; melancholy, dwelling on the memory of past glorious days. Yes, past, alas! And who can tell when these happy hours may return? those charming meetings? where the whole circle have but one heart and one soul — all those delightful musical evenings, which can only be remembered, not described. Where are all those inspired moments? All gone — and gone for long.

You must not be surprised, dear lady, that I have delayed writing to express my gratitude. I found everything at home in confusion; for three days I did not know whether I was Kapellmeister or Kapell-servant; nothing could console me; my apartments were all in confusion; my pianoforte, which I formerly loved so dearly, was perverse and disobedient, and rather irritated than soothed me. I slept very little, and even my dreams persecuted me, for while asleep I was under the pleasant delusion that I was listening to the opera of *Le Nozze di Figaro*, when the blustering north wind woke me and almost blew my nightcap off my head.

I lost 20 pounds in weight in three days, for the effects of my good fare at Vienna disappeared on the journey. Alas! alas! thought I to myself, when forced to eat at the restaurateur's, instead of capital beef, a slice of a cow 50 years old; instead of a ragout with little balls of force meat, an old sheep with yellow carrots; instead of a Bohemian pheasant, a tough grill; and instead of good and juicy oranges, Hungarian salad; instead of pastry, dry apple-fritters, and hazelnuts, &c. Alas, alas! thought I again to myself, would that I now had many a morsel that I despised in Vienna! Here in Estoras no one asks me: Would you like some chocolate, with milk or without? Will you take some coffee, with or without cream? What can I offer you, my good Haydn? Will you have vanilla ice or pineapple? If I had only a piece of good Parmesan cheese, particularly in Lent, to enable me to swallow more easily the black dumplings and puffs! I gave our porter this very day a commission to send me a couple of pounds.

Forgive me, dear lady, for taking up your time in this very first letter with so wretched a scrawl and such stupid nonsense; you must forgive a man spoiled by the Viennese. Now, however, I begin to accustom myself by degrees to country life, and yesterday I studied for the first time, and somewhat in the Haydn style too.

No doubt you have been more industrious than myself. The pleasing adagio from the quartet has probably now received its true expression from your fair fingers. I trust that my good Fräulein Peperl [4] may be frequently reminded of her master by often singing over the cantata, and that she will pay particular attention to distinct articulation and correct vocalization, for it would be a sin if so fine a voice were to remain imprisoned in the breast. I beg, therefore, for a frequent smile or else I shall be most vexed. I advise M. François [5] too to cultivate his musical talents. Even if he sings in his dressing-gown, it will do well enough, and I will often write something new to encourage him. I again kiss your hands in gratitude for all the kindness you have shown me and I remain, with the greatest lifelong esteem, etc.

[FRANZ JOSEPH HAYDN]

To the Managers of the *Esterházy* Estate
[*Eisenstadt*, 1796 or 1797]
Gentlemen:

I see by the legal papers forwarded to me, and the enclosure from His Highness the Prince Esterházy's Office of Management, that, in consequence of Lungmayer's *inability* to pay his debt, I am condemned to do so; [6] pray, why? Because I am supposed to be *able* to pay. Would to God this were the case! But I swear by the *Kyrie eleison* which I am at this moment composing for my fourth Prince [7] that since the death of my second Prince, [8] of blessed memory, I have fallen into the same state of inability as Lungmayer himself, only with this difference: that he has descended from a horse to the back of an ass, whereas I have remained on the horse, but without saddle or bridle. I beg, therefore, gentlemen, you will at least have patience till I have finished the 'Dona nobis pacem, and

4 Daughter of Frau von Genzinger.
5 Son of Frau von Genzinger.
6 Haydn had endorsed several notes made by Lungmayer, steward of the Esterházy Estate.
7 Prince Miklós Esterházy II.
8 Prince Miklós Jozsef Esterházy.

till the Prince's major-domo Lungmayer shall have ceased to receive his salary from the poorly paid music director Haydn (who has spent twenty-six years in the Prince's service), and shall begin to receive the salary justly due to him from his most gracious Prince. For surely nothing can be more sad or incongruous than that one servant should pay another servant, that is, the Kapellmeister pay the major-domo. If I should presently, by my own efforts (*for flatter or beg I cannot*), or by the voluntary impulse of my gracious Prince, be placed in a *better* position, I will not fail to comply with the above demand.

Most respectfully and humbly,
Franz J. Haydn
Doctor of Oxford and Kapellmeister
to Prince Esterházy

◦▸◦▸◦▸◦▸◦▸◦▸

To Messrs. *Breitkopf* & *Härtel*

June 12, 1799

My business unhappily multiplies with my years, and yet it almost seems as if with the decrease of my mental powers, my inclination and impulse to work increase. Oh God! how much yet remains to be done in this splendid art, even by a man like myself! The world, indeed, pays me many compliments, even on the fire of my last works; but no one could believe the strain and effort it costs me to produce these, inasmuch as many a day my feeble memory and the unstrung state of my nerves so completely crush me to the earth that I fall into the most melancholy condition, so much so that for days afterwards I am incapable of finding one single idea, till at length my heart is revived by Providence, when I seat myself at the piano and begin once more to hammer away at it. Then all goes well, God be praised!

Yesterday I received another packet of musical newspapers. The manner in which this work is published does you infinite credit, etc., etc. As for myself, now an old man, I only wish and hope that the critics may not handle my *Creation* with too great severity and be too hard on it. They may possibly find the musical orthography faulty in various passages, and perhaps other things also that for so many years I have been accustomed to consider as minor points; but the genuine connoisseur will see the real cause as readily as I do,

and willingly cast aside such stumbling blocks. This, however, is
entirely *inter nos*, or I might be accused of conceit and arrogance,
from which, however, my heavenly Father has preserved me all my
life long.

[FRANZ JOSEPH HAYDN]

⊹⊱⊹⊱⊹⊱⊹⊱⊹⊱⊹⊱⊹

To the Members of the *Bergen Musical Union*[9]

Vienna, September 22, 1802

Gentlemen:

It was indeed a most pleasing surprise to me to receive
such a flattering letter from a place where I could have no idea that
the fruits of my poor talents were known. When I now see, however, not only that my name is familiar to you, but that my compositions are performed by you with approval and satisfaction, the
warmest wishes of my heart are thus fulfilled; and these are to be
considered by every nation where my work may penetrate as a not
wholly unworthy priest of this sacred art. You tranquillize me on
the point so far as regards your fatherland, and still further, you
give me the pleasing conviction (which cannot fail to be the most
fruitful consolation of my declining years) that I am often the enviable source from which you, and so many families susceptible of
true feeling, derive pleasure and enjoyment in domestic life. What
happiness this thought causes me!

Often when contending with the obstacles of every sort opposed to my works, often when my powers of both body and mind
failed and I felt it a hard matter to persevere in the course I had entered on, a secret feeling within me whispered: "There are but few
contented and happy men here below; everywhere grief and care
prevail; perhaps your labours may one day be the source from
which the weary and worn, or the man burdened with affairs, may
derive a few moments' rest and refreshment." What a powerful motive to press onwards! And this is why I now look back with heart-
felt cheerful satisfaction on the works to which I devoted such a
long succession of years and such persevering efforts and exertions.

And now I thank you in the fullness of my heart for your
kindly thoughts of me and beg you to forgive my answer's having

9 A society of amateur musicians in Rügen on the Baltic, who sent Haydn a letter
of appreciation after performing *The Creation*.

been somewhat delayed. Feeble health, the inseparable companion of the grey-haired man of seventy, and also pressing business deprived me till now of this pleasure. Perhaps nature may yet accord me the gratification of composing a little memorial of myself to send to you, from which you may gather the feelings of a gradually decaying veteran who would fain even after death survive in the charming circle of which you draw so pleasing a picture.

I have the honour to be, with highest consideration,

Your obedient servant,
JOSEPH HAYDN

JOHANN CHRISTOPH FRIEDRICH BACH

Leipzig, 1732 — Bückeburg, 1795

❖➤❖➤❖➤❖➤❖➤❖

To *Heinrich Wilhelm von Gerstenberg*

Bückeburg, April 1, 1773

Right Honourable Baron, most esteemed Master:

I can hardly assure you sufficiently of the great pleasure I felt upon receiving your esteemed letter, only I was somewhat embarrassed at your special kindness. That beautiful creation of yours the *Mohrenmädchen* [1] deserved much finer garb than she received; however, it was done with the best intentions on my part, and while at this time I little merit the approbation of such connoisseurs of music, I was so greatly affected by it that I shall endeavour to become ever more deserving of it.

The question Your Honour has asked me: why it is that our sonatas must have two fast movements and one slow, I know no other way of answering than as follows: A fugue is called a fugue precisely because it is worked out according to prescribed rules. The old suite for the clavier would not have been named thus, had it not pleased our forefathers to fashion such a combination from a prelude, allemande, etc., and the rest of the pieces composing the work that they called Suite for the Clavier. I understand just as little why the order in this type of composition must consist of the prelude, through the allemande, courante, saraband, and in conclusion the gigue.

A composition that would convey your idea of describing the history of Cleopatra would not be imposible, but in my present haste just a few objections come to mind:

1. Anyone desirous of playing the composition will need to have very precise knowledge of the whole story.

---

1 *Lied eines Mohren*, poem by Gerstenberg with music by J. C. F. Bach, had recently been completed and was published in 1776 as the cantata *Die Amerikanerin.*

2. How many clavier-players have proper execution?
3. Of these, only the smallest number would be capable of performing this piece with the proper execution.
4. I find that otherwise excellent claviers are not yet capable of expressing very movingly a picture of this sort which lacks words; and finally, such a composition would be nothing but *descriptive fantasies*, which, according to my small musical insight, would be the only permissible title for this piece.

Undoubtedly general character and general passions can be made understandable on the clavier to a certain extent. I do not know whether Your Honour is acquainted with a Sonata à 3 for two violins and bass by my brother [2] in Hamburg, which has appeared in print. Therein he sought to express a discourse between *Melancolico* and *Sanguineo* and, quite apart from the great pains he took with this, one would not have grasped the significance of a single section had he not made his meaning clear in words. And I do not believe we would be any more successful with our Cleopatra. Will you, honoured sir, give me your opinions on my judgment?

For the rest, I cherish as a real honour this opportunity of making your acquaintance through correspondence and very much entreat its continuance. With this hope I humbly send you my compliments, and most respectfully I have the honour to remain, sir, your most humble and obedient servant,

J. C. F. BACH

---

2 C. P. E. Bach.

JOHANN CHRISTIAN BACH

Leipzig, 1735 — London, 1782

❧❧❧❧❧❧❧❧

To *Giambattista Martini* [1]

Milan, June 24, 1757

Most Reverend Father, esteemed Master:

I cannot think that a letter written some time ago to Your Reverence has been lost, and so conclude that your many occupations have delayed your esteemed reply, which I look forward to receiving with much anticipation. When you write, will you tell me whether in *a cappella* music consecutive fourths are allowed between the parts, though the bass moves in contrary motion? I found a not disagreeable instance in a score of Signor Perti [2] and have followed his example, but feel that I am being strongly criticized for doing so.

In the second place, please tell me whether one may proceed from the third to the fifth by direct motion, or use consecutive fourths in 8-part *a cappella* music. Lastly, why must one end a minor composition on a major chord? Pardon, Your Reverence, the trouble I give you. I should not dare to inconvenience you did I not remember your generous promise to assist me in any difficulties I may meet with. I beg you to continue your favour to me, and declare myself Your Reverence's, my most revered patron's

Most humble and devoted servant,

J. C. BACH.

---

1 Former teacher of J. C. Bach, "the London Bach."
2 Giacomo Antonio Perti (1661–1756), composer, chiefly of church music.

ANDRÉ ERNESTE GRÉTRY

Liége, 1742 — Montmorency, 1813

❖❀❖❀❖❀❖❀❖❀❖

To *Giambattista Martini*

Paris, March 3, 1768

Reverend Father:

       I have the honour of sending you the two volumes of the *Dictionary* by Jean Jacques,[1] or rather I have already sent you one volume. The man I mentioned who was going to Turin could not do me the favour of taking both — his travelling-bag was too full. Now I await the earliest opportunity to send you the second volume. It will give me the greatest pleasure to receive the second volume of your work,[2] which is so highly praised and esteemed here. Further, Abbé Arnaud expresses his thanks to you for your attention and requested me to inform you that he will write shortly. He will grant your request concerning Monsieur Rameau.

       The *Dictionary* that I sent you is harshly criticized. You will easily recognize the principal reason: namely, that Monsieur Rousseau is the enemy of Monsieur Rameau, although the former makes use of his system and promotes French music, which has frenetic admirers here.

       I do not know whether Your Reverence is acquainted with the reason for this falling out between these two great men. You should know that Monsieur Rameau was present once while Jean Jacques was directing a rehearsal of a French opera [3] he wrote. When it was over, the audience paid him great compliments, but he rather scorned them and remarked that the opinion of that great man (who was standing in a corner) interested him more than anything else. He then requested Monsieur Rameau to pronounce judgment. Monsieur Rameau declared — after inquiring three or four times whether

---

1 *Dictionnaire de musique* (1767), by J. J. Rousseau.
2 *Storia della Musica* (1757).
3 *Les Muses galantes* (1747).

he desired the truth, and each time Monsieur Rousseau replied in the affirmative — that there were parts in it worthy of the greatest masters, but also other parts that a student of four months would not have written. Further, that the recitatives had come from a different pen than the arias. Monsieur Rousseau flew into a rage and burst into tears at the insult. Since that time, they say, they have been enemies, and in the *Dictionary* you will observe that he certainly does not spare him. You see it is a childish quarrel, but great men interest us in everything they do.

> I have the honour to remain, with all respect, Your Reverence's Most humble and obedient servant,
>
> GRÉTRY

KARL STAMITZ

Mannheim, 1746 — Jena, 1801

◦❯◦❮◦❯◦❮◦❯◦❮◦❯◦❮◦

To King *Friedrich Wilhelm II* of *Prussia*

Greiz en Vogtland, April 12, 1791

Sire!

In accordance with Your Majesty's commands, I have the honour to present four selected compositions. A *Symphonie à double orchestres,* the first I ever composed in my life.

Next is a *Symphonie figurée en quatre parties;* the idea for this comes from Versailles in 1772. That year the summer was not at all agreeable, but toward the beginning of October the weather was lovely and every morning the Queen used to go walking in the country. For this I imitated a pastoral. Toward evening a storm springs up, and the night is very dark. But the next day brings fine weather again and the King continues the hunt he ordered the day before.

The third piece is an *Echo à deux orchestres,* for which the second orchestra is closed up in another room.

The fourth, an *Ouverture d'un bal masqué,* I composed at The Hague for Their Most Serene Highnesses the Prince and Princess of Orange. It was performed in the presence of the Grand Duke of Russia. They deigned to express their pleasure, especially the Prince, who graciously considered this piece his favourite.

Since the Ambassador of Turkey is now in Berlin and Your Majesty will certainly desire to honour him with several different kinds of entertainment, and the Turks are fond of this very noisy music, I thought it well to send you these pieces. I would have offered Your Majesty the last three pieces a long time ago, but they were in no state for me to have ventured to present them until now.

Sire, I most humbly request that when these pieces are per-

formed, the orchestra be arranged in the manner I have indicated [1]
so as to create the proper effect and meet with your entire satisfaction. I shall attain the height of happiness should these compositions receive the approval of Your Majesty, who is so great a critic
and connoisseur. I have the honour of commending myself to your
august protection and am, with the deepest respect, Sire,

Your Majesty's most humble and obedient servant,
CHARLES STAMITZ

1 Sketches of orchestral arrangement by Stamitz:

Symphonie à double orchestres

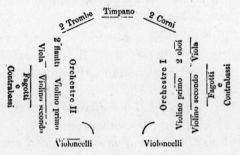

Symphonie figurée en quatre parties

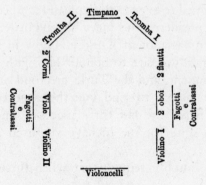

MUZIO CLEMENTI

Rome, 1752 — Evesham, 1832

❂❂❂❂❂❂❂❂

To *F. W. Collard* [1]

Vienna, April 22, 1807

Dear Collard,

By a little management, and without committing myself, I have at last made a complete conquest of that *haughty beauty*, Beethoven; who first began at public places to grin and coquet with me, which of course I took care not to discourage; then slid into familiar chat, till meeting him by chance one day in the street — "Where do you lodge?" says he; "I have not seen you this *long* while!" — upon which I gave him my address. Two days after I found on my table his card, brought by himself, from the maid's description of his lovely form. This will do, thought I. Three days after that he calls again and finds me at home. Conceive then the mutual ecstasy of such a meeting! I took pretty good care to improve it to *our house's* advantage, therefore as soon as decency would allow, after praising very handsomely some of his compositions: "Are you engaged with any publisher in London?" "No," says he. "Suppose, then, that you prefer *me*?" "With all my heart." "Done. What have you ready?" "I'll bring you a list."

In short, I agreed with him to take in MS. three Quartets, a Symphony, an Overture,[2] a Concerto for the Violin, which is beautiful, and which, at my request, he will adapt for the pianoforte, with and without additional keys; and a Concerto for the Pianoforte,[3] for *all* which we are to pay him two hundred pounds sterling. The property, however, is only for the British Dominions. Today sets off a courier for London through Russia, and he will bring over to you two or three of the mentioned articles. Remember that the

---

1 Member of the music-publishing firm, Clementi & Co.
2 The Rasoumowsky Quartets, op. 59; Fourth Symphony; *Coriolanus.*
3 Piano Concerto No. 4 in G major.

[65]

Violin Concerto he will adapt himself and send it as soon as he can. The Quartets, etc. you may get Cramer or some other very clever fellow to adapt for the pianoforte. The Symphony and the Overture are wonderfully fine, so that I think I have made a very good bargain. What do you think? I have likewise engaged him to compose two sonatas and a fantasia for the pianoforte, which he is to deliver to our house for sixty pounds sterling (mind I have treated for Pounds, not Guineas). In short, he has promised to treat with no one but me for the British Dominions. In proportion as you receive his compositions you are to remit him the money; that is, he considers the whole as consisting of six articles, viz. three quartets, symphony, overture, pianoforte concerto, violin concerto, and the adaptation of said concerto, for which he is to receive £200.

[MUZIO CLEMENTI]

WOLFGANG AMADEUS MOZART

Salzburg, 1756 — Vienna, 1791

❂❂❂❂❂❂❂❂

To *Hieronymus von Colloredo*, Archbishop of *Salzburg* [1]

Salzburg, August 1, 1777

Your Grace, Most Worthy Prince of the Holy Roman Empire:

I will not presume to trouble Your Grace with a full description of our unhappy circumstances, which my father has set forth most accurately in his very humble petition that was handed to you on March 14, 1777. As, however, your most gracious decision was never conveyed to him, my father intended last June once more most respectfully to beg Your Grace to allow us to travel for a few months in order to enable us to make some money; and he would have done so if you had not given orders that in view of the imminent visit of His Majesty the Emperor your orchestra should practise various works with a view to their performance.

Later my father again applied for leave of absence, which Your Grace refused to grant, though you permitted me, who am in any case only a half-time servant, to travel alone. Our situation is pressing and my father has therefore decided to let me go alone. But to this course also Your Grace has been pleased to raise certain objections.

Most gracious Prince and Lord! Parents endeavour to place their children in a position to earn their own bread; and in this they follow alike their own interest and that of the state. The greater the talents that children have received from God, the more they are bound to use them for the improvement of their own and their parents' circumstances, so that they may at the same time assist them and take thought of their own future progress. The gospel teaches us to use our talents in this way. My conscience tells me that I owe

---

1 Leopold Mozart was Court Composer and Assistant Kapellmeister, Wolfgang was Concertmaster, in the Archbishop's service.

it to God to be grateful to my father, who has spent his time un-wearyingly upon my education, so that I may lighten his burden, look after myself, and later on be able to support my sister. For I should be sorry to think that she should have spent so many hours at the harpsichord and not be able to make good use of her training.

Your Grace will therefore be so good as to allow me to ask you most humbly for my discharge, of which I should like to take advantage before autumn, so that I may not be obliged to face the bad weather of the ensuing months of winter. Your Grace will not misunderstand this petition, seeing that when I asked you for per-mission to travel to Vienna three years ago, you graciously declared that I had nothing to hope for in Salzburg and would do better to seek my fortune elsewhere. I thank Your Grace for all the favours I have received from you and, in the hope of being able to serve you later on with greater success, I am

Your most humble and obedient servant,[2]
WOLFGANG AMADÉ MOZART

❂❁❂❁❂❁❂❁❂

To his father

Augsburg, October 23, 1777

Mamma is reading your letter now. Last Sunday I attended Mass in the Heiligkreuzkirche and at ten o'clock I went to Herr Stein. That was on the 19th. We rehearsed a few symphonies for the concert. Afterwards I lunched with my uncle at the Heilig-kreuz Monastery. During the meal we had some music. In spite of their poor fiddling I prefer the monastery players to the Augsburg orchestra. I performed a symphony and played Vanhall's Violin Concerto in B flat, which was unanimously applauded. The Dean, who is a cousin of Eberlin, by name Zeschinger, is a fine, jolly fellow and knows Papa quite well. In the evening at supper I played my Strasbourg Concerto [K. 218], which went like oil. Everyone praised my beautiful, pure tone. Afterwards they brought in a small clavichord and I improvised and then played a sonata and the Fischer Variations [K. 179].

Then the others whispered to the Dean that he should just hear me play something in the organ style. I asked him to give me a theme. He declined, but one of the monks gave me one. I put it

---

2 The Archbishop, on August 28, 1777, granted Mozart permission to travel; his father was not permitted to leave.

through its paces and in the middle (the fugue was in G minor) I started off in the major key and played something quite lively, though in the same tempo; and after that the theme over again, but this time arseways. Finally it occurred to me, could I not use my lively time as a theme for a fugue? I did not waste much time in asking, but did so at once, and it went as neatly as if Daser [3] had fitted it. The Dean was absolutely staggered. "Why, it's simply phenomenal, that's all I can say," he said. "I should never have believed what I have heard. You are a first-rate fellow. My Abbot told me, it is true, that he had never in his life heard anyone play the organ so smoothly and so soundly." (For he had heard me play a few days before when the Dean was away.) At last someone produced a sonata in fugal style and wanted me to play it. But I said: "Gentlemen, this is too much. Let me tell you, I shall certainly not be able to play that sonata at sight." "Yes, that I can well believe," said the Dean very pressingly, for he was my strong supporter. "It is too much to expect. No one could tackle that." "However," I said, "I should like to try it." I heard the Dean muttering behind me all the time: "Oh, you little rascal, oh, you villain, oh, you — !" I played until eleven o'clock, for I was bombarded and besieged with themes for fugues.

When I was at Stein's house the other day he put before me a sonata by Beecke — I think I have told you that already. That reminds me, now for his little daughter.[4] Anyone who sees and hears her play and can keep from laughing must, like her father, be made of stone. For instead of sitting in the middle of the clavier, she sits right opposite the treble, as it gives her more chance of flopping about and making grimaces. She rolls her eyes and smirks. When a passage is repeated, she plays it more slowly the second time. If it has to be played a third time, then she plays it even more slowly. When a passage is being played, the arm must be raised as high as possible, and according as the notes in the passage are stressed, the arm, not the fingers, must do this, and that too with great emphasis in a heavy and clumsy manner. But the best joke of all is that when she comes to a passage which ought to flow like oil and which necessitates a change of finger, she does not bother her head about it, but when the moment arrives, she just leaves out the notes, raises her hand, and starts off again quite comfortable — a method by which she is much more likely to strike a wrong note, which often produces a curious effect.

3 A tailor in Salzburg.

4 Maria Anna (Nannette) Stein, child prodigy.

I am simply writing this in order to give Papa some idea of clavier-playing and clavier-teaching, so that he may derive some profit from it later on. Herr Stein is quite crazy about his daughter, who is eight and a half and who now learns everything by heart. She may succeed, for she has a great talent for music. But she will not make progress by this method — for she will never acquire great rapidity, since she definitely does all she can to make her hands heavy. Further, she will never acquire the most essential, the most difficult, and the chief requisite of music, which is time, because from her earliest years she has done her utmost not to play in time.

Herr Stein and I discussed this point for two hours at least and I have almost converted him, for he now asks my advice on everything. He used to be quite crazy about Beecke; but now he sees and hears that I am the better player, that I do not make grimaces, and yet play with such expression that, as he himself confesses, no one up to the present has been able to get such good results out of his pianofortes. Everyone is amazed that I can always keep strict time. What these people cannot grasp is that in "tempo rubato" in an Adagio, the left hand should go on playing in strict time. With them the left hand always follows suit. Count Wolfegg and several other passionate admirers of Beecke publicly admitted at a concert the other day that I had wiped the floor with him. The Count kept running about in the hall, exclaiming: "I have never heard anything like this in my life." And he said to me: "I really must tell you, I have never heard you play as you played today. I shall tell your father so too as soon as I return to Salzburg."

Now what does Papa think we played immediately after the symphony? Why, the Concerto for three claviers [K. 242]. Herr Demmler played the first, I the second, and Herr Stein the third. Then I gave a solo, my last Sonata in D [K. 284], written for Baron Dürnitz, and after that my Concerto in B flat [K. 238]. I then played another solo, quite in the style of the organ, a Fugue in C minor, and then all of a sudden a magnificent Sonata in C major, out of my head, and a rondo to finish up with. There was a regular din of applause. Herr Stein was so amazed that he could only make faces and grimaces. As for Herr Demmler, he couldn't stop laughing. He is a quaint fellow, for when he likes anything very much, all he does is to burst into fits of laughter. In my case he even started to curse. Addio. I kiss Papa's hands and embrace my sister with my whole heart. I am your most obedient son,

WOLFGANG AMADÉ MOZART

To his cousin, *Maria Anna Thekla Mozart*

Mannheim, December 3, 1777

Ma très chère Cousine:

Before I write to you, I must go to the closet. Well, that's over. Ah! At last I feel lighter, a weight is off my heart; and now I can guzzle again. Oh, oh, when you've emptied yourself, life is far more worth living. Your letter of November 25 would have reached me safely if you hadn't written that you had pains in your head, throat, and arms; but as you say that now, at the moment, for the present, for the nonce, at this instant you feel no more pains, I have safely received your letter of November 26. Yes, yes, my dearest Miss Cousin, thus has it been since days of old, Tom has the purse and Dick has the gold; and what do you hold it with? with your ☞, don't you? Huzza, coppersmith, come, be a man, catch if you can, lick my arse, coppersmith. Yes, and true it is that whosoever believes it is happy and whosoever does not will go to heaven, but straight, and not in the way I am writing. You see now that I can write just as I like, both fair and untidy, both straight and crooked. The other day I was in a bad humour and I wrote a fair, straight, and serious hand; today I am in good spirits and I am writing an untidy, crooked, and jolly one. So all depends now on what you prefer. You must make the choice (I have no medium article to offer you) between fair and untidy, straight and crooked, serious and jolly, the three first or the three last. I expect to hear your decision in your next letter. My decision is taken; when it's necessary, I go somewhere; but it all depends on circumstances. If I have diarrhœa, I run: and if I can't contain myself any longer, I shit into my trousers. God preserve thee, foot, on the window-sill lies the hamstring.

I am much obliged to you, my dear Miss Cousin, for the compliments from your Fräulein Freysinger, which your dear Fräulein Juliana has been so kind as to send me. You say: "I could tell you a great deal more, but too much is more than enough." In *one* letter it is too much, I admit, but one can write a great deal by instalments. You see what I mean? As for the sonata, she must possess herself in patience for a little longer. If it had been for my dear coz, it would have been finished long ago. Who knows whether Mlle Freysinger hasn't forgotten all about it? All the same, I'll get it done as soon as possible, write a letter to accompany it, and beg my dear coz to deliver them safely. Apropos, since I left Augsburg, I have not taken off my trousers, except at night before going to bed. What will you think when you hear that I am still in Mannheim, dug in? It is due to my not having left and gone somewhere else! But now I think that I shall soon leave Mannheim. Yet Augsburg, through you, can continue to write to me and address letters to Mannheim until further notice. My uncle, my aunt, and my cousin send their greetings to my mamma and to me. They are anxious about us and thought that we must be ill, as they had received the day before yesterday our letter of November 26, and today, December 3, they have had the pleasure of replying to me. So I am to keep my promise to you? Ah, you are glad to hear this. Be sure you don't forget to compose the Munich for sonata, for what one has once performed, one must promise, one must always be a man of one's word. Well, let's be serious.

I must tell you something very briefly. I did not lunch at home today, but with a certain Mr. Wendling. Now, you must know that he always takes his lunch at two o'clock, that he is married and has a daughter, who, however, is always ailing. His wife is singing in the new opera and he plays on the flute. Well, can you believe it, but when it was half past one we all, except the daughter, who stayed in bed, we all, I say, sat down to table and began to eat.

Please give a whole arseful of greetings from us both to all our good friends. Our remembrances to your parents will be found on page 3, line 12. Well, I've no more news to give you, save that an old cow has shit some new muck. So now adieu, Anna Maria Schlosser, née Schlüsselmacher. Take care of yourself and continue to love me. Write without delay, for it is cold today, and keep your promise too or else forsooth I'll spue. Adieu, mon Dieu, I send you a great dollop of kisses, slap bang wollop!

Mannheim
without slime,
The 3rd of December,
Today's not an Ember,
1777 in dark obscurity,
From now to all eternity
          Amen.

Ma très chère cousine,
Were you never in Berlin?
Your cousin of virtues rare
In weather foul or fair
          W. A. MOZART,
Who shits without a fart.

To his father

Vienna, September 26, 1781

Mon très cher Père:

Forgive me for having made you pay an extra
heavy postage fee the other day. But I happened to have nothing
important to tell you and I thought that it would afford you pleasure if I gave you some idea of my opera.[5] As the original text began
with a monologue, I asked Herr Stephanie to make a little arietta
out of it, and then to put in a duet instead of making the two chatter
together after Osmin's short song. As we have given the part of
Osmin to Herr Fischer, who certainly has an excellent bass voice
(in spite of the fact that the Archbishop told me that he sang too low
for a bass and that I assured him that he would sing higher next
time), we must take advantage of it, particularly as he has the whole
Viennese public on his side. But in the original libretto Osmin has
only this short song and nothing else to sing, except in the trio and
the finale; so he has been given an aria in Act I, and he is to have
another in Act II.

I have explained to Stephanie the words I require for this aria
— indeed, I had finished composing most of the music for it before
Stephanie knew anything whatever about it. I am enclosing only
the beginning and the end, which is bound to have a good effect.
Osmin's rage is rendered comical by the accompaniment of the
Turkish music. In working out the aria I have given full scope now
and then to Fischer's beautiful deep notes (in spite of our Salzburg
Midas). The passage *"Drum beim Barte des Propheten"* is, indeed,
in the same tempo, but with quick notes; but as Osmin's rage gradually increases, there comes (just when the aria seems to be at an end)
the "allegro assai," which is in a totally different meter and in a different key; this is bound to be very effective. For just as a man in
such a towering rage oversteps all the bounds of order, moderation,
and propriety and completely forgets himself, so must the music too
forget itself. But as passions, whether violent or not, must never be
expressed in such a way as to invite disgust, and as music, even in the
most terrible situations, must never offend the ear, but must please
the hearer, or, in other words, must never cease to be MUSIC, I have
gone from F (the key in which the aria is written), not into a re-

---

5 *Die Entführung aus dem Serail.*

mote key, but into a related one, not, however, into its nearest relative, D minor, but into the more remote A minor.

Let me now turn to Belmonte's aria in A major, "*O wie ängstlich, o wie feurig.*" Would you like to know how I have expressed it — and even indicated his throbbing heart? By the two violins playing octaves. This is the favourite aria of all those who have heard it, and it is mine also. I wrote it expressly to suit Adamberger's voice. You feel the trembling — the faltering — you see how his throbbing breast begins to swell; this I have expressed by a crescendo. You hear the whispering and the sighing — which I have indicated by the first violins with mutes and a flute playing in unison.

The Janissary chorus is, as such, all that can be desired; that is, short, lively, and written to please the Viennese. I have sacrificed Constanze's aria a little to the flexible throat of Mlle Cavalieri, "*Trennung war mein banges Los und nun Schwimmt mein Aug' in Tränen.*" I have tried to express her feelings, as far as an Italian bravura aria will allow it. I have changed the "*Hui*" to "*schnell,*" so it now runs thus — "*Doch wie schnell schwand meine Freude.*" I really don't know what our German poets are thinking of. Even if they do not understand the theatre, or at all events operas, yet they should not make their characters talk as if they were addressing a herd of swine. Hui, sow!

Now for the trio at the close of Act I. Pedrillo has passed off his master as an architect — to give him an opportunity of meeting his Constanze in the garden. Bassa Selim has taken him into his service. Osmin, the steward, knows nothing of this and, being a rude churl and a sworn foe to all strangers, is impertinent and refuses to let them into the garden. It opens quite abruptly — and because the words lend themselves to it, I have made it a fairly respectable piece of real three-part writing. Then the major key begins at once pianissimo — it must go very quickly — and wind up with a great deal of noise, which is always appropriate at the end of an act. The more noise the better, so that the audience may not have time to cool down with their applause.

I have sent you only four bars of the overture, which is very short with alternate fortes and pianos, the Turkish music always coming in at the fortes. The overture modulates through different keys; and I doubt whether anyone, even if his previous night has been a sleepless one, could go to sleep over it. Now comes the rub! The first act was finished more than three weeks ago, as was also one aria in Act II and the drunken duet (*per i signori viennesi*) which consists entirely of my Turkish tattoo. But I cannot compose any more, because the whole story is being altered — and, to tell the truth, at my own request. At the beginning of Act III there is a charming quintet or rather finale, but I should prefer to have it at the end of Act II. In order to make this practicable, great changes must be made, in fact an entirely new plot must be introduced — and Stephanie is up to the eyes in other work. So we must have a little patience. Everyone abuses Stephanie. It may be that in my case he is only very friendly to my face. But after all he is arranging the libretto for me — and, what is more, as I want it — exactly — and, by Heaven, I do not ask anything more of him.

Well, how I have been chattering to you about my opera! But I cannot help it. Please send me the march that I mentioned the other day. Gilowsky says that Daubrawaick will soon be here. Fräulein von Aurnhammer and I are longing to have the two double concertos. I hope we shall not wait as vainly as the Jews for their Messiah. Well, adieu. Farewell. I kiss your hands a thousand times and embrace with all my heart my dear sister, whose health, I hope, is improving, and am ever your most obedient son

W. A. Mozart

To his father

Vienna, December 15, 1781

Mon très cher Père:

I have this moment received your letter of the 12th. Herr von Daubrawaick will bring you this letter, the watch, the Munich opera,[6] the six engraved sonatas,[7] the sonata for two claviers,[8] and the cadenzas. As for the Princess Württemberg and myself, all is over.[9] The Emperor has spoiled everything, for he cares for no one but Salieri. The Archduke Maximilian recommended *me* to her and she replied that had it rested with her, she would never have engaged anyone else, but that on account of her singing the Emperor had suggested Salieri. She added that she was

6 *Idomeneo.*
7 For violin and clavier, K. 296, 376–380.
8 K. 448, composed in November 1781.
9 Mozart had expected to give her clavier lessons.

extremely sorry. What you tell me about the house of Württemberg and yourself may possibly prove useful to me.

Dearest Father, you demand an explanation of the words in the closing sentence of my last letter! [10] Oh, how gladly would I have opened my heart to you long ago, but I was deterred by the reproaches you might have made to me for *thinking of such a thing at an unseasonable time* — although indeed thinking can never be unseasonable. Meanwhile I am very anxious to secure here a small but *certain* income, which, together with what chance may provide, will enable me to live here quite comfortably — and then — to marry!

You are horrified at the idea? But I entreat you, dearest, most beloved Father, to listen to me. I have been obliged to reveal my intentions to you. You must therefore allow me to disclose to you my reasons, which, moreover, are very well founded. The voice of nature speaks as loud in me as in others, louder, perhaps, than in many a big strong lout of a fellow. I simply cannot live as most young men do in these days. In the first place, I have too much religion; in the second place, I have too great a love of my neighbour and too high a feeling of honour to seduce an innocent girl; and, in the third place, I have too much horror and disgust, too much dread and fear of diseases, and too much care for my health to fool about with whores. So I can swear that I have never had relations of that sort with any woman. Besides, if such a thing had occurred, I should not have concealed it from you; for, after all, to err is natural enough in a man, and to err *once* would be mere weakness — although, indeed, I should not undertake to promise that if I had erred once in this way, I should stop short at one slip. However, I stake my life on the truth of what I have told you.

I am well aware that this reason (powerful as it is) is not urgent enough. But owing to my disposition, which is more inclined to a peaceful and domesticated existence than to revelry, I, who from my youth up have never been accustomed to look after my own belongings, linen, clothes, and so forth, cannot think of any-

---

10 Vienna, December 5, 1781: "You say that I must not forget you! That you rejoice to think that I do not gives me the greatest pleasure. But if you could believe it possible that I should forget you, that indeed would pain me dreadfully. You say that I must remember that I have an immortal soul. Not only do I think it, but I firmly believe it. If it were not so, wherein would consist the difference between men and beasts? Just because I both know and most firmly believe this, I have not been able to carry out all your wishes exactly in the way you expected. Now farewell!"

thing more necessary to me than a wife. I assure you that I am often
obliged to spend unnecessarily, simply because I do not pay attention to things. I am absolutely convinced that I should manage better
with a wife (on the same income that I have now) than I do by myself. And how many useless expenses would be avoided! True, other
expenses would have to be met, but — one knows what they are and
can be prepared for them — in short, one leads a well-ordered existence. A bachelor, in my opinion, is only half alive. Such are my
views and I cannot help it. I have thought the matter over and reflected sufficiently, and I shall not change my mind.

But who is the object of my love? Do not be horrified again,
I entreat you. Surely not one of the Webers? Yes, one of the Webers
— but not Josefa, nor Sophie, but Constanze, the middle one. In no
other family have I ever come across such differences of character.
The eldest is a lazy, gross, perfidious woman, and as cunning as a
fox. Mme Lange [11] is a false, malicious person and a coquette. The
youngest — is still too young to be anything in particular — she is
just a good-natured, but feather-headed creature! May God protect
her from seduction! But the middle one, my good, dear Constanze,
is the martyr of the family and, probably for that very reason, is the
kindest-hearted, the cleverest, and, in short, the best of them all.
She makes herself responsible for the whole household and yet in
their opinion she does nothing right.

Oh, my most beloved Father, I could fill whole sheets with
descriptions of all the scenes that I have witnessed in that house. If
you want to read them, I shall do so in my next letter. But before
I cease to plague you with my chatter, I must make you better acquainted with the character of my dear Constanze. She is not ugly,
but at the same time far from beautiful. Her whole beauty consists
in two little black eyes and a pretty figure. She has no wit, but she
has enough common sense to enable her to fulfil her duties as a wife
and mother. It is a downright lie that she is inclined to be extravagant. On the contrary, she is accustomed to be shabbily dressed, for
the little that her mother has been able to do for her children she has
done for the two others, but never for Constanze. True, she would
like to be neatly and cleanly dressed, but not smartly, and most
things that a woman needs she is able to make for herself; and she
dresses her own hair every day. Moreover, she understands housekeeping and has the kindest heart in the world. I love her and she

---

11 Another Weber sister.

loves me with all her heart. Tell me whether I could wish myself a better wife.

One thing more I must tell you, which is that when I resigned the Archbishop's service, our love had not yet begun. It was born of her tender care and attentions when I was living in their house.

Accordingly, all that I desire is to have a small assured income (of which, thank God, I have good hopes), and then I shall never cease entreating you to allow me to save this poor girl — and to make myself and her — and, if I may say so, all of us very happy. For you surely are happy when I am? And you are to enjoy one half of *my fixed income*. My dearest Father, I have opened my heart to you and explained my remarks. It is now my turn to beg you to explain yours in your last letter. You say that I cannot imagine that you were aware *a proposal which had been made to me and to which I, at the time when you heard of it, had not yet replied*. I do not understand one word of this — I know of no such proposal. Please take pity on your son! I kiss your hands a thousand times and am ever your most obedient son,[12]

W. A. MOZART

To *Michael Puchberg*

Vienna, July 12–14, 1789

*Dearest most beloved Friend
and most honourable B. O.:*[13]

Great God! I would not wish my worst enemy to be in my present position. And if you, most beloved friend and brother, forsake me, we are altogether lost, *both my unfortunate and blameless self* and my poor sick wife and child. Only the other day when I was with you I was longing to open my heart to you, but I had not the courage to do so — and indeed I should still not have the courage — for, as it is, I only dare write, and tremble as I do so — and I should not even dare to write, were I not certain that you know me, that you are aware of my circumstances, and that you are wholly convinced of my *innocence* so far as my unfortunate and most distressing situation is concerned.

Good God! I am coming to you not with thanks but with fresh

---

12 Mozart and Constanze Weber were married on August 4, 1782.
13 Brother in the Order of Masons; Mozart had become a Mason in 1784.

entreaties! Instead of paying my debts I am asking for more money! If you really know me, you must sympathize with my anguish in having to do so. I need not tell you once more that owing to my unfortunate illness I have been prevented from earning anything. But I must mention that in spite of my wretched condition I decided to give subscription concerts at home in order to be able to meet at least my present great and frequent expenses, for I was absolutely convinced of your friendly assistance. But even this has failed. Unfortunately fate is so much against me, *though only in Vienna*, that even when I want to, I cannot make any money.

A fortnight ago I sent round a list for subscribers and so far the only name on it is that of Baron van Swieten! Now that (the 13th) my dear little wife seems to be improving every day, I should be able to set to work again, if this blow, this heavy blow, had not come. At any rate, people are consoling me by telling me that she is better — although the night before last she was suffering so much — and I on her account — that I was stunned and despairing. But last night (the 14th) she slept so well and has felt so much easier all the morning that I am very hopeful; and at last I am beginning to feel incined for work. I am now faced, however, with misfortunes of another kind, though, it is true, only for the moment.

Dearest, most beloved friend and brother — you know *my present circumstances*, but you also know my *prospects*. So let things remain as we arranged; that is, *thus or thus*, you understand what I mean. Meanwhile I am composing six easy clavier sonatas [14] for Princess Frederike and six quartets [15] for the King, all of which Kozeluch is engraving at my expense. At the same time the two dedications will bring me in something. In a month or two my fate must be decided *in every detail*. Therefore, most beloved friend, you will not be risking anything so far as I am concerned. So it all depends, my only friend, upon whether you will or can lend me another 500 gulden. Until my affairs are settled, I undertake to pay back ten gulden a month; and then, as this is bound to happen in a few months, I shall pay back the whole sum with whatever interest you may demand, and at the same time acknowledge myself to be your debtor for life. That, alas, I shall have to remain, for I shall never be able to thank you sufficiently for your friendship and affection. Thank God, that is over. Now you know all. Do not be offended by my confiding in you and remember that unless you help

---

14 He finished only one of these: K. 576, his last.
15 He completed only three: K. 575 (1789), K. 589 and 590 (1790).

me, the honour, the peace of mind, and perhaps the very life of your friend and brother Mason will be ruined.

> Ever your most grateful servant, true friend and brother
> W. A. MOZART

At home, July 14, 1789

Oh God! — I can hardly bring myself to dispatch this letter! — and yet I must! If this illness had not befallen me, I should not have been obliged to beg so shamelessly from my only friend. Yet I hope for your forgiveness, for you know both the good *and the bad prospects of my situation*. The bad is temporary; the good will certainly persist, once the momentary evil has been alleviated. Adieu. For God's sake forgive me, only forgive me! — and — Adieu!

❁❁❁❁❁❁❁❁❁

To his wife

Vienna, July 7, 1791

Dearest, most beloved little Wife:

You will forgive me, I know, for only sending you *one letter* a day. The reason is that I must keep hold of —— and not let him escape. I am at his house every day at seven o'clock in the morning.

I hope you got my letter of yesterday. I did not go to see the balloon, for it is the sort of thing that one can imagine. Besides, I thought that this time, too, nothing would come of it. But goodness! How the Viennese are rejoicing! They are as full of his praises now as they have been up to the present of abuses.

There is something in your letters that I cannot read and something I cannot understand. You say: "I am certain that my — little husband will be in the Prater today in a numerous com. etc." I presume that "com." stands for "company" — but what you mean by "numerous company" I cannot think.

Tell Sauermayer [16] from me that I have not had time to be for ever running off to his Primus and that whenever I did go he was never at home. Just give him the three gulden, so that he may not cry.

My one wish now is that my affairs should be settled, so that I can be with you again. You cannot imagine how I have been aching for you all this long while. I can't describe what I have been

---

16 Nickname for Franz Xaver Süssmayr, friend and pupil of Mozart.

feeling — a kind of emptiness, which hurts me dreadfully — a kind of longing, which is never satisfied, which never ceases, and which persists — nay, rather increases — daily. When I think how merry we were together at Baden — like children — and what sad, weary hours I am spending here! Even my work gives me no pleasure, because I am accustomed to stop working now and then and exchange a few words with you. Alas! this pleasure is not longer possible. If I go to the piano and sing something out of my opera,[17] I have to stop at once, for this stirs my emotions too deeply. Basta! The very hour after I finish this business I shall be off and away from here. I have no news to tell you. The illuminations at Baden were, I dare say, a little premature — as the truth is precisely the contrary. I shall inquire at the court chemist's, where the electuary may perhaps be obtained. If so, I shall send it to you at once. Meanwhile, if it is necessary, I should advise you to take *tartar* rather than *brandy*. Adieu, dearest little wife.

Ever your
MOZART

---

17 *The Magic Flute.*

LUDWIG VAN BEETHOVEN

Bonn, 1770 — *Vienna*, 1827

❀❀❀❀❀❀❀❀

To *Karl Amenda* [1]

Vienna, June 1, 1801

My dear, good Amenda, my cordial friend, I received and read your last letter with mixed pain and pleasure. To what shall I compare your fidelity, your attachment to me? Oh, it is so beautiful that you have always been true to me, and I know how to single you out and keep you above all others. You are not a Viennese friend, no, you are one of those who spring from the ground of my native land. How often do I wish you were with me, for your Beethoven is living an unhappy life, quarrelling with nature and its creator, often cursing the latter because He surrendered His creatures to the merest accident, which sometimes broke or destroyed the most beautiful blossoms.

Know that my noblest faculty, my hearing, has greatly deteriorated. When you were still with me I felt the symptoms, but kept silent; now it is continually growing worse, and whether or not a cure is possible has become a question; but it is said to be due to my bowels, and so far as they are concerned I am nearly restored to health. I hope, indeed, that my hearing will also improve, but I am dubious because such diseases are the most incurable. How sad is my lot! I must avoid all things that are dear to me and live among such miserable and egotistical men as —— and —— and others. I must say that among them all Lichnowsky [2] is the most satisfactory, since last year he settled an income of 600 florins on me and the good sale of my works enables me to live without care. I could sell everything that I compose five times over and at a good price. I have written considerably of late, and as I hear that you have ordered a pianoforte from —— I will send you various things in the box of the instrument so that it need not cost you much.

1 Amateur violinist who became friendly with Beethoven in Vienna in 1798.
2 Prince Karl Lichnowsky, one of Beethoven's greatest admirers and most generous patrons.

To my comfort there has lately come a man with whom I can share the pleasures of association, an unselfish friendship; he is one of the friends of my youth. I have often spoken of you to him and told him that since I left my fatherland you have been the only choice of my heart. —— is not very satisfactory to him — he is and always will be too weak for friendship. I use him and —— only as instruments on which I play when I please, but they can never become witnesses of my whole internal and external activities or real participants [in my feelings]. I estimate them at only what they are worth to me.

Oh, how happy could I be if my hearing were completely restored; then would I hurry to you, but as it is I must refrain from everything and the most beautiful years of my life must pass without accomplishing the promise of my talent and powers. A sad resignation to which I must resort, although, indeed, I am resolved to rise superior to every obstacle. But how will that be possible? Yes, Amenda, if my infirmity shows itself to be incurable in half a year, I shall appeal to you; you must abandon everything and come to me. My affliction causes me the least trouble in playing and composing, the most in association with others, and you must be my companion. I am sure my fortune will not desert me. What might I not essay? Since you have been gone I have composed everything except operas and church music. You will not deny me; you will help your friend bear his cares and affliction. I have also greatly bettered my pianoforte-playing and I hope the journey will, perhaps, make your fortune; afterwards you will remain with me.

I have received all of your letters, and despite the fact that I answered so few, you were always with me and my heart still beats as tenderly for you as ever it did. I beg you to keep the matter of my deafness a profound secret to *be confided to nobody no matter who it is.* Write to me very often. Your letters, no matter how short, comfort me, do me good, and I shall soon expect another from you, my dear fellow. Do not lend your quartet [3] to anybody, because I have changed it greatly, having just learned how to write quartets properly, as you will observe when you receive it. Now farewell, my dear, good fellow; if you think I can do something for you here, command me as a matter of course.

Your faithful and truly affectionate
L. V. BEETHOVEN

---

3 Op. 18, no. 1, which Beethoven had presented to Amenda in June 1799.

[*The Heiligenstadt Testament*]

To his brothers

Heiligenstadt, October 6, 1802

For my brothers Carl and [Johann] Beethoven to be read and executed after my death.

O ye men who think or say that I am malevolent, stubborn or misanthropic, how greatly do ye wrong me, you do not know the secret causes of my seeming, from childhood my heart and mind were disposed to the gentle feeling of goodwill, I was even eager to accomplish great deeds, but reflect now that for 6 years I have been in a hopeless case, aggravated by senseless physicians, cheated year after year in the hope of improvement, finally compelled to face the prospect of a *lasting malady* (whose cure will take years or, perhaps, be impossible), born with an ardent and lively temperament, even susceptible to the diversions of society, I was compelled early to isolate myself, to live in loneliness, when I at times tried to forget all this, oh, how harshly was I repulsed by the doubly sad experience of my bad hearing, and yet it was impossible for me to say to men: speak louder, shout, for I am deaf. Ah, how could I possibly admit an infirmity in the *one sense* that should have been more perfect in me than in others, a sense that I once possessed in highest perfection, a perfection such as few surely in my profession enjoy or ever have enjoyed —

Oh, I cannot do it, therefore forgive me when you see me draw back when I would gladly mingle with you, my misfortune is doubly painful because it must lead to my being misunderstood, for me there can be no recreation in society of my fellows, refined intercourse, mutual exchange of thought, only just as little as the greatest needs command may I mix with society. I must live like an exile, if I approach near to people a hot terror seizes upon me, a fear that I may be subjected to the danger of letting my condition be observed — thus it has been during the last half year, which I spent in the country, commanded by my intelligent physician to spare my hearing as much as possible, in this almost meeting my present natural disposition, although I sometimes ran counter to it yielding to my inclination for society, but what a humiliation when one stood beside me and heard a flute in the distance and *I heard nothing* or someone heard *the shepherd singing* and again I heard nothing, such incidents brought me to the verge of despair, but little more and I would have put an end to my life — only art it was that withheld me; ah, it seemed impossible to leave the world until I had produced all that I felt called upon to produce, and so I endured this wretched existence — truly wretched, an excitable body which a sudden change can throw from the best into the worst state — Patience it is said I must now choose for my guide, I have done so, I hope my determination will remain firm to endure until it pleases the inexorable *parcæ* to break the thread, perhaps I shall get better, perhaps not, I am prepared.

Forced already in my 28th year to become a philosopher, oh, it is not easy, less easy for the artist than for anyone else — Divine One thou lookest into my inmost soul, thou knowest it, thou knowest that love of man and desire to do good live therein. O men, when some day you read these words, reflect that ye did me wrong and let the unfortunate one comfort himself and find one of his kind who despite all the obstacles of nature yet did all that was in his power to be accepted among worthy artists and men. You my brothers Carl and [Johann] as soon as I am dead if Dr. Schmid is still alive ask him in my name to describe my malady and attach this document to the history of my illness so that so far as is possible at least the world may become reconciled with me after my death. At the same time I declare you two to be the heirs to my small fortune (if so it can be called), divide it fairly, bear with and help each other, what injury you have done me you know was long ago forgiven. To you, brother Carl, I give special thanks for the attachment you have displayed toward me of late. It is my wish that your lives may be better and freer from care than I have had, recommend *virtue* to your children, it alone can give happiness, not money, I speak from experience, it was virtue that upheld me in misery, to it next to my art I owe the fact that I did not end my life by suicide —

Farewell and love each other — I thank all my friends, particularly *Prince Lichnowsky* and *Professor Schmid* — I desire that the instruments from Prince L.[4] be preserved by one of you but let no quarrel result from this, so soon as they can serve you a better purpose sell them, how glad will I be if I can still be helpful to you in my grave — with joy I hasten toward death — if it comes before I shall have had an opportunity to show all my artistic capacities it will still come too early for me despite my hard fate and I shall probably wish that it had come later — but even then I am satisfied, will

---

4 A set of string quartet instruments given him by Prince Lichnowsky.

it not free me from a state of endless suffering? Come when thou wilt I shall meet thee bravely — Farewell and do not wholly forget me when I am dead, I deserve this of you in having often in life thought of you how to make you happy, be so —

LUDWIG VAN BEETHOVEN

Heiligenstadt, October 10, 1802, thus do I take my farewell of thee — and indeed sadly — yes that beloved hope — which I brought with me when I came here to be cured at least in a degree — I must wholly abandon, as the leaves of autumn fall and are withered so hope has been blighted, almost as I came — I go away — even the high courage — which often inspired me in the beautiful days of summer — has disappeared — O Providence — grant me at last but one day of pure *joy* — it is so long since real joy echoed in my heart — oh, when — oh, when, O Divine One — shall I feel it again in the temple of nature and of men — Never? no — oh, that would be too hard.

⊙⊱⊙⊱⊙⊱⊙⊱⊙⊱⊙

To the Immortal Beloved [5]

[*Teplitz*], July 6, [1806] [6]

My angel, my all, my very self — only a few words today and at that with pencil (with yours) — not till tomorrow will my lodgings be definitively determined upon — what a useless waste of time. Why this deep sorrow where necessity speaks — can our love endure except through sacrifices — except through not demanding everything — can you change it that you are not wholly mine, I not wholly thine? Oh, God! look out into the beauties of nature and comfort yourself with that which must be — love demands everything and that very justly — *thus it is with me so far as you are concerned, and you with me.* If we were wholly united you would feel the pain of it as little as I.

My journey was a fearful one; I did not reach here until 4 o'clock yesterday morning; lacking horses the post-coach chose another route — but what an awful one! At the stage before the last I was warned not to travel at night — made fearful of a forest, but that only made me the more eager and I was wrong; the coach must

---

5 This letter was discovered in Beethoven's rooms immediately after his death. It is thought to have been intended for Giulietta Guicciardi, Bettina Brentano, or Amalie Sebald.

6 According to Thayer; other music historians place it between 1802 and 1812.

needs break down on the wretched road, a bottomless mud road — without such postilions as I had with me I should have stuck in the road. Esterházy, travelling the usual road hitherward, had the same fate with eight horses that I had with four — yet I got some pleasure out of it, as I always do when I successfully overcome difficulties.

Now a quick change to things internal from things external. We shall soon surely see each other; moreover, I cannot communicate to you the observations I have made during the last few days touching my own life — if our hearts were always close together I would make none of the kind. My heart is full of many things to say to you — Ah! — there are moments when I feel that speech is nothing after all — cheer up — remain my true, my only treasure, my all as I am yours; the gods must send us the rest that which shall be best for us.

Your faithful
LUDWIG
Evening, Monday, July 6

You are suffering, my dearest creature — only now have I learned that letters must be posted very early in the morning. Mondays, Thursdays — the only days on which the mail-coach goes from here to K[arlsbad]. You are suffering — Ah! wherever I am, there you are also. I shall arrange affairs between us so that I shall live and live with you, what a life!!!! thus!!!! thus without you — pursued by the goodness of mankind hither and thither — which I as little try to deserve as I deserve it. Humility of man toward man — it pains me — and when I consider myself in connection with the universe, what am I and what is he whom we call the greatest — and yet — herein lies the divine in man. I weep when I reflect that you will probably not receive the first intelligence from me until Saturday — much as you love me, I love you more — but do not ever conceal your thoughts from me — good night — as I am taking the baths I must go to bed. Oh, God! so near so far! Is our love not truly a celestial edifice — firm as heaven's vault.

Good morning, on July 7

Though still in bed my thoughts go out to you, my Immortal Beloved, now and then joyfully, then sadly, waiting to learn whether or not fate will hear us. I can live only wholly with you or not at all — yes, I am resolved to wander so long away from you until I can fly to your arms and say that I am really at home, send my soul enwrapped in you into the land of spirits. — Yes, unhappily it must be so — you will be the more resolved since you know my fidelity —

to you, no one can ever again possess my heart — none — never —
Oh, God, why is it necessary to part from one whom one so loves
and yet my life in V[ienna] is now a wretched life — your love
makes me at once the happiest and the unhappiest of men — at my
age I need a steady, quiet life — can that be under our conditions?
My angel, I have just been told that the mail-coach goes every day
— and I must close at once so that you may receive the l[etter] at
once. Be calm, only by a calm consideration of our existence can we
achieve our purpose to live together — be calm — love me — today
— yesterday — what tearful longings for you — you — you — my
life — my all — farewell — Oh, continue to love me — never mis-
judge the most faithful heart of your beloved L.

> ever thine
> ever mine
> ever for each other.

❖❖❖❖❖❖❖❖

To *Johann Wolfgang von Goethe*

Vienna, April 12, 1811

Only a moment's time offers me the urgent opportunity inasmuch as a friend of mine who is a great admirer of yours (like myself) is hastily departing from here, to thank you for the long time
that I have known you (for I know you since my childhood) —
that is so little for so much — Bettina Brentano has assured me that
you will graciously, even kindly receive me, but how can I think of
such a reception when I can only approach you with the greatest
reverence and with an unutterably deep feeling for your glorious
creations — you will soon receive the music to *Egmont* [7] from Leipzig through Breitkopf & Härtel, this glorious *Egmont* which I read
so ardently, thought over and experienced again and gave out in
music — I would greatly like to have your judgment on it and your
blame, too . . . will be beneficial to me and my art, and be accepted
as gladly as the highest praise.

> Your Excellency's
> Great admirer,
> LUDWIG VAN BEETHOVEN

---

7 First performed May 24, 1810.

To *Emilie M.*[8]

Teplitz, July 17, 1812

Dear good Emilie,
my dear friend:

I am late in answering your letter — my excuse is a great deal of business and constant illness. The fact that I am here for a health cure proves the truthfulness of my excuse.

Do not snatch away the laurel wreaths from Handel, Haydn, and Mozart, for they deserve them; as yet I do not. I shall keep your pocketbook with the other many tokens of esteem I have received and which I do not merit. Continue; do not merely practise art but penetrate to the very heart of it — this it deserves — for only art and science elevate man to the Godhead. If you want to know something at any time, write me without hesitation, dear Emilie. The true artist is not proud. He senses dimly how far he is from his goal, and though others may admire him, he feels sad not to have reached the point where his better genius lights the way like a distant sun.

I would sooner come and visit you and your people than many rich folk who display inner poverty. If one day I should come to H., I will call on you at your home. I recognize no other superiorities in man than those which cause him to rank among better men; where I find this is my home.

Dear Emilie, if you wish to write me, address me here directly where I shall be for the next four weeks, or to Vienna, it doesn't matter. Regard me as your friend and the friend of your family.

LUDWIG VAN BEETHOVEN

❧❀❧❀❧❀❧❀❧❀

To *Ignaz von Mosel*[9]

1817

I am very pleased that you share my opinion in regard to the terms designating the measure of time that were handed down to us when music was still in an age of barbarism. For instance, what could be more meaningless than *Allegro*, which definitely means *merry*,

---

8 A child of ten or twelve. Beethoven writes in reply to a letter of appreciation and a pocketbook she sent him.
9 Music critic, one of the managers of the Court Theatre in Vienna (1772–1844).

and frequently how far off we are from that conception of this tempo, so that the piece itself expresses something quite contrary to that term! As regards the four principal tempo indications, which indicate neither truthfully nor correctly the importance of the four principal movements, we can easily lay them aside.

However, it is another matter with the words that indicate the character of a composition; these we cannot give up since they are virtually indicative of *the soul of the piece*, whereas the time refers more or less to the body. For my part, I have frequently thought of abandoning those meaningless terms: Allegro, Andante, Adagio, Presto, and now Maelzel's [10] metronome gives us the best opportunity for this. I hereby give you *my word* that I shall *no longer* use them in my new compositions. Another question is whether by this means we can bring the M[etronome] into general use — which is so necessary. I have no doubt they will shout that I am a *despot*, which would be worth it if it served the cause; anyway, that would be better than accusing me of *feudalism*. My opinion is that the best thing for our country, once music has become a national necessity and every village schoolmaster has to promote the use of the metronome, would be for Maelzel to try to bring out by subscription a certain number of metronomes at higher prices, and when the number covers his expenses, he will be able to supply the other necessary metronomes for the national musical needs at so cheap a rate that we can expect them to be used in the most general and extensive fashion.

It is self-evident, of course, that some people must place themselves at the head of such a movement to give it stimulus. In so far as my influence can be of help to you, you may certainly count on me, and with pleasure I await the post you will assign to me therein.

Sir, with great esteem,

Yours most devotedly,

LUDWIG VAN BEETHOVEN

---

10 Johann Nepomuk Maelzel (1772–1838), Viennese mechanic and inventor of the metronome.

To *Johann Wolfgang von Goethe*

Vienna, February 8, 1823

Your Excellency:

Still living as I have lived from my youthful years in your immortal, never aging works, and never forgetting the happy hours spent in your company, it nevertheless happens that I must recall myself to your recollection — I hope that you received the dedication to Your Excellency of *Meerstille und glück-liche Fahrt* composed by me. Because of their contrast they seemed to me adapted for music in which the same quality appears; how gladly would I know whether I have fittingly united my harmonies with yours; advice too, which would be accepted as very truth, would be extremely welcome to me, for I love the latter above all things and it shall never be said of me *veritas odium parit*. It is very possible that a number of your poems, which must ever remain unique, set to music by me, will soon be published, among them *Rastlose Liebe*. How highly would I value some general observations from you on the composition or setting to music of your poems!

Now a request to Y. E. I have composed a Grand Mass,[11] which, however, I do not want to publish at present, but which is to be sent to the principal courts. The honorarium for the same is 50 ducats only. I have addressed myself in the matter to the Grand-Ducal Weimarian Embassy, which has accepted the appeal to His Serene Highness and promised to deliver it. The Mass can also be used as an oratorio, and who does not know that the benevolent societies are suffering from the lack of such things? My request consists in this: that Y. E. call the attention of His Serene Highness the Grand Duke to this matter so that His Highness may subscribe for the Mass. The Grand-Ducal Weimarian Embassy gave me to understand that it would be very beneficial if the Grand Duke could be induced to regard the matter favourably in advance.

I have written much but accumulated scarcely anything, and now I am no longer alone but have for more than six years been father to a son of my deceased brother, a promising youth in his sixteenth year, wholly devoted to science and already at home in the rich shafts of Hellenism; but in these countries such things cost a great deal and, in the case of young students, not only the present

---

11 *Missa Solemnis.*

but also the future must be borne in mind, and as much as I formerly kept my thoughts directed aloft I must now extend my glances *downwards*.

My income is all outgo — the condition of my health for years had not permitted that I make artistic journeys or seize upon the many things that yield money! — If my health should be completely restored I might expect other and better things. Y. E. must not think that it is because I am asking a favour that I have dedicated the *Meerstille und glückliche Fahrt* to you — this was already done in May 1822, and this method of making the Mass known was not thought of till a few weeks ago. The respect, love, and esteem that I have cherished for the only and immortal Goethe since the days of my youth have remained with me. Things like this are not easily put into words, especially by a bungler like myself, who has always been bent only on making tones his own, but a singular feeling impels me always to tell you this, inasmuch as I live in your works. I know that you will not refuse to help an artist who feels only too keenly how far mere *monetary reward* is from *her* [art] now that he is compelled by *need* and constrained to work and labour *because of others for others*. The good is always plain to us and therefore I know that Y. E. will not deny my request.

A few words from you would fill me with happiness.

I remain, Your Excellency, with the sincerest and most unbounded respect,

BEETHOVEN

To *Ignaz Moscheles* [12]

Vienna, March 18, 1827

I can hardly put into words the feelings I had when I read your letter of March 1. This magnanimity on the part of the Philharmonic Society has moved me to the very depths of my heart. I beg you, therefore, dear Moscheles, to convey my deepest thanks to the Philharmonic Society for their unusual sympathy and support. Tell these worthy gentlemen that when God restores my health to me again,[13] I shall attempt to express my gratitude through new works and that I leave it to the Society to select what they would like me

12 Renowned pianist then residing in London.
13 Beethoven died on March 26, 1827.

to write for them. A symphony, completely sketched, lies in my desk together with a new overture and also something else.

In regard to the concert that the Philharmonic has decided to arrange in my behalf, I urgently request them not to abandon the idea. In short, I shall endeavour to fulfil everything the Society may request and I have never approached any work of mine with such love as would happen in this case. May Heaven only give me back my health soon and I shall prove to the generous Englishmen how much I appreciate their sympathy with my sad fate.

I found I had to draw the entire amount of 1,000 florins at once since I happened to be in the disagreeable position of having to borrow money. I shall never forget your very generous behaviour and I am going to send my thanks to Sir Smart and Mr. Stumpff very shortly. I ask you to turn over the metronomized Ninth Symphony to the Philharmonic Society. The markings are enclosed herewith. With highest esteem,

Your friend,
BEETHOVEN

GASPARO SPONTINI

Majolati, 1774 — Majolati, 1851

✥❀✥❀✥❀✥❀✥❀✥

To *Antonio Salieri*

Paris, April 9, 1816

Honoured Master:

At last, thanks to your efforts, the musical world and especially the composers have obtained what they sought and desired for a long time to establish: the tempi of their music. Yesterday, at a meeting of the foremost composers of Paris (where I also had the honour to be present), they expressed great admiration for the perfected chronometer of Herr Maelzel,[1] who asserted that this was the result of frequent encouragement and judicious advice from the celebrated Maestro Salieri, whose friendship I have the good fortune to possess.

A twofold interest induced us then and there to make a rigid examination of this instrument, and the more closely we examined it, the more we discovered its perfection and the immeasurable interest it will arouse as soon as it becomes commonly known and employed. Italy, Germany, France, and England will commend the inventor as the originator of a machine that truly restores all the intentions of the composer and prevents the public from distorting his intentions as has been done up to the present time.

Following your precedent, we have all signed a manifesto expressing our utter admiration for an invention that music had lacked up to now and that many had sought in vain. Accept, dear master, my particular gratitude as well as that of the assembled composers, whose interpreter I am.

Your most obliged servant and friend,
SPONTINI

---

1 The metronome.

LOUIS SPOHR

Brunswick, 1784 — *Kassel,* 1859

❖❖❖❖❖❖❖❖❖

To *Moritz Hauptmann* [1]

Kassel, June 11, 1853

Dear Friend:

Herewith I am sending you the manuscript of the Bach *Inventions* and the three-part *Sinfonias*.[2] Will you retain the interesting titles when you have them published?

Yesterday they gave *Tannhäuser* for the third time and we had a full house again. The uproar aroused by the new *Leipzig Musikzeitung* attracted a lot of curious people here. Last night there was a lady in the loge next to my wife who kept telling her neighbours what she had read in that paper and she remarked that in this work Richard Wagner had created a completely new *catastrophe* in music. Others said: "This is no music at all," and left after the second act.

But the opera has gained many admirers because of its subject matter and seriousness, and when I compare it with other productions of recent years, I admire it also. Much that was extremely offensive to me at the beginning I have already got used to after a few more hearings, but I'm always repelled by its lack of rhythm and well-rounded phrases. This production is really exceptionally good and we shall hear few so precise in Germany. Last night not a single note was omitted in the enormously difficult ensemble of singers in the second act.

Still, that doesn't prevent its being really terrifying music in some parts, especially just before the part where Elizabeth throws herself on the singers rushing in on Tannhäuser. Imagine the faces Haydn and Mozart would make if they had to listen just once to the hellish noises that now pass for music!

---

1 Pupil of Spohr and one of the founders of the Bach Gesellschaft.
2 For clavier.

The intonation in the pilgrims' choruses (but in this perform-ance they were supported by clarinets and bassoons piano) was so pure that for the first time I felt somewhat reconciled to the far-fetched and unnatural modulations. It is astonishing what the human ear can gradually get used to! After this experience I can under-stand how Mendelssohn, who was fed largely on Bach's music from the time he was a boy, could write such harsh harmonies, in fact downright cacophony. But of course that's nothing compared to what Schumann is doing.

This year I hope to finish my business in London early enough for us to return around the middle of July. Then you and your family will still be here and I hope we can spend some time together.

Cordial greetings from my wife to your wife.

As ever,
Louis Spohr

CARL MARIA VON WEBER

Eutin, 1786 — *London,* 1826

❖❖❖❖❖❖❖❖❖

To *Hans Georg Nägeli* [1]

Mannheim, May 1, 1810

As my circumstances are altered and I have once more devoted myself entirely to art, I take advantage of the first moment of time that offers, to renew the connection already established between us by Herr von Wangenheim, and likewise to thank you for your favourable opinion of my compositions.

But I cannot refrain from touching on a point too important for me to be passed over in silence. You seem from my quartet [2] and caprice [3] to discover in me an imitator of Beethoven, and flattering as this may appear to many, it is far from agreeable to me. In the first place, I hate everything that bears the stamp of imitation, and, secondly, my views differ far too much from those of Beethoven ever to come into contact with him. The fiery, nay, almost incredible, inventive faculty that inspires him is attended by so many complications in the arrangement of his ideas that it is only his earlier compositions that interest me; the later ones, on the contrary, appear to me only a confused chaos, an unintelligible struggle after novelty, from which occasional heavenly flashes of genius dart forth, showing how great he might be if he chose to control his luxuriant fancy.

Though I certainly can't boast of the great genius of Beethoven, still I think I can vindicate both the logic and the phraseology of my music, each individual piece causing a definite impression. For it seems to me that the aim of an artistic composition is to deduce the character of the whole from individual thoughts, and that, amid the greatest diversity, still unity, displayed by the first principle or

---

1 Publisher and writer on music (1773–1836).
2 Piano Quartet in B flat.
3 *Momento Capriccioso* for piano, op. 12 (1808).

theme, should always shine forth. An amusing article on this subject is given in the *Morgenblatt*, No. 309, published December 27, 1809, which may serve further to illustrate my views.

It so happened that, besides the quartet I had the honour to send you, nothing but the caprice was written out, whence you probably concluded that all my compositions bear the stamp of the bizarre. I hope, however, that when I have the pleasure of sending you some of my other works, you will not fail to perceive at least my efforts to attain clearness, harmony, and feeling.

As you declined publishing the quartet, I sold it to Herr Simrock, and therefore request you to return it to me as soon as possible, to my address, C. M. v. Weber, Darmstadt, at Herr Kammerrat Hoffmann's. Herr von Wagenheim told me that you wished to have something from me for your *Pianoforte-Repertorium*,[4] and I beg you will decide in what style it is to be. I should very much like to see a work of mine published by your respected firm, and as I have a store of compositions of every kind, I beg you will write to me and say what would best suit you.

I must press for a speedy answer, for, being about to undertake a distant journey, I cannot stay much longer in these parts. I trust you will have no cause to regret having entered into nearer connection with me, and begging you to excuse this scrawl, I have the honour to be, etc.,

C. M. v. WEBER

०१०१०१०१०१०

To *Johann Gänsbacher* [5]

Dresden, March 10, 1817

Beloved Brother:

I ought long ago to have written to you and announced my appointment (as Royal Saxon Kapellmeister and director of the German opera), which I received in Berlin on December 27, 1816, but I have really had too much to do. I am at length fairly settled, and all my fine projects for travelling dissolved into thin air. I have indeed annual leave of absence, but if I marry, God willing,

---

4 *Répertoire des clavecinistes*, periodical of contemporary piano compositions, founded by Nägeli in 1803.

5 Fellow pupil, with Weber and Meyerbeer, of Vogler; at that time Kapellmeister at St. Stephen's in Vienna.

in the autumn, all expeditions will be more difficult and I shall no doubt become a regular *Philistine*. I was obliged to begin my career here with much annoyance, and many struggles against cabals; and in fact I was several times on the point of setting off again; but all this seems eventually to have done good, in so far that it is now evident to them they have to do with a man who will not permit himself to be trifled with and who has sufficient independence not to submit to any kind of neglect or want of respect. Everything is at present going on smoothly, and those who do not like me at all events respect me.

Even the Italians have become pacific, from seeing that I am more likely to promote their interests than to undermine them. Art has no fatherland; and all that is beautiful ought to be prized by us, no matter what clime or region has produced it. Thus I have every reason to be satisfied, and my sole wish is that Heaven may soon bestow on me tolerable singers, for as yet I have actually none at all. Things go on miserably in Prague, where everything is hastening to decay. My *Silvana* [6] was given there, and created the most tremendous furore, while all deplore my loss and the golden time of the opera when I was with them.[7] Yes, yes! it serves them right, for at that period nothing I did was good enough for them. I mean soon to set to work at a new opera that the well-known poet Friedrich Kind has written for me, the *Jägersbraut*,[8] a very romantic, mysterious, and beautiful work.

My life here, on the whole, is very solitary, and, indeed, I may say rather dull also, for though I know a number of people and am esteemed by all, still a true friend is wanting and I have no one whatever with whom I can converse on musical subjects, which is melancholy enough. I hope, dear brother, that you will soon pay me a visit, when we can talk and work together famously; you will live with me, and our life will be like heaven itself. Our holidays begin a fortnight hence, when I intend to make a run to Prague and take the people by surprise, an idea that delights me beyond measure. It seems that poor *D minor* [9] has met with many misfortunes, but you are probably better informed than I on these points; the half of her crops and her château have been burned. I wrote to her, but have got no answer as yet. I have news from Meyerbeer, who is in Milan;

---

6 Opera, 1810.

7 He was Kapellmeister at the Prague Opera 1813–16.

8 Later called *Der Freischütz*, first performed at Berlin, June 18, 1821.

9 Nickname of a friend in Prague.

he is to remain all this year in Italy, where his address is: *Ferma in posta, Venezia*. He seems to have been working hard, and has written both a French and a German opera. Bärmann [10] and Madame Harlas will probably soon visit me, as they propose making a journey to Berlin. I have heard nothing of Gottfried [11] for a long time. No doubt, Schlesinger [12] has meanwhile written to you. Send to him or to me the exact opus, title, and dedication of the three works. Do be industrious, dear brother, for your works are certain to sell, and you can thus make a good sum yearly.

My appointment is only for one year, which is the usual form, and though there never has been an instance of its not being followed by a life appointment, still I know my star too well not to dread, at least, some difficulties; but as God wills! [13] I place my trust in Him, and fear nothing, although henceforth I shall have more than myself to provide for. The arrangement with my Lina's [14] mother is at last completed; she is to go to her son in Mayence, and I am to allow her 100 dollars a year; it was better to make this sacrifice, and to have rest and peace at home. Write to me soon how you get on in Vienna; guard well your liberty, and do not allow *F major* [15] to beguile you into making any promises. Independence is noblest and best for a man. It is said that Pixis is to leave Prague, and also most of the members of the orchestra and the theatre. Madame Liebich is to marry Herr Stöger. Clam tore up a bill for 40,000 florins; that was indeed being a true friend. The prices are raised, but the theatre empty. The departure of Mademoiselle Brandt, and, please God, Madame Grünbaum also (if I can secure her), will give the final *coup de grâce*. May God guard you, dear brother; write to me soon how you are and what you are doing, and ever continue your love for your faithfully attached brother,

WEBER

---

10 Heinrich Joseph Bärmann (1784–1847), clarinettist.
11 Gottfried Weber (1779–1839), lawyer and musician.
12 Director of music publishing firm.
13 Weber retained this appointment until his death.
14 Caroline Brandt, his future wife.
15 Nickname of friend in Prague.

To *Johann Gänsbacher*

Dresden, March 28, 1821

Brother of my heart:

What joy your welcome letter of February 22 caused me! I would have answered it by return of post had I not wished to give you some pleasure in return, so I now enclose printed evidence that it is my highest delight to tell the world something about you. I need not tell you the interest my Lina takes in you. We are very much concerned lest you should be obliged to go to Italy; so pray set our fears at rest as soon as possible. It is indeed long since we met, and I can as yet see no glimpse of hope in this respect, and you have even less command of your time than I have. Only be industrious and write a good deal; I don't know why, but it always seems to me that your doing so may one day have an important influence on your fate. Man is thus constituted, and even the most ardent and glowing requires an impetus for his art.

I have all sorts of things to tell you about myself. Last year I travelled from August to November, going to Hamburg and on to Copenhagen, which turned out happily in every point of view, my reception everywhere being far beyond my most sanguine hopes, and I also made plenty of money. But I was obliged to leave my good Lina in Hamburg, as she expected her confinement, and a sea voyage was thought a risk for her. Man proposes, and God disposes; for notwithstanding these precautions, she had a premature confinement, but was so admirably nursed by kind people that by the time I returned from Copenhagen I found her quite brisk again; the good creature, too, not having written me one word on the subject to avoid alarming me. During our journey there had been great changes in Dresden. Count Vizthum, our intendant, had taken leave of us, and Herr von Könneritz from Vienna had stepped into his place. He is the kind of man who goes with the stream and is quite in the hands of the Italians, and thus I see vanish for ever all that I have with such difficulty accomplished for German opera during the last four years. There were times when I felt utterly miserable and desperate, but I now endeavour to take the matter as lightly as possible; I have the comfort of knowing that I have done my duty as an honest man, and the rest I leave to God.

I am going to Berlin the end of April to conduct my new opera, *Der Freischütz*, with which the theatre there is to open. From there

I go with my Lina to Alexisbad, which is necessary both for her and for me. I hope also about that time to see Meyerbeer again in Berlin. God grant that in Germany he may be what he formerly was and not think in the same style in which he composes when in Italy. I heard yesterday that B. A. Weber [16] is dead. It is very possible that I may be offered his situation, but I should be very unwilling to leave Dresden, though many things are exceedingly painful to my feelings — our royal family are indeed truly excellent, when well known — but as God wills.

I have just looked at your letter and am shocked to find that you have had no news of me since the end of 1818. My dear brother, in the meantime I was at the point of death, and during the whole summer of 1819 dangerously ill; then my wife had another premature confinement, so instead of children I have a dog and a monkey — but God will no doubt replace our loss. My health since then has become very fragile and I cannot yet get rid of a teasing cough; well, no doubt it will pass away in time.

Bärmann passed through here before Christmas, when you were often spoken of. I got letters from the Junghs two days ago; he has just recovered from inflammation of the lungs, and his wife has had another girl. He also wrote to me about your ring, and hopes to hear from yourself. The old mother has got the arrears of her pension, which amount to a good round sum. I believe they require it all; may Heaven preserve him to his large family! I have heard nothing whatever of *D minor* or *F major*. Naumann's *Vater Unser* is being engraved, and the subscribers can soon have it, for a louis d'or, I believe. Only the pianoforte arrangement of my *Kampf und Sieg* [17] is engraved; so I await your orders on the subject; perhaps you might also make use of the cantata that I wrote for the jubilee of our King,[18] which might be given with other words as a harvest thanksgiving.

I am at present engaged in a grand comic opera,[19] and an *opera seria* is to follow, with recitative throughout.[20] Were you not glad to hear that Dietrichstein and Mosel had become directors in Vienna? At last that Imperial city will no longer be quite closed

16 Bernhard Anselm Weber (1766–March 23, 1821), Imperial Prussian Kapellmeister.
17 Cantata (1815) commemorating the victory at Waterloo.
18 *Jubelkantate, Erhebt den Lobgesang* (1818), celebrating the fiftieth anniversary
   of the accession of King Friedrich August I.
19 *Die drei Pintos*, never completed.
20 *Euryanthe*.

against nature and talent, and what is really good will be preferred, instead of always Rossini. Moreover, I hope he will no longer be considered a standard, for he is cutting his own throat. May Heaven only send peace from a political point of view! A favourite plan of mine has long been to go from here to Munich, and thence by Salzburg and Innsbruck to Milan, and home by Vienna; but who can now venture to make any calculations? Besides, it could not be till next year, and by that time there may be many changes. May God dispose the hearts of our rulers to peace!

Dear old Hänsel, farewell — may God keep you in the same health that you now, to my great satisfaction, enjoy! My Lina sends you her regards. I trust we shall ever continue the same, except indeed in writing — a point on which we might both easily improve. May each of us frequently take up the pen to send mutually happy tidings, for it is too tiresome to do nothing but complain. I embrace you, and believe me, with a loving brother's heart,

Ever your
WEBER

CARL CZERNY

Vienna, 1791 — Vienna, 1857

⊹⊹⊹⊹⊹⊹⊹⊹⊹

To *Johann Peter Pixis* [1]

Vienna, June 8, 1824

Esteemed Friend:

My deepest thanks for your gracious letter and the agreeable surprise of your splendid composition. I have just received it, and a first glance already shows me what beautiful effects you have created in this genre, as graceful as it is new. Nothing will give me greater pleasure than to hear it performed by worthy hands and I shall do all I can to shorten the delay in presenting this pleasure to the greater public. It really does me good to learn of your prosperity in Paris, where they must be delighted to have an intelligent and highly gifted instrumental virtuoso — something that has been all too little cultivated in that celebrated capital, according to all accounts. There is no doubt that the longer you remain there, the more you will be appreciated.

I can write you no more significant news about music in our dear Vienna than that Beethoven finally gave his long-awaited concert. He astonished everyone in the most amazing manner since everybody feared that after a loss of hearing lasting ten years he would be able to produce nothing but dry, abstract, unimaginative compositions. His new symphony,[2] to a great extent, breathes forth such a fresh, lively — indeed, youthful — spirit, and as much strength, novelty, and beauty as anything else that has ever come forth from the brain of this original man. Although of course he jolted the old graybeards several times. Moscheles and Kalkbrenner have earned all the glory here that they deserve, and everything else is pretty much *in statu quo.*

I have already found occasion to transmit your remembrances

---

1 Pianist and composer (1788–1874).
2 The Ninth.

to our mutual acquaintances, especially at Frau von Weyrother's, where I now have the pleasure of teaching little Natalie, who is indebted to you for so much musical education. While I thank you once more for your generous remembrance, which I so greatly esteem, until we can greet each other in person (whether in the Tuilleries or the Paternostergässchen) I beg you to receive the assurance of the very great respect with which I remain your true and devoted friend,

CARL CZERNY

੦੧੦੧੦੧੦੧੦੧੦

To *Franz Liszt* [3]

Vienna, July 14, 1824

Dear Franzi:

With the greatest pleasure I hear on all sides that you are just as successful in the capital of noble England and arouse as much attention and approbation as you did previously in Paris. This is all the more to your credit since the inhabitants of London have the most excellent pianists of our time and they may perhaps have surer standards for evaluating our art than the French.

I am delighted that my dear little friend, having redoubled his efforts and paid proper attention to study and to performance, and to correct behaviour as well, will be worthy of the great honour of ranking among the foremost artists of our time in the most esteemed publications.

You will not forget that the greater the enthusiasm and acclaim of the public, the more difficult and important it is to maintain this, and that even if one can elicit special applause from that glittering part of the great world by means of petty trifles and childishness, the opinion of one great master and authority is worth more and lasts longer than the agreeable prattle of the crowd.

London is particularly advantageous for you at the present time since Ries, I hear, has already taken his departure from musical life, and Moscheles is still detained in Bohemia; also Kalkbrenner told me himself that he is leaving soon for a rest at his estate on the Loire.

I have seen notices in several journals about a little eight-year-

---

3 Liszt, then thirteen years old, was on a concert tour in London. Previously he had studied piano with Czerny in Vienna.

old boy — Aspull, I believe the name is — who is said to play uncommonly well. Have you heard him? Before I knew that our little Zisy had stolen away and was on the sea bound for London, I sent you a package of music through Prince Paul Esterházy in Paris, which includes my latest works and several other things suitable for performance. I addressed it to your Paris lodgings and wrote your father to have it fetched from the Austrian Embassy. I hope you have received it.

My *Allegri di Bravura* for Mr. Boosey are now ready and I await the most favourable opportunity to send them to London. If you see Mr. Boosey, tell him I am very anxious for him to let me know as soon as possible whether he can publish this jointly with Herr Peters in Leipzig and if he is willing to agree on an honorarium of 50 ducats for the whole work. In any case, he cannot prevent its being reprinted in Germany, and if he accepts my proposal, it will be to both his and my advantage.

I am now working with the greatest diligence and shall soon have some things published, including some *Variations brillantes* on *Gott erhalte Franz den Kaiser* with orchestral accompaniment, which I shall send you, little Franzi, as soon as I can.

1000 times adieu to your dear parents and to yourself. May you be upright and virtuous, happy and healthy, and come to Vienna soon and see that we receive news of you shortly. I remain your true friend,

CARL CZERNY

GIACOMO MEYERBEER

Berlin, 1791 — Paris, 1864

❋❋❋❋❋❋❋❋

To *Franz Liszt*

Berlin, February 8, 1852

Dear and illustrious colleague:

Monsieur Schlesinger has spoken to me about a letter you wrote him in which you say that you have composed a large piano composition on the Anabaptists' hymn from *Le Prophète*,[1] and that you intend to dedicate this work to me when it is published, but first you wish to write to me directly.

I shall not wait for the arrival of that letter to tell you how happy I am that one of my songs impresses you as worthy to be used as a motif for one of your piano compositions, destined to be heard throughout Europe and intoxicate those who have the good fortune to hear them played by your wonderful, poetic fingers. However, I feel even more honoured at the mark of sympathy you offer me in dedicating your work to me, for if it is an honour to see my name linked with yours, it is even more agreeable to me that you make it known in this manner that we are friends.

Let me say in passing that some people believe and some critics have even written me that, just as in the case of Luther's chorale and *Les Huguenots*,[2] I had stolen a chorale of the period for the Anabaptists. Since I am not in the habit of refuting what the papers erroneously print about me, I permitted that error to circulate, as I have done so many others. But I insist that *you*, dear and illustrious colleague, should know there is nothing in it. The Anabaptists' hymn, good or bad as it may be, grew from my own terrain and I tried to give it the colour of a hymn of the period, that is all.

Monsieur le Marquis de la Ferrière, who has had the privilege of hearing your latest compositions, as well as the piano concerto,

---

1 Opera, 1849.
2 Opera, 1836.

the overtures, and the music for *Prometheus*, recently spoke to me about them with the greatest enthusiasm, which made me doubly regret my inability to be present at their performance last summer. Since then I have been frequently tempted to go to Weimar and enjoy that pleasure. But the serious illness I sustained last summer, which just missed carrying me off, still compels me to exercise great caution and not undertake a journey during the winter twice as far as to Dresden, the only journey I have dared to hazard since my illness. Otherwise I also would have come to Weimar to hear the first performance of your celebrated friend Berlioz's *Benvenuto Cellini*, inasmuch as I read in the papers that he was to conduct his great work himself. Will you extend my good wishes to him?

I do not have the privilege of knowing Madame la Princesse de Wittgenstein [3] personally, but everything I have heard from those who have seen her — the superiority of her mind, her fine intelligence, her noble and elevated character, her poetic imagination — make me acutely regretful that I have been deprived of this honour. Until I have the honour of being presented personally by you, kindly offer her my cordial and deferential respects. Deign to accept, dear colleague, the expression of whole-hearted devotion from your admirer,

G. MEYERBEER

---

3 Liszt's mistress.

GIOACCHINO ROSSINI

Pesaro, 1792 — Passy (Paris), 1868

❂❂❂❂❂❂❂❂❂❂

To *Leopoldo Cicognara*

February 12, 1817

Dear Leopoldo:

These are my opinions on the present state of music. Ever since the five notes were added to the cembalo I have said that a fatal revolution would come about in this art, which at that time had reached perfection; for experience has shown that when one desires to attain the best, one achieves the worst.

Formerly Haydn began to corrupt purity of taste by introducing into his works strange chords, artificial passages, and daring innovations. He still preserved so much sublimity and ancient beauty, however, that his errors could be forgiven. Then came Cramer and Beethoven with their compositions so lacking in unity and naturalness and so full of oddities and personal caprice that they completely corrupted the quality of instrumental music. In opera at the present time Mayr [1] has replaced the simple and majestic measures of Sarti, Paisiello, and Cimarosa [2] with his ingenious though vicious harmonies, and the accompaniment drowning out the melody, and he is imitated by the young opera-composers of the new German school.

Many of our singers born outside of Italy have renounced purity of musical taste (for which Italy has always been the centre) to please the capitals of Europe and they have adopted the unwholesome style of the foreigners. When they returned to Italy they brought with them and spread the germs of bad taste. The Marchettis, Davids, Antanis, Todis, and Billingtons were preferred to the divine Pacchierotti, to the Rubinellis, the Crescentinis, Pozzis, Bantis, and Babbinis. Corruption already seemed to have reached its

---

1 Johann Simon Mayr (1763–1843).
2 Leading Italian opera-composers of the eighteenth century.

zenith in the musician Velluti, who, more than anyone else, abused the supreme gifts nature bestowed upon him when the appearance of Catalani demonstrated that there is nothing bad that could not be worse.

Warblings, wild leaps and jumps, trills, misuse of semitones, notes all tangled up — this is the kind of singing that now holds sway. That is why the measure, the essential part of music, without which melody is unintelligible and harmony becomes disordered, is neglected and violated by singers. They arouse our astonishment rather than our emotion, and whereas in better times the performers tried to make their instruments sing, our singers now try to make their voices play. In the meantime the crowd, applauding such poor style, does to music what the Jesuits did to poetry and oratory when they preferred Lucan to Virgil, and Seneca to Cicero.

These are my opinions on the present state of music, and I confess that I have very little hope of seeing this divine art emerge from the corruption in which it lies, unless there be a total overthrow of social institutions. And the remedy, you see, would be worse than the evil. Adieu. Your

G. R.

◌⬧◌⬧◌⬧◌⬧◌⬧◌

To *Ferdinando Guidicini*

February 12, 1851

Dear Signor Guidicini:

Thank you for your kind note asking my opinion on a musical question. But the question is more a matter of words than of substance and I shall reply very briefly.

I maintain that in order to perform his part well, the good singer should be nothing but an able *interpreter* of the ideas of the master, the composer, and he should try to express them with great skill and all the brilliance of which they are susceptible. Therefore the performers should be nothing but accurate *executants* of what is written down. In short, the composer and the poet are the only true *creators*. Sometimes a clever singer will burst into additional ornamentation and would like to call this his creation, but it often happens that this creation is false, and even more often that it ruins the composer's ideas, robbing them of the simplicity of expression they should have.

The French use the term *créer un rôle* — an example of French vanity — which should be applied to those singers who demand a leading part in a new opera, hoping to prove thereby that they will set the example to be followed later by other singers who perform the same part. Here, too, the word *create* seems rather inappropriate since *to create* means *to dig up from nowhere.* Instead, the singer works with something already made, he follows the poetry and the music, which are not his creations.

That is what it occurred to me to say and it seems sufficient in response to your request. Nothing remains but to send you my greetings.

With great esteem, most affectionately,

R.

ⓞﻮⓞﻮⓞﻮⓞﻮⓞﻮⓞ

To *Giuseppe Bellentari* [3]

Florence, December 28, 1853

The so-called Swan of Pesaro to the
  Eagle of the Sausage-Dealers

When you provided me with your own specially prepared *zamponi* and *cappelletti* you elected to soar on one of your highest flights and it is only proper that I should raise up a loud cry of thanks to you, as it were, from the depths of the ancestral marshes of old Padua. I found the collection of your works perfect in every respect, and all whose good fortune it was to enjoy the splendid delicacy of your celebrated products applauded your proficiency.

I shall not set your praise to music, for as I have already written you, in the midst of all the hubbub of the harmonic world I maintain myself as an ex-composer. Good for me and better for you. You know how to strike certain keys to please the palate, a surer judge than the ear, since in its outermost points it is based on sensitivity of touch, which is the beginning of all manifestation of life.

I strike only a few of these keys to please you — namely, my most grateful appreciation for your trouble — and may it serve to inspire you to ever higher flights, in order to win the laurel wreath with which it pleased you to crown your most grateful servant,

GIOACCHINO ROSSINI

---

3 Sausage-dealer in Modena.

To *Giovanni Pacini*

Passy (Paris), April 8, 1864

Beloved Friend:

Giorgione, Titian, Van Dyck, and Velasquez could not paint a better likeness of me than the one sketched at the beginning of your very kind letter of April 2. By this I mean the smile with which you thought I would grant your request for a short instrumental composition for the (so celebrated) Quartet Society of Florence. Indeed, I did not smile, but shed a little tear at the thought of not being able to grant your flattering request, and since I have to inform you of the reason for my refusal, "I shall do as he who weeps and speaks."

I abandoned my musical career in 1829; the long silence has made me lose the ability to compose and my knowledge of instruments. At present I am a simple fourth-rate pianist, and although, as you see, I have described myself very modestly, the pianists of all the nations (who flatter me in my presence) wage a harsh and bitter war (behind my back) so that I never find students despite the moderate price of twenty sous per lesson. Nor can I put myself forward when I am not asked and thus I live (as a pianist) under the public's whip. My Giovanni! "If you do not weep what does make you weep?" I have said all and now I am finished.

I was certain that you would be willing to do the cantata for me and the honour of my compatriots. I was not surprised, since I know your heart and I thank you a thousand times for this new proof of affection that you tender me.

I am reading with the greatest pleasure your *Memoirs* in the paper forwarded to me by Guidi. You are a devil! You always have the youthful spirit; may God keep it for you for many years to come. Be prepared to fight for the mass in execution of your holy project. Keep me warm in your heart and believe that no one surpasses me in the great admiration and affection I hold toward you. My wife gratefully returns your greetings and she wishes, together with myself, to be remembered to your wife.

[Gioacchino Rossini]

To *Franz Liszt*

Passy (Paris), June 23, 1865

Venerable Father,[4] *dearest friend:*

By return of post I reply to your precious letter of the 17th, which proved to me that time and distance have not weakened your affection for the old man of Pesaro. I write you in my mother tongue, that being the best suited to bring forth and express my heart's sentiments. I began to love and admire you in Vienna in 1822 (how sweet is that memory to me!). The succeeding years have only increased my affection for you; your decision to enter upon an ecclesiastical career did not surprise me, it edified me. Oh, my dearest Father Liszt, permit me to offer you my most sincere congratulations on the holy decision you have made, assuring you the best possible future. I am certain, moreover, that you will not abandon music, in which God made you so great, and that heavenly harmony will always remain your most faithful companion on this earth.

Speaking of music, I do not know whether you have heard that I composed a *Messa di Gloria* in four parts which was performed in the palace of my friend Count Pillet-Will. This Mass was sung by talented artists of both sexes and accompanied by two pianos and a harmonium. The foremost composers of Paris (including my poor colleague Meyerbeer, who was then still alive) praised it highly, far beyond its merit.

Now they want me to orchestrate it so that it can be performed in one of the Paris churches. But I feel a repugnance to undertaking this task since I have put all my feeble knowledge of music into this composition and I wrote it with sincere religious feeling. There exists (so they tell me) a fatal bull by a former Pope that prohibits the mixture of the two sexes in the church.[5] Can I ever consent to hear my poor notes sung by little boys in the first grade, all out of tune, rather than by women who have been raised up *ad hoc* for sacred music and, musically speaking, with their clear, white-winged voices, seem like the celestial angels? If it were granted to

---

4 Liszt had taken minor orders in April of that year and thereafter was known as the Abbé Liszt.

5 Although no such bull had ever been issued, from the early beginnings of Christianity it was traditional for women to be prohibited from taking part in the liturgical offices of the church. A *motu proprio* reaffirming this custom was issued by Pope Pius X, November 22, 1903.

me to live in the Vatican as you do, I should throw myself at the feet of my adored Pius IX to request the favour of a new bull permitting women to sing in church together with men.

This would give new life to sacred music, which is in full decline. I am certain that if His Holiness, who so loves music and to whom my name is not unknown, were to issue such a bull, he would win new glory in paradise, and the Catholics of all nations would bless him for this act of justice and true harmonic conscience. Our sacred religion, though it be trampled on by wretches, will nevertheless always retain its full glory, and music will always remain the primary aid for the devout.

As a valiant Father, my dear friend, join with me and let us try to obtain from His Holiness a favour that must lie doubly in your heart, both as servant of God and as musician. I realize that I have taken too much of your time and shall conclude by blessing you and declaring that no one loves you more than

G. Rossini

FRANZ SCHUBERT

Vienna, 1797 — Vienna, 1828

◇┼◇┼◇┼◇┼◇┼◇┼◇

To *Franz von Schober* and other friends

Zelez [*Hungary*], September 8, 1818

Dear Schober: *Dear Senn:*

Dear Spaun: *Dear Streinsberg:*

Dear Mayrhofer: *Dear Wayss:*

Dear Weidlich:

     How infinitely happy your letters, separately and together, make me is beyond telling. I was attending a cattle auction when they brought me in your fat budget. I opened it and, catching sight of Schober's name, gave vent to a loud cry of joy. With childish pleasure and laughing to myself all the time, I read it through in a room near by. It was as though my dearest friends were really within arm's reach again! But now I must answer you all in the proper order.

Dear Schobert:

     I see that this alteration in your name holds good. Well, dear Schobert, your letter was from beginning to end very precious and delightful, and especially the last sheet. Yes, indeed, the last sheet sent me into the seventh heaven of joy. You are a splendid fellow (in Swedish of course), and, believe me, my friend, you will not fail, for your understanding of art is the finest and sincerest imaginable. That you should look upon this change as a small one pleases me very much: for a long time now you have had one foot in our particular inferno. The fact that the management of the Opera House in Vienna is so stupid and produces the finest operas but none of mine makes me pretty furious.

     Here in Zelez [1] I have to be everything at once. Composer, editor, audience, and goodness knows what besides. There is not a

---

1 Schubert was then music-teacher to the family of Count Johann Esterházy.

soul here with a genuine interest in music except, perhaps, now and then, the Countess (if I am not mistaken). So I am all alone with my beloved and must hide her in my room, in my pianoforte, and in my own heart. Although this is often very depressing, yet on the other hand it inspires me toward greater things. Do not be afraid that I shall stay away longer than I absolutely must. Several new songs — and I hope very successful ones — have come into being during this time.

That the bird of Greece [2] should be fluttering his wings in Upper Austria does not surprise me at all, since it is his own country and he is on a holiday. I wish I were with him. I should certainly know how to make good use of my time. But that you — by nature a sensible fellow — should imagine my brother to be wandering about there alone, with neither guide nor companion, does surprise me very much. First, since an artist likes best of all to be left to himself; 2nd, since there are too many lovely districts in Upper Austria for him not to be able to discover the most beautiful; 3rd, since he has an agreeable acquaintance in Herr Forstmeyer in Linz. He must know quite certainly, therefore, what he is about.

If you could manage a greeting to Max when his melancholia is better, I should be infinitely glad. And since you will shortly be seeing your mother and sister, please give them my kindest regards. It is quite possible that this letter will not reach you in Vienna in time, for I only received yours at the beginning of September, just when you were due to leave. I will then have it sent on to you. I am very glad, among other things, that Milder is, for you, irreplaceable. I feel the same about her too. She sings best and trills worst of all.

Now a description for you all:

Our castle is by no means one of the largest, but it is very attractively built. It is surrounded by a lovely garden. I live in the estate agent's house. It is fairly quiet except for some forty geese, which at times set up such a cackling that one cannot hear oneself speak. All the people about me are thoroughly kind-hearted. It is rare for a nobleman's household to run as smoothly as this one. The agent, a Slav from Slavonia and a good fellow, very much fancies his former musical talents. He can blow on the flute two German dances in a masterly fashion. His son, a student of philosophy, has just arrived on his holidays, and I hope I shall get on very well with him. His wife is just like any other woman who wants to be taken

---

2 Allusion to his friend Vogl's love of the classics. Vogl was a singer at the Vienna Opera.

for a lady. The steward is perfectly suited to his job: a man of extraordinary perspicacity in whatever concerns his own purse and pocket. The doctor, twenty-four years old, and a really able man, is as full of ailments as an old lady. A great deal of it put on. The surgeon, whom I like best of all, a venerable old man of seventy-five, always happy and serene. God grant to all such a fortunate old age! The magistrate a very unaffected and pleasant man. A cheerful old bachelor, companion to the Count, and a good musician, often comes to see me. The chef, the lady's maid, the chambermaid, the lodge-keeper, etc., and two coachmen are all good folk. The chef, rather a loose fellow; the lady's maid, 30 years old; the chambermaid very pretty, and often in my company; the children's nurse a nice old body; the lodge-keeper my rival. The two grooms are better suited to the stables than to human society. The Count is rather a rough sort of man, the Countess proud, but a more sensitive nature, the little Countesses good children. So far I have been spared any invitation to the dining room. I can think of nothing more to tell you now. I need hardly say to all of you who know me that with my naturally frank disposition I get along very well with all these people.

Dear Spaun, I am heartily glad that you are able at last to build palaces for little clerks of the Court Chancery to run about in. You probably mean by this a choral quartet. Remember me to Herr Gahy.

Dear Mayerhofer [*sic*], you cannot be longing for November much more than I am. Stop being so seedy, or at least give up taking medicine, and the other will follow of itself.

For Hans Senn to read too if he pleases: as above.

Maybe friend Streinsberg is already dead: and that is why he cannot write. Let friend Weidlich tack his name on to his own coat-tails.

Good old Waiss remembers me with gratitude. He is an excellent man.

And now, dear friends, good-bye. Write to me very soon. My best and favourite form of entertainment is to read your letters through a dozen times.

Greetings to my dear parents, and tell them how much I long for a letter from them. With enduring love,

Your faithful friend,
FRANZ SCHUBERT

To *Leopold Kupelwieser*

[*Vienna*], March 31, 1824

Dear Kupelwieser:

    I have been longing to write to you for a long time past, but could never hit upon the when and where. Now comes an opportunity through Smirsch, and at last I am able to pour out my whole heart to someone again. You are so good and faithful, you are sure to forgive me things that others would only take very much amiss. — To be brief, I feel myself to be the most unfortunate and the most wretched man in the whole world. Picture to yourself someone whose health is permanently injured, and who, in sheer despair, does everything to make it worse instead of better; picture to yourself, I say, someone whose most brilliant hopes have come to nothing, someone to whom love and friendship are at most a source of bitterness, someone whose inspiration (whose creative inspiration at least) for all that is beautiful threatens to fail, and then ask yourself if that is not a wretched and unhappy being.

    "*Meine Ruh' ist hin, mein Herz ist schwer, Ich finde sie nimmer und nimmer mehr.*" [3] That could be my daily song now, for every night when I go to sleep I hope never to wake again, and each morning I am only recalled to the griefs of yesterday. So I pass my days, joyless and friendless, except when Schwind comes now and again to see me and brings with him a ray of light from those sweet days that are no more.

    Our Society (Reading Society), as you will already know, has dealt itself its own death-blow by swelling its ranks with a rowdy chorus of beer-drinkers and sausage-eaters, and it is being dissolved in two days' time — though I myself have scarcely ever attended it since you went away. Leidesdorf, whom I have got to know very well, is a really earnest and good-hearted man, but of such a melancholy disposition that I am afraid his company in this respect may have influenced me rather too much. Things are going badly with him as with me, and therefore we never have any money. They declared that it was impossible to make use of your brother's opera [4] — he made a mistake in leaving the theatre — and, together with my music, it was not accepted. Castelli's opera *The Conspirators* has been set to music in Berlin by a local composer and enthusiasti-

---

3 From Goethe's *Faust*.
4 Schubert's *Fierrabras*, libretto by Josef Kupelwieser (1823).

cally received; so it seems that I have composed two more operas for nothing! [5] I have written very few new songs, but against that I have tried my hand at several kinds of instrumental music and composed two quartets for violins, viola, and violoncello, an octet, and I want to write yet another quartet and so prepare the way for a big symphony.

The latest news in Vienna is that Beethoven is giving a concert, at which his new symphony, three selections from the new Mass, and a new overture will be performed. — I too should like to give a similar concert next year, God willing. I must end now so as not to use up too much paper, and kiss you 1,000 times. If you were to write and tell me about your present mood of inspiration and about the rest of your life, nothing would better please

Your faithful friend,
FRANZ SCHUBERT
Fare well! Right well!

⭑⭑⭑⭑⭑

To the *Emperor Francis II*

Vienna, April 7, 1826

Your Majesty!
Most gracious Emperor!

With the deepest submission the under-signed humbly begs Your Majesty graciously to bestow upon him the vacant position of Vice-Kapellmeister to the court, and supports his application with the following qualifications:

(1) The undersigned was born in Vienna, is the son of a school-teacher, and is twenty-nine years of age.

(2) He enjoyed the privilege of being for five years, a court chorister at the Imperial and Royal College School.

(3) He received a complete course of instruction in compo-sition from the late Chief Kapellmeister to the court, Herr Anton Salieri, and is fully qualified, therefore, to fill any post as Kapell-meister.

(4) His name is well known, not only in Vienna but through-out Germany, as a composer of songs and instrumental music.

(5) He has also written and arranged five Masses for both

---

5 Schubert had composed *Die Verschworenen* on the same text.

smaller and larger orchestras, and these have already been performed in various churches in Vienna.

(6) Finally, he is at the present time without employment, and hopes in the security of a permanent position to be able to realize at last those high musical aspirations which he has ever kept before him.

Should Your Majesty be graciously pleased to grant this request, the undersigned would strive to the utmost to give full satisfaction.[6]

Your Majesty's most obedient humble servant,
FRANZ SCHUBERT

✿⁍✿⁍✿⁍✿⁍✿⁍✿

To *Franz von Schober*

Vienna, November 12, 1828

Dear Schober:

I am ill. I have had nothing to eat or drink for eleven days now, and can only wander feebly and uncertainly between armchair and bed. Rinna is treating me. If I take any food I cannot retain it at all.

So please be so good as to come to my aid in this desperate condition with something to read. I have read Cooper's *Last of the Mohicans, The Spy*, and *The Pioneers*. If by any chance you have anything else of his, I beg you to leave it for me at the coffee-house with Frau von Bogner. My brother, who is conscientiousness itself, will bring it over without fail. Or indeed anything else.[7]

Your friend,
SCHUBERT

---

6 After a year's delay Schubert's application was rejected.
7 Schubert died on November 19, 1828.

VINCENZO BELLINI

Catania (Sicily), 1801 — *Puteaux,* 1835

❖❂❖❂❖❂❖❂❖❂❖

To *Jean Battista Perucchini*

Milan, December 31, 1831

My dear Perucchini:

      It seems impossible that I haven't had so much as a line from you since December 26.[1] Of course you could also reproach me, for I should have sent you the reviews of the performance. My poor *Norma* has been persecuted so cruelly — you see they wanted to crush it at birth and all the papers cried failure, utter failure! A powerful faction, supported by the enormous sums of money spent by that madwoman [2] — am I clear? — because in a few days a Pacini opera was to follow — am I clear?

      My dear Perucchini, money and the most diabolical intrigues may hide the truth for a time, but in the end it will shine forth again in its own true light, and it was my good fortune to have the truth revealed, in part during the first performance, and in its entirety during the second and third. The proof is the enormous crowd in the theatre — it is always filled to the rafters — and the silence, especially in the second act, just as it was in Venice during the last scene of *I Capuleti.*[3] So there is my failure!

      Those parts which will always be effective, and a sure hit after three performances, are the Introduction, which consists of a chorus, the first part of the Donzelli cavatina (neither the public nor I like the second part), the entire scene and exit of La Pasta, and a duet between La Grisi and Donzelli, which we shall be able to put on the level of the finale of the Donzelli cavatina. The first act closes with a terzetto after a duet between the two ladies. The first night it went fine up to the duet, but in the terzetto, the singers were so worn out

---

1 First performance of *Norma* at La Scala, Milan, December 26, 1831.
2 Countess Samayloff, ardent supporter of Giovanni Pacini, (1796–1867).
3 Bellini's *I Capuletti ed i Montecchi;* first performance, 1830.

that they couldn't get a note out and the first act finished cold. But at the second and third performances the audience began to appreciate it, since the execution was much improved, and it won me a call on stage.

I haven't told you about the second act, which, except for the first night, has stirred up a general furore. It consists of a delicate duet between the two ladies, a soldiers' chorus, a hymn of war, a duet between La Pasta and Donzelli, and a finale consisting of a concert piece and stretto. These last two pieces are so new and effective that they have silenced no matter how many enemies I may have had, and I assure you that I myself think them the finest pieces I've written.

The papers will have to contradict themselves, especially the *Gazetta*, and the public is so indignant that who knows how many articles will be inserted to change this. Enough. I am most satisfied with the result, and especially for having triumphed over so many scheming and envious people.

If you hear some selections from this opera, you will understand with what fervor I wrote it, and also my assertions concerning it. Don't show this letter to anyone. You are my heart's delight.

I leave Milan this week and am going to Naples, where I expect news of you. I shall be back here possibly in April, and we may see each other this coming year. In the meantime accept the sincere good wishes of your loving friend, and give my regards to your family and all our friends.

Most affectionately,
BELLINI

HECTOR BERLIOZ

La Côte-Saint-André, 1803 — Paris, 1869

❊⳾❊⳾❊⳾❊⳾❊⳾❊⳾❊

To his uncle

Paris, February 18, 1825

My dear Uncle:

You will no doubt be surprised at the purpose of this letter. I entreat you to act as mediator between my father and myself.[1] His great friendship for you makes me hope that he will heed your advice, and the similarity of your opinions with his cannot fail to make him realize that if you plead my cause, you must think it reasonable.

This is what I have to say on my own behalf. First, Papa considers himself a man of perfect judgment, which gives him, he says, a great advantage over my habitual state of enthusiasm when it comes to seeing things in their true light. In his last letter he begins by telling me that "I'm wrong to think my perseverance will ever be able to wear him out or that my success can ever reconcile him." This means that even if I were to become a Gluck or a Mozart, he would never consent to my being a musician.

Is it good judgment to reason that way? Just imagine the consequences of such an opinion. I told him one day that if all fathers behaved the way he does, there would never be any poets, or painters, or architects, or sculptors, or composers in Europe. He replied: "What a disaster!"

Do you call that good judgment? Perhaps you might say that if all fathers shared my father's opinions, that could not annihilate the arts, because men born in the lowest classes of society who have nothing to lose could take on the dangers of such a thorny career. But I reply that if these men agreed with my father, they would naturally decide that instead of subjecting their careers to any risk,

---

1 The son of a doctor, Berlioz was sent to Paris in 1822 to study medicine. Instead, much against his father's wishes, he entered the Conservatoire.

[123]

it would be better to take up a sure thing like carpentry or shoe-making, and so on. Then the arts would be destroyed and I hardly think it necessary to ask whether this would be an affliction for civilized countries.

My father goes on to say that enthusiasm destroys all the qualities of the heart and makes men possessed by it weak, immoral, selfish, and contemptible. For example he cites La Fontaine, who abandoned his wife and children. But without going into detail about why the celebrated writer of fables behaved in this way (everybody knows the reasons), I cite the examples of Boileau and the great Corneille, of Racine, Gluck, Grétry, Lesueur, and innumerable others. All contemporaries agree over and over again on the qualities that make men good, regardless of their genius, and surely if the authors of *Horace* and *Athalie*, and the composers of *Iphigénie en Tauride*, *Sylvain*, and *Les Bardes* [2] were not possessed by the demon of enthusiasm, I don't know what to call the fire that inspired them.

You will no doubt ask me, dear Uncle, on what I base my hopes of success. I think the time when I become a brilliant success in the theatre is very far off, but I have high hopes of a *Messe Solennelle* which will be performed four or five months from now. I wanted to have it played sooner, as you may have heard, but getting together so many indispensable artists, and having a work performed that will never be given frequently, have been insurmountable obstacles. I have just retouched the score and have pruned it of all the most difficult parts. I showed it to Monsieur Lesueur again, and after spending four days going over it carefully, he returned it to me and said: "It is extremely discouraging that your parents should wish to stop you; I no longer have the slightest doubt of your success in music and it is evident that you are destined for greatness. This work shows remarkable imagination and a wealth of ideas that astonishes me. The trouble is that you have too many. Be moderate. Try to be more simple." And this is what he said about my Mass to someone who repeated it to me: "That boy has the devil's own imagination; his Mass is astonishing! There are so many ideas in it that I could make ten of my scores with this one of his. But it is stronger than he is; he absolutely must fire his first broadside. He wants to overwhelm the world with his power and burst upon it like a bolt of lightning."

I've heard similar things from the conductor at the Opéra, who

---

2 Operas by Gluck, Grétry, and Lesueur, respectively.

studied my score for a week and then hired me to conduct a performance. I received a letter of praise and advice from Monsieur Lefebvre, the organist at St. Roch, who was present during a rehearsal we started but did not finish, the day before I was to give a Mass in that church. Someone I know spoke to him about me, and Monsieur Lefebvre said, among other things: "In a few years, perhaps, he will be the greatest composer we have."

All this has encouraged me a good deal, but what I am counting on principally is a certain power I feel within myself, a fire and ardour that I cannot define and that are directed straight toward one point: great music, dramatic or religious. I could not experience the same feeling toward light music and I wouldn't walk six steps to hear an operetta.

To sum up — it seems that Papa, far from being a man of good judgment, is so carried away by his imagination that at present he writes me about things he wouldn't even have thought of a year ago. It seems obvious that I shall succeed. It is certain that nothing can make me change my direction, and since my father considers me a madman it is no longer I who can cure him of his prejudices.

This is why, dear Uncle, I beg you to reflect carefully, setting aside all prejudice, and plead my cause less for my sake than to restore tranquillity to the most loving of fathers. If you take my side, I shall not despair of regaining the happiness that his affliction has caused me to lose.

Your affectionate nephew,
H. BERLIOZ

❀❀❀❀❀❀❀

To *Humbert Ferrand*

Paris, October 30, 1829

O Ferrand, Ferrand, my friend, where are you? This morning we had the first rehearsal of *Les Francs-Juges*. Forty-two violins, and a total of a hundred and ten performers! I am writing to you from the Lemardelay restaurant while I am waiting for my dessert. Nothing, I swear to you, nothing is so terrifically fearful as my Overture to *Les Francs-Juges*. O Ferrand, my dear friend, you would understand me; where are you? It is a hymn to despair, the most deplorable, horrible, tender despair that can be imagined. Habeneck,[3] who

3 François Antoine Habeneck (1781–1849), conductor of the Paris Opéra.

conducted my immense orchestra, was really afraid of his task. They had never seen anything so difficult, but apparently they did not think ill of it, for at the end of the overture they overwhelmed me, not only with frantic applause, but also with sounds almost as terrifying as those of my orchestra. O Ferrand, Ferrand, why are you not here?

I am going to the Opéra at once in search of a harmonica; they brought me one this morning that was too low, and we could not make use of it. The sextet out of *Faust* goes splendidly, my very sylphs are enchanted. The Overture to *Waverley* does not go well yet; we will rehearse it again tomorrow, and it *shall* go. And the *Jugement dernier*, as you know it, but with the addition of a recitative accompanied by four pair of kettle drums in harmony. O Ferrand, Ferrand, a hundred and twenty leagues!

Yesterday I was too ill to walk; today the demons of the infernal regions who dictated *Les Francs-Juges* have given me incredible strength. This evening I must run all over Paris. The Beethoven concerto is a prodigious, astounding, sublime conception! I do not know how to express my admiration.

Oh, the sylphs!

I have composed a *pianissimo* solo for the big drum in *Les Francs-Juges*.

In a word, it is terrifying! All the fury and tenderness that my heart contains are in this overture.

O Ferrand!

[HECTOR BERLIOZ]

❂❂❂❂❂❂❂❂❂

To *Johann Vesque von Püttlingen* [4]

Paris, March 31, 1851

Dear Friend:

Thanks a thousand times for your remembrance and the excellent idea you had of sending me your new work. I have already read it avidly and enjoyed the purely musical part of the work very much. My ignorance of the language unfortunately prevents me from appreciating the qualities of expression that I have no doubt it contains, apart from the melodies, and I am unable to grasp the close bond between the music and the poetry.

---

4 Austrian official (1803–83). Composed under the pseudonym J. Hoven. Berlioz became acquainted with him in Vienna in 1845.

I am going to see poor Heine one of these days and know he will be glad to hear that you published this collection without neglecting to mention his name, as so many others have done. He is still at death's door and his brain is as lively as ever. He gives the impression of standing at the window of his tomb to look out once more upon this world of which he is no longer a part and which he scoffs at. Once when I was there recently, he heard me being announced and shouted from his bed this sad and charming epigram: "Why, Berlioz, so you haven't forgotten me! Always original!" Alas! What great originality in this horrible Paris when one does not forget those missing, or the half-dead, or the dead!

Have no doubt, my dear de Vesque, that I am at least that original. I often think of you and all the tokens of affection you gave me during our visit in Vienna and they are as near and dear to me as if I had received them yesterday.

But the life I lead here! The incessant whirl, never a moment of leisure or quiet reverie, always running about or working at top speed, always buzzing, vibrating, full of boiling indignation — every morning, after several hours of more or less troubled sleep, to have to return to this cold, nervous world, quivering like a red-hot iron plunged into water, and always tripping over that infernal riffraff. Oh, if I were free! The least bit free! How joyfully I would set out for Palma or Teneriffe, to sleep in the sweet sunlight of those blessed isles among the good people who live there, unmindful of the fever of art! Oh, the sea, the sea, open space, bright light, warmth, rich tropical vegetation, silence — the animal life!

My dear friend, forgive me for bursting into this senseless reproach. As you see, I am really ill. Remember me to your charming family and Madame de Vesque's family and to your brother. Always your very devoted and affectionate

HECTOR BERLIOZ

❂❂❂❂❂❂❂❂❂

To *Franz Liszt*

London, June 25, 1855

I haven't had two minutes to write you until now, the London whirl has kept me so busy this year.[5] Today, Sunday, permits me

---

5 This letter was written during Berlioz's last visit to London, while he was guest conductor of the New Philharmonic. Wagner was also in London at the time as guest conductor of the rival organization, the London Philharmonic Society.

a little more peace and I am taking advantage of it. We have been talking a lot about you with Wagner lately and you can imagine with how much affection, for, on my word of honour, I believe he loves you as much as I do myself.

He will doubtless tell you about his stay in London and all that he has to endure from hostile prejudice. He is superb in his warm-heartedness, his fervour, and I swear that even his fury enraptures me. It seems as if fate prevents me from hearing any of his latest works. The day when, by request of Prince Albert, he conducted his Overture to *Tannhäuser* at the Hanover Square Rooms, I had to run a frightful chorus rehearsal at the same time for the New Phil-harmonic concert that I was to conduct two days later. They were doing the choruses from the first four parts of *Roméo* and it was so extraordinarily execrable that in spite of Dr. Wilde, who found the whole thing well sung, I ought to have put an end to the horror by suppressing the singing entirely. Despite some *actual absences* in the orchestra, the first two parts of *Roméo* went well. In fact the "*Fête*" was given with such verve that for the first time since the symphony was written it was encored with a great Hurrah! by all the vast audience of Exeter Hall. There were plenty of slips in the Scherzo.

I shall remain in London a few more days for a concert they plan to have me conduct at Covent Garden after our last Philhar-monic. Wagner will be finished with his concerts at Hanover Square tomorrow, Monday, and will leave the following day. We are dining together before the concert. There is something singu-larly attractive about him, and even if we both are irascible, at least we complement each other. (Explain this to Cornelius.) Wagner tells me you are leaving for Hungary soon, so write six lines to me in London, where I shall be until July 7, or in Paris. Some rather peculiar propositions have been offered me here; I'll tell you about them later; they don't seem acceptable.

Meyerbeer has just arrived; his star is rising toward Covent Garden, but it rises slowly. It seems his recitatives torture the singers horribly. Even Papa Lablache [6] the other day gave vent to an out-burst of anger or despair because of them. Good-bye, they are look-ing for me at Champion Hill. I promised to spend part of the day there.

---

6 Luigi Lablache, operatic basso.

Monday morning

I have returned from my rural excursion; that is, I returned last night. Klindworth [7] was there. He played a delicious and melancholy piece of his and afterwards we sang — he, the two daughters of the house, a young German painter, and I — five-part pieces by Purcell. The ladies seemed to know them like their Bible, but they pleased Klindworth and me only tolerably. The others drank it up like consecrated milk. There is a musical feeling at the bottom of these English organizations, but it is a conservative feeling, religious above all, and anti-passionate.

Wagner has lowered himself in the opinion of the London public by seeming to do little for Mendelssohn. Now, for most people Mendelssohn is a Handel and a half! On the other hand, if I didn't have the same weakness in respect to other composers whom I despise with the force of a 120-cannon, I should say that Wagner errs in not finding the puritanical Mendelssohn a rich and fine personality. When a master is a master and has continually, on every occasion, honoured and respected Art, we must honour and respect him also, whatever divergence there may be between the line he has followed and ours. Wagner could use the same argument against me if he knew whom I loathe [8] so much, but I shall guard against telling him. When I hear or see certain pieces by that coarse master, I content myself with clenching my teeth until I return home and am alone, and then I relieve myself by heaping curses upon him. People are not perfect.

Adieu, adieu, place all my imperfections at the feet of the Princess,[9] who will have no objection, I hope, to honouring them with a glance of pity.

Yours,

H. BERLIOZ

To *Richard Wagner*

Paris, September 10, 1855

My dear Wagner:

Your letter gave me very great pleasure. You are quite right in deploring my ignorance of the German language, and in regard to what you say about the impossibility of my appreciating

7 Karl Klindworth (1830–1916), pianist and editor.
8 Probably Rossini.
9 Princess Sayn-Wittgenstein, Liszt's mistress.

your works in my present circumstances. I am continually saying it myself. The flower of expression invariably withers under the weight of translation, however delicately the translation may be effected. In *real music* there are accents that require their special words, as there are words that need their special accents. To separate one from the other, or to give them their approximate meanings, is like having a puppy attacked by a goat, or vice versa. But what is to be done? I experience a diabolical difficulty in learning languages, and I have been hard pushed to manage a few words of English and Italian.

So you are at last on the highroad to melt glaciers in composing your *Nibelungen!* To write thus in the presence of mighty nature must be superb! That is another source of enjoyment that is denied to me! Lovely landscapes, lofty summits, and the grand aspects of the sea completely absorb me instead of rousing within me the power of thought. I feel them, but I cannot express myself. I can only paint the moon when I see her image reflected at the bottom of a well.

I should be very much pleased to send you the scores you have been good enough to ask me for; unfortunately, I have not had any of them from my publishers for a long time. But there are two or three — the *Te Deum, L'Enfance du Christ,* and *Lélio* (lyric mono-drama) — that will appear in a few weeks, and in any case I can send you those.

I have your *Lohengrin;* if you could let me have *Tannhäuser,* you would confer a pleasure on me. The meeting you propose would be a fête, but I must not let myself think of it. I am compelled to make journeys which are anything but pleasure trips in order to gain a livelihood, as Paris gives me nothing but Dead Sea fruit.

It is all one — if we live a hundred years longer, I imagine we shall know many things and many men. Old Demiurgos must laugh from behind his grey beard at the farce he makes us play. But I will not abuse him; he is a friend of yours and I know you take his part. A mingled flight of many-hued ideas has come to me, together with the desire to send them to you. I have no time. Write me down an ass until further orders.

[HECTOR BERLIOZ]

To *Humbert Ferrand*

Paris, November 10, 1864

My dear Humbert:

As it seems that my letters are a source of pleasure to you, I do not see why I should deny myself the happiness of writing to you. What can I do better? Positively nothing. I always feel less unhappy after having chatted with you or heard from you. I have an ever increasing admiration for our civilization with its mails, its telegraphs, its steam, its electricity, those slaves to human will, which allow thought to be transmitted with such rapidity.

Some means should also be discovered for preventing thought from being so sad as a rule. The only one we know of at present is to be young, beloved, free, and a lover of the beauties of nature and mighty art. You and I are neither young, nor beloved, nor free, nor even in good health, so we must needs content ourselves and rejoice over what is left to us. Hippocrates said: *ars longa;* we should say: *ars æterna*, and we should prostrate ourselves before its eternity.

True it is that this adoration of art renders us cruelly exacting, and makes everyday life, which, alas! is the real life, press twice as heavily upon us. What are we to do? To hope? To despair? To resign ourselves? To sleep? To die? Not so. After all, by faith alone we are saved; by faith only we are lost. "All the world's a stage." What world? The earth? The world of fashion? And are there players, too, in the other worlds? Are the dramas there as sad or as visible as among us? Are their audiences as tardy in enlightenment, and have their audiences time to grow old before their eyes are opened so that they see clearly?

The pitching and the rolling of the heart — inevitable ideas! A wretched ship which knows that even the compass gets out of order during the storm! *Sunt lacrymæ rerum.*

Would you believe, my dear Humbert, that I cannot make up my mind about the past? I cannot understand why I did not know Virgil; it seems to me that I see him, mild, affable, and accessible, dreaming in his Sicilian villa. And Shakespeare, that mighty indifferent man, impassable as a mirror. And yet he must have been endowed with an immense, universal pity. And Beethoven, contemptuous and uncouth, yet gifted with such profound sensibility. It seems to me that I should have forgiven him everything, contempt, brutality, and all. And Gluck the superb!

Send me the march from *Alceste* with your words; I will find means of having it stereotyped without any expense to you. You will not get paid for your poetry, but you will be none the less abused for having composed it.

Last week, M. Blanche, the doctor of the lunatic asylum at Passy, invited a goodly array of savants and artists to celebrate the anniversary of the first performance of *Troyens*. I was invited without having the slightest suspicion of what was contemplated. Gounod, *Doli fabricator Epeus*, was there; and with his weak voice, but deep feeling, sang the duet "*O nuit d'ivresse.*" Madame Berthe Bauderali sang the music of Dido, and then Gounod gave us the song of Hylos, unaccompanied. A young lady sang the dance music, and I was made to recite, without music, Dido's scene: "*Va, ma sœur, l'implorer.*" I assure you, the Virgilian passage produced an immense effect.

Terque quaterque manu pectus percussa decorum
Flarentesque abscissa comas.

Everybody knew the score almost by heart. We missed you.
[HECTOR BERLIOZ]

MIKHAIL IVANOVICH GLINKA

Selna (Smolensk), 1804 — Berlin, 1857

☩☩☩☩☩☩☩☩

To *Nestor Kukolnik* [1]

Paris, April 18, 1845

Dear Nestor:

Although I realize that you are busier than ever, I don't suppose you will object to my writing you these few lines. I am leaving Paris shortly and thought it my duty to give you a little information on my visit here. I arrived here the end of June, witnessed the July celebration, and my first months here — that is, until the beginning of the long and dreary autumn — my life was that of a traveller. The new impressions, the street life, the *bals champêtres*, the theatre, the picturesqueness of these surroundings took up all my time. During November, December, and most of January my nerves were bad, and I tell you that I did not much care for the celebrations here with their noisy attractions. They lack the picturesque quality of the Italian carnival and remind me of the hustle and bustle of our Shrovetide celebration. The first few rays of the spring sunshine revived me not only physically but in spirit.

I've happened to meet several congenial people here and have made some friends, only a few, of course, but sincere and talented. Undoubtedly my most valuable acquaintance is Hector Berlioz. One of the main reasons I came here was to become better acquainted with his compositions, which are praised to heaven by some people and so harshly criticized by others. Fortune has been kind to me. Not only have I heard Berlioz's music in concert and rehearsal but I've come to know this composer quite well, in my opinion the foremost of our time (in his genre, to be sure), and I have become his friend, so far as it is possible to be a friend of such an eccentric character.

It seems to me that in the domain of fantasy no one has more

---

1 Writer; librettist for part of Glinka's *Ruslan and Lyudmila*.

colossal inventive faculty, and his works, in addition to their other merits, are absolutely original. Breadth in the total structure, development of detail, compact harmonic tissue, and that tremendously powerful orchestration — unheard-of up to now — these are the characteristics of Berlioz's music. In drama, carried away by his fantastic temperament, he wanders off, lacks naturalness, and does not ring true. Among his works that I've heard, the ones I like best are the Overture from *Les Francs-Juges*, the Scherzo of Queen Mab from *Roméo et Juliette*, the Pilgrims' March from *Childe Harold*, also the *Dies Iræ* and the *Tuba Mirum* from the *Messe des morts*. All these pages produced an indescribable effect on me. Right now, at home, I have several of his unpublished manuscripts, which I am studying with sheer pleasure.

I have given Heidenreich my opinion on the Conservatoire concerts. He must have told you about it. I want to add that I have heard their orchestra in the "Pastoral" Symphony. It was very good — too good, I think. They bring out each detail with so much attention and such refinement of nuance that the total effect suffers.

The papers and notices I sent you will inform you of my Paris debut. Here are a few details. In Berlioz's third concert, the aria *"Spolie Tchistoïe"* [2] got a great deal of applause. Soloieva started a bit low but soon took hold of herself. My *"Lezghinka,"* [3] which, as you know, was written for two orchestras and arranged for one, really an enormous one, lost much of its effect and I am not sure whether it was the arrangement or the execution that made it rather unsuccessful. The result did not come up to my nor Berlioz's expectation. He likes this piece very much and chose it himself. In the fourth concert Soloieva did not sing so well and in the one I gave at the Salle Herz she lost her head completely in the middle of the duet from the *I Puritani* and was unable to appear in the rest of the pieces. Marras saved the situation by singing the cavatina from *Elisir d'Amore*, which was not on the program. He does this beautifully. Fifty-two musicians from the Italian Theatre played my things in first-rate style and they were well received, especially the scherzo in the form of a waltz. They play this everywhere and it's going to be published, along with my romance *Il Desiderio*.

The attempts at translation have not been successful, and I've had to restrict myself to minor things. But aside from the fact that concerts have to include only music that is understood at a single

2 From *Life for the Czar* (1836).
3 From *Ruslan and Lyudmila* (1842).

hearing, I did not wish to make my debut here with anything other than pieces that were *composed in Russia and for Russia*. I am pleased with *ce succès d'oiseau de passage*, especially since Berlioz, Herz,[4] and others have seen my scores. Berlioz wrote a long article about me which was published in the *Débats*,[5] and it will show you that my *amour-propre* as a composer has been fully satisfied.

Gretsch is going to print a short description of my concert in the *Nordische Biene*, together with a translation of the letter Berlioz sent me two weeks before the concert, which will serve as proof of the sincerity of his opinions. I have already sent my sister the *Journal des débats* and I shall send other articles as they appear. When you receive them, I beg you to be careful about the translation and to have them printed in the *Nordische Biene* and the other papers most widely read throughout Russia. Don't work on them yourself, but commission someone to do it.

All in all, I'm very pleased with my trip. Paris is a wonderful city. The variety of its intellectual pleasures is inexhaustible and one can live the way one wants to here. I can't remember any period of my life more agreeable than the past few months I've spent here. From the artistic point of view, my study of Berlioz's music and my acquaintance with the Parisian public have led me to important conclusions. I have decided to add a few (and if my health permits, many) orchestral concert pieces to my repertoire, which are to be called *Picturesque Fantasies*.

Up to the present time, instrumental music has been divided into two separate branches: quartets and symphonies, which few appreciate and which frighten the bulk of the audience because of their complexity — and then, concertos, variations, and so on, which tire the ear with their heaviness and lack of organization. It seems to me that we shall be able to reconcile the requirements of art with the demands of our century, and profiting by the tremendous improvement in instrument-manufacture and musical execution, we shall be able to write pieces that are agreeable to both the connoisseur and the general public.

I have already started work. I am writing a coda for my *"Tchernomor"* March;[6] it is well liked here, but it needs a coda. In Spain I shall start on the Fantasies I have in mind. The originality of the melodies there will help me a great deal, especially since nobody has

---

4 Henri Herz (1803–88), pianist and composer.
5 *Journal des débats*, April 16, 1845.
6 From *Ruslan and Lyudmila*.

yet done anything in this field, and my unbridled imagination needs, in addition to originality, a text and a definite foundation. Then and there I shall see whether I can attempt a Spanish opera; at any rate, I shall make an effort to translate my impressions into sound.

If you can spare your friend a few minutes and reply to this letter, I promise to write you from time to time about everything of interest that occurs on this trip, which I plan to start very soon. My mother wrote me she is sending some money, which should arrive in about five days, and in ten days or so I expect to leave. I am not travelling in any hit-or-miss fashion, so to speak — I have learned enough Spanish to express and understand almost everything and I also have a great many letters of introduction. But the best part is that for the last two months I've had a Spanish servant, who is more of a companion than a servant, and I like him very much.

Until autumn, or September, I shall be in the vicinity of Madrid, then I'm going to Granada and spend the fall and winter in Andalusia. My nerves need warmth and sunshine although Paris was good for my health except for the extraordinary dampness.

Forgive me, Nestor, for having been silent for so long and please write a few lines to cheer me up when you can. My regards to our friends, and give them this address which I'm adding in French: *M. Michel de Glinka, Madrid en Espagne.* Warmest greetings to Amalie Ivanova. Tell Heidenreich I'll write him one of these days.

MIKHAIL IVANOVICH

FELIX MENDELSSOHN

Hamburg, 1809 — Leipzig, 1847

❂❂❂❂❂❂❂❂

To *Carl Friedrich Zelter* [1]

Munich, June 22, 1830

Dear Professor:

    I have wished to write to you for a long time and once more express my gratitude. But it is difficult for me to say thanks in writing; the words seem so cold and formal while what I enjoyed so greatly and want to thank you for still appears so vividly to me. When you introduced me nine years ago into Goethe's house you were perfectly aware of how great a happiness your kindness had in store for me. But I could not know that myself at the time, nor could I fully appreciate a gift whose value was not yet clear to me. But now that I have experienced greater delight and comfort with Goethe and his family than ever before, now that I have lived through a number of unforgettable days, when every hour brought nothing but elation, joy, and pride — now at last I know how to appreciate it. Nevertheless, I cannot thank you as I ought. You did not do it in order to be thanked, and so you will excuse my speaking about it, even though my words have not the tone I should like to give them and are not adequate for their purpose. Well, I am sure you know how I feel.

    I have often played to Goethe in the morning hours. He wanted to get an idea of how music has developed and wishes to hear the music of different composers in chronological order. He seemed rather wary of Beethoven; but I could not spare him this acquaintance because he had to hear "where sounds had turned to," and so I played for him the first movement of the C minor Symphony, which he liked very much. He was delighted with the overture by Johann Sebastian Bach, the one in D major with the trum-

---

1 Director of the Berlin Singakademie and Mendelssohn's former teacher (1758–1872).

pets, which I played on the piano as well as I could; "in the beginning it sounds so distinguished and pompous, one really sees the crowd of smartly attired people walking down the steps of a broad staircase." And I also played the Inventions and quite a few pieces of the *Well-Tempered Clavichord*.

One day he asked me if I would not care to pay a compliment to craftsmanship and call on the organist, who might let me see and hear the organ in the cathedral. I said yes, of course I would, and the instrument gave me great pleasure. I was told that you, too, had given your expert opinion on the repair work, and that therefore it had been done better than on any repaired organ I know of. Owing to the long narrow space in which it is housed, the pedal-pipe is fitted deep in the rear; none the less the full organ sounds ample and strong, the tone does not tremble in the least, and this shows that there must be plenty of wind. The pedal is in perfect proportion to the manual and there is no lack of beautiful soft voices of various kinds. The organist offered me the choice of hearing something scholarly or something for "people" (because he said that for people one had to compose only easy and bad music), so I asked for something scholarly. But it was not much to be proud of; he modulated around enough to make one giddy, but nothing unusual came of it; he made a number of entries, but no fugue was forthcoming. When my turn came to play to him, I started with the D minor Toccata of Sebastian and remarked that this was at the same time scholarly and something for "people" too, at least for some of them; but mind, hardly had I begun to play when the superintendent dispatched his valet upstairs with the message that this playing had to be stopped right away because it was a week-day and he could not study with that much noise going on. Goethe was very much amused by this story.

Here in Munich the musicians behave exactly like that organist; they believe that good music may be considered a heaven-sent gift, but just *in abstracte*, and as soon as they sit down to play they produce the stupidest, silliest stuff imaginable, and when people do not like it they pretend that it was still too highbrow. Even the best pianists had no idea that Mozart and Haydn had also composed for the piano; they had just the faintest notion of Beethoven and consider the music of Kalkbrenner, Field, and Hummel classical and scholarly. On the other hand, having played myself several times, I found the audience so receptive and open-minded that I felt doubly vexed by those frivolities. Recently, at a soirée given by a Countess, who is supposed to lead in fashion, I had an outbreak. The young ladies, quite able to perform adequate pieces very nicely, tried to break their fingers with juggler's tricks and rope-dancer's feats of Herz's; when I was asked to play, I thought: Well, if you get bored, it serves you right; and started right out with the C-sharp minor Sonata of Beethoven.[2] When I finished, I noticed that the impression had been enormous; the ladies were weeping, the gentlemen hotly discussing the importance of the work. I had to write down a number of Beethoven sonatas for the female pianists who wanted to study them. Next morning the Countess summoned her piano-teacher and desired from him an edition of good, really good music, by Mozart, Beethoven, and Weber. This story went around in Munich, and the good-natured musicians were much pleased that I had set myself up as the preacher in the desert. Subsequently I gave a long sermon to the leading pianist and reproached her for having contributed nothing toward the knowledge and appreciation of the works of the great masters here and for having just followed the popular trend instead of guiding the taste of the public — and she vowed to improve. Since that time I play only what I really like, however serious, and everybody listens to me with attention.

I am delighted to make so much music here, and though I have little time left to compose and to think, this gay life inspires me with many new ideas and proves to be cheering and refreshing. I have a sacred piece in mind; as soon as I find time to write it down, I shall mail it to you. Good-bye for today, dear Professor Zelter. With the most cordial greetings for you and yours and the best wishes for your health and happiness,

Always your faithful
F. M. B.

❂❂❂❂❂❂❂

To *Ignaz Moscheles*

Düsseldorf, February 7, 1834

My own poverty in novel passages for the piano struck me very much in the *Rondo brillant*,[3] which I wish to dedicate to you; these are what cause me to demur and to torment myself; and I fear you will remark this. In other respects there is a good deal in it that I like, and some passages please me exceedingly; but how I am

---

2 Op. 27, no. 2; the so-called "Moonlight."
3 Op. 29, for piano and orchestra, 1834 (dedicated to Moscheles).

to set about composing a methodical *tranquil* piece (and I well remember you advised me strongly to do this last spring) I really cannot tell. All that I now have in my head for the piano is about as *tranquil* as Cheapside, and even when I control myself and begin to extemporize very soberly, I gradually break loose again. On the other hand, the *scena* that I am now writing for the Philharmonic is, I fear, becoming much too tame; but it is needless to carp so much at myself, and I work hard: by my saying this you will see that I am well and in good spirits.

Dear Madame Moscheles, when you, however, advise me to remain quite indifferent toward the public and toward critics, I must in turn ask: Am I not, in my profession, an *anti-public-caring* musician, and an *anti-critical* one into the bargain? What is Hecuba to me, or critics either? (I mean the press, or rather pressure); and if an overture to Lord Eldon were to suggest itself to me, in the form of a reversed canon, or a double fugue with a *cantus firmus*, I should persist in writing it, though it would certainly not be popular — far more, therefore, a "lovely Melusina," [4] who is, however, a very different object; only it would be fatal indeed were I to find that I could no longer succeed in having my works performed; but as you say there is no fear of this, then I say, Long live the public and the critics! but I intend to live too, and to go to England next year if possible.

Your observations on Neukomm's [5] music find a complete response in my own heart. What does astonish me is that a man of so much taste and cultivation should not, with such qualifications, write more elegant and refined music; for, without referring to the ideas or the basis of his works, they appear to me most carelessly composed, and even commonplace. He also employs brass instruments recklessly, which ought, through discretion even, to be sparingly used, to say nothing of artistic considerations.

Among other things, I am particularly pleased by the mode in which Handel, toward the close, rushes in with his kettle-drums and trumpets, as if he himself were belabouring them. There is no one who would not be struck by it; and it seems to me far better to *imitate* this than to overexcite and stimulate the audience, who before the close have become quite accustomed to all this cayenne pepper.

---

4 Overture, *Lovely Melusina,* op. 32 (1833).
5 Sigismund Neukomm (1778–1858).

I have just looked through Cherubini's new opera,[6] and though I was quite enchanted with many parts of it, still I cannot but deeply lament that he so often adopts that new corrupt Parisian fashion, as if the instruments were nothing and the effect everything — flinging about three or four trombones as if it were the audience who had skins of parchment instead of the drums; and then in his finales he winds up with hideous chords, and a tumult and crash most grievous to listen to. Compare with these some of his earlier pieces, such as *Lodoiska*, and *Medea*, etc., etc., where there is as much difference in brightness and genius as between a living man and a scarecrow; so I am not surprised that the opera did not please. Those who like the original Cherubini cannot fail to be provoked at the way in which he yields to the fashion of the day and to the taste of the public; and those who do not like the original Cherubini find far too much of his own style still left to satisfy them either, no matter what pains he may take to do so — he always peeps forth again in the very first three notes. Then they call this *rococo, perruque*, etc., etc.

[FELIX MENDELSSOHN]

੦੩੦੩੦੩੦੩੦੩੦

To the Committee of the *Lower Rhine* Music Festival
Leipzig, January 18, 1838

I am deeply grateful for the invitation contained in your letter of the 8th of January. Your kind remembrance is not less prized by me than the prospect of again attending such a pleasant festival and deriving from it as much enjoyment as that for which I have already to thank the Rhenish Musical Festivals. I therefore accept your invitation with sincere delight, if God grants health to me and mine and if we can agree on the selection of the music to the full satisfaction of both parties. The more successful the previous Cologne festival was with regard to the arrangement of the pieces performed, especially in Handel's work with the organ, the more important it seems to me to have at least *one* piece in the program by which this year's festival may be distinguished from others and by means of which progress may, as far as possible, be manifested.

For this purpose I consider it absolutely necessary to have the name of Sebastian Bach on the program, if only for one short piece;

---

6 *Ali Baba* (1833).

for it is certainly high time that at these festivals, on which the name of Handel has shed such lustre, another immortal master, who is in no one point inferior to any other master and in many points superior to all, should not longer be forgotten. The same scruples that exist in opposition to this must also have existed in former years with regard to the works of Handel, and you are all grateful to those who, disregarding these obstacles, revealed to you such treasures of sublimity and elevation. Earn for yourself, then, similar thanks from the Rhenish friends of music by making a beginning, which is indeed difficult (for this I do not deny) and must be proceeded with cautiously, but which will certainly be attended with the best results and universally imitated. For when anything of Bach's has been once performed, it will be easy to discover that it is beautiful and to perform it again; the only difficulty is the beginning.

The proposal that I wish to make to you on this subject is to introduce into this musical festival a short Psalm of Bach's (about twenty minutes or half an hour in length), and if you are afraid of doing this on the second day, from the dread of scaring away the public, whom this learned name might alarm, then do so on the first day and give in addition a rather shorter oratorio of Handel's. It is pretty certain that no fewer people will come to hear Handel, for those who do not fear the one will be equally disposed to like the other, and there are still three or four totally unknown and truly admirable oratorios of his, which would not occupy more than an hour and a half, or scarcely two hours at most, and would be a welcome novelty to all lovers of music.

I first became acquainted with these works by the splendid gift of the previous committee,[7] and I should be very glad were you to derive any benefit from these volumes for this year's festival. With regard to the second day, I may first inquire whether you intend to apply to Cherubini for his grand Requiem; it must be translated, and is entirely for men's voices, but as it will last only an hour, or even less, that would not much matter, and according to the universal verdict it is a splendid work. At present, however, the chief object seems to me to be the first point in this letter, and I therefore beg you will arrange about it as soon as possible.

[FELIX MENDELSSOHN]

---

7 Arnold's edition of Handel, in 32 volumes.

To *Conrad Schleinitz*

Berlin, August 1, 1838

Dear Schleinitz:

What you write me about your increased business rejoices me much. You know how often we have talked the subject over, and I cannot share your sentiment that any one profession is preferable to another. I always think that whatever an intelligent man gives his heart to and firmly grasps must become a noble vocation; and personally I only dislike those in which there is nothing personal and in which all individuality disappears; as, for example, the military profession in peace, of which we have instances here. But with regard to the others, it is more or less untrue. When one profession is compared with another, the one is usually taken in its naked reality, and the other in the most beautiful ideality, and then the decision is quickly made.

And how easy it is for an artist to feel such reality in his sphere and then to esteem *practical* men happy who have studied and known the different relations of men toward each other, and who help others to live by their own life and progress, and at once see the fruits of all that is tangible, useful, and benevolent instituted by them; and just on this account an upright man has the hardest stand to make, knowing that the public are more attracted by outward show than by truth. But individual failures and strife must not be allowed to have their growth in the heart; there must be something to occupy and to elevate it far above these isolated external things. This speaks strongly in favour of my opinion, for it is the best part of every calling, and common to all: to yours, to mine, and to every other.

Where is it that you find beauty when I am working at a quartet or a symphony? Merely in that portion of myself that I transfer to it or can succeed in expressing; and you can do this in as full measure as any man, in your defence of a culprit, or in a case of libel, or in any one thing that entirely engrosses you, and that is the great point. If you can only give utterance to your inmost thoughts, and if these inmost thoughts become more and more worthy of being expressed — all the rest is indifferent. I thank you, therefore, for the report you give me of your occupations, and hope you will often send me equally good tidings.

Your

FELIX MENDELSSOHN BARTHOLDY

To *Ignaz Moscheles*

Leipzig, November 30, 1839

. . . Your Paris letter gave me much pleasure although what it describes is anything but pleasant. What a curious state of things seems to prevail there! To tell the truth, I never felt very sympathetically disposed toward it; and all I have heard lately, through you and others, does not tend to improve my opinion. Vanity and outward show nowhere seem to play so prominent a part; and the fact that people assume poses not only to become stars, to acquire decorations and wear stiff neckties, but also to reveal their interest in high art, and a soul replete with enthusiasm, does not mend matters.

When I read your description of the soirée at the Kalkbrenners', I see and hear it all: that anxiety to shine at the piano, that greed for a poor little round of applause, the shallowness that underlies it all and is as pretentious as if such petty exhibitions were events of world-wide importance! To read about it is more than enough for me. After all, I prefer the German philistine, with his nightcap and tobacco; although I am not the one to stand up in his defence, especially since the events in Hanover, which I followed with great interest and which, I am sorry to say, do not reflect much credit on the German fatherland. So, on the whole, there is not much to be proud of on either side; and one cannot help being doubly grateful for that art which has a life of its own, far away from everything — a solitude to which we can flee and be happy. . . .

I want to write a new concerto, but so far it is swimming about in my head in a shapeless condition. A new oratorio, too, I have begun; but how it is to end, and what is to come in the middle, heaven only knows. I should so like to show you my trio; [8] it has grown quite dear to me, and I am confident there are things in it with which you would be satisfied. The publishers are pressing me to let them have it; I only wish I could just play it once to you before. . . .

I declined to give anything to Pott [9] in furtherance of his scheme; nor would you have done so had you known all their doings and dealings in Germany with regard to monuments. They speculate with the names of great men in order to give themselves great

---

8 Op. 49, in D minor.
9 August Pott (1806–83), violinist.

names; they do a deal of trumpeting in the papers, and treat us to ever so much bad music with real trumpets. If they wish to honour Handel in Halle, Mozart in Salzburg, and Beethoven in Bonn by founding good orchestras and performing their works properly and intelligently, I am their man. But I do not care for their stones and blocks as long as their orchestras are only stumbling-blocks, nor for their conservatories in which there is nothing worth conserving.

My present hobby is the improvement of our poor orchestra.[10] After no end of letter-writing, soliciting, and importuning I have succeeded in getting the salaries raised by five hundred taler; and before I leave them I mean to get them double that amount. If that is granted, I shall not mind their setting up a monument to Sebastian Bach in front of the St. Thomas School; but first, mind you, the grant! You see, I am a regular small-beer Leipziger. But really you would be touched if you could see and hear for yourself how my good fellows put heart and soul into their work and strive to do their best.

I am very glad you improved your acquaintance and friendship with Chopin. He is certainly the most gifted of them all, and his playing has real charm. They say Liszt is coming here, and I should be very glad; for notwithstanding his unpalatable contributions to the papers, I am thoroughly impressed by both his playing and his striking personality. Berlioz's program that you sent me is a very silly production. I wish I could see any pluck or originality in it, but to me it seems simply vapid and insipid. Has not Onslow [11] written anything new? And old Cherubini? There is a man for you! I have got his *Abencérages* [12] and am again and again enjoying his sparkling fire, his clever and unexpected transitions, and the neatness and grace with which he writes. I am truly grateful to this fine old gentleman. It is all so free, so bold and bright.

Now I must end, my dear friend. I have been jumbling everything together, and chatting away as if I were sitting next to you by the piano. . . . Write to me and let me know what you are doing and what composing; and, above all, tell me that you are my friend, as I am your

F. M. B.

---

10 Mendelssohn was conductor of the Gewandhaus concerts.
11 George Onslow (1784–1853), violinist.
12 Opera, composed 1813.

To *Marc-André Souchay* [13]

Berlin, October 15, 1841

. . . There is so much talk about music, and yet so little is said. For my part, I believe that words do not suffice for such a purpose, and if I found they did suffice I would finally have nothing more to do with music. People often complain that music is too ambiguous; that what they should think when they hear it is so unclear, whereas everyone understands words. With me it is exactly the reverse, and not only with regard to an entire speech, but also with individual words. These, too, seem to me so ambiguous, so vague, so easily misunderstood in comparison with genuine music, which fills the soul with a thousand things better than words.

The thoughts that are expressed to me by music that I love are not too indefinite to be put into words, but on the contrary, too definite. And so I find in every effort to express such thoughts that something is right but at the same time that something is lacking in all of them; and so I feel, too, with yours. This, however, is not your fault, but the fault of the words, which are incapable of anything better. If you ask me what I was thinking of when I wrote it, I would say: just the song as it stands. And if I happen to have had certain words in mind for one or another of these songs, I would never want to tell them to anyone, because the same words never mean the same things to different people. Only the song can say the same thing, can arouse the same feelings in one person as in another, a feeling that is not expressed, however, by the same words.

Resignation, melancholy, the praise of God, a hunting song, do not conjure up the same thoughts in everybody. Resignation is to one what melancholy is to another; the third can form no lively conception of either. Why, to anyone who is by nature a keen sportsman, a hunting song and the praise of God would come to pretty much the same thing, and to him the sound of the hunting horn would actually be the praise of God, while to us it would be nothing but a hunting song. And however long we might discuss it with him, we should never get any farther. Words have many meanings, but music we could both understand correctly. Will you allow this to serve as an answer to your question?

At all events, it is the only one I can give, although these, too, are nothing, after all, but ambiguous words!

[FELIX MENDELSSOHN]

---

13 Souchay had asked Mendelssohn the meanings of some of his *Songs without Words*.

FRÉDÉRIC CHOPIN

Zelazowa Wola, 1810 — Paris, 1849

❀❀❀❀❀❀❀❀

To *Joseph Elsner* [1]

Paris, December 14, 1831

Dear Pan Elsner:

  Your letter brought me fresh proof of the fatherly interest and sincere good wishes you are still kind enough to continue toward the most faithful of your pupils. In 1830, though I realized how much I still lacked, and the long road ahead I still had to travel to reach any of your standards, I still dared to think: "At least I shall get a little closer to him and if not a Cubit, then perhaps a Spindleshanks [2] may come out of my brain." But today, having lost all such hope, I have to think of clearing a path for myself in the world as a pianist, and I must put off until later those higher artistic aims your letter so rightly presents.

  In order to be a great composer, one needs an enormous amount of knowledge, which, as you taught me, one does not acquire from listening only to other people's work, but even more from listening to one's own. There are many talented young men, pupils of the Paris Conservatoire, who are waiting with folded hands for the performance of their operas, symphonies, and cantatas, which thus far only Cherubini and Lesueur have seen on paper. (I'm not speaking of the little theatres, though it's equally difficult to get in there, too, and when you do, as Thomas did at Leopoldstadt, the result is of little artistic importance though one may be very talented.)

  Meyerbeer, well known as an opera-composer for ten years, had to work and pay his way in Paris for three years before (at last they had had enough of Auber) he managed to produce his *Robert*

---

1 Chopin's former teacher at the Warsaw Conservatory.

2 Two characters in Elsner's opera *King Cubit;* the nicknames of two ancient Polish kings.

[147]

le Diable, which is creating a furore in Paris at present. It seems to me that in order to enter the musical world, a man is fortunate to be at the same time a composer and an actor.

Here and there in Germany I am known as a pianist; certain music journals have mentioned my concerts, expressing the hope that I may soon take my place among the foremost virtuosi of that instrument (which means: *disce puer faciam te*, my Lord). Today I find an unequalled opportunity to fulfil the promise innate in me; why should I not seize it? In Germany I do not know anyone who can teach me anything about piano and though there were some people who thought I still lacked something, they didn't know what it was, and I myself could not see the beam in my own eye which still keeps me from looking higher. Three years is too long, much too long, even Kalkbrenner,[3] having examined me more closely, admits it, which should convince you that a real virtuoso who deserves his fame knows no jealousy. But I would have been willing to spend three years working if this enabled me to make great progress in my undertaking. I am so determined not to become a copy of Kalkbrenner that nothing can interfere with my idea and desire, perhaps audacious, but at least high-minded, to create a new world for myself, and if I work, it is to achieve a more solid standing.

Ries [4] found it easier to obtain laurels for his *Braut* in Berlin and Frankfurt because he was known as a pianist. How long was Spohr known only as a violinist before he wrote *Jessonda*, *Faust*, and so on? I hope, sir, that you will not refuse me your blessing when you learn by what principles I am inspired and what my plans are.

No doubt my parents will have told you about my concert's being postponed to the 25th. I had a lot of trouble arranging it, and if it were not for Paër,[5] Kalkbrenner, and especially Norblin [6] (who sends his best regards), I should not be able to give it so soon (they say that two months is a very short time in Paris). Baillot,[7] who is very agreeable and courteous, will play the Beethoven quintet, and Kalkbrenner will play the Duo with me accompanied by four pianos. Reich [8] I know only by sight; you know how eager I

---

3 Friedrich Kalkbrenner (1788–1849), piano virtuoso and teacher.
4 Ferdinand Ries (1784–1838), teacher and composer.
5 Ferdinand Paër (1771–1839), composer and conductor.
6 Louis Norblin (1781–1854), cello-teacher at the Paris Conservatoire.
7 Pierre Baillot (1771–1842), violinist.
8 Anton Reicha (1770–1836), composer.

was to meet him, but I know several of his pupils, who gave me a very different impression of him. He is not fond of music; he doesn't even go to the Conservatoire concerts and he does not like to talk about music with anyone. During his lessons he keeps looking at his watch, and so on. Cherubini, too, keeps babbling continually about cholera and revolutions. These gentlemen are dried-up marionettes whom one must regard with respect and learn something from their music. Fétis,[9] whom I know, lives in the suburbs and comes into Paris only for lessons; otherwise he would have been locked up in Sainte Pélagie long ago because of his debts. You probably know that in Paris debtors must be arrested in their homes, so he doesn't stay at his Paris place but in the suburbs, where the law cannot touch him for a while.

The number of people among the masses here who are interested in all kinds of music is amazing. Three orchestras: the Academy, the Italian, and Fédau's, they are excellent; Rossini is the *regisseur* of his own opera, which is the best noted in Europe. Lablache, Rubini, Pasta (who is away now), Malibran, Devrient, Schröder, Santini, and others arouse our admiration and enchant us on the grandest scale three times a week. Nourrit, Levasseur, Derivis, Mme Cinti-Damoreau, Mlle Dorus sustain the level of the Opéra, while Cholet, Mlle Casimir, Prevost are wonderful at the Opéra Comique; in short, only here can one learn what singing is. Today, most assuredly, not Pasta but Malibran (Garcia) is the foremost singer in Europe — really marvellous! Walenty Radziwill raves about her and in this connection we often talk about how much you would admire her! Lesueur thanks you for your remembrances and asks me to send you his warmest greetings; he always speaks of you in the kindest way and keeps asking — "*et que fait notre bon Monsieur Elsner — racontez-moi de ses nouvelles*," and immediately mentions the Requiem you sent him. All of us here love and admire you, starting with me and ending with your godson, Antonij Orlowski, who, it seems, won't get his operetta performed very soon, because the *sujet* is not of the best, and besides, the theatre is closed until the new year. The King is not throwing his money away, and all in all these times are difficult for artists; only the English pay. I could go on writing until tomorrow, but I've bored you enough already. Accept, sir, the assurance of my gratitude and the respect with which I shall for ever remain your most faithful pupil,

F. F. CHOPIN

9 François Joseph Fétis (1784–1871), theorist and music historian.

To *Dominik Dziewanowski*

[*Paris*, 1832]

Dear Domus:

If I had a friend (with a big, crooked nose, I'm not talking about any other friend) who used to kill horseflies with me at Szafarnia many years ago, and who had convinced me of his love, and if that friend were to leave the country and not write a single word, I should have the lowest opinion of him. And even if afterwards he begged me for forgiveness with tears in his eyes, I would not forgive him. But I, Fryc, am brazen enough to defend my negligence and give you a sign of life after this long silence, like a horsefly that takes its head out of the water when nobody asks it to.

But I won't try to explain. I would rather confess my guilt, which perhaps may seem more serious from this distance than it really is, for I am terribly distracted and torn every which way at once. Now that I've been introduced into high society, I associate with ambassadors, princes, ministers, and I don't know how this miracle came about, because I certainly didn't try to get there. At present it is absolutely indispensable for me since good taste is supposed to depend on this. You immediately have greater talent if you've played at the English or Austrian Embassy, and you play better if Princess Vaudemont (the last descendant of the old Montmorency family) was your protector — (I can't say *is your protector* because the old thing died a week ago). She was the sort of lady like our now deceased Zielonkowa or Lady Polanecka; people of the court used to call on her, she did a lot of good, and during the revolution she hid many aristocrats. After the first July days she was the first person to present herself at the court of Louis Philippe. She was surrounded by a great crowd of little black and white dogs, canaries, parrots; and also had the drollest monkey in the world, which would bite the other countesses at her receptions.

I already enjoy the friendship of the artists here although this is my first year among them. The proof of their regard is that they dedicate their pieces to me, even people with tremendous reputations, before I dedicate mine to them. Pixis dedicated his last Variations for a military band to me. Also people compose variations on my themes and Kalkbrenner wrote some variations on my mazurka [op. 7, no. 1]. The Conservatoire students and the pupils of Moscheles, Herz, and Kalkbrenner — in a word, accomplished virtuosi — take lessons from me and link my name with that of Field.[10] In short, if I were even more stupid than I am, I would think I had reached the culminating-point of my career, but I know how much I still lack in order to achieve perfection, and the more so since I live only among first-rate artists and recognize their shortcomings.

But I'm ashamed of having written all this nonsense. I've been boasting like a child, or rather like someone who hurries to defend himself before he is attacked. I would cross out the whole thing but have no time to start another letter. Anyway, perhaps you have not forgotten what my character is like and you will remember that I am now what I was formerly, with this difference, that I have only one whisker on my cheek, the other refuses to grow.

Today I have to give five lessons; no doubt you think I'm making a fortune. Carriages and white gloves cost more than I earn and without them I would not be in good taste. I love the Carlists; I detest the Philippists; I myself am a revolutionary; money means nothing to me and nothing is important to me except friendship, for which I pray and beseech you.

FRYDERYK

---

10 John Field (1782–1837), pianist and composer.

ROBERT SCHUMANN

Zwickau, 1810 — *Endenich,* 1856

❋❋❋❋❋❋❋❋

To *Friedrich Wieck* [1]

Heidelberg, November 6, 1829

I have but just laid aside Hummel's [2] Concerto in A minor, my dear master. It was the work of a moment to pull down my blind, light my cigar, pull up the table, and bury my face in my hand, and in a flash I was transported to the corner of the Reichsstrasse, my music under my arm, ready for my piano lesson. Ah! what possessed me to leave Leipzig? There I had access to the Olympus of music, and you, its priest, at hand to lift the veil with gentle decision from the eyes of the dazzled novice.

Here it is very much as I expected.[3] There is on the whole a great love for music, but little talent. Here and there an antiquated critic or two, but little creative power. As you know, I have small taste for crude theory and have been going my own way quietly, improvising a good deal, but playing very little from notes. I have begun several symphonies, but have finished nothing. Now and again I squeeze in a Schubert waltz between Roman law and the Pandects, and the trio haunts my dreams, bringing back the heavenly hour when I first heard it at your house. I think I may say I have not lost much ground; neither have I made any appreciable progress — practically a standstill, I admit. Still, I feel that my touch is much fuller in forte, more supple and responsive in piano, although I may have lost in fluency and precision. Without undue vanity, I cannot help feeling modestly conscious of my superiority over all the other Heidelberg pianists. . . .

I am now working up the last movement of Hummel's F-sharp minor Sonata. It is truly a titanic work, epic in character, describing

---

1 Schumann's former piano-teacher and his future father-in-law.
2 Johann Nepomuk Hummel (1778–1837).
3 Schumann was studying law at the University of Heidelberg.

the mighty struggles of a giant mind and its eventual resignation. I shall play you only this at Easter, so you may make it a test of my progress.

There is a strong party, in which I figure, now forming against Thibaut.[4] You would hardly believe what delightful, refreshing hours I have spent with him, and yet how his one-sided and really pedantic views on music grieve me, knowing, as I do, his broadmindedness in jurisprudence and the irresistible power of his brilliant, dominating intellect.

I returned from my tour in Switzerland and Italy a fortnight ago, poorer by a few napoleons, but richer by my increased knowledge of the world and a store of precious memories. I declare you can have no notion of Italian music until you have heard it under the Italian skies which called it into being. How often did I think of you in the Scala Theatre at Milan! How charmed I was with Rossini, or rather with Pasta's interpretation! I leave her name unqualified to show my respect — I might say, my adoration. In the Leipzig concert-room I sometimes experienced a thrill of awe in the presence of the genius of music, but Italy has taught me to love it. Only once in my whole life have I had an impression of the actual presence of God, of gazing reverently and unrebuked into His face; this was at Milan as I listened to Pasta — and Rossini! Do not smile, dear master, for I speak seriously. But this was my sole musical treat in Italy. Their music is, in the ordinary way, hardly fit to listen to. You have no conception of the sort of slapdash facility with which they reel off everything. . . .

Schubert is still my one and only love, the more so as he has everything in common with my one and only Jean Paul. To play his compositions is with me like reading one of Jean Paul's novels. . . . There is no other music that presents so bewildering a psychological problem in its train of ideas, its apparently abrupt transitions. It is rare to find a composer who can stamp his individuality plainly on such a heterogeneous collection of tone-pictures, and still rarer are those who write, as Schubert did, as their hearts prompt them. Schubert unburdened his heart on a sheet of music-paper just as others leave the impression of passing moods in their journals. His soul was so steeped in music that he wrote notes where others use words — so, at least, I venture to think.

Some years back I began a book on the æsthetics of sound and made some way with it; but I soon realized that I had neither enough

---

4 Professor of law at the University of Heidelberg.

ripe judgment nor a sufficiently objective attitude, consequently sometimes finding what others had missed and vice versa. But if you only knew my perpetual state of ferment! Why, I might have arrived at op. 100 with my symphonies had I written them out. I feel so entirely in my element with a full orchestra; even if my mortal enemies were marshalled before me, I could lead them, master them, surround them, or repulse them. Circumstances rather than principles keep me from undue presumption, though I occasionally take a high tone with people who provoke it. But there are times when my soul so overflows with melody that it is impossible to write anything down; at such times I could laugh in the face of any art critic who should tell me that I had better write nothing, since I cannot excel, and boldly say he knew nothing about it. Forgive these wonderful revelations.

And now for the favours I have to ask. The first and most pressing is — write to me; the second — very soon. Your letters mean positively as much to me here as the Leipzig concerts I have to miss. So you have had Paganini at Leipzig, and heard him four times! Really, that *four* is too tantalizing. . . .

[ROBERT SCHUMANN]

To his mother

Heidelberg, July 30, 1830
5 a. m.

Good morning, Mamma!

How shall I describe my bliss at this moment: the spirit-lamp is hissing under the coffee-pot, the sky is indescribably clear and rosy, and the keen spirit of the morning fills me with its presence. Besides, your letter lies before me and reveals a perfect treasury of good feeling, common sense, and virtue. My cigar tastes uncommonly good; in short, the world is very lovely at times, if one could only always get up early.

There is plenty of blue sky and sunshine in my life at present, but my guide, Rosen, is wanting. Two more of my best friends, the von Herzogenbergs from Pomerania, went off to Italy a week ago, and so I often feel very lonely, which sometimes makes me happy and sometimes miserable — it just depends. One can get on better without a sweetheart than without a friend; and sometimes I get into a regular fever when I think of myself.

My *whole life* has been a twenty years' struggle between poetry and prose, or, if you like to call it so, music and law. There is just as high a standard to be reached in practical life as in art. In the former the ideal consists in the hope of plenty of work and a large, extensive practice; but what sort of prospect would there be in Saxony for a fellow like myself, who is not of noble birth, has neither money nor interest, and has no affection for legal squabbles and pettiness?

At Leipzig I did not trouble my head about my career, but went dreaming and dawdling on and never did any real good. Here I have worked harder, but both there and here have been getting more and more attached to art. Now I am standing at the crossroads and am scared at the question: "Which way to choose?" But the fact is — now do not be angry at what I am going to say, for I will but whisper it — it always seems to me as if you were putting obstacles in my way. You had very good reasons for doing so, and I understand them all perfectly, and we both agreed in calling art an "uncertain future" and "a doubtful way of earning one's bread." There certainly can be no greater misery than to look forward to a hopeless, shallow, miserable existence which one has prepared for oneself. But neither is it easy to enter upon a career diametrically opposed to one's whole education, and to do it requires patience, confidence, and quick decision.

I am still at the height of youth and imagination, with plenty of capabilities for cultivating and ennobling art, and have come to the conclusion that with patience and perseverance, and a good master, I should in six years be as good as any pianist, for pianoforte-playing is mere mechanism and execution. Occasionally I have much imagination and possibly some creative power — now comes the question: "To be or not to be," for you can only do *one* thing well in this life, and I am always saying to myself: "Make up your mind to do one thing thoroughly well, and with patience and perseverance you are bound to accomplish something." This battle against myself is now raging more fiercely than ever, my good mother. Sometimes I am daring and confident in my own strength and power, but sometimes I tremble to think of the long way I have traversed and of the endless road that lies before me. As to Thibaut, he long ago recommended me to take up art. I should be very glad if you would write to him, and he would be very pleased too, but unfortunately he went off to Rome some time ago, so probably I shall never speak to him again.

If I stick to law I must undoubtedly stay here for another winter to hear Thibaut lecture on the Pandects, as every law-student is bound to do. If I am to go in for music, I must leave this at once and go to Leipzig, where Wieck, whom I could thoroughly trust and who can tell me what I am worth, would then carry on my education. Afterwards I ought to go to Vienna for a year and, if possible, study under Moscheles.

Now I have a favour to ask of you, my dear mother, which I hope you will grant me. *Write yourself to Wieck and ask him point-blank what he thinks of me and my career.* Please let me have a SPEEDY answer, deciding the question, so that I can hurry up my departure from Heidelberg, although I shall be very sorry to leave it and my many kind friends and favourite haunts. *If you like you can enclose this letter to Wieck. In any case the question must be decided before Michaelmas,* and then I shall pursue my object in life, whatever it may be, with fresh vigour and without tears. You must admit that this is the most important letter I have ever written, so I trust you will not hesitate to comply with my request, for there is *no time* to be lost.[5]

Good-bye, dear Mother, and do not fret. In this case Heaven will only help us if we help ourselves.

Ever your most loving son,
ROBERT SCHUMANN

◐Ю◐Ю◐Ю◐Ю◐

To *Clara Wieck*

Leipzig, April 13, 1838

How full of music I am now, and always such lovely melodies! Only fancy, since my last letter I have finished another whole book of new things. You and one of your ideas are the principal subject, and I shall call them "Kreisleriana," and dedicate them to you;[6] yes, to you and to nobody else; and you will smile so sweetly when you see yourself in them. Even to myself my music now seems wonderfully intricate in spite of its simplicity; its eloquence comes straight from the heart, and everyone is affected when I play before people, as I often do now, and like to do. And when you are standing by me, as I sit by the piano, then we shall both cry like children — I know I shall be quite overcome.

That Fantasia of Liszt's was the most wonderful thing I have

---

5 Several weeks later Schumann returned to Leipzig to study with Wieck.
6 Actually dedicated to Chopin.

ever heard you play. Play him the Toccata, and the Études, which
he does not know yet, and call his attention to the Paganini Études.
The *Kinderscenen* will probably be finished by the time you arrive;
I am very fond of them, and make a great impression when I play
them, especially upon myself. The next things to be printed are
some Fantasies, but to distinguish them from the *Fantasiestücke* I
have called them *Ruine, Siegesbogen und Sternbild*, and *Dich-
tungen*. It was a long time before I could think of that last word.
It strikes me as being a very refined and most characteristic title for
a piece of music.

But you must have patience with me sometimes, and often
scold me. I have got plenty of faults, though fewer than I used to
have. Our having had to wait so long has had some advantages: we
shall have got over a good deal that other people experience after
marriage. I have just noticed that marriage is a very musical word,
and a fifth too: E–H–E.[7] But to return to my faults; I have got one
detestable habit: namely, showing my affection for people I love
most by playing them all sorts of tricks. For instance, supposing
there is a letter that I ought to have answered long ago. You might
say: "Dear R., do answer that letter, it has been lying there such a
long time" — but do you suppose I should do it? No such thing. I
would sooner make all sorts of pretty excuses, etc. Then I have got
another very saucy trick; I am one of the greatest admirers of beautiful women; I simply delight in them, and revel in praising your
sex. So if ever we are walking together through the streets of Vienna and meet somebody pretty, and I should exclaim: "Oh, Clara,
look at that divine creature," or something of that sort, you mustn't
be alarmed, or scold.

Now just look at your old Robert. Is he not just the same
trifler, joker, and teller of ghost stories? But I can be very serious
too, and sometimes for days together; but don't let that alarm you,
for it is only when my mind is at work and I am full of ideas about
music and my compositions. I am affected by everything that goes
on in the world, and think it all over in my own way, politics, literature, and people, and then I long to express my feelings and find an
outlet for them in music. That is why my compositions are sometimes difficult to understand, because they are connected with distant interests; and sometimes striking, because everything extraordinary that happens impresses me, and impels me to express it in
music.

---

7 *Ehe* — marriage. H stands for the note B; E to B is a fifth.

And that is why so few modern compositions satisfy me, because, apart from all their faults of construction, they deal in musical sentiment of the lowest order and in commonplace lyrical effusions. The best of what is done here does not equal my earliest musical efforts. Theirs may be a flower, but mine is a poem, and infinitely more spiritual; theirs is a mere natural impulse, mine the result of poetical consciousness. I do not realize all this while I am composing; it only comes to me afterwards; you, who are at the top of the tree, will understand what I mean. And I cannot talk about it; in fact, I can only speak of music in broken sentences, though I think a great deal about it.

In short, you will find me very serious sometimes and will not know what to make of me. Then, you must not watch me too closely when I am composing; that would drive me to desperation; and for my part, I will promise you, too, only very seldom to listen at your door. Well, we shall indeed lead a life of poetry and blossoms, and we will play and compose together like angels and bring gladness to mankind. . . .

I have not been to see Mendelssohn very often, he generally comes to me. He is certainly the most eminent man I have met. I have heard people say that he is not sincere with me. I should be much grieved to think so, as I feel that I have become very fond of him, and have let him see it. . . . I know exactly what he is to me in music, and could go on learning from him for years. But he can also learn something from me. If I had grown up under the same circumstances as he did and had been destined for music from childhood, I should now beat every one of you; I can feel that in the energy of my ideas. Well, everyone's life has something peculiar about it, and I will not complain of mine. My father, a man whom you would have honoured if you had only seen him, saw through me very early and intended me for a musician, but my mother would not allow it.[8] Afterwards, however, she spoke very kindly and even approvingly of my change of career.

[Robert Schumann]

---

8 August Schumann died in 1826.

To *Gustav Adolf Keferstein* [9]

Leipzig, January 31, 1840

Most honoured Sir and Friend:

I received your friendly letter and its interesting enclosures this morning. I have only been able to glance at the latter; the former I will answer at once, with a few grateful lines.

A long pause lies between this and my last letter, as also much joy and sorrow, musical and mortal. When the editor has a holiday, the composer takes his turn; and circumstances of a most agitating nature have claimed much of my time and strength. So you must excuse my long silence.

I have often — dare I confess it? — doubted if you took the same interest in the efforts of the junior portion of the musical world that I once observed. A remark recently made by you in a Stuttgart paper confirmed my suspicion. You said: "From Bach and Kuhnau we first learn the source of Mozart and Haydn's music, but not where the new generation get theirs." Such, at least, was the idea. But I don't quite agree with you. Mozart and Haydn knew Bach but partially, on single sides; and it is by no means clear how a more intimate knowledge of him would have affected their productions. But the inventiveness, the poetry and humour of the new school of music draw their inspiration largely from Bach. Mendelssohn, Bennett, Chopin, Hiller, and all the romanticists (I mean the Germans) approach Bach much more nearly than Mozart; for they all are thoroughly acquainted with him. I myself bow daily before this lofty spirit, aspiring to purify and strengthen myself through him. Then Kuhnau, honourable and delightful as he may be, should not be ranked with Bach. Even had Kuhnau written the *Well-Tempered Clavichord*, he would be but the hundredth part of Bach. In my estimation, Bach is incomparable, incommensurable. No one (Marx [10] excepted) has written of Bach so well as my old Zelter: he, usually so gruff, grows gentle as a coaxing child when he speaks of Bach. But enough: pardon my writing to you what would better befit my *Zeitschrift*.[11] You are right about the Berlin man: he was very saucy. Still, if you knew his music, you'd judge him more mildly. He is one of the most dauntless geniuses I ever knew.

9 Writer on music, usually under the pseudonyms K. Stein and Peregrinus Jocosus.
10 A. B. Marx (1795–1866), writer on music.
11 *Neue Zeitschrift für Musik*, founded by Schumann in 1834.

Didn't you say Beethoven's theory of counterpoint was compared with Bach's in that review? I don't exactly remember.

I am sorry you receive the *Zeitschrift* so late. It contains a great deal that ought to be read and profited by at once. I should like another contribution from you. The honorarium is two louis d'or per printed page. Becket, the organist, tells me that you wrote him "that the *Zeitschrift* was to be given up." That will never be until the force of circumstances obliges me to resign the post of editor. On the contrary, the *Zeitschrift* gains influence every year and holds such a position that the loss of one hundred subscribers would not affect it at all.

And now one private prayer: I know no one more kind or better informed than you to whom I may apply. But promise me, most honoured friend, that you will tell no third party.

Perhaps you know that Clara is my betrothed. . . . Clara's illustrious position as a musician often makes me think how petty mine is; and although she is not ambitious, and loves me simply as a man and musician, still I think it would please her could I attain higher rank, in an official sense. Permit me to ask: Is it difficult to become a doctor in Jena? Should I have to pass an examination? and in what? To whom ought I to apply? Would not my position as editor of a paper (which has been established for seven years), my position as a composer, and my constant effort after truth assist me to obtain this title? Tell me your *candid* opinion, and grant my request to observe strict silence on the matter.

Feel ever kindly toward me and gladden me with a speedy answer.

Yours most truly,
R. SCHUMANN

Perhaps you haven't seen my new compositions — *Kreisleriana*, a second sonata, *Novellettes, Kinderscenen?* I'll send them to you if you'll write me.

✛✛✛✛✛✛✛

To *Felix Mendelssohn*

Dresden, October 22, 1845

Dear Mendelssohn:

You must now be well in the middle of my symphony.[12] Do you still remember the first rehearsal of it in the

---

12 Symphony in B flat, op. 38. Mendelssohn was conductor of the Gewandhaus concerts in Leipzig.

year 1841 — and the stopped trumpets and horns at the beginning? It sounded as if the orchestra had a cold in its head; I can't help laughing when I think of it. And now let me thank you for again thinking about my piece and again taking trouble over it. It is with the greatest pleasure that I think of that first evening's performance. How beautifully it went, better than I have ever heard it since! I might perhaps repeat the experience tomorrow, but I dare not come. I am sorry to say that I have not yet regained my full strength; every divergence from my simple regime upsets me and induces morbid irritability. That is why I reluctantly stayed away when my wife was with you. I must avoid every form of gaiety. There is nothing for it but to go on hoping, and that I am determined to do.

Clara told me with genuine pleasure how good and kind you had been. You know she is an old admirer of yours and is happy at your least sign of approval. For her untiring zeal and energy in her art she really deserves everyone's love and encouragement; then, as a woman, she is indeed a gift from heaven. So, you see, she came back from Leipzig quite delighted, frankly admitting that you were the chief cause of her delight. Lately we have been absorbed in your organ sonatas, unfortunately with the piano as substitute; but we should have discovered that they were yours without the name on the cover. They are stamped on every page with that striving after perfection which makes me look to you as my model. Then the poetry and originality of the form! Each sonata is rounded off to a complete picture. Bach's music gives me the impression of himself seated at the organ, but yours brings me a vision of a Cecilia fingering the keys. How charming that that should be your wife's name, too! The fifth and sixth struck me as being the most important. One thing is certain, dear Mendelssohn, no one but you writes harmonies so pure, harmonies ever increasing in purity and spiritual beauty. Have I been praising you again? May I?

What, indeed, does the world in general (many so-called musicians included) understand of pure harmony? There is Wagner, who has just finished another opera.[13] He is certainly a clever fellow, full of crazy ideas and audacious to a degree. Society still raves over *Rienzi*. Yet he cannot write or think out four consecutive bars of beautiful, hardly of good music. All these young musicians are weak in harmony, in the art of four-part writing. How can enduring work be produced in that way? And now we can see the whole score in print, fifths, octaves, and all. It is too late now to alter and

---

13 *Tannhäuser.*

scratch out, however much he may wish it. The music is no fraction better than *Rienzi*, but duller and more unnatural, if anything. If one says anything of the sort it is always put down to envy, and that is why I only say it to you, knowing you have long been of the same opinion. . . .

[ROBERT SCHUMANN]

○)○)○)○)○)○)○)○

To his wife

Endenich, September 14, 1854

How pleased I was to see your handwriting, dearest Clara. Thank you for writing on this day of all days,[14] and for your loving remembrance of me and that of the dear children. Give the little ones my love and kisses. Oh, that I could have a sight of you, a word with you all! But the distance is too great. I should be glad to know from you how you are living, and where; whether you play as gloriously as ever; whether Marie and Elise continue to make progress, and whether they still sing. Have you still the same Klemm piano? Where have my collection of (printed) scores and my manuscripts (the *Requiem* [15] and the *Sängers Fluch*,[16] for instance) been put? Where is our album with the autographs of Goethe, Jean Paul, Mozart, Beethoven, and Weber, and the various letters addressed to you and myself? Where is the *Neue Zeitschrift für Musik* and my correspondence? Have you still all the letters I wrote you, and the love-verses I sent to you in Paris from Vienna? Could you send me anything to read? Scherenberg's poems, for instance, some back volumes of my paper, and the *Musikalisch Haus-und-Lebens-regeln*? [17] I also feel the want of manuscript-paper, as I sometimes feel inclined to write a little music.

My life here is very simple. I take my chief pleasure in the view of Bonn, and, when I am there, in the Siebengebirge and Godesberg. You will remember sitting there in the glare of the sun, and being seized with a cramp as you worked at the *Page*.[18] I should like to

---

14 After attempting suicide in February 1854, Schumann was committed to a mental hospital at Endenich, where he spent the last two years of his life. "This day of all days" — his wife's birthday.

15 *Requiem für Mignon*, op. 98.

16 Ballad for solos, chorus, and orchestra, op. 139, published after his death.

17 *Advice to Young Musicians*, published as a supplement to the *Album for the Young*.

18 A song by Schumann, *Vom Pagen und der Königstochter*, op. 140.

know too, dear Clara, whether you have by chance sent me clothes or cigars? I particularly want to know this. Tell me more details about the children. Do they still play Beethoven, Mozart, and pieces out of my *Jugendalbum*? Does Julie keep up her playing, and how are Ludwig, Ferdinand, and sweet Eugenie shaping?

How I wish I could listen to your beautiful playing again! Was it all a dream — our tour in Holland last winter, your brilliant reception everywhere, particularly at Rotterdam, and the torches carried in our honour. You played the E-flat Concerto, Beethoven's sonatas in C major and F minor, Chopin's studies, Mendelssohn's *Songs without Words*, and my new *Konzertstück* in D in such glorious fashion. Do you remember how I once heard, in the night, a theme in E flat, on which I composed variations? Will you send them, and perhaps a few of your own compositions with the rest?

I am full of questions and petitions. If I could but come and voice them in person! If you think it desirable to draw a veil over any of the questions I have raised, please do so.

And now good-bye, dearest Clara, and dear children all. Write to me soon.

Your faithful
ROBERT

FRANZ LISZT

Raiding, 1811 — Bayreuth, 1886

❂❂❂❂❂❂❂❂❂❂

To *Robert Schumann*

[May 1838]

My dear Monsieur Schumann:

I shall not attempt to tell you how grateful and touched I am by your friendly letter. Mademoiselle Wieck,[1] whom I have been so happy to meet here, will express to you better than I can all the sympathy, all the admiring affection I have for you. I have been such a nomad lately that the pieces you were kind enough to address to me at Milan only reached me on the eve of my departure from Venice about a fortnight ago; and since then we have been talking so much of you, day and night, that it hardly occurred to me to write to you. Today, however, to my great astonishment, I get a fresh token of your friendly remembrance, and I certainly will not delay in thanking you many times for it, so I have just left a charming party of pretty women in order to write these few lines to you. But the truth is you need hardly thank me for this little sacrifice, for it is a great pleasure to me to be able to have a little chat with you.

The *Carnaval* and the *Fantasiestücke* have interested me exceedingly. I play them really with delight, and God knows that I can't say as much of many things. To speak frankly and freely, it is absolutely only Chopin's compositions and yours that have a powerful interest for me. The rest do not deserve the honour of being mentioned — at least, with a few exceptions — to be conciliatory, like Eusebius.[2]

In six weeks to two months I shall send you my twelve *Études* and a half-dozen *Fantasiestücke* (*Impressions et Poèmes*) — I con-

---

1 Clara Wieck, later Schumann's wife.
2 Schumann's pen-name in his articles in the *Neue Zeitschrift für Musik*.

sider them less bad than others of my making. I shall be happy to think that they do not displease you.

In a fortnight I am returning to Venice. I shall be back in Milan at the time of the coronation (toward the end of August). Next winter I expect to pass in Rome, if the cholera or some other plague does not prevent me. I will not induce you to come to Italy. Your sympathies would be too deeply wounded there. If they have even heard that Beethoven and Weber ever existed, it is as much as they have done. Won't you have what you sent me printed? Haslinger would take it gladly, I think, and it would be a great pleasure to me to see my name associated with yours.

If I might make a request, I would ask you to write some trios, or a quintet or septet. It seems to me that you would do that admirably, and for a long time nothing remarkable in that line has been published. If ever you determine to do so, let me know at once, as I should be anxious to have the honour of making them known to the public.

Adieu, my dear Monsieur Schumann; keep me always in affectionate remembrance, and accept once more my warm sympathy and devotion.

F. Liszt

❂❂❂❂❂❂❂❂❂

To the *Comtesse Marie d'Agoult* [3]

London, June 1840

"I can't do anything else at this moment and probably always but live completely alone." That's what you had to tell me! Six years of the most absolute devotion have brought you only to this result. . . . And thus many of your words! Yesterday (to recall only one day) the whole way from Ascot to Richmond you did not utter a single word that was not an offence, an outrage. But what good is it to return to such sad things, to count up one by one all the wounds in our hearts? Perhaps you will add these words to those you will no longer admit. My words have changed so much. You say so, at any rate.

Midnight

Love is not justice. Love is not duty. It is not pleasure, either, but it mysteriously contains all these things. There are a thousand

---

3 Daniel Stern was her pen-name.

ways of experiencing it, a thousand ways of practising it, but for those whose heart is utterly and infinitely thirsty, there is one, eternally one, without beginning or end. If it is manifested anywhere on earth, it is above all in this complete trust of one in the other, in this supreme conviction of our angelic nature, inaccessible to any taint, impenetrable to everything outside of it. So let us not argue about words (or even about things), let us not bargain, let us not measure. If love is still at the bottom of our hearts, all has been said; if it has disappeared, there is nothing more to say.

It is hard to countermand Alava. I have invited Polez and shall tell Reeve. As for me, it is doubtful that I shall come; I have so much to do here. If you feel well enough Monday morning and are on your way, then come; otherwise not. In any case I shall order the loge because I shall be obliged to play.

Adieu, I feel extremely tired. I'd like to talk with you longer, but the memory of your words constrains and chills me. Good night. Sleep well. A thousand ideas bother and irritate me. Shall I be able to talk to you? I don't know, but perhaps this time again my words will win you over? Adieu, I do not despair.

[FRANZ LISZT]

❖❁❖❁❖❁❖❁❖

To *Wilhelm von Lenz* [4]

Weimar, December 2, 1852

I am doubly in your debt, my dear Lenz (you will allow me, will you not, to follow your example by dropping the *Mr.*?), first for your book, so thoroughly imbued with that sincere and earnest passion for the Beautiful without which one can never penetrate to the heart of works of genius; and secondly for your friendly letter, which reached me shortly after I had got your book, the notice of which had very much excited my curiosity.

That I have put off replying to you till now is not merely on account of my numerous occupations, which usually preclude my having the pleasure of correspondence, but chiefly on account of you and your remarkable work, which I wanted to read at leisure in order to get from it the whole substance of its contents. You cannot find it amiss that it has given me much to reflect upon, and

---

4 Councillor of State at the Russian court and writer on music. His book, *Beethoven and His Three Styles*, which Liszt discusses in this letter, had appeared a few months before.

you will easily understand that I shall have much to say to you on this subject — so much that to explain all my thoughts I should have to make another book to match yours — or, better still, resume our lessons of twenty years ago, when the master learned so much from the pupil, — discuss pieces in hand, the meaning, value, import, of a large number of ideas, phrases, episodes, rhythms, harmonic progressions, developments, artifices; I should have to have a good long talk with you, in fact, about minims and crochets, quavers and semi-quavers — not forgetting the rests, which, if you please, are by no means a trifling chapter when one professes to go in seriously for music, and for Beethoven in particular.

The friendly remembrance that you have kept of our talks, under the name of lessons, in the rue Montholon is very dear to me, and the flattering testimony your book gives to those past hours encourages me to invite you to continue them at Weimar, where it would be at once so pleasant and so interesting to see you for some weeks or months ad libitum, so that we might mutually edify ourselves with Beethoven. Just as we did twenty years ago, we shall agree at once, I am certain, in the generality of cases; and, more than we were then, we shall each of us be in a position to make further steps forward in the esoteric region of art.

For the present allow me, at the risk of often repeating myself hereafter, to compliment you most sincerely on your volume, which will be a chosen book and a work of predilection for people of taste, and particularly for those who feel and understand music. Artists and amateurs, professors and pupils, critics and virtuosi, composers and theorists — all will have something to gain from it and a part to take in this feast of attractive instruction that you have prepared for them. What ingenious traits, what living touches, what well-dealt blows, what new and judiciously adapted imagery should I not have to quote were I to enter in detail into your pages, so different from what one usually reads on similar subjects!

In your arguments, and in the intrinsic and extrinsic proofs you adduce, what weight, without heaviness, what solidity, without stiffness, of strong and wholesome criticism, without pedantry! Ideas are plentiful in this by turns incisive, brilliant, reflected, and spontaneous style, in which learning comes in to enhance and steady the flow of a lively and luxuriant imagination. To all the refinement and subtle divination common to Slavic genius, you ally the patient research and learned scruples that characterize the German explorer. You assume alternately the gait of the mole and of the eagle — and

everything you do succeeds wonderfully, because amid your subterranean manœuvres and your airy flights you constantly preserve,
as your own inalienable property, so much wit and knowledge,
good sense and free fancy. If you had asked me to find a motto for
your book I should have proposed this,

"Inciter et initier,"

as best summing up, according to my ideas, the aim that you fulfil
by your twofold talent of distinguished writer and musician *ex pro-
fesso*.

It is really curious to observe how the well-known saying: "It
is from the north that light comes to us today," has been verified
lately with regard to musical literature. After Mr. Oulibicheff had
endowed us with a Mozart,[5] here come you with a Beethoven.
Without attempting to compare two works that are in so many respects as different and separate as the two heroes chosen by their
respective historiographers, it is nevertheless natural that your name
should be frequently associated with that of Mr. Oulibicheff — for
each is an honour to Art and to his country. This circumstance,
however, does not do away with your right to lecture Mr. Oulibicheff very wittily, and with a thorough knowledge of the subject,
for having made of Mozart a sort of Dali Lama, beyond which there
is nothing. In all this polemical part (pp. 26, 27, etc.), as in many
other cases, I am entirely of your opinion, with all due justice to the
talents and merits of your compatriot. From a reading of the two
works, *Mozart* and *Beethoven*, it is evident that, if the studies, pre-
dilections, and habits of mind of Mr. Oulibicheff have perfectly
predisposed him to accomplish an excellent work in its entirety,
yours, my dear Lenz, have led you to a sort of intimacy, the famili-
arity of which nourished a sort of religious exaltation, with the
genius of Beethoven.

Mr. Oulibicheff in his method proceeds more as proprietor
and professor; you more as poet and lawyer. But whatever may be
said about this or that hiatus in your work, the plan of which has
confined you disadvantageously to the analysis of the piano sonatas,
and however much people may think themselves justified in cavilling at you about the distribution of your materials, the chief merit,
which none could refuse you without injustice, is that you have
really understood Beethoven and have succeeded in making your

5 Alexandre Dimitrievitch Oulibicheff: *Nouvelle Biographie de Mozart* (1844).

imagination adequate to his by your intuitive penetration into the secrets of his genius.

For us musicians, Beethoven's work is like the pillar of cloud and fire that guided the Israelites through the desert — a pillar of cloud to guide us by day, a pillar of fire to guide us by night, "*so that we may progress both day and night.*" His obscurity and his light trace for us equally the path we have to follow; they are each of them a perpetual commandment, an infallible revelation. Were it my place to categorize the different periods of the great master's thoughts, as manifested in his sonatas, symphonies, and quartets, I should certainly not fix the division into *three styles*, which is now pretty generally adopted and which you have followed; but, simply recording the questions that have been raised hitherto, I should frankly weigh the *great* question which is the axis of criticism and of musical æstheticism at the point to which Beethoven has led us — namely, in how far is traditional or recognized form a necessary determinant for the organism of thought?

The solution of this question, evolved from the works of Beethoven himself, would lead me to divide this work, not into three styles or periods — the words *style* and *period* being here only corollary subordinate terms, of a vague and equivocal meaning — but quite logically into two categories: the first, that in which traditional and recognized form contains and governs the thought of the master; and the second, that in which the thought stretches, breaks, re-creates, and fashions the form and style according to its needs and inspirations. Doubtless in proceeding thus we arrive in a direct line at those incessant problems of *authority* and *liberty*. But why should they alarm us? In the region of liberal arts they do not, happily, bring in any of the dangers and disasters that their oscillations occasion in the political and social world; for in the domain of the Beautiful, Genius alone is the authority, and hence, Dualism disappearing, the notions of authority and liberty are brought back to their original identity. — Manzoni, in defining genius as "a stronger imprint of divinity," has eloquently expressed this very truth.

This is indeed a long letter, my dear Lenz, and as yet I am only at the preliminaries. Let us then pass on to the Deluge — and come and see me at Weimar, where we can chat as long and fully as we like of these things in the shade of our fine park. If a thrush chances to come and sing I shall take advantage of the circumstance to make, *en passant*, some groundless quarrels with you on some inappropriate terms that one meets with here and there in your book — as, for example, the employment of the word *scale* (ut, fa, la, etc.) instead of *arpeggio chord;* or, again, on your inexcusable want of gallantry, which leads you maliciously to bracket the title of "Mamselle" (!) with such and such a *Diva,* a proceeding that will draw down upon you the wrath of these divinities and of their numerous admirers.

But I can assure you beforehand that there are far more nightingales than thrushes in our park; and, similarly, in your book the greater number of pages, judiciously thought out and brilliantly written, carry the day so well in worth and valour over any thinly scattered inattentions or negligences that I join with my whole heart in the concert of praise to which you have a right.

Pray accept, my dear Lenz, the most sincere expressions of feeling and best thanks of

Your very affectionate and obliged
F. LISZT

To the *Baron Beaulieu-Marconnay* [6]

[Weimar] May 21, 1855

Dear Baron:

It is not precisely a distraction, still less a forgetfulness, with which I might be reproached as regards the program of this evening's concert. The indications which Her Royal Highness the Grand Duchess condescends to give me are too precious to me for me not to be most anxious to fulfil at least all my duties.

If, then, one of Beethoven's symphonies does not figure in to-day's program, it is because I thought I could better satisfy thus the intentions of H.R.H., and I permitted myself to guess what she has not taken the occasion to explain this time. The predilection of His Majesty the King of Saxony for Beethoven's symphonies assuredly does honour to his taste for the beautiful in music, and no one could more truly agree with that than I. I will only observe, on the one side, that Beethoven's symphonies are extremely well known, and, on the other, that these admirable works are performed at Dresden by an orchestra having at its disposal far more considerable means than we have here, and that consequently our performance would run the risk of appearing rather *provincial* to His Majesty.

---

6 Intendant of the Court Theatre at Weimar. Liszt had accepted the position of
   conductor there with the express purpose of fostering modern music.

Moreover if Dresden, following the example of Paris, London, Leipzig, Berlin, and a hundred other cities, stops at Beethoven (to whom, while he was living, they much preferred Haydn and Mozart), that is no reason why Weimar — I mean musical Weimar, which I make the modest pretension of representing — should keep absolutely to that. There is without doubt nothing better than to respect, admire, and study the illustrious dead; but why not also sometimes live with the living? We have tried this plan with Wagner, Berlioz, Schumann, and some others, and it would seem that it has not succeeded so badly up to now for there to be any occasion for us to alter our minds without urgent cause, and to put ourselves at the tail — of many other tails!

The significance of the musical movement of which Weimar is the real centre lies precisely in this initiative, of which the public does not generally understand much, but which none the less acquires its part of importance in the development of contemporary Art.

For the rest, dear Baron, I hasten to make all straight for this evening by following your advice, and I will ask Messrs. Singer and Cossman to play with me Beethoven's magnificent trio (in B flat — dedicated to the Archduke Rudolph) as No. 3 on the program.

A thousand affectionate compliments, and yours ever,

F. LISZT

RICHARD WAGNER

Leipzig, 1813 — Venice, 1883

❋❋❋❋❋❋❋❋

To *Theodor Apel*

Magdeburg, October 26, 1835

You will be wondering that you have received no answer from me as yet to your last two letters. I wrote you one immediately with an enclosure for F. Mendelssohn-Bartholdy and had actually got some oiled linen so as to send him a big parcel of compositions through you (you shall have the letter, already sealed, when next you are here), but I changed my mind entirely and sent you nothing, for I am now taking leave, once and for all, of the concert hall. I may perhaps even not take your advice that I should send a good overture to Leipzig. I don't want to be anyone's hanger-on, and your reports of Mendelssohn have finally dissuaded me.

Adieu, ye solid splendours, I give myself up to the tinsel of the stage! I am now a composer of operas only, and am casting myself, body and soul and all my hopes, into my opera,[1] at which I am hard at work now. The practice of this art absorbs me now entirely, and during the short time I have been back here I have been well rewarded for it. I am now entirely responsible for the opera here[2] and have just luckily discovered and brought to light a couple of young talents who will let the theatrical world hear of them some time. Who could have thought of Minna's[3] sister, lost in obscurity at Braunschweig? I engaged the girl for her beautiful alto voice and I have now rehearsed her in Romeo.[4] Few beginners have made such a sensation as she — people went absolutely mad over her. The opera had to be repeated at once to a house full to bursting, and tears were as plentiful as at a performance by Devrient. I have likewise hunted out a little tenor called Schreiber and am training him to the great

---

1 *Das Liebesverbot* (1836).
2 He was music director at the Magdeburg Theatre.
3 Minna Planer, later his wife.
4 Bellini's opera *I Capuletti ed i Montecchi.*

satisfaction of the public. That's something to rejoice about! And it's all my work! I am becoming vain as a conductor, too, you see! I am producing my operas promptly and on time. We are rehearsing new operas — *Jessonda* (quite new here!) — *Norma, Lestocq*[5] ought to follow upon one another merrily. That is where our un-exampled business method comes in — the salaries are paid exactly and punctually. Everything is going well — well! And I delight in being absolute ruler of the opera! Perhaps I shall do as well as Men-delssohn — but I am only in Magdeburg and he is in Leipzig — that's the difference. However, I haven't finished yet! I feel full of vigour! I am not going to bother about Leipzig — I am thinking of attempt-ing something quite different, Berlin, in fact, where I contemplate getting my *Liebesverbot* first produced.[6] More of this anon, but I may just say that I am not hankering in the least after you and your honours.

The 27th

I was interrupted yesterday. It is noticeable in your last letter that you tend to think our modern ideas need revising. The modern position as regards love, etc., no longer meets with your approval, perhaps never has done. My present bourgeois post presses a little heavily on me, too, and I could almost be weak enough to submit again to all sorts of superannuated conceptions, but that my un-shakable convictions about the present position of art have a most stimulating effect on my social views. So with my music — I shall never, never acclaim our Germanism again, and your Leipzig with all its classic *gloire* can never drag me back to it. We have stuffed our stomachs with too much rotten matter. It seemed to me very opportune that I should at this moment be busy about a German work again. I am rehearsing *Jessonda*, and how I shy away again from reactionary ideas! The opera fills me once more with utter disgust; the soft Bellini is a veritable Hercules compared with this great, lengthy, pedantic, sentimental Spohr. A little while ago it occurred to me to compose an overture to *Romeo and Juliet*. I was thinking out a rough plan when — would you believe it? — Bellini's stale, insipid overture with its battlefield of a crescendo turned up of itself in my sketch!

Fräulein Haas is very ill. Don't bother your head about Minna — I am leaving it all to fate. She loves me, and her love is worth very much to me now. She is the pivot of my life and gives it consistency

---

5 By Spohr, Bellini, and Auber, respectively.
6 It was produced only once, at Magdeburg, March 29, 1836.

and warmth. I cannot relinquish her. I only know this, dear Theodor, that you know nothing at all of the sweetness of such a connection. There is nothing low, unworthy, or enervating about it. Our epicureanism is pure and strong — it is not a vulgar amour. We love each other and trust each other and leave the rest to fate. You, of course, know nothing of this, and truly only with an actress could one live in such a relationship. This disregard of the ideas of conventional society can exist only where the whole basis of life is imaginative freedom and poetic licence. I have got a nice friendly sitting-room and a splendid grand piano, which I got cheap, and with these all would be well if I had not got to live within such horribly strict limits. I don't mean to complain about it, but when I reflect that all this is insufficient to atone for the immediate past, I could rage! You can imagine how penuriously I live when I have to pay off 30 taler a month — that is really bitter. And now just listen; since you once settled to give me a certain sum, don't leave me in the lurch this first of the month. I reckon on you — else I'm bankrupt — and listen again — if it should be a little more than before I should certainly not complain — you may believe me! Now we'll see what comes of it — it can't be too much! What a life I'm leading! No, I'm extremely respectable and am getting a heavenly reputation. There are rubs here and there of course, but I'm willing to put up with them if I can make something by it. Haven't I become nice and tame? — and I'm a good conductor, too — deuce take me if I don't flatter myself a little on that head. If I can only get a bit of a name with my opera I shall do well enough. Now write to me and don't take things ill — you know I'm an ass! . . .

[RICHARD WAGNER]

❀❁❀❁❀❁❀❁❀

To *Karl Gaillard* [7]

Dresden, January 30, 1844

It is chiefly people who know only *Der fliegende Holländer* who doubt if I should write the librettos for my own operas. They argue that I am unequal to the task because of the difficulties I certainly created for myself in this subject. Those who know *Rienzi*, however, judge otherwise and assert that I could have found no more fortunate libretto than this self-made one. I really lay no claim to a poet's reputation and assure you I at first took to writing for myself

---

7 Editor of the *Berliner musikalische Zeitung*.

of necessity, since no good librettos were offered me. I could not now, however, compose on another's operatic text for the following reasons. It is not my way to choose some story or other at pleasure, get it versified, and then begin to consider how to make suitable music for it. For this mode of procedure I should need to be twice inspired, which is impossible.

The way I set to work is quite different. In the first place I am only attracted to matter the poetic and musical significance of which strike me simultaneously. Before I go on to write a verse or plot or scene I am already intoxicated by the musical aroma of my subject. I have every note, every characteristic motif in my head, so that when the versification is complete and the scenes arranged, the opera is practically finished for me; the detailed musical treatment is just a peaceful meditative after-labour, the real moment of creation having long preceded it.

Furthermore, subject matter ought to be selected that is capable of musical treatment only. I would never take a subject that might be used just as well by an able playwright for spoken drama. As a musician I can choose subjects, develop situations and contrasts, which must for ever remain outside the province of the poet as playwright. Here and now we arrive at the point where opera and drama should definitely part company, each amicably pursuing its own distinct path. It is the province of the present-day dramatist to give expression and spiritual meaning to the material interests of our own times, but to the operatic poet and composer falls the task of conjuring up the holy spirit of poetry as it comes down to us in the sagas and legends of past ages. For music affords a medium of synthesis which the poet alone, particularly in association with the stage, has not at command. Here is the way to raise opera to a higher level from the debasement into which it has fallen as the result of our expecting composers to take as their subjects commonplaces, intrigues, etc., things that modern comedy and drama without music are far more successful in presenting.

For my next opera I have chosen the beautiful and characteristic saga of the knight Tannhäuser, who lingered in the Venusberg and went to Rome to seek absolution! I have amalgamated this saga with the story of the tournament of song at the Wartburg, where Tannhäuser takes the place of Heinrich von Ofterdingen. By this combination I get a rich subject of drama. I think it will be quite clear that only a musician could handle this subject. . . .

[RICHARD WAGNER]

To *Eduard Hanslick* [8]

Dresden, January 1, 1847

. . . The trend, so favourable to me, of your comprehensive discourse [9] on my *Tannhäuser* best pleases me as evidence of the impression my work made upon yourself. I must truthfully confess, if you would like to know my real feelings upon reading your paper, that it was a most anxious experience. Whether I read praise or blame of myself I always feel as if someone were seizing and examining my entrails. Neither have I outgrown a certain maidenly bashfulness as though my soul were my body. A public performance of one of my operas is still an occasion of such boundless emotional turmoil that I have frequently tried to prevent performances when I have felt unequal to this interior conflict.

I am fully convinced that blame is far more useful to the artist's self than praise. The man who is ruined by criticism deserves his fall — only he who accepts it as a challenge has true inward power. But it is, nevertheless, clear that the true artist in whom Nature herself has implanted passion at its strongest for a spur is bound to feel either praise or blame very acutely.

As I create with ever heightened artistic consciousness I am more and more impelled to make a whole man. I want to create flesh and blood and limbs, a being who freely and truly lives and moves, and I am often amazed when I see how many perceive only the flesh and examine its softness or hardness. Let me speak more plainly. To touch on one sphere only, nothing has satisfied me better than the effect upon the public at most performances of *Tannhäuser* . . . of the whole scene of the Song Contest. I have known each of the songs in it to be received with the liveliest interest, rising to unwonted heights of excitement during the last songs and at the outburst of horror in the assembly that closes the scene. I tell you this observation has immensely pleased me, because as an instance of extreme naïveté in the public it proves to me that the noblest ends are attainable. Very few could be sure whether they had the musician or the poet to thank for this impression and I need only leave it an open question.

I naturally have no special ambition to see my poetry cast into the shade by my music, but I would certainly be guilty of a lie were I to pretend that my music was at the mercy of my poetry. I cannot

8 Music critic and writer on æsthetics (1825–1904).
9 In *Allgemeine Wiener Musikzeitung,* 1846.

make use of any poetic matter that is not first conditioned by music. My Song Contest, even though the poetic element predominates in it, could not have expressed my higher intentions without music.

But a work of art does not exist till it becomes apparent; in drama this means performance upon the stage. As far as lies in my power I mean to master this aspect and I value my capacity to do so effectively almost equally with the other faculties of my creative gift. . . .

I would not care to venture a decision as yet as to whether music is, of its essence, able exactly to render the meaning of a poem, however musical the latter may be. Gluck's poems certainly make no very extreme demands upon the passionate possibilities of the music, being more or less confined to a certain limited pathos — that of the tragedies of Racine — and wherever this ought to have been overstepped, Gluck's music fails unmistakably to rise to the occasion. The poems of Mozart's operas are still less concerned with the deepest realities of human nature. Donna Anna is a single exception, but the possibilities are far from exhausted even there. Spontini in the second act of *La Vestale* (the Julia scene) and Weber in portions of *Euryanthe* (for instance the moment after the betrayal of her secret to Eglantine, etc.) have nothing better with which to meet the occasion than "diminished-seventh music," and I, for my part, can only recognize here a limitation in our forefathers' musical achievements.

It is indisputable that we are far from having attained the highest and truest in opera as measured by these models — I speak of the dramatic work of art as a whole, not of the purely musical aspect — and in this conviction and relying on powers that I am more inclined to despair of than to overestimate in myself, I regard my present and forthcoming works simply as experiments to ascertain the possibilities of opera. . . .

A world of difference separates us, as shown by your estimate of Meyerbeer. I can say this without the least embarrassment, for I am personally friendly with him and have every reason to value him as a sympathetic and amiable person. But when I want to sum up everything that repels me in the trade of opera-composition as being intellectually muddled and technically feeble, I comprehend it under the word *Meyerbeer*, and all the more so since I recognize in Meyerbeer's music an extraordinary knack of getting a superficial effect, a thing that hinders the true development of art by offering gratification divorced from spirituality. He who strays into the realm of the trivial has to pay for it by the loss of his higher nature, but he who deliberately seeks the trivial is — fortunate, for he has nothing wherewith to pay. . . .

[RICHARD WAGNER]

◎◑◎◑◎◑◎◑◎◑◎

To *Franz Liszt*

Zurich, April 18, 1851

. . . I did not wish to write to you at once, preferring to write more fully and more calmly on a favourable day. Then came the number of the *Illustrierte Zeitung* for the 12th of April and once again I read through your printed article! [10] It will be hard indeed for me to convey to you what an impression your work of friendship makes on me just now! . . .

How curiously things happen between us! If I could but describe the love that binds me to you! . . . You are a wonderful man and our love is wonderful! If we had not loved each other we must have hated each other intensely. I must now out with everything, which I meant to write to you with studied moderation, just as it comes into my head. I shall begin on my *Siegfried* early in May, come what will! Away with all guarantees of my livelihood, I shall not starve. I have at last got a publisher for my book — Avenarius of Leipzig; he is paying me 100 taler; it is precious little, but I do not think I can get any more. You will put by an odd halfpenny for me now and then. . . . Frau Ritter of Dresden does what she can from time to time; in the winter I shall earn a few louis d'or again by conducting symphonies — and so in the end I shall manage to cheat the Devil if only my wife can keep calm. So, then, we will leave Madame the Grand Duchess in peace. *I* cannot and may not ask anything of her even in a roundabout way.

You ask me about *Judaism*.[11] You know for certain that the article is mine; why, then, ask me? I appeared pseudonymously, not out of fear, but to avoid the question being dragged by the Jews into the region of naked personalities. I have cherished a long-repressed resentment about this Jew business, and the grudge is as

10 Liszt had sent the manuscript of his essay on *Lohengrin* to Wagner; it was published April 12, 1851 in the *Illustrierte Zeitung*, Leipzig.

11 *Das Judentum in der Musik* appeared on September 3 and 6, 1850 in the *Neue Zeitschrift für Musik* under the pseudonym R. Freigedank.

necessary to my nature as gall is to blood. An incentive came when their accursed scribblings annoyed me intensely, so at last I let fly. It seems I have struck home alarmingly, and that is as I would have it, for I really only wanted to give them just such a fright. That they will remain our masters is as certain as that, not our princes, but our bankers and the philistines are our lords now.

My attitude toward Meyerbeer is now a peculiar one. I do not hate him, he is infinitely repugnant to me. This everlastingly amiable complaisant fellow reminds me of the most muddy, I might almost say the most degraded, period of my life, when he used to make a show of protecting me. It was the period of intrigues and back stairs, when we are made fools of by patrons for whom we inwardly care not a rap. That is an utterly dishonourable relationship. . . . I do not reproach Meyerbeer in the least for the intentional ineffectiveness of his good offices for me — on the contrary, I am glad not to be so deeply his debtor as, for example, B[erlioz]. But it was time I severed my dishonest connection with him. Outwardly I had not the least inducement to do so, for even the discovery that he did not mean honestly by me could not surprise me, nor indeed put me in the right, for at bottom I had to reproach myself with having intentionally deceived myself in him. It was from within that the impulse came to me to relinquish every consideration of ordinary self-interest with regard to him. As an artist I cannot exist in my own eyes and those of my friends, I cannot think and feel, without realizing and publicly confessing my complete antagonism to Meyerbeer; and I am driven to proclaim it by sheer despair when I find again, even in my friends, the erroneous opinion that I have anything whatever in common with Meyerbeer. . . .

[RICHARD WAGNER]

To *August Röckel* [12]

Zurich, January 25, 1854

. . . I come back to the point that you seem to me to be happier in your lot than I am in mine. Every line of your letter shows me that you are in health. I assure you of my joyful amazement at it! That you can write me a five-page letter assures me, too, of an

---

12 Music director at the Dresden Court Theatre until 1849, when he was imprisoned for his political activities in Dresden.

improvement in your personal conditions for which I am heartily glad, even though I must assert that I can imagine circumstances in which I could refuse any and every amelioration of existence without grieving very much for what I was renouncing.

One thing excels all others — freedom! But what is freedom? Is it — as our politicians believe — licence? No indeed! Freedom is *integrity*. Whosoever is true — that is, completely at one with his nature in accordance with the law of his being — he is *free*. Outward compulsion really attains its end only when it destroys the integrity of its victim, when the latter becomes a hypocrite and tries to make himself and others believe him other than he really is. That is true slavery. But the victim of constraint need never let it come to this, and the man who preserves his integrity — even under compulsion — preserves his essential freedom also; at least he is certainly more free than one who no longer notices the constraint of which our world is full, because his soul is wholly submissive, and who has defaced himself by submission.

I believe that this integrity is in essence the whole of that truth spoken of in our philosophies and theologies. . . . Therefore to be consumed with love of absolute truth is to surrender oneself to absolute reality upon the emotional side — to experience the joys and sorrows of the begetting, growth, and blossom-time of life, its withering and dissolution, refusing nothing — to desire life only that we may live in delight and in anguish — and so die. This alone is to "be consumed with love of truth." But to make this self-immolation possible we must utterly abandon the search for the whole. The whole only reveals itself to us through separate phenomena, for it is these alone that we, are able to perceive in the full sense of the word. We can only really understand a phenomenon when we can let ourselves be wholly absorbed in it, as we must also be able to absorb it wholly into us. "How is this marvellous process most fully achieved?" asks Nature. Only through *Love*! — everything which I am unable to love remains outside myself and I outside it; the philosopher may flatter himself that he understands this, but not the real man. Now, the full reality of love is only possible between the sexes. It is only as man and woman that we mortals can love most really, while all other loves are mere derivatives, originating in it, connected with it, or æsthetic counterfeits of it. . . .

Enough! I dare send you this confession in your loneliness without fear of awakening distress in you by thus imparting my views. Not you alone, but I too — and all of us — are living at present in circumstances and conditions that only permit of substitutes and makeshifts. For you no less than for me the truest, most real love can only be a concept, an inspiration. I have come to my thirty-sixth year before divining the true meaning of the æsthetic impulse in myself. Till then I took art to be the end and life the means. . . .

It only remains to describe what, from my point of view, I cannot but feel bound to do in order to draw mankind . . . — myself and mankind together — nearer to the goal that I have described, without the use of those means which I have once and for all forsworn. My art is to help me do it, and the particular work of art that I have to frame to this end is my *Nibelung* poem. I am inclined to think that the reason much of it remained unintelligible to you is to be sought less in any obscurity in the present form of the poem than in your own point of view, sincerely held, yet very divergent from mine. . . . For me my poem has the following meaning: the representation of reality as defined by me above. — Instead of the words "a dark day dawns for the gods. Thy glorious race shall yet end in shame, unless thou surrender the ring!" — We must learn to die, and to die in the fullest sense of the word; dread of the end is the source of all lovelessness and it is engendered only where love is already fading. How came it that this highest blessing of all things living so vanished from the race of men that at last all the acts of humanity came to be rooted and grounded solely in fear of the end? My poem supplies the answer. It shows Nature as she really is, undistorted, all her actual various antitheses comprising things mutually repellent. But the ultimate source of disaster is not in Alberich's repulse by the Rhine maidens. . . . Alberich and his ring could not harm the gods were these not already ripe for evil. Where, then, is the root of this evil? Look at the first scene between Wotan and Fricka, which leads finally to Act II of *Die Walküre*. The strong chain that binds those two, forged from love's instinctive error in desiring to prolong itself through inevitable change, in asking mutual guarantees in opposition to the law of eternal transmutation and renewal in the world of phenomena, constrains them both to the mutual torment of lovelessness. Accordingly the whole course of the drama demonstrates the necessity of recognizing and submitting to the multiplicity, the ever changing aspects, the eternal renewals of reality and of life. Wotan rises to the tragic dignity of *willing* his own destruction. This is the whole lesson we have to learn from human history — to will the thing that must be and ourselves to fulfil it. The creative power of this highest, self-annihilating will finds ultimate issue in Siegfried, the man fearless and steadfast in love. — That is all.

In detail the poem tells of the power of evil, the true poison of love, under the similitude of the gold stolen from nature and mis-used, the Nibelungen ring. The curse resting upon the ring can never be lifted till it is restored to nature, till the gold is once again sunk in the waters of the Rhine. This, too, Wotan learns to recog-nize only at the very end, at the term of his tragic story. It was he who, in his greed of power, utterly ignored what Loki had early told him so often and so movingly. He first learned to believe in the power of the curse through Fafner's death, but it was not till the ring came to be the ruin of Siegfried that he understood that only through the restitution of the spoils could the evil be annulled, and accordingly made his own wished-for annihilation a condition of the wiping out of that most ancient wrong. Experience is every-thing. Siegfried alone (man by himself) is not the perfect "man." He is but the half and not till Brünnhilde is with him does he become a saviour. One solitary cannot do everything; numbers are needed, and suffering, self-immolating woman is at length the true and con-scious saviour; for love is indeed the "eternal feminine" itself. — So much for the universal and greatest aspects of the drama; they com-prise many others more particular and more defined.

I cannot but think that you likewise have taken this to be my meaning, only it seems to me that you attribute more value to the middle and intermediary members of the great chain than really be-longs to them as such, and, moreover, that you had been driven to do this in order to justify from my poem a preconceived philosophy peculiar to *you*. On the whole I do not accept certain objections made by you on the score of lack of clarity in specified instances. On the contrary, I believe it was a true instinct that led me to guard against an excessive zeal for making things clear, for I have felt un-mistakably that to make my intention too obvious would be to hinder a proper understanding; in drama — as in art generally — the way to produce an effect is not by a statement of opinion, but by a presentation of the instinctive. And this is just what distinguished my poetic matter from the political matter that at present monopo-lizes the field. . . .

What most astonishes me, coming from you, is the question: "When the Rhinegold is given back to the Rhine, why do the gods perish nevertheless?" — I believe that a good production of the drama would completely satisfy the simplest mind on this point.

The downfall of the gods does *not* proceed from counterpoints — things that can generally be explained, twisted and turned (one need only set a political jurist on the job as advocate) — no, we feel in our inmost souls, as does Wotan, that their destruction is of necessity. The object was, then, to justify this necessity *emotionally*, and this happens quite naturally if the whole action of the drama with all its simple and natural motives is followed sympathetically from beginning to end. When Wotan at last declares this necessity, he is only saying what we ourselves have already recognized. At the end of *Das Rheingold* when Loki cries after the gods as they enter Valhalla: "Swiftly ye speed to your end, ye who dream that your throne is established!" he expresses in that moment no more than the feeling of anyone who follows this prelude with interest, not hypercritically or analytically, and duly allowing the incidents to work upon his emotions. . . .

The composition — now complete — of the difficult and momentous *Rheingold* has brought me once again a great sense of certitude, but I perceive anew how much there is, by the very nature of my poetic intent, that can be revealed through the music alone. *I* can no longer look at the poem without music. In time I think I shall be able to tell you about the composition. For the present, only this much — that it has become a close-knit unity; there will be scarcely an orchestral note that does not proceed from a preconceived motive. . . .

How I am ever to achieve production is a tremendous problem, to be sure. Still, I shall make the attempt in due time, as I can see before me no other adequate object in life. I feel fairly certain that the purely mechanical side of the enterprise could be contrived. But — my performers?! There I heave a deep sigh! Of course I must insist upon young players not yet entirely spoiled by our operatic stage. I would not even *consider* so-called "celebrities." I shall have to see first how I am to train my young people. I should prefer to have my company together for a year without letting them appear in public, work with them day by day, give them a humane and artistic training, and let them ripen gradually for their task. Accordingly I could not look for a first performance before the summer of 1858 [13] even under the most favourable conditions. Let the time be as long as it will, however, I feel a constant urge to give myself a reason for living through intense concentration of a goal of my very own, . . .

I am not so out of touch with Nature as you think, even though

13 This did not actually occur until 1876.

I am no longer personally in a position for scientific intercourse with her. Herwegh [14] has to do this on my behalf. He lives here too and has long pursued nature studies very thoroughly, and through him, my friend, I learn very beautiful and important things about Nature, who governs me in the many and great things of life. It is only when she is supposed to take the place for me of life itself — that is, love — that I turn from her. . . .

[RICHARD WAGNER]

⊙⦂⦂⦂⦂⦂⦂⦂⊙

To *Otto Wesendonck* [15]

London [March 21, 1855]

. . . London [16] is a very great and wealthy city and the English are exceptionally shrewd, circumspect, and intelligent, but I, unlucky man that I am, have really nothing to do with them. . . . If I chose to be comfortably installed here as conductor of the Philharmonic for a number of years, undoubtedly I could easily get the appointment, for these people see that I am a good conductor, but that would be *all* the satisfaction I should get here; beyond that there is nothing. There is not the remotest prospect of arousing any particular interest (especially at court) in my operas or in a good sound German theatre. The Queen's taste, for instance, is trivial to the last degree and sympathy with the unusual is the last thing likely from anyone here. You can see it is so from the very nature of the people. True art is something utterly foreign to them and they are not to be touched outside the sphere of income and expenditure.

For instance, the equanimity with which these people listened to the singing of a wearisome duet thirty seconds after the close of the "Eroica" was an altogether new experience for me; everyone assured me that no one was in the least scandalized by it — and the duet was applauded just like the symphony! This by the way! — I placed all my hopes of satisfaction in my dealings with the orchestra, which is very devoted to me, and in the hope of a fine performance for its own sake. In particular I counted very much on being allowed *two* rehearsals for the next concert, as I hoped it would

---

14 Georg Herwegh (1817–75), poet.
15 Wagner's principal backer during his Zurich period.
16 Wagner had been invited to London to conduct some concerts of the Philharmonic Society.

give me the opportunity of getting the orchestra really well in hand. But yesterday's first rehearsal dashed that hope as it showed me that *two* rehearsals are too few for my purpose. I had to pass over many important points and I see that I shall never be able to make up in just *one* more rehearsal, so I shall have to be satisfied with no more than a relatively good performance of the Ninth Symphony.

As to selections from my *Lohengrin*, I have felt this time, to my deep distress, how wretched it is for me to have to keep on appearing before the public with such extremely meagre extracts from this work. I felt I was making myself ridiculous, for I know how little people can learn of me and my work from these sample snippets with which I go travelling round like a *commis voyageur*. And to think that I am wasting these my best years like this, utterly hampered and circumscribed in my artistic activities! I would far rather forgo every attempt at outside activity, for no one but myself knows the torture I suffer by it! Under such conditions, my sole remaining satisfaction would be to have done something for my lot on the practical side. I should be glad if I could do so, but how, short of stealing? How fat my purse will grow through my concert honorarium here we have yet to see; in spite of my expensive lodgings I contemplate no actual extravagance and hope to save. But that's all, now and for ever! An Act of Parliament has been passed recently according to which there is no longer to be copyright in works that have already appeared abroad, but only in those written in England and for England and first published here. So the first thing to greet me here was an elegant translation of the "Evening Star" and Lohengrin's "Rebuke to Elsa," published by Ewer, and I am assured that a further complete selection of my vocal pieces is contemplated immediately. It appears that everyone has the right to reprint them at pleasure. Consequently I very much regret that I recently paid carriage for having these things sent to me for England.

Dearest friend, give up trying to make me "independent." All my life I shall be a ragamuffin — particularly according to English ideas — and accordingly can only hope no one will depend on me; anyone who does so will have a hard time of it. That's the long and the short of the matter. But perhaps I shall soon give up art altogether, and in that case all will be well. It is that alone that from time to time fills me with illusions which can only result in evil for me. Periodically it induces a frivolous mood in me and, as you know, frivolity is good for no one, least of all for those who give themselves up to it. Only a little more, I assure you, and I shall have come to the point of putting a final stop to that particular source of all folly in my life. I have cause enough. The agonies my art inflicts on me far outweigh the rare enchantments it affords me. Only a little — only one thing, indeed — and I give this game up too. Then — something will probably be done, but by other ways than most would be prepared to believe. . . .

Apart from this, my dearest London acquaintance up till now is the first violin here, Sainton, a native of Toulouse, ardent, kind-hearted, and lovable. My call to London is due to him alone. He has lived four years in close friendship with a German, Lüders. The latter has read my writings on art and became so predisposed toward me that, to the best of his ability, he made them known to Sainton, and the two thereupon decided that there was no doubt of my being an able man. So when Sainton proposed me to the directors and had to say how he knew me, he lied and said he had personally seen me conduct, for, as he said to me — the true reason for his conviction about me would have been unintelligible to these people. After the first rehearsal, when Sainton embraced me ecstatically, I could not help calling him a *téméraire* who might think himself lucky he had not caused offence this time! I like this man very much. . . .

A man like that in London among Englishmen is a perfect oasis in the desert. On the other hand, anything more offensive than the genuine English type I cannot conceive. They are one and all of the sheeplike type, and the Englishman's practical brains are just as reliable as the sheep's instinct for finding its fodder in the meadow. It finds its fodder, sure enough, but unhappily the whole fair field and the blue sky above are non-existent to its senses of perception. How wretched must he seem among them who, on the contrary, sees only meadow and sky but is bad at perceiving the yarrow!

I also very much like a young musician, Klindworth, introduced to me by Liszt. If the fellow only had a tenor voice, he would be a complete Siegfried. . . .

[RICHARD WAGNER]

❂❂❂❂❂❂❂❂

To *August Röckel*

Zurich, August 23, 1856

. . . It is seldom, probably, that any man has held concepts so widely divergent from his intuitions, has been such a stranger to himself, as I, who am forced to admit that I have only arrived at last at an understanding of my own works of art — that is to say, formed an intellectual conception of them, elucidated them to the satisfaction of my own reason — by the aid of another, who has furnished me with concepts perfectly correlative with my intuitions. The period during which I created in response to these inner intuitions began with *Der fliegende Holländer; Tannhäuser* and *Lohengrin* followed, and if there is any one imaginative principle underlying them, it is surely the high tragedy of renunciation, the deliberate, reasoned, ultimately necessary negation of the will, in which alone is salvation. It is this underlying quality that gives inspiration to my poetry and my music; without it their actual power to stir the emotions would be non-existent. Now, nothing is more striking than the fact that all the ideas I had formed by way of speculation and in an attempt to attain an understanding of life cut clean across these basic intuitions. While as an artist my intuitions had such compelling certainty that all my creations were moulded thereby, as a philosopher I was attempting to construct an entirely contrary explanation of the universe, an explanation that, though most stoutly upheld, was always being dismissed cavalierly by my instinctive objective artistic perceptions, much to my own astonishment.

My most startling experience of this kind came to me, as it must have done, in regard to the *Nibelungen*. I shaped the poem at a time when I had built myself a conceptual universe upon the Hellenic-optimistic model, which I believed entirely possible of realization if mankind would only will it, and in it I attempted ingeniously to bridge for myself the problem as to why, in that case, they do not actually will it. I recollect now having evolved the character of my Siegfried to this very end, with the will to present a life without sorrow; but I counted on expressing myself still more plainly through the presentation of the whole Nibelung myth, with its exposure of a first wrong, from which springs a whole world of evil, which therefore perishes, and so teaches us all a lesson on how we should recognize the evil, tear it out by the roots, and establish a righteous world in its stead. And all the time I scarcely noticed that in the execution, indeed at bottom even in the planning of my design, I was unconsciously following a quite different and far deeper perception and, instead of a phase of world evolution, had discerned the nature of the universe itself in all its conceivable phases and had recognized its nothingness; whence it naturally happened that, since I was faithful not to my concepts but to my intuitions, something emerged quite different from what I had actually proposed.

And yet I recollect that I at last succeeded in making my intention tell, by force as it were, in one single passage (in the significant last words of Brünnhilde in which she tells the bystanders to look away from the evil thing, property, to the only satisfying thing, love), without (unfortunately!) actually quite coming to an understanding with myself as to this "love," which, after all, as we see, appears in the course of the myth as an utterly devastating force. In this one passage, then, I was blinded by the interposition of my *conscious* intentions. Well, curiously enough, this passage continually tormented me and it required the great revolution in my rational concepts, ultimately affected through Schopenhauer, to disclose to me the cause of my trouble and to give my poem a fitting keystone — a sincere recognition of the true underlying nature of things — without, on that account, rendering my work in the least propagandist. . . .

I am an artist and nothing but an artist — that is my blessing and my curse; if it were not so, I should gladly be a saint and know my life settled in the simplest way for me; and so I run hither and thither, poor fool, to find peace, that complex peace of an undisturbed sufficiently comfortable life, in order to — do nothing but work — be free to be an artist. This is such a difficult thing to obtain that I often have a hearty laugh at myself and my everlasting hunt for peace. . . .

[RICHARD WAGNER]

To *Mathilde Wesendonck* [17]

Venice, January 19, 1859

. . . My poetic conceptions have always been so far in advance of my experience that I can regard my moral education as determined and effected almost solely by these occupations. *Der fliegende Holländer, Tannhäuser*, the *Nibelungen*, Wotan were all in my brain before they became part of my experience. But it will not be difficult for you to appreciate in what a remarkable relation I now stand to *Tristan*. I say openly (for this work belongs, if not to the world, at least to all purified souls) that never was an idea so clearly embodied in experience. How far the two — the idea and the experience — were mutually predeterminative is a subject of such marvellous subtlety that the ordinary processes of thought can only

17 Wife of Otto Wesendonck and intimate friend of Wagner.

present it in inadequate and distorted form. And now — with my spirit full of intuitions of Safitri, *Parsifal* striving to take imaginative shape — when I bend brooding in formative stillness over the completion of my artistic creation in *Tristan*, who can imagine the wonder that fills me and so wraps me from this world that I am almost persuaded that I have already overcome it? *You* can guess it! *You* know it! Yes, and probably you alone! . . .

I hear from Dresden that I am expected to go there under a safe-conduct, appear in person before the courts, and stand my trial, in return for which, even in case of condemnation, I might be sure of receiving the King's pardon. Well, that would be all very well for a man who could attain all he wanted to make his life happy by such a submission, after undergoing the disgusting chicanery of the judicial inquiry. But — my God! — what should *I* gain by it? For the very doubtful satisfaction of a few possible performances of my works, I should have this absolutely certain annoyance, worry, and overstrain, all the more inevitable now that ten years of seclusion have made me intensely sensitive to contact with this horrible traffic in art which I should still have to employ as means to my end! Accordingly I have not acceded to these Dresden suggestions. To tell the truth, while I work my feet hardly touch solid earth! I could not allow any of my new works to be performed without taking part personally. The Grand Duke of Baden seems to be the prince who is most active and faithful in my interests. He has let me know that I can count with certainty on producing *Tristan* under my own direction at Karlsruhe. They would like to give it on September 6, the birthday of the Grand Duke.

I should not object to that, and the persistent interest of this amiable young prince has warmed my heart toward him. We shall see whether he carries his purpose through and — whether I am ready. I have yet a great deal of serious work before me. Still, I hope now to be able to go on without interruption. I shall certainly not have it finished before June. After that if circumstances are unchanged I think of leaving Venice and seeking my Swiss mountains again. . . .

Karl Ritter came back on New Year's Day and comes to see me every evening at 8 o'clock. He tells me that he found my wife looking somewhat better. On the whole things seem to be going tolerably well with her and I take care that she lacks nothing for her comfort. . . .

[RICHARD WAGNER]

To *Bertha Goldwag* [18]

Lucerne, February 1, 1867

Dear Miss Bertha:

Please let me know how much money I should have to send you for a house robe made according to the enclosed specifications. It is to be pink, like one of the enclosed samples — which I numbered 1) and 2), so that you can let me know the cost of each, as I suppose that they vary in price. The material of No. 2 is somewhat stiff, and skimpy on the underside, but I like the colour. An exact estimate, then.

Of the blue satin (I am returning the enclosed sample), which, I hope, is not too expensive, I'll take 18 yards. In case the money for the new expenditures is not sufficient, I am sending you another 25 taler, which you will kindly place to my account. With the blue satin send another 10 fl. worth of the very narrow blonde ribbon for shirt trimming; you know, about an inch wide.

Frau von Bülow [19] is expecting your bill for the portfolio, which she will settle immediately.

Now then — how much will the house robe as described cost me?

Best regards,

Yours sincerely,
RICH. WAGNER

[Enclosure]

Pink satin. Filled with eiderdown and quilted in squares like the grey and red quilt you made for me; just the same thickness, light, not heavy; top and underside material to be stitched together, of course. Lined with lightweight white satin. Use six widths for a very wide hem. Add a separate — not sewed on to the quilting! — shirred ruffle of the same material, going all around the hem; from the waist downward this ruffle should increase in width, forming a shirred insertion to finish off the front.

Make a close study of the drawing for this: [20] the trimming or ruffle, which must be of especially rich and fine workmanship, should be about half a yard wide on each side at the bottom. Then rising evenly toward the waist, it should lose itself in the regular

18 Wagner's seamstress.
19 Cosima Liszt von Bülow, his future wife.
20 The autograph of this letter included two pen drawings by Wagner of the robe and the sash.

width of the shirred ruffle encircling the waist. Along the ruffle, three to four beautiful bows of the same material. The same sleeves as you made for me the last time in Geneva, with a richly shirred border; one bow in front and a broader, generous bow inside at the bottom, where the sleeve hangs down.

Also a broad sash, 5 yards long, having the full width of the material at the ends, a bit narrower only in the centre. The shoulders narrower, so that the sleeves won't sag, you understand. Remember, six widths at the bottom (seamed) and another half yard of ruffle on each side in front. That makes a total of six widths and one yard at the bottom.

☯☯☯☯☯☯☯

To *Friedrich Nietzsche* [21]

[Triebschen, winter, 1870]

Dear Friend:

It is a wonderful comfort to be able to interchange letters of this kind! I have no one with whom I can discuss things so seriously as with you — the *only one* [22] excepted. God knows what I should do without you two! When, after a period of deep dejection, I come back to my work, I am often thrown into a mood of sheer good humour simply because I cannot comprehend it and am therefore obliged to laugh about it. At such times the reason for all this comes to me like a flash, but to attempt to analyse this feeling and endeavour to express it in terms of "Socratic wisdom" would require an unlimited amount of time and the elimination of all other claims upon me.

Division of labour is a good thing. You, for example, could assume a large part, in fact the half of my objectives, and (perhaps!) thereby be fulfilling your *own* destiny. Only think what a poor showing I have made as a philologist, and what a fortunate thing it is that you are on about the same terms with music. Had you decided to become a musician, you would have been, more or less, what I should have become had I persistently clung to philology. As matters now stand, philology exerts a great influence over me; in fact, as an adjunct of prime importance, it even directs me in my

---

21 Nietzsche was then Professor of Classical Philology at the University of Basel; he had recently sent Wagner copies of two lectures: "On the Greek Music Drama," and "Socrates and Tragedy."

22 Wagner's second wife, Cosima Liszt von Bülow.

capacity as a musician. On the other hand, you remain a philologist and allow your life to be directed by music.

What I am now saying is meant very seriously. In fact, it was you yourself who gave me the idea of the unworthy circle in which a philologist by profession is doomed to revolve at the present time, and you have assuredly learned from me something of all the mathematical rubbish among which an absolute musician (even under the most favourable circumstances) is obliged to fritter away his time. Now you have an opportunity of proving the utility of philology, by helping me to bring about the grand "renaissance" in which Plato will embrace Homer, and Homer, imbued with Plato's spirit, will become, more than ever before, the truly supreme Homer.

These are just random thoughts that occur to me, but never so hopefully as since I have taken so strong a liking to you, and never so clearly — and (as you see) never so clamorous for expression — as since you read us your "centaurs." [23] Therefore do not doubt the impression created upon me by your work. A very serious and profound wish has been awakened in me, the nature of which will also be clear to you, for should you not cherish the same wish, you will never be able to carry it to fulfilment.

But we must talk all this over. Therefore — I think — in short, you must come to Triebschen next Saturday. Your sleeping-room, the "Gallerie," is ready and *"Der Rauchfang ist Dir auch gewiss"* [24] — in other words: *auf Wiedersehen!*

With all my heart,
Yours,
R. W

---

23 Refers to a remark of Nietzsche: "Science, art, and philosophy have grown so closely together in my works that I shall most likely give birth to a 'centaur' one of these days."

24 From Goethe's *Faust*, Part I.

GIUSEPPE VERDI

Le Roncole, 1813 — Sant' Agata, 1901

❁⟩❁⟩❁⟩❁⟩❁⟩❁

To *Camille du Locle* [1]

Genoa, December 7, 1869

My dear du Locle:

Thank you for *Froufrou.* I read the play in one sitting. If, as the *Revue* says, the whole thing were as distinguished and original as the first three acts are, it would be extremely fine; but the last two acts descend to the commonplace, though they are effective, extraordinarily so. Good as *Froufrou* is, I would, if I had to work for Paris, prefer to Meilhac's and Halévy's *cuisine* (as you call it), another, a more refined, more piquant one: that of Sardou, with du Locle to write the verse!

But *hélas!* it's neither the hard work of writing an opera nor the taste of the Parisian public that holds me back, but the certainty that I can never succeed in having my music done in Paris the way I want it. How curious that a composer must always find all his plans crossed and his ideas misunderstood! In your opera houses (this is not meant to be an epigram) there are too many connoisseurs! Everyone wants to pass judgment according to the light of his own wisdom, according to his own taste, and, worst of all, according to a *system*, without taking any account of the character and individuality of the composer. Everyone wants to express an opinion, give voice to a doubt, and if a composer lives long enough in this atmosphere of doubt, he cannot help being shaken in his convictions, and then he begins to correct and alter his work, or rather to spoil it. And so instead of a work in one piece, the final result is a *mosaic*, and however fine, it remains a *mosaic*.

You may reply that a lot of masterpieces have come out of your Opéra this way. Well, they may be masterpieces; but allow

---

1 Librettist for part of Verdi's *Don Carlos* and the French version of *Aïda;* at this time director of the Paris Opéra.

me to say that they would be much more nearly perfect if this piece-meal work and these corrections were not obvious at every turn. Most certainly no one will deny the genius of Rossini. Well, in spite of his genius, *William Tell* betrays the fatal atmosphere of the Paris Opéra; sometimes, if not as frequently as with other composers, you have the feeling that there is too much here, too little there, that the work does not flow with the freedom and assurance of say, the *Barber*. I have no intention of belittling what you have achieved. All I mean is that it's quite impossible for me to crawl under the Caudine yoke of your French theatres again.

I know perfectly well that success is impossible for me if I cannot write as my heart dictates, free of any outside influence whatsoever, without having to keep in mind that I'm writing for Paris and not for the inhabitants of, say, the moon. Furthermore, the singers would have to sing as I wish, not as they wish, and the chorus, which, to be sure, is extremely capable, would have to show the same goodwill. A single will would have to rule throughout: my own. That may seem rather tyrannical to you, and perhaps it is. But if the work is an organic whole, it is built on a single idea and everything must contribute to the achievement of this unity. You may perhaps say that nothing stands in the way of all that in Paris. No! In Italy it can be done, or at least I can always do it; but in France: no. For example, if I come into the foyer of an Italian theatre with a new work, no one ventures to utter an opinion, to pass judgment, before understanding everything thoroughly. And no one would even dare to make inappropriate requests. There is respect for the work and for the composer, and decisions are left to the public.

In the foyer of the Opéra, on the other hand, everybody starts to whisper after the first four chords: *Oh, ce n'est pas bon . . . c'est commun, ce n'est pas de bon goût. . . . Ça n'ira pas à Paris.* What do such pitiable words as *commun . . . de bon goût . . . Paris* mean, if you're dealing with a real work of art, which should belong to the whole world!

The conclusion from all this is that I'm no composer for Paris. I don't know whether it's for lack of talent or not, but in any case my ideas of art are too different from those held in your country.

I believe in *inspiration:* you people believe in construction. I don't object to your *criterion*, for the sake of argument, but I desire the *enthusiasm* that you lack, in feeling and judging. I strive for *art*, in whatever form it may appear, but never for the *amusement*, *artifice*, or *system* which you prefer. Am I wrong? Am I right? However it may be, I have reason enough to say that my ideas are completely different from yours, and still more: my backbone isn't pliable enough for me to give way and deny my convictions, which are profound and deeply rooted in me. And I should feel very badly, my dear du Locle, if I wrote an opera for you which you might have to withdraw after a dozen performances, as Perrin did with *Don Carlos*.

If I were twenty years younger, I should say to you: "Perhaps later the character of your theatres will take a turn that will bring it nearer to my views." But time is rushing past, and for the present it's impossible for us to understand each other, unless something completely unforeseen should happen, which I can't imagine. If you come here (as you wrote my wife you might), we will talk about this much more in detail. If you don't come, I shall probably go to Paris for a while at the end of February. If you come to Genoa, we unfortunately can't offer you the ravioli again, for we haven't our Genoese cook any more. But in any case we won't let you die of hunger, and you'll be sure to find two friends who are fond of you and to whom your presence will be a real treat. Many greetings from us both to your charming Maria and a kiss for little Claire.

[GIUSEPPE VERDI]

❂❂❂❂❂❂❂❂

To *Clarina Maffei* [2]

Sant' Agata, September 30, 1870

The disaster of France fills my heart, as well as yours, with despair. Yes, the *blague*, the impertinence, the presumption of the French was and is (in spite of all their misfortune) unbearable. But, after all, France gave the modern world its freedom and civilization. And if it falls, let us not deceive ourselves, all our liberties will fall, and then falls our civilization too. Let our littérateurs and our politicians praise the knowledge and science and even (God forgive them) the art of these victors. But if they would look a little below the surface, they would see that the old blood of the Goths still flows in their veins, that they are monstrously proud, hard, intolerant, rapacious beyond measure, and scornful of everything that is not German. A people of intellect without heart — a strong people,

2 Close friend of Verdi. Her salon was a favourite gathering-place for Italian nationalists.

but they have no grace. And that King who is always talking about God and divine providence, with whose help he is destroying the best part of Europe! He thinks he is predestined to reform the morals and punish the vices of the modern world!!! What a fine messenger of God he is!

Old Attila (another emissary of God!) halted before the majesty of the capital of the old world. But this one here is about to bombard the capital of the modern world! And now that Bismarck is trying to make us believe Paris will be spared, I am more afraid than ever that it will be at least partly laid in ruins. Why? . . . I cannot imagine. Perhaps so that there may no longer be any such beautiful capital, since they themselves will never succeed in building its equal. Poor Paris! And last April I saw it still so gay, so beautiful, so shining!

What now? . . . I should have preferred to have our government follow a more generous policy and pay a debt of gratitude. A hundred thousand of our men might have saved France. Anyhow I would rather have signed a peace after being defeated along with France than to have been a passive spectator. That we are doing this will expose us to contempt some day. We shall not escape the European war and it will engulf us. It will not come tomorrow, but it is coming. An excuse is easily found . . . perhaps Rome . . . the Mediterranean . . . and then what about the Adriatic, which they have already proclaimed a German sea?

The business in Rome is a great event, but it leaves me cold, perhaps because I feel that it might lead to internal as well as external disaster; because I can't reconcile the idea of Parliament with the College of Cardinals, a free press with the Inquisition, civil law with the Syllabus; and because I am frightened at the way our government just goes ahead any old way, hoping that time will take care of everything.

If tomorrow we should have a shrewd, adroit pope, a really crafty fellow, such as Rome has often had, he would ruin us. A *pope* and a *king of Italy* — I can't bear to see the two together, even in this letter. The paper is giving out. Forgive this tirade! It is a release for me. I am very pessimistic. Even so I haven't told you half my qualms and fears. Farewell!

[GIUSEPPE VERDI]

To *Francesco Florimo*

Genoa, January 4, 1871

Dear Florimo:

If anything could flatter my vanity, it is the invitation to become Director of the Conservatory in Naples, as sent to me through you from the teachers of the Conservatory and other musicians of your city. It is very painful for me not to be able to answer this demonstration of confidence as I should like to. But with pressure of business, my habits, my love of independence, it would be impossible for me to undertake so weighty an office. You may say: "And what about art?" Of course; but I have done my best for art, and if I am to be able to go on doing something from time to time, I must be free of all other obligations. Otherwise you can imagine how very proud I should be to occupy the place held by such fathers of tradition as Alessandro Scarlatti, Durante, and Leo. It would be an honour for me to instruct the students in the weighty, vigorous, and lucid teachings of those fathers. I should have been able to stand, so to speak, with one foot in the past and the other in the present and future (for I am not afraid of the "Music of the Future"). And I should have said to the young pupils: "Practise the fugue constantly and persistently until you are weary of it and your hands are supple and strong enough to bend the music to your will. Thus you will learn assurance in composition, proper part-writing, unforced modulation. Study Palestrina and some few of his contemporaries. Then skip everything up to Marcello, and pay particular attention to the *recitatives*. Attend but few performances of contemporary opera, and don't be seduced by the profusion of harmonic and instrumental beauties, or by the chord of the diminished seventh, that easy subterfuge for all of us who can't write four measures without half a dozen sevenths."

When they have gone thus far and have achieved a broad literary background I would say finally to these young students: "Now lay your hands on your heart and go ahead and write. If you have the stuff of artists in you, you will be composers. In any case, you will not swell the legion of modern imitators and neurotics who seek and seek but never really find, although they may do some good things." In singing I would have modern declamation taught along with time-honoured studies. But to apply these few deceptively simple principles, it would be necessary to supervise the instruction so closely that twelve months a year would be almost too

little. I have a house, business, property, and all, here — tell me yourself: how could I do it?

So, my dear Florimo, will you express to your colleagues and
the other musicians in your beautiful Naples my deep regrets that
I cannot accept an offer that does me such honour? I hope you may
be able to find a man who is, above all, learned and a strict teacher.
Liberties and mistakes in counterpoint can be condoned and are
even sometimes quite good . . . in the theatre. But not in the conservatory. Let us turn back to the old masters: progress will be the
result.

A warm farewell! I remain devotedly yours,
[GIUSEPPE VERDI]

To *Opprandino Arrivabene*

Sant' Agata, July 17, 1875

I cannot tell you how we are to escape from this musical ferment. One person wants to be a melodist like Bellini, another a harmonist like Meyerbeer. I want to be neither the one nor the other,
and if I had my say, a young man beginning to compose would never
think about being a melodist, harmonist, realist, idealist, musician of
the future, or whatever other pedantic formulas the Devil may
have invented. Melody and harmony should be simply the means in
the hand of the artist to make music; and if ever the day comes when
people no longer talk about melody and harmony, about German
and Italian schools, about the past and the future of music, then the
kingdom of art will probably begin.

Another evil of our times is that all the young men's works are
the offspring of fear. No one writes as his heart dictates. Instead,
when young men set out to write, they have but one thought: to be
sure not to offend the public, and to get into the critics' good graces.

You will tell me that I owe my success to the union of both
schools. I have never had anything of the sort in my mind. All this
is an old story, which is gone through by others after a certain
period.

[GIUSEPPE VERDI]

To *Giulio Ricordi*

April 20, 1878

We are all working, without meaning to, for the downfall of our theatre. Perhaps I myself, perhaps you and the others are at it too. And if I wanted to say something that sounds foolish, I should say that the Italian quartet societies were the first cause; and a more recent cause was the success of the performances (not the works) given by the Scala orchestra in Paris. I've said it — don't stone me! To give all the reasons would take up too much time. But why in the name of all that's holy must we do German art if we are living in Italy? Twelve or fifteen years ago I was elected president of a concert society, I don't remember whether in Milan or elsewhere. I refused, and I asked: "Why not form a society for vocal music? That's alive in Italy — the rest is an art for Germans." Perhaps that sounded as foolish then as it does now; but a society for vocal music, which would let us hear Palestrina, the best of his contemporaries, Marcello, and such people, would have preserved for us our love of song, as it is expressed in opera.

Now everything is supposed to be based on orchestration, on harmony. The alpha and omega is Beethoven's Ninth Symphony, marvellous in the first three movements, very badly set in the last. No one will ever approach the sublimity of the first movement, but it will be an easy task to write as badly for voices as is done in the last movement. And supported by the authority of Beethoven they will all shout: "That's the way to do it. . . ."

Never mind! Let them go on as they have begun. It may even be better so; but a "better" that undoubtedly means the end of opera. Art belongs to all nations — nobody believes that more firmly than I. But it is practised by individuals; and since the Germans have other artistic methods than we have, their art is basically different from ours. We cannot compose like the Germans, or at least we ought not to; nor they like us. Let the Germans assimilate our artistic substance, as Haydn and Mozart did in their time; yet they remained predominantly symphonic musicians. And it is perfectly proper for Rossini to have taken over certain formal elements from Mozart; he is still a melodist for all that. But if we let fashion, love of innovation, and an alleged scientific spirit tempt us to surrender the native quality of our own art, the free natural certainty of our work and perception, our bright golden light, then we are simply being stupid and senseless.

[GIUSEPPE VERDI]

To *Opprandino Arrivabene*

June 5, 1882

Berlioz was a poor, sick man who raged at everyone, was bitter and malicious. He was greatly and subtly gifted. He had a real feeling for instrumentation, anticipated Wagner in many instrumental effects. (The Wagnerites won't admit it, but it is true.) He had no moderation. He lacked the calm and what I may call the balance that produce complete works of art. He always went to extremes, even when he was doing admirable things.

His present successes in Paris are in good part justified and deserved; but reaction is even more largely responsible. When he was alive they treated him so miserably! Now he is dead: Hosanna!

[GIUSEPPE VERDI]

❂❂❂❂❂❂❂❂

To *Opprandino Arrivabene*

June 10, 1884

I have heard the composer Puccini well spoken of. I have seen a letter, too, reporting all kinds of good things about him. He follows the new tendencies, which is only natural, but he keeps strictly to melody, and that is neither new nor old. But it seems that he is predominantly a symphonist: no harm in that. Only here one must be careful. Opera is opera, symphony is symphony; and I don't think it is a good idea to insert a symphonic piece into an opera just for the pleasure of letting the orchestra cut loose once in a while.

I say this just by the way, so don't attach any importance to it; I am not even absolutely sure I have said a true thing, but I am sure I have said something that runs counter to the spirit of the times. Each age has its own stamp.

History will decide later what ages were good, what ages bad. Who knows how many people in the seventeenth century admired Achillini's sonnet, *Sudate, o fuochi*, more than a canto of Dante?

But whatever may be good or bad, you in the meantime must keep your good health and your good humour, and that for a long time to come!

[GIUSEPPE VERDI]

To *Opprandino Arrivabene*

Milan, May 2, 1885

I have the number of *Ars Nova* that you sent me. I have not had time to read it carefully; but so far as I can see, it is one of the usual screeds that do not discuss, but simply pronounce judgment with unbelievable intolerance. On the last page I see, among other things: "If you suppose that music is the expression of feelings of love, grief, etc., give it up. . . . It is not for you!"

And why, pray tell, must I not suppose that music is the expression of love, grief, etc.?

The fellow begins by citing as the *non plus ultra* of music Bach's Mass, Beethoven's Ninth Symphony, and the Mass of Pope Marcellus. Personally I should not be at all surprised if somebody were to tell me, for instance, that Bach's Mass is a trifle dry; that the Ninth Symphony is badly written at some points, and that among the nine symphonies he prefers certain movements that are not in the Ninth; and that there are even better things in Palestrina than in his Mass of Pope Marcellus.

Why not? Simply because someone holds that opinion, why can he not be one of the elect, and why is music necessarily not for him?

Anyway, I am not going to argue. I don't know anything and don't want to know anything. But I do know that if the great man of the *Ars Nova* should be born among us, he would abjure much of the past, and disdain the pretentious utopias of the present, which do no more than substitute new faults and conventions for the faults and conventions of other days, clothing intellectual emptiness in baroque garments.

And now keep well and cheerful, which is much more important to us than *Ars Nova*.

[GIUSEPPE VERDI]

ROBERT FRANZ

Halle, 1815 — Halle, 1892

❖❖❖❖❖❖❖❖

To *Franz Liszt*

Halle, December 26, 1858

Esteemed Doctor:

While I offer you my deepest thanks for your kind letter which arrived at my house like a beautiful Christmas gift, I shall also tell you that I am in agreement with your proposals. When everything is ready I shall send you the copies with the two accompanying notes, and once again I shall accept your generous assistance in this transaction with the most grateful sense of obligation. I do hope, however, that I shall not bring dishonour to your recommendation — I have composed the songs[1] with particular pleasure.

Of course today there is a certain risk in writing music to Goethe's poetry; there are already many different kinds in existence, some of them celebrated compositions. Nevertheless, it seems to me that up to the present time our art has not done full justice to many examples of Goethe's lyric poetry. This poetry does not represent overwhelming passion to the extent that people are inclined to believe. It is rather a true impression of this and consequently presumes, one might say, a certain empathy on the part of the individual, clarified by tranquillity. Goethe's style, so delicate, pellucid, and smooth-flowing, frequently leads one astray into a one-sided treatment. The musical expression evaporates into an absolute, melodic form that is more suitable for a general mood than for a self-participating subject. I have always taken care to compose from a concrete situation, in keeping with Goethe's personality, and, I confess, must leave the world to decide whether or not it can sense this in my music.

I am especially eager to have your opinion in regard to a cer-

---

1 Op. 33, *Whistling.*

tain piece — its subject is that wonderful poem from the *Italienische Reise: "Cupido, loser, eigensinniger Knabe."* Everyone to whom I have showed the piece has criticized it without being able to show me anything better. With the best intention in the world I recognize no humour in the text. If anything, it seems to me to involve the deepest personal suffering of the poet, and while Goethe tries hard to detach himself jokingly from his feelings, I fear he has not shaken off the little god by this means.

But I am talking about matters that can interest you only when you see the volume of songs — forgive my ineptitude. With warmest greetings to you. Remember me to the Princess.[2] I remain, with all love and esteem, your

ROBERT FRANZ

To *Franz Liszt*

Halle, March 18, 1873

Most Esteemed Doctor:

Your letter heaps upon me favour after favour and in return I have nothing to offer but a grateful heart, which will beat for you as long as I live. The introduction of my songs in Pest in itself is a most comforting event, but the fact that *you* have done me this service means that scarcely any doubt concerning their value can arise in future. Will you offer my thanks to the two ladies Frau von Semsey and Frau Dunkl [3] for their most generous efforts on my behalf? This message will doubtless mean more to them than if I personally tried to satisfy my obligations.

I have given Rissé your opinion on the *Studie;* no doubt this will greatly stimulate him in the pursuit of his literary works. I had already communicated with him before in connection with some of my own works, which, of course, necessitated many preliminary studies.

Up to the present, people have generally pointed out my leaning toward Bach and Handel, Schubert and Schumann. Of course I would not for a moment deny that these four masters have had a profound influence on my development, but I cannot think of them

---

2 Princess Sayn-Wittgenstein, Liszt's mistress.

3 The artists who performed at a benefit concert for Franz in Budapest, March 2, 1873, which Liszt arranged.

as the foundation of my style. Rather, this is to be sought and easily found in the old Protestant chorale, which dominated, almost exclusively, my entire youthful period. The structure of my cantilena, the support by the bass parts, the treatment of the middle voices, the handling of keys and harmonic relationships, finally the cross-play of expression in the old church modes are the outward forms in which these connections are demonstrated unequivocally. On the other hand, all sorts of transcendental tendencies could be observed as the ideal point of contact. Still, if one focuses on the fact that the Protestant chorale had its roots in the old German folk-song, new factors enter into the picture that satisfactorily explain many new phenomena.

Bach and Handel, who should be designated as the culminating-point of the Protestant chorale, have done me the great service of showing me how to expand my forms of expression; Schubert and Schumann, on the other hand, have helped me to find myself in relation to the present.

This short sketch of the genesis of my development is hardly based on illusions; even a fairly exact demonstration would be possible. But this opens up a perspective that places great difficulties in the way of a scholarly treatment of the subject; one would have to bring in here the various kinds of styles of long past epochs — a problem that very few would be able to cope with nowadays — even people like yourself, before whose genius time and space disappear. Formerly I myself was unable to see things so clearly, but at present the idea of having a serious settlement with the past is uppermost in my mind.

Consequently I set the above remarks before you, esteemed Doctor, since no one is better able to penetrate their value or lack of it more keenly than you. Do not be annoyed at me for having troubled you with these verbose analyses — they are not completely without interest, and it was that which gave me the courage to present them for your opinion. Should we meet again in person, as seems so pleasant in prospect, I shall take the liberty of stating a few curious facts to you which illustrate these opinions.

With everlasting gratitude and reverence,
ROBERT FRANZ

CHARLES GOUNOD

Paris, 1818 — *Paris,* 1893

❖❖❖❖❖❖❖❖

To *Pigny* [1]

London, September–October 1870

Yes, my dear fellow, you are perfectly right. The peace proposals Prussia dreams of are a crying shame. But the shame, thank God, lies wholly with the proposing party. They bring glory to those who reject them. Like you, I feel, I will not say humiliated, but cut to the very heart by the horrible misfortunes that have befallen our poor unhappy France. So much so that I keep wondering, every hour of the day, whether the duty of those who are called to the honour and happiness of defending our country is not less heavy than that which you and I have to perform, and which no man would choose if he felt he must blush for the performance of it.

Alas, dear friend, this once, at all events, in history, Frenchmen in general have spilt their noble blood so gallantly that the shame of those who only think of their own personal safety clings to themselves alone. But the glory of victory nowadays (for the first time, perhaps, in the world's history) is won by machinery rather than by men, and disasters will be weighed in the same balance. The Prussians have not been braver than we. We have been less fortunate than they.

You know already, and I say it again, if you decide to re-enter any gate of Paris, I will not let you go alone. Family life means something more than mere family dinner.

Well, here we are at last, dear friend, in our new dwelling, after eighteen days spent in the enjoyment of the simplest and sincerest hospitality. Some Englishmen there are who will not let us Frenchmen feel we are in England. The manner in which our kind friend Brown has shared our trouble proves it.

But the external peace we have found here gives us no inward

1 Gounod's brother-in-law.

calm. The longer this horrible bloody war of pride and extermination lasts, the more do I feel my very heart-strings wrung with grief for my unhappy country, and anything that seems to rouse me from my sad contemplation of our beloved France, far from comforting me, as with kindness, stings like an insult.

Oh, most unhappy earth! Wretched home of the human race where barbarism not only still exists, but is taken for glory, and permitted to obscure the pure and beneficent rays of the only true glory in existence, the glory of love, of science, and of genius! Humanity still lingers, it would seem, under the grim shadow of chaos, amid the monstrosities of the iron age; and instead of driving their weapons into the earth to benefit their fellow creatures, men plunge them into one another's hearts to decide the ownership of the actual soil. Barbarians! Savages!

Ah, dear fellow, let us make an end, or I shall go on for ever, for very sorrow.

The dear ones near me, who are dear to you too, are well. Would we could have hidden them a little less far off — in Paris!

Your brother,
Ch. Gounod

❦❧❦❧❦❧❦❧

To *Pigny*

London, April 14, 1871

Dear Friend:

Your letter of the 12th has just reached me, and I reply at once in the hope that my answer may be at Versailles in time to welcome you on your return to the dear fraternal roof, and that thus your two brothers may each greet you after his fashion — one in his peaceful garden, the other by these few lines from the other side of the sea; one opening his door to you, the other stretching out his arms; both taking you to their hearts. How large is the place you hold there, you know very well.

Alas! dear friend, dear brother, I too hear the terrible guns whose booming grieves your soul and breaks your heart, as well it may! As step by step I follow the progress of events and the various phases of this conflict, or rather of the utter bedlam that causes and maintains it, I watch the gradual disappearance — I will not say of my illusions (the word is not too worthy to express my meaning, nor should I mourn over it as I do), but of my hopes, present or near, at all events, of the approaching erection of a new *storey* in the building of the moral habitation men call "Liberty," the only dwelling, after all, worthy of the human race.

No, again I say it, these are no illusions that are fading from our sight! Liberty is no dream; it is our Canaan, a true land of promise. But, like the Jews, we shall only see it afar off. To enter it we must become God's own people. Liberty is as real as heaven. It is a heaven on earth — the country of the elect; but it must be earned, and conquered, not by oppression, but by self-devotion; not by pillage, but by generosity; not by taking life, but by bestowing it, in the moral as well as the material sense. Morally above all; for once that is well understood and ascertained, the material side of the question will take care of itself. The man's hygiene must come first, his animal welfare second — that is the just and therefore the logical course.

When I consider the outcome (so far, at least) of all the moral gifts, all the advances on trust, as it were, of which humanity, political and social, has been the recipient up to the present day, I cannot help observing that it has been treated like a spoiled child. I feel inclined to doubt whether a wise and opportune distribution of all those gifts which cannot be appreciated and utilized till the human race comes of age has not been anticipated with reckless and imprudent prodigality.

We still stand in need of *overseers*. Well, master for master, take it all in all, I would rather have *one* than *two hundred thousand*. You can always get rid of one tyrant (natural death, what we call *la belle mort* will do that for you); but a collective tyranny, compact, endlessly reproductive, feeding and fattening perpetually on its own victims! — I can never believe that is God's chosen model of human evolution. Now, if we carry the argument to its conclusion, we come to this: "Liberty is merely the voluntary and conscious accomplishment of justice." And as justice is obedience to eternal and unchanging laws, it follows that where there is freedom, there must be submission. This is the end of the argument, and the basis of all life. I should go on twaddling for ever (and so would you), but I must not forget mine is not the only letter this envelope is to hold.

So I will send my affectionate love to you and Berthe.

Your brother,
CH. GOUNOD

To *Oscar Comettant*

London, May 6, 1874

My dear Friend:

I read your last article dealing with the Choral Symphony with the greatest pleasure. It's possibly the best and most delightful you've written. Well and good! That's the way I like to see this supreme master discussed — as one of the prophets. In regard to this immortal work, last year's May 1st issue of the English musical journal *The Orchestra* has an article entitled "Rescoring Beethoven." Though I agree with many of the observations the author makes in this article, may I add a few on this subject that may interest you?

I do not know the Beethoven Choral Symphony "according to Wagner"; the only one I know is "according to Beethoven" and that is enough for me. I have heard and read this gigantic work many times and I have never felt the slightest need for any correction in reading or listening to it. Furthermore, as a matter of principle, much as one may admire Wagner and even if one were another Beethoven (about as likely as there being another Dante or Michelangelo), I do not agree that anyone has the right to correct the masters. We don't redraw or repaint Raphael and Leonardo da Vinci — aside from the fact that it would be a calamity to substitute a foreign touch for that of these great geniuses, who, I should think, knew what they were doing and why.

But to return to the particular example of the Choral Symphony, I can't see at all what this presumption of changing the text is based on. First of all, as regards the purely instrumental part of the work — the first three movements and the beginning of the fourth — Beethoven had such profound knowledge and prodigious mastery of orchestral resources, of the tone colour and qualities of the different instruments, that I cannot understand how anyone could think for a moment of offering him any advice on this subject. For this we need Monsieur Wagner, who gives lessons to everybody, to Beethoven just as to Mozart and Rossini.

I have heard the Ninth Symphony conducted by Habeneck, the celebrated founder and director of the orchestra of the Société des Concerts of the Paris Conservatoire. The only change (not in the prescribed instrumentation but in nuance) that this learned conductor permitted was a mezzo forte instead of a forte in the long unison of strings that accompanies the thirds and sixths in the melancholy passage of the Scherzo.

The purpose of this slight change was to absorb the sonority of the flutes, clarinets, and bassoons (beneath the force of a large number of strings), which carry the melodic design above the continuous energetic rumbling of the main rhythm.

As for the vocal part (solos and choruses) which ends this incomparable work, so sublime, so unique, so majestic, I emphatically deny that the performers or audience have ever pronounced a definite or final *non possumus* against it. *Non possumus* is the word for all the early discouragement; it greeted the first appearance of all the innovations; they used it against the Beethoven symphonies when they were introduced into France. They said the same thing about Meyerbeer and *Robert le diable*, *Les Huguenots*, and *Le Prophète*. Recently they have even used it in Germany in connection with the latest works of Monsieur Richard Wagner; the artists and singers said it was impossible to remember and sing them. They said it and many are still saying it about the great last quartets of Beethoven. Eventually time smooths out the difficulties, and just as in many other problems, what seemed impossible yesterday is easy today.

It is true that the vocal part of the Ninth is difficult to perform and that the way in which the voices are treated calls for an aptitude and knowledge of music well above that of the average singer and chorus. However, I might say that, contrary to the assertions advanced by the critic, with whom I disagree, in 1842, at Vienna in Austria, I heard Otto Nicolai conduct the Choral Symphony with 1,200 musicians (450 instrumentalists and 750 voices) and it was *admirable* from every point of view: ensemble, solidity, precision of attack, rhythm, perfect intonation, and observation of nuance even in the highest notes and the most ticklish passages.

It is true that in Germany, the register and timbre of their soprano voices are particularly well adapted to attacking and holding high notes, which partly explains the superiority of performance as regards precision and purity of intonation. But one should also consider that the German educational system makes it compulsory to practise reading music in all the schools, and that knowledge of music contributes a good deal to a sure performance. Thus, if we wish to prove that the vocal part of this symphony is perfectly executable, though as Rossini used to say, it may be "badly fingered for the voice," we must have choruses and vocalists who not only have good voices, but, what is more important, know how to read music, and I must say that this last condition is not very well satisfied in England.

However that may be, let us not touch the works of the great; it is an example of dangerous discourtesy and irreverence, to which there would never be an end. Let us not put our hands on the hands of that great race, for posterity should be able to view their noble lines and solid structure and majestic elegance without any veil. Let us remember that it is better to let a great master retain his own imperfections, if there are any, than to impose our own upon him.

[CHARLES GOUNOD]

ÉDOUARD LALO

Lille, 1823 — Paris, 1892

☙❧❧❧❧❧❧❧

To *Pablo de Sarasate* [1]

Paris, October 28, 1878

Dear Friend:

Today I am writing to you in a state of inexpressible stupefaction! The reason is Brahms's Second Symphony in D. I read it through yesterday morning and I heard it the same day at the Concert Populaire. And this is the man whom some rank above, and others beside, Schumann! Schumann, the great poet, powerful, inspired, whose every note is individual — and the author of the Second Symphony in D — it's absolutely grotesque.

Brahms is a second-rate mind. He has dug up every corner in modern harmony and counterpoint — that's his only importance. He is not a born musician, his invention is always insignificant or derivative, and in his latest symphony the pastiche is especially flagrant. I have carefully kept up with all his chamber music; it holds together well because it is based on solid study, but his invention is hesitant, and one senses a man who is searching right and left for what he does not find in himself; further, under the pretext of increasing the sonority, there is an intolerable abuse of unison (Beethoven understood harmony well enough to appreciate the unison, but with his gift for sonority he did not need this ridiculous method).

Finally came the Piano Quintet. In the ensemble of this work there is an outburst that made me hope that the composer had at last found himself. Alas, the works that followed, always strongly steeped in laboured research, are absolutely insignificant as to invention. Since these last chamber-music compositions I have seen nothing by this man, and before yesterday's concert I had never heard his orchestral works.

---

1 Violin virtuoso (1844–1908) for whom Lalo wrote his First Violin Concerto.

Perhaps you will tell me that Pasdeloup's [2] performance is not good. Maybe so, but it is the same for everyone, and Pasdeloup has worked very hard on this symphony, which, as a matter of fact, is not difficult. Now, at the same concert they played Mozart's G-minor Symphony, which seems like a dwarf when placed next to an orchestral page by Beethoven. Beside the Brahms symphony it seemed like a colossus. The first and last movements show paltry and old-fashioned invention and they are full of patches of Mendelssohn and Beethoven in all the themes serving as basis for development. The Andante is in contrast to these two puerile movements, but it is no less boring; it gives me the impression of some one who puts on an air of terrible and profound conviction to keep repeating sentences like the following in a cavernous voice: "The flash of this sabre is the most beautiful light of my life! The chariot of state navigates on a volcano!" The Scherzo is a nice little genre piece.

As for Brahms's instrumentation — I am completely dumbfounded. He understands nothing about selecting timbres; he orchestrates like a pianist, and if one of us had written such mediocre orchestration, the rest of us would say: "My dear fellow, you have possibilities, but hurry back to the schoolroom."

To sum up, the quintet, which I thought would be the point of departure of a vigorous old boy who, finally coming into his full power, was going to give us a series of remarkable works, is, on the contrary, the apogee of a composer who had done nothing but stumble around, and his latest symphony is below the level of his weakest quartet.

A stupid scene occurred at this concert; people whistled and hissed; these were the same idiots who had just encored an absurd guitar piece by Taubert.[3] Well, I applauded as hard as I could, only because extremes attract extremes, and I think it monstrous for imbeciles to whistle at an artist whose value I dispute because his partisans overrate him, but who, nevertheless, has an incontestable value. As for his symphony, I tell you again, it deserves neither applause nor catcalls. The same evening I saw Saint-Saëns; his opinion of the symphony is the same as mine.

This is a very long letter, but it will show you what regard the musicians on the other side of the Rhine had for Brahms and his reputation since all of them went out of their way to admire the

---

2 Jules Étienne Pasdeloup (1819–87), conductor of the Concerts Populaires.
3 Karl Gottfried Taubert (1811–91).

mountain that had been promised them; it isn't their fault if the mountain gave birth to only a mouse.

Where are you? What are you doing? Where are you going? Send me your itinerary. With all my heart,

É. LALO

⊙⁣⊙⁣⊙⁣⊙⁣⊙⁣⊙⁣⊙

To *Pablo de Sarasate*

November 21 ,1878

My very dear Friend:

If you knew how much pleasure your letter gave me and how much it diverted me from all my troubles you wouldn't have kept me waiting so long. Though I should be used to your malady of silence, I waited anxiously, and since I had asked you for news of *La Norvégienne*,[4] I kept counting the days. When nothing arrived I finally became convinced that you hadn't liked it and that I had ruined the orchestration, and that you were putting off from day to day the moment of telling me about this annoying hitch. Luckily there was nothing in it, and your letter gave me a little of the gaiety that has been missing since the Escudier failure.[5]

Tell Max Bruch I thank him for this act of artistic brotherliness, and if he needs me in Paris, I shall be at his disposal. Tell him I beg him not to pass final judgment on the orchestration of the *Fantaisie*, which I have not heard. The combination of various orchestral timbres with a solo violin is very difficult if one doesn't want to be flat and insignificant and you know I haven't written a single piece you play without making enormous improvements after the first rehearsal. I'm very curious to know if the experience I've acquired has helped me in this piece. I'm a little anxious because this *Fantaisie* is not at all like the symphony or the concerto and it is a new test.

Give me the pleasure and favour of listening closely to the orchestra; take notes on the smallest details and send me your criticisms; I have confidence in your judgment. As for you, I know what the " lion of the violin " can do — you play this like an en-

---

4 *Fantaisie norvégienne*, for violin and orchestra; later changed to *Rhapsodie norvégienne* for orchestra, first performed October 26, 1879, Paris.

5 Léon Escudier (1808–81), Paris music-publisher and editor, was director of the Théâtre-Italien from 1876 until its failure in 1878.

raged devil, and I am certain of success with you. If I have any fears, it's only because of my conscience as a composer.

As for business, sell the piece for as much as you can get. The more they pay, the more one is esteemed, says the proverb, and a piece played by you is the very best publicity for the publishers.

As for Brahms, what you tell me about the respect for his name in Germany doesn't surprise me. The Germans make a fetish of everything that belongs to them and they bring such ardent conviction to the defence and exaltation of the men they admire that those who don't share their convictions are imbeciles. We French have the opposite fault, but that is no reason for going the whole hog in every case, the genius of Brahms being one of them. To be a genius, first one would have to have the personal poetry and invention of Schumann or Schubert; Brahms has neither one nor the other. Just one of Beethoven's last quartets makes him a genius. All the works of Brahms makes him a very talented man, nothing more.

In his Second Symphony there is flagrant plagiarism of Schubert and Mendelssohn, and while he was imitating the latter, he certainly ought to have borrowed a little of his luminous orchestration; the symphony would have been less doughy. The form of this symphony is old, its invention poor, and the orchestration is that of a student who doesn't know whether to use a clarinet or an oboe. If they were not such fetishists, the intelligent German musicians would agree with this opinion; they are rich enough in immense musical glory not to have to exalt into a genius a talented man, the top of whose head barely reaches the ankles of their giants.

I had quite an argument on this subject at the Szarvadys'. "You didn't understand it," she said to me with her air of incontestable superiority; "You have to hear this masterpiece several times." Now, Madame Szarvady had heard this masterpiece just once, but, with her vast intelligence, she admired each note. You know that Madame Szarvady invented Brahms and she doesn't want anyone to touch her invention; she is a fetishist of the first order. I got exasperated and demolished her fetish by exaggerating my criticisms, as always happens in such cases, and I am nothing but a wretched musician incapable of understanding the sublimities of art.

That's where German fetishism leads. Blind and irrational passion can impose its ardent convictions on boobies, but Mount Valérien is not Mount Blanc, and Brahms will never be a Schumann.

Our best wishes, with all my heart,

É. LALO

BEDŘICH SMETANA

Leitomischl, 1824 — Prague, 1884

⊛)⊕)⊕)⊕)⊕)⊕)⊕)⊕)⊕)⊕

To *Franz Liszt*

Prague, March 23, 1848

Sir:

   Trusting in your well-known goodness and magnanimity, I am taking the liberty of dedicating to you this little product of my imagination.[1] To be sure, I should have first sought your permission, but I am completely unknown, even among my neighbours, and I had to venture this step to see whether or not the composition would be worthy of your acceptance. Permit me to tell you first what has decided me to take advantage of your kindness.

   From my childhood on, I devoted myself to the study of literature, and despite my ardent interest in music, I was compelled to pursue it mostly as simple recreation and enjoyment. And the sort of instruction I received! When I was seventeen I knew neither what C double-sharp nor D double-flat was, and harmony was completely unknown territory to me. Despite that I composed.

   When I was nineteen I broke the chains that bound me to my studies and with the greatest diligence devoted myself to music under the direction of a very thorough teacher, Joseph Proksch of Prague. Now I am twenty-four, and by this time I have studied all branches of music and completed a great many exercises, so that I have acquired a certain facility. But I am poor, helpless, friendless, and I have had to pay dearly for my lessons. Only this year, for the first time, after economizing for a long time and obtaining a few positions as a result of a public performance and some small acknowledgment of my humble talent, have I been able to pay half of my long-standing debt. But when shall I be able to pay the other half?

   My employment pays me 12 florins a month, so that I have

---

1 *Six Character Pieces for Piano*, op. 1.

barely enough not to die of starvation. I cannot have my compositions published since I would have to pay for this myself and unfortunately cannot spare the money. Anyway I believe I could hardly live on my compositions. The protection I sought gave promise of a great deal, but thus far nobody has done anything for me. Yes, I must tell you that I was close to desperation when I received word that my parents had sunk so low that they were almost beggars. Oh, sir, what wouldn't I have done to help them! In my great need, helpless, with no prospect of assistance, suddenly I noticed the name Liszt on a sheet of music lying on my table, and like a flash of lightning the idea came into my head of confiding everything to you, that incomparable artist whose generosity re-echoes throughout the world. To introduce my humble talent to you, I wrote these *Character Pieces*, my first work, which perhaps may help to bring me some attention.

Now I humbly beg you to be kind enough to accept this work and to have it published. Dare I hope that your name will place this work before the public, that your name will be the foundation of my future happiness and the object of my eternal gratitude? I cannot describe my impatience, my anxiety, until I know your decision, and I beg you please not to postpone it and leave me in the throes of this agonizing uncertainty.

I venture still another request. My present condition is terrible. May God keep other artists from such a life! Yet I could very easily obtain for myself an existence that would make me the happiest man on earth, and whereby I would be able to fulfil the only wish I have — to take care of my poor parents until their death, if only I could have some assistance for my plan to establish a music school. The one here in Prague already has almost one hundred students from last year. Moreover, the ordinary musicians say that they have more than eighty students who pay 400 florins monthly. If only I had enough money to be able to rent lodgings and buy at least two instruments, I should be able to earn my living, have my parents with me, and be the happiest man on earth. I am both a creative and a performing artist and I have *no* instrument. A friend helps me out by letting me use his; indeed, my lot is not enviable. Thus, even if I may seem presumptuous, I make bold to beg you for a loan of 400 florins, which I solemnly swear, *on my life*, to repay you. I have no guarantees other than myself and my word, which is more sacred to me, and perhaps even more dependable, than 100 guarantees.

I beg you not to take my boldness in bad part. I have confessed my need and poverty to no one but you, and in whom can an artist confide if not in another artist? The rich and the aristocrats regard the poor devil without pity and let him starve to death. With the greatest anxiety I ask you once again, and I hope not in vain, not to postpone your reply, no matter whether it decide my good fortune or misfortune, but quickly to deliver me from my uncertainty, for in a few weeks perhaps there may be no Smetana. I live at No. $\frac{548}{I}$ Alstädter Ring, second floor back.

I hope, sir, that you will forgive me for having taken up your time, but it is necessary for you to have some knowledge of one who is requesting your assistance.[2] I remain, most respectfully,

Your humble servant,
[BEDŘICH SMETANA]

To *Josef Srb* [3]

Jabkenice *[Bohemia]* April 12, 1878

Esteemed Sir:

I am sending along the score of my string quartet;[4] it is my manuscript and has been in my hands up to now. I should like you to copy the parts for yourself and keep them as your property, but to return the manuscript to me as soon as the parts are copied. Dr. Procházka must have the Trio for piano, violin, and cello.

Concerning the style of my quartet, I shall gladly leave judgment on this to others and I will not be angry at all if they do not like it, for it is contrary to the conventional style of quartet music. I had no intention of composing a quartet according to a formula or according to the usual conception of form. I worked long enough in this as a young student of musical theory to become thoroughly familiar with it and to master it. With me, the form of each composition is determined by its subject. Consequently this quartet created its own form. I wanted to picture in tones the course of my life.

First Movement: The inclination to art in my youth, romanticism predominating, the unspeakable yearning for something I could not express or definitely imagine, and also a sort of warning of

---

2 Liszt helped him open a music school.
3 Writer on music.
4 *From My Life* (1876).

my future disaster: ; this is the origin of the long

sustained tone in the finale: . It is that fateful whistling of the highest tones in my ear which in 1874 was announcing
my deafness. I allowed myself this little game because it was so cata-
strophic for me.

Second Movement: The quasi Polka carries me back in retro-
spection to the happy life of my youth when, as a composer of dance
music, I frequented the gay world, where I was known as a passionate dancer. Middle Section: "Meno vivo," D-flat major, is the one
that, in the opinion of performers of this quartet, is absolutely impossible to perform! It is supposed to be impossible to produce clarity of chords. In this section I paint in tones my impressions of the
aristocratic circles in which I lived for many years. I gave the indi-

cation in small notes : "più facile," with the violins and

viola playing more lightly, and I ask you to try both ways, and if
you find it possible to use the first, original manner without sac-
rificing the clarity of chords, please keep that one, for I like it better.
I think this movement is the main reason these gentlemen hesitate
to play this quartet, rather than their objections to the orchestral
style.

Third Movement: "Largo sostenuto"; this brings to mind the
bliss of my first love for the girl who later was to become my faithful wife.

Fourth Movement: Perception of the beauty of national music,
happiness resulting from this interrupted by my ominous catastrophe
— the beginning of my deafness; the view into a tragic future, a
slender ray of hope for improvement, but remembrance of the first
beginnings of my path still creates a painful feeling.

That was approximately the aim of the work, which is almost
intimate, and that is why it is written purposely for four instruments, as though in a small friendly circle they are discussing among
themselves what so obviously troubles me. That's all.

I am expecting your brochure the *History of the Conservatory*.[5] It is high time to proclaim that the Conservatory promotes
German compositions exclusively, often worthless trash, and com-

5 *A Short History of the Prague Conservatory* (1878).
6 *Hubička*, opera (1876).

pletely ignores native works no matter how much better they may be.

Mr. Krejči is sitting terribly high but he should take care not to become dizzy and fall way down! I wrote Dr. Strakatý asking him to let me copy the piano score of *The Kiss*,[6] as I have no other copy than the one I sent him, but thus far I have received no reply.

Concerning folk songs other than ours, I shall see if I have some Scandinavian ones, and if so, I shall send them along.

I was pleased to hear that the chorus *Sea Song* [7] was performed in the last concert of the *Hlahol* [choral society].

With hearty greetings and all my respects,
Your devoted
BEDŘ. SMETANA

---

7 *Piseň na moři* (1877).

ANTON BRUCKNER

Ansfelden, 1824 — Vienna, 1896

☙❀☙❀☙❀☙❀☙

To Baron *Hans von Wohlzogen*

[1884]

Esteemed Baron:

It was around the beginning of September in 1873 (Crown Prince Friedrich was then in Bayreuth) when I asked the Master's permission to show him my Second in C minor and my Third in D minor. The recently deceased man refused because of lack of time (building the theatre [1]) and said he was unable to look at any scores and had even been forced to put aside the *Nibelungen*.

When I replied: "Master, I have no right to steal even fifteen minutes of your time," but thought that, with his keen penetration, a mere glance at the themes would suffice to know how matters stood, the Master slapped me on the back, told me to come along, led me into the salon, and looked at the Second Symphony. "Very fine," he said, although he thought it was too tame (they had scared me so much in Vienna at first), and then he took up the Third (in D minor) saying: "Look, look, what's this?" and he went through the entire seventh section (he was especially struck by the trumpet); then he said: "Leave this work here with me and I shall examine it more carefully after dinner" (it was twelve o'clock). I thought to myself: do I dare utter the request that Wagner provokes in me? Very timidly, my heart throbbing, I said to the Master whom I loved so ardently: "Master! there is something in my heart that I do not trust myself to say."

"Out with it," said the Master, "you know how much I like you." I expressed my request but only on condition that it would be agreeable to the Master, for I did not wish to desecrate his illustrious name. The Master said: "You are invited to Wahnfried at five

---

1 The Festspielhaus at Bayreuth, specially designed by Wagner for the performance of his works.

[220]

o'clock in the evening; you will find me there, and after I have examined your D-minor Symphony more closely, *we shall talk about this matter*."

At five o'clock I was at the theatre they were building at Wahnfried. The Master of Masters hurried over to me, held out his arms, and warmly embraced me. "Dear friend," he said, "the dedication is all settled; this work of yours will give me *uncommonly great* pleasure." Then I had the good fortune to sit with the Master for two and a half hours, during which he talked about musical relationships in Vienna, brought me beer, and led me into the garden and showed me his *grave!!!* Afterwards he, or rather I, the lucky one, was permitted to accompany him into one of the houses. The next day he sent me his wishes for a good journey, adding "the way the trumpet begins the theme!"

In Vienna and Bayreuth he often asked me whether the symphony had been performed yet, saying: "Play it, play it." In 1882 the Master, who was then already suffering, took my hand and said: "Rely on me. I myself will play your symphony and all your works." I said: "Oh, Master!" to which he replied: "Have you been to *Parsifal*? How did you like it?" While he held my hand, I bent down on my knee, kissing and pressing his noble hand to my mouth, and said: "Oh Master, I worship you!" The Master replied: "Calm yourself, Bruckner; good night!" Those were his last words to me.

The next day the Master, who was sitting behind me at *Parsifal*, rebuked me once because I was applauding too violently.

Esteemed Baron, I beg you to guard this with the greatest care. It is my most precious legacy — *until up there!!!*

Esteemed Baron, your most gratefully,
A. BRUCKNER

My stomach!!!

JOHANNES BRAHMS

Hamburg, 1833 — *Vienna,* 1897

❂❂❂❂❂❂❂❂❂❂

To *Clara Schumann*

Detmold, October 11, 1857

My Clara:

What a pleasant surprise you gave me yesterday evening! I returned home an hour before my *Singverein* and I found your parcel awaiting me — first the beautiful letter so nice and long, and then the magnificent present. I cannot reconcile myself to your spending so much money, but apart from that I acknowledge that the gift has given me the greatest pleasure. It is so exquisitely taste-ful and practical and provokes such pleasant expectations of letters such as the one that I found enclosed. A thousand thanks, and more thanks still for your letter.

I can see you looking out of your letter and smiling at me. My dear Clara, you really must try hard to keep your melancholy within bounds and see that it does not last too long. Life is precious and such moods as the one you are in consume us body and soul. Do not imagine that life has little more in store for you. It is not true. It is true only of a very few people. If you abandon yourself entirely to your present depression you will not enjoy happy intervals as much as you might. The more you endeavour to go through times of sorrow calmly and accustom yourself to doing so, the more you will enjoy the happier times that are sure to follow. Why do you suppose that man was given the divine gift of hope? And you do not even need to be anxious in your hope, for you know perfectly well that pleasant months will follow the present unpleasant ones, just as they do every period of unhappiness. Do not make light of what I say, because I mean it. Body and soul are ruined by persisting in melancholy, and one must at all costs overcome it or not let it come into being. It is just as if one fed one's body on the most unhealthful food and comforted oneself with the reflection that in the summer one would try the milk cure. For a while the latter might do good, but the body would be debilitated and would quickly perish. . . .

You must seriously try to alter, my dearest Clara. Every morning make the determined resolution to spend the day more equably and happily. Passions are not natural to mankind, they are always exceptions or excrescences. The man in whom they overstep the limits should regard himself as an invalid and seek a medicine for his life and for his health. The ideal and the genuine man is calm both in his joy and in his sorrow. Passions must quickly pass or else they must be hunted out. Consider yourself for the moment, my dear Clara, as a serious invalid and without necessarily being anxious, but, on the contrary, with calm and perseverance, try to look after yourself. Forgive all this chatter, but I have never learned to arrange my thoughts and to express them clearly. Just think all this over and act accordingly, and then everything will be better and you will feel happier every day, and all those who belong to you will be made happier through you.

Yesterday I had the *Singverein*. While practising I felt as if I had already been at the work for twenty-five years. My voice is of no little use to me on these occasions, because I have to shout so loud, and it is an advantage that, like every other, I exploit to the full. My voice sounds quite majestic. While the choir is singing I exercise it and yell above the din, really only on my own account in order to get practice. We intend to do the *Zigeunerleben* [1] and I am sure it will soon go splendidly. How childishly easy such things are compared with old church music, and my *Salve Regina* [2] is easy as such things go. This piece would please you very much. I can't tell you very much about Rovetta except that he lived about 1640. Both pieces please the singers very much, and they are taking great pains with them. The *Zigeunerleben* is exquisite and sounds wonderful. Yesterday with Bargheer I had to accompany the Prince in his songs. I hope it won't often happen. . . .

I cannot agree with you about Debrois's essay. What he writes about me (as the charming principal figure) I found sensible beyond expectation, with the exception of one or two obvious absurdities, as, for instance, when he says that my B-minor Var. [3] was not intentionally based upon the corresponding piece by your husband. Surely it is as plain as a pikestaff! N. B. the piece in question follows

---

1 By Robert Schumann.

2 By Giovanni Rovetta (1605–68), Venetian composer.

3 In op. 9, Variations for pianoforte on a theme by Schumann in F-sharp minor.

upon the theme in F-sharp minor, so the whole thing is quite simple. About Joachim he only talks nonsense. The unfortunate part about Debrois is that here and there he makes such amateurish blunders that the people of Leipzig could cut him up frightfully. But whoever wishes to write against this Liszt clique must talk nonsense. For these people hold their own thanks only to the lowest and most confused personalities and gossip, and one must expose all this if one wishes to destroy their lair. The most stupid part of it is that this little fellow Debrois insists on regarding himself as the apex of the musical world. Who today can ever be in a position to say that anything has reached its limit when it can never have any limit at all? Little people have always wanted to put full stops after geniuses, even after Mozart, if we go back to an earlier generation. . . . Only a creative genius can be convincing in art. . . .

Send me a description of your new abode soon. I am still capable of being surprised. Every day I think of the joy I shall have in going to Hamburg at the New Year. Now I shall exult inwardly. With hearty greetings, my beloved Clara, and remembrances to Woldemar,

Your

JOHANNES

Go for walks and look through Woldemar's things carefully and sympathetically.

◓◔◓◔◓◔◓◔◓◔

To *George Henschel*

Vienna, February 1880

Dear H.:

Your letter reaches me just as I am happening to be at home for a few days; a very rare occurrence this winter, worse luck! *Post festum* my best congratulations upon the success of your concert, which indeed must have been splendid. The question in your letter received today is somewhat obscure, indistinct; I hardly know what to answer: "If the indications by figures of the tempi in my Requiem should be strictly adhered to?"

Well — just as with all other music. I think here as well as with all other music the metronome is of no value. As far at least as my experience goes, everybody has, sooner or later, withdrawn his metronome marks. Those that can be found in my works — good friends have talked me into putting them there, for I myself have never

believed that my blood and a mechanical instrument go well together. The so-called "elastic" tempo is moreover not a new invention. *"Con discrezione"* should be added to that as to many other
things.

Is this an answer? I know no better one; but what I do know is
that I indicate (without figures) my tempi, modestly, to be sure,
but with the greatest care and clearness.

Remember me kindly to Mr. Goldschmidt,[4] and tell him,
please, that there is only one thing in the coming performance I dislike thinking of, and that is that No. 5 will not be sung by his wife.[5]
I do wish I could have heard that once from her!

In haste and with kindest greeting,
Yours,

[JOHANNES BRAHMS]

* * *

To *Clara Schumann*

Ischl, August 1894

I hope Frl. Eugenie did me the credit of believing that I would
have written to her at once and exhaustively if I had been able to say
anything about how to learn transposing. I regard it chiefly as a matter of practice and habit. Anybody who has to accompany singers
every day soon learns it, and I would therefore recommend this
above all. Then let her try her hand at waltzes and easy Haydn symphonies for four hands and things of that sort. The principal thing
seems to me to be to treat the matter lightly and with skill. Of course
a thorough knowledge of harmony is also very useful for that sort
of thing (but how anyone can give lessons in harmony for years I
have never been able to understand). That you continue to study
my beloved songs is a great joy to me. . . .

Has it ever occurred to you that the last of the songs comes in
my Opus 1,[6] and did anything strike you in this connection? It really
ought to mean something. It ought to represent the snake that bites
its own tail; that is to say, to express symbolically that the tale is
told, the circle closed. But I know what good resolutions are, and I

---

4 Otto Goldschmidt, conductor, who was preparing a performance of Brahms's
   Requiem.
5 Mrs. Otto Goldschmidt was Jenny Lind.
6 *"Verstohlen geht der Mond auf,"* in *Deutsche Volkslieder* (1894), was used for
   the theme of the second movement of op. 1, Piano Sonata in C major (1853).

only think of them and don't say them aloud to myself. At present, now that my sixtieth year has passed, I should like to be as sensible as I was at twenty. At that time the publishers of Frankfurt tempted me in vain to have something printed. In vain did Kranz offer me all the money which I as a poor young man had such difficulty in earning. Why this was so it is not so easy to explain. At sixty it is probably high time to stop, but again without any particular reason!!

But in any case I am going to give myself a treat very shortly, I am expecting the visit of the clarinet-player Mühlfeld and will try two sonatas [7] with him, so it is possible that we may celebrate your birthday with music. I don't say solemnize! I wish you could be with us, for he plays very beautifully. If you could extemporize a little in F minor and E-flat major you would probably chance on the two sonatas. I would send them to you, because you could play them quite comfortably, but the clarinet would have to be transposed and that would spoil your pleasure. Thus in this letter I have managed successfully to come back to where it started, and so I will close, with most affectionate greetings to you all,

Wholly yours,

JOHANNES

---

7 Op. 120: Two Sonatas for clarinet and piano, in F minor and E flat.

ALEXANDER BORODIN

St. Petersburg, 1834 — St. Petersburg, 1887

❊⧆❊⧆❊⧆❊⧆❊⧆❊

To *Lyubov Ivanovna Karmalina*

Esteemed Lyubov Ivanovna:

Moscow, June 1, 1876

Many thanks for remembering and for the desire to exchange thoughts. . . . Your curious opinion of our musical circle pleases me a great deal, even though I do not agree with it. But it seems to me that our differences of opinion are more superficial than fundamental. Our understanding of the words "the dissolution of the circle" differs. You, too, find great distinction among us and you say that the works of the members of the circle are so diverse and dissimilar in character, spirit, etc., that this constitutes the "dissolution." (It is understood that there is no personal enmity or dislike of each other and that there could not be any since our mutual respect binds us together as people.) And if I find such dissolution natural, it is only because it always happens thus in all branches of human activity.

According to the degree of development the individual has reached, he begins to stand out over and above the school, depending on what he has inherited. The eggs laid by a hen are all alike; the chicks hatched from the egg are less alike, and when they grow up, they don't resemble one another at all — one becomes the aggressive black cock, another the meek white hen. That's the way it is here. The general character of the circle remains the same just as in the example of the chicken genus and its communal life. Later on, every one of us, as a full-grown cock or hen, develops his own personal characteristics, his own individuality. Thank Heaven! If people think that we parted with Balakirev as people, then they think wrongly. We all love him as fervently as we did before and we spare neither time nor effort to keep up our former relationship. At an urgent request of the ever energetic and warm-hearted Lyudmila

[227]

Ivanovna, Balakirev has begun the completion of his *Tamara*. God grant him success! As for the rest of us, we continue to be interested in the manifestation of each other's musical activity, and it is only natural that not everything is acceptable to all of us, partly because tastes and opinions necessarily differ, and partly because each of us during various periods of development changes his opinions and tastes. This is perfectly natural.

If I did not reply to your kind and affectionate letter immediately, it was because it reached me at a moment of feverish activity. At the close of the year I am so bothered by commissions, examination committees, reports, theses, laboratory work, etc.,[1] that I am incapable of friendly correspondence. At this point I am like that character in one of Shakespeare's historical plays who answers every question: "Anon, anon, sir!" During this time I am the most unmusical of men and completely forget that I ever occupied myself with music. Since your letter deals chiefly with music, I postponed answering it until the beginning of vacation.

You ask for news of *Igor*. When I talk about this work I have to laugh at myself. It always reminds me of the magician Finn in *Ruslan*,[2] who, though consumed with passionate love for Naina, forgets that time is passing, and cannot bring himself to decide his fate until both he and his betrothed have grown grey with age. I am like him in attempting to write a heroic Russian opera while time flies by with the speed of an express train. Days, weeks, months, whole winters pass without my being able to get to work seriously. It isn't that I could not find a couple of hours a day, but because I do not have the leisure of mind to withdraw from occupations and preoccupations that have nothing to do with music.

One must have time to concentrate, to get into the right mood, or else the creation of a sustained work is impossible. For this I have only part of the summer at my disposal. In the winter I can compose only when I am ill and have to give up my lectures and laboratory work. So, reversing the usual custom, my friends never say to me: "I hope you are well," but "I hope you are ill." During Christmas I had influenza and could not go to the laboratory. I stayed home and wrote the Thanksgiving Chorus for the last act of *Igor*. I also wrote Yaroslavna's lament when I was slightly ill.

In all, I have written one act and a half out of four. I am satis-

---

1 Borodin was professor of chemistry at the St. Petersburg Academy of Medicine and Surgery.
2 *Ruslan and Lyudmila*, by Glinka.

fied with what I have done, and my friends are too. The Thanks-giving Chorus, performed by the orchestra of the Free School, was a great success and it is a significant omen for the rest of the work.

As a composer who seeks to remain anonymous, I am shy about confessing my musical activity. This is understandable enough. For others it is their chief business, their occupation and aim in life. For me it is relaxation, a pastime that distracts me from my principal business, my professorship. I do not follow Cui's example. I love my profession and my science, the Academy and my students. My teaching is of a practical nature and therefore takes up much of my time. I have to be constantly in touch with my pupils, male and fe-male, because in order to direct the work of young people one must always be close to them. I have the interests of the Academy at heart. If, on the one hand, I want to complete my opera, on the other hand I am afraid of devoting myself to it too assiduously and thus throwing my scientific work into the shadow.

But now, since the performance of the chorus from *Igor*, the public knows I am composing an opera. There is no longer anything to conceal or to be ashamed of. Like a girl who has lost her inno-cence and by that fact has acquired a certain kind of liberty, come what may, I now must finish the work. The kind wishes of my friends and the great interest on the part of the opera company, the Petrovs, Vasilyevs, Kondralyevs, etc., will have their influence.

I must observe, however, that, from the operatic standpoint, I have always differed from my friends. By nature and disposition I do not care for recitative. Though according to some critics I do not handle it altogether badly, I am far more attracted to melody and cantilena. I am more and more drawn to definite and concrete forms. The very manner in which I treat operatic material is differ-ent. In opera, as in decorative art, minute and trifling details are out of place and only bold outlines are necessary. Everything should be clear and direct, suitable for practical performance from the vocal and instrumental standpoint. The voices should come first and the orchestra be secondary. I cannot judge how far I shall be successful but my opera will be closer to *Ruslan* than to *The Stone Guest* [3] — that I can promise.

It is curious the way all the members of our circle agree in their praise of my work. While controversy rages among us on every other subject, thus far everyone is pleased with *Igor* — Mus-sorgsky, the ultra-realist; Cui, the innovator of lyric drama; Rimsky-

3 By Alexander Dargomizhsky (1813–69).

Korsakov, our master, who is so strict regarding form and tradition; and even Vladimir Stasov, our valiant defender of everything that bears the stamp of novelty or greatness.

Such is the history of child *Igor*, illegitimate and prematurely born. From this unlawful offspring I pass on to my lawful wife. Katerina Sergeyevna thanks you for the kind messages you sent, and sends her best regards to you and your husband; she was unable to see him because she was ill. As a rule her health is very bad, which saddens our home, so pleasant in every other respect. . . .

A. BORODIN

MODEST MUSSORGSKY

Karevo (Pskov), 1835 — St. Petersburg, 1881

❂❀❂❀❂❀❂❀❂❀❂

To *Arsenii Golenishchev-Kutuzov* [1]

St. Petersburg, March 2, 1874

My dear Arsenii:

Forgive my long silence. The trouble is that I am rather out of sorts with you. The folk scene [2] you sent me pleases me, for the most part, and what is more significant is that in the depths of my conscience I am becoming convinced of your creative powers. Yes, my dear friend, you have taken precisely the right approach toward historical drama. Getting a thorough understanding of the facts, nosing into things, going back into the very depths and attacking things with your brains, not once, twice, but a hundred times — until you know you are right. That is how historical drama must be approached. Now, is this really so — is it only under such conditions that historical drama can be created? Let's get settled comfortably and talk.

People grow. Therefore human society also grows. The conformity of the demands of a developed person (in the sense of time) with those of the society that has developed from him (also in the sense of time) is a harmony that is much sought after, and the way to achieve it is through relentless struggle, wherever it may appear. For a modern artist the ideal of abstraction as the personal task of the artist is only half or a small fraction of the work so far as creativity is concerned. Inadvertently he arrives at this abstraction as a means of orientation or even through self-preservation. Even though the creation take root in a firm soil, under these conditions the mere ideal of abstraction must not and cannot satisfy the rebellious and searching spirit of the true artist. An ideal must materialize in the

---

1 Poet. Mussorgsky wrote several songs based on his works.
2 From Golenishchev-Kutuzov's dramatic chronicle *Discord*.

spirit of the time. The artist must command his public (imperceptibly, painlessly, without compulsion) to comprehend in its entirety the event he has selected, and to be inspired by it. He must command with love, as he does a woman he passionately adores.

An artistic revelation of the spirit of an epoch requires that the public be reminded as little as possible of habits, manner of speech, and means of expression indigenous to that public. The more remote and completely truthful (but not obvious) the horizon, the more fully and easily will the public grasp it and be inspired by it.

Arsenii, you are strong but not industrious. Delve into the thing that unsheathes your Achilles' heel. Kenevich [3] promised to write you about some books that will be helpful (*The Book of Insurrections* and *The Story of What Really Happened*) — precious books, my dear friend. You have no doubt understood me. Let's put on our hats, button up our caftans, and *au revoir*. If it is not inconvenient, remind your *maman* now and then that her good, kind heart seems very near to me even at a distance. I worshipped my own dear mother, whom I have lost for ever. [4]

[MODEST MUSSORGSKY]

◘◑◘◑◘◑◘◑◘◑◘

To *Arsenii Golenishchev-Kutuzov*

August 15, 1877

Dear Arsenii:

You sent me just a bit more and I shall remain grateful for that little bit until we meet again. I have, my friend, plunged rather successfully into *Sorochinsk*. With God's help and redoubled effort in the future I hope to complete an opera *The Fair at Sorochinsk*, whether good or bad, the season after next.

I did not start with the first act, which requires great concentration and a certain amount of liberty scenically, (my vacation hasn't started yet), but with the second act, which is the core of the entire opera. As you will recall, this act immediately follows the Intermezzo (*Night on Bare Mountain* — it will be called *The Dream of the Youth*). The scene of Khivra with the slipper, and the scene of Khivra with the priest's son and guests — all this has been composed.

---

3 Vladislav Theophilevich Kenevich (1831–79), writer and scholar.
4 His mother had died in 1865.

Now I shall set to work on the core: the tale of the Red Overcoat. It's an extremely difficult task.

You know, my friend, that your modest Modest cannot refrain from carefully searching the author and he is bold enough to reproduce in music what might slip the attention of another, immodest musician. This isn't the first time I'm becoming acquainted with Gogol; there was *Marriage* [5] and therefore his capricious prose does not frighten me. *Marriage* was an exercise within the scope of the musician, or more precisely the non-musician who wished to understand the meanderings of human expression in a direct, accurate presentation, as interpreted by the ingenious Gogol. It is a chamber study.

On a large scale it will be necessary for the speeches of the actors (each according to his own nature, his habits, and "dramatic inevitability") to be presented to the audience in relief. It will be necessary for the audience to understand all the non-artistic business of everyday human existence, and at the same time for this to be interesting artistically. Imagine, my dear friend, that everything you've read in the speeches by Gogol's characters will have to be interpreted from the stage by my characters in musical language, with nothing of Gogol changed. There have been many attempts to take the fortress by storm and this seemed to frighten many musicians, but if one can manage to capture only a small window in that impregnable fortress, one is inspired and very happy. You see, one wants to communicate many, many truths.

If only we could succeed in communicating a small shred of the truth! How great Gogol was! The pleasure of setting Pushkin to music (in *Boris*) is revived again in setting Gogol to music (in *Sorochinsk*). Pushkin wrote *Boris* in dramatic form, but not for the stage. Gogol wrote *The Fair at Sorochinsk* in the form of a story, and certainly not for the stage. But with their great creative power both these giants outlined the contours of scenic action so sharply that only the colour has to be filled in. Only woe to him who decides to take Pushkin or Gogol merely as text.

You, my friend, know the way your modest Modest has treated your artistic creations. Your modest friend is the same in his attitude toward Gogol. Since the sphere of words is the creation of the true sensitive nature of the artist, the musician is obliged to treat this creation " courteously," penetrating into its very substance, for that is the essence of what the musician intends to portray in musical

---

5 One-act opera, 1868.

form. *The truly genuine artistic cannot be capricious* since it cannot easily be portrayed in another form, and on its own account it demands profound study and sacred love. And when the artistic kinship of artists succeeds in any field of art, the path is a good one! You know this, Your Excellency, please do not be cross.

Well, dear Arsenii, that is what I've been doing. The publishers in Mother Russia are sometimes awful. Jurgenson at first liked the idea of publishing *Macabre*, but since then has remained obstinately silent. Here's something that will please you. At L. I. Shestakova's your very beautiful "The General" [6] was performed twice by Lody. (I take it upon myself to report, Your Excellency, that all who heard it trembled with delight.) You cannot imagine how strikingly unique your portrayal is when it is done by a tenor! One can hear a kind of transfiguring, inexorable love of death. To put it more precisely, it is death — coldly passionate amorous death — taking delight in death. Unheard-of freshness of impression! And P. A. Lyudin did your marvellous portrayal with such feeling! That singer is a real artist. Yes, after the war . . .

I forgot to tell you that I have written a Biblical portrait entitled *Joshua*,[7] exactly according to the Bible, and I was guided by the map of the victorious march of Joshua through Canaan. This little piece is based on themes that you know but won't recognize. That is, you won't recognize your modest Modest having set to work with the aim of ploughing through a subject. Well, I've told you everything, my friend. I will add that in *Sorochinsk*, the story about the Red Overcoat is the finale of the second act. Which means, God willing, one act of *Sorochinsk* will be ready soon.[8] The scenario is finished and that is important, extremely important — thanks to that clever A. Y. Vorobyeva-Petrova.

[MODEST MUSSORGSKY]

---

6 Song by Mussorgsky from *Dances of Death* (1875).
7 *Joshua Navin* for chorus and orchestra.
8 This opera was never completed.

CAMILLE SAINT–SAËNS

Paris, 1835 — Algiers, 1921

◉◉◉◉◉◉◉◉◉

To *Camille Bellaigue*

Cairo, January 30, 1907

My dear Friend:

With a mind as intelligent as yours, how can you be taken in by the mirages of the Wagnerites? How is it you don't see all the speciousness in that fantastic phraseology? Don't you see how inferior to you all that is? Wagner's works bringing about innovations in customs, in government, in education, in social relationships? Wagner "repudiating the bias and pretensions of the old music of static emotional states" — you say this is truth itself, and I shall have to take your word for it since I can't understand how an impassioned phrase expresses the evolution of passion rather than its lasting state. If this means that Wagner has expressed desire very well, then it's a lot of fuss about nothing.

Wagner as *redeemer!* Wagner writing for the masses! Excuse me for laughing. Nietzsche is perfectly right about this. The aspirations of the people are very small and easily satisfied. Melodrama, farce, and in music facile and vulgar melody — that's what they like. The only work by Wagner the least bit popular is *Tannhäuser* because it has tunes, ensembles, and even vulgarity.

The more I observe, the more I realize that works of art can have no significance other than an æsthetic one; in fact, that is what keeps them from being immoral — once they are conceded to have any beauty. You can find examples easily enough. *Les Huguenots* and *La Juive* are apologies for the Reformation and for Hebraism and veritable prosecuting attorney's speeches against Catholicism. No one gives this a thought when they are performed, and no Catholic has ever been shocked by them.

Would you say that it's different in the case of Richard? After hearing *Tristan*, have you ever been tempted to kill yourself, the

[235]

better to love Madame Bellaigue, and do you think she would relish that sort of love? I leave it to her judgment.

I would say that when they try to get works of art out of the realm of art, it means getting them into the realm of madness. Richard Strauss is now showing us the way.

[CAMILLE SAINT-SAËNS]

To *Camille Bellaigue*

Cairo, February 4, 1907

My dear Friend:

I am astonished — forgive me — at all you find in Palestrinian art. I myself see in it only an impassive and inexpressive art with some intention, some *indication* of expression in rare instances — in a word, the purest expression of that *art for art's sake* you don't want. Whether you like it or not, it comes down to this: art for art's sake, or, to speak clearly, form loved and cultivated for itself, is the principle and the very essence of art. The search for expression, legitimate and inevitable as it may be, is the germ of decadence, which begins the moment the search for expression takes precedence over the search for perfection of form.

Now, it happens that religious art, requiring purity and beauty above all (the kind of music in which feeling appears only in the state of brief and accessory indications) and in which the cult of form predominates — this music whose flaccid tonality hesitating between ancient modality and modern tonality seems to give off an extra-human character — such music is wonderfully suited to the church.

If the principle I have just set forth were untrue, if the search for expression constituted progress in art, the Laocoön would be superior to the Hermes of Praxiteles.

To return to the school of Palestrina, either you are reading things into it that are not there, or I do not know how to see — which is quite possible. But you will never be able to make me believe that the theme of the Pope Marcellus Mass expresses "Lord, have mercy on us."

Those "molto espressivo" directions which the Schola Cantorum keeps planting in the corners of their editions is a monstrous error, I think. Inflicting whining on that music means perverting it.

[CAMILLE SAINT-SAËNS]

MILI BALAKIREV

Nizhni-Novgorod, 1837 — St. Petersburg, 1910

❖❖❖❖❖❖❖❖❖

To *Piotr Ilyich Tchaikovsky*

[December] 1869

Since your overture [1] is practically finished and is to be performed soon, I shall tell you very frankly what I think of the themes
you sent me (I'm not using the word in Zaremba's sense). I do not
care for the first theme at all though perhaps it improves in the development, I don't know, but in the crude state in which I see it,
it has neither strength nor beauty and it does not sufficiently suggest
the character of Father Laurence. Here something like one of Liszt's
chorales (*The Night Ride, Hunnenschlacht, St. Elizabeth*) would
be very appropriate, something in the old Catholic Church style
and suitable for the Orthodox Church.

Your theme is very different — it is in the style of a quartet by
Haydn, that genius of burgher music, and it stimulates a terrible
thirst for beer. There is nothing of old-worldliness or Catholicism
about it; it's more the type of Gogol's *Comrade Kunz*, who wanted
to cut off his nose to save the money he spent on snuff. But perhaps
in the development your theme may turn out very differently, in
which case I shall eat my words.

The B-minor theme seems to me not so much a theme as a
lovely introduction for one, and after the agitated section in C
major, something very powerful and energetic should follow. I am
taking it for granted that it will really be done that way, and that
you were too lazy to write out the context.

The first theme in D-flat major is very pretty but rather spineless. The second, in the same key, is simply fascinating. I play it very
often and I could hug you for it. It has the sweetness of love, its
tenderness, its longing — in short, so much that must appeal to the
heart of that immoral German, Albrecht. I have only one objection;

---

1 *Romeo and Juliet*, first performed on March 4, 1870.

[237]

it does not sufficiently suggest an inner, mystical, spiritual love, but rather a fantastic and passionate glow, even with its slight nuance of Italian sentiment. Romeo and Juliet were not Persian lovers but Europeans. I don't know whether you will understand what I'm driving at. Whenever I talk about music I always feel the lack of appropriate words and I have to take recourse in comparison to explain myself. Offhand I can mention something in which spiritual love is expressed very well, as I see it, the second theme in Schumann's overture, *Die Braut von Messina*. This theme has its weak aspects too; it is morbid and rather sentimental at the end, but the underlying emotion is genuine.

In conclusion I shall tell you that I am most impatient to receive the entire score so that I can get a just impression of your skilful overture, which thus far is your best work. The fact that you dedicated it to me gives me the greatest pleasure. This is the first of your compositions that contains so many beautiful things that one doesn't hesitate to pronounce it good as a whole. You can't compare it with that old Melchizedek who got so drunk with sorrow that he had to dance his disgusting trepak in Arbatsky Square.[2] Send me the copied score soon, I am very eager to see it.

[Mili Balakirev]

---

2 A reference to Tchaikovsky's *Fate*.

GEORGES BIZET

Paris, 1838 — Bougival, 1875

To *Edmond Galabert* and **G**.

Vesinet, October 1866

You are both loves. I was deeply touched by your token of affection and trust in me and I read and reread your journal. It is delightful in its rambling way, charming in portraying so wonderfully the state of your minds during this trip which seems so young and spontaneous and fantastic and tender and full of caprice — I almost wanted to say of sad gaiety. You made me feel young again, don't laugh, and I remembered my travels in the Apennines. But you have a great advantage over me, you know that, you devils! And if your good hearts didn't soften your harshness, you would crush me with all your philosophy, which has never failed and never will. . . .

I understand perfectly everything you say about religion. I agree with you, but see here, let us not be unjust. We agree on a principle that, I believe, can be expressed this way: Religion is a means for the strong to exploit the weak, religion is the cloak of ambition, injustice, and vice. This progress you speak of proceeds slowly but surely; little by little it destroys all the superstitions. The truth becomes disengaged, science is popularized, religion is shaken. Soon it will fall — in several centuries — which is to say tomorrow.

That will be fine, but we should not forget that this religion, which you can do without, you, I, and several other people, has been the admirable instrument of progress. It is religion, especially the Catholic, that taught us the precepts that make it possible for us to do without it today. Ungrateful children — we murder the breast that nourished us because the food it offers us today is no longer worthy of us. We condemn that false clarity which, however, gradually accustomed our eyes to see the light. Without it we should have remained for ever blind from the cradle on.

Don't you believe that a splendid imposter like Moses made possible a significant advance in philosophy, and therefore humanity? Look at that sublime absurdity entitled the Bible. Isn't it easy to pick out from all that fine rubbish the preponderant part of the truths we know today? At that time it was necessary to clothe them in the costumes of the period; it was necessary to make them cover delivery from evil, lies, and imposture. Dogma and religion have had a fortunate and decisive influence on man. If you object on the grounds of the persecutions, the crimes and infamies committed in its name, I reply that humanity has burned its fingers in the candle. Millions of men slaughtered by other men, a drop of water in the ocean — nothing! No doubt man is not yet strong enough to cut himself off from belief. It is sad, but what can one do?

Religion is a policeman. Later on we shall also be able to manage without policemen and judges. We have already advanced a great deal, since this policeman is almost enough for us. Ask Society which it prefers — to do without policemen or without bishops. Give it an opportunity to decide, take a vote, and you will see that a large majority favours the policeman. Today the tricorne is powerful enough to restrain evil passions. The tricorne would not have had the slightest effect on the Hebrews, who didn't in the least understand what philosophy was. They needed altars, Mount Sinais with Bengal fires, and so on. One had to appeal to their eyes; later it sufficed to appeal to their imagination. Later still, the only thing we shall have to deal with is reason. I believe that the entire future belongs to the perfecting of our social contract (they're always stupidly mixing it up with politics). Once Society is perfected, no more injustice, no more discontent, no more crimes against the social contract, no more priests, policemen, crimes, adulteries, prostitution, no more quick emotions or passions, wait — no more music, no more poetry, no more Legion of Honour, no more newspapers (for this, hurrah!), especially no more theatre, no more illusion, and no more art! Confound it! It's your fault. But unhappy as you are, your relentless and inevitable progress destroys art. My poor art! Galabert is furious; I'm sure he believes none of this.

The societies most tainted with superstition have been the great promoters of art: Egypt and its architecture, Greece and its plastic art, the Renaissance and Raphael — Phidias, Mozart, Beethoven, Veronese, Weber, the madmen! The fantastic, hell, paradise, jinn, phantoms, ghosts, elves, that is the domain of art! Prove to me that we shall have art based on reason and truth and exactitude and I shall come over to your camp, bag and baggage. But I seek in vain; I see nothing but Roland at Roncevaux.[1] Not enough, and still there is a bishop, Roland's horn, and so on.

As a musician, I tell you that if you were to suppress adultery, fanaticism, crime, evil, the supernatural, there would no longer be the means for writing one note. Good Lord! Art certainly has its philosophy but you have to skin the meaning of the words to define it. *The science of knowledge.* That's what it is, except that it is completely the opposite! I am a miserable philosopher (as you see), yet I assure you that I would write better music if I believed in everything that is not true! In short, to sum up, art declines as reason advances. You don't believe this, but *it's true!* Just show me a Homer or a Dante today. With what? The imagination thrives on chimeras, visions. Suppress the chimeras and good-night imagination. No more art! Science everywhere! And if you ask me what harm in this, I shall stop and argue no further, *because you are right.* But it's a shame, a damn shame. Literature will be saved by philosophy. We shall have Voltaires. That's consoling, but we shall have some Jean-Jacques just the same, for you don't change the stuff of which man is made, and I have a horror of that hodge-podge of vice, sentimentality, philosophy, and genius which produces a Rousseau. A three-headed calf! A man with thirty-six faces. Faugh! Let's not discuss it further. A hysteric, cynic, hypocrite, republican, and sensitive into the bargain! George Sand imitates him — a terrible punishment! (Between us, I much prefer Robespierre, though he was almost without talent.) Phew! I won't reread this, for if I did, I wouldn't be able to send you this drivel, and Edmond's anger would be wasted. . . .

My dear Edmond, write me some counterpoint in syncopation "as if it were raining." Contribute to the propagation of the species, and then compose. Choose very ideal subjects, the more absurd, the better. Thanks again for your too short journal; it is a foretaste of the quartet.

Why doesn't G. try something for the theatre? True, it's a risky career, but why not ignore the risk? Adieu, good-bye to you, my dear Edmond, whom I love with the best of my heart, and to you, G., whom I already know so well without having seen you. If you have a photograph of yourself, send it to me, otherwise I shall wait until you come. An idea — in this letter I have slipped in a

---

1 *Roland à Roncevaux*, opera by Auguste Mermet (1864), based on the *Chanson de Roland*.

reproduction of a very bad subject with highly irregular features, strongly inclined to the pleasures prohibited by the true and healthy philosophy that is yours. This I admit, but I am always attracted by what is young, sincere, honest, pure, truthful, good, and intelligent, as you two are — and, without character, the best of the least perfect of men.

[GEORGES BIZET]

To *Paul Lacombe* [2]

Paris, March 11, 1867

Dear Sir:

Thank you. Your letter gave me real pleasure. If anything can make up for the indifference of a bored and apathetic public, it is surely the approbation and sympathy of men of taste and intelligence like you, who devote the major part of their existence to the cultivation of the noblest art. We both speak the same language, a language foreign, alas, to most of those who consider themselves artists. In principle our ideas are the same. Only the difference in our situations may sometimes lead to trifling disagreements between us. I am eclectic. I lived in Italy for three years and got accustomed, not to the disgraceful goings-on in music in that country, but to the temperament of some of her composers. Furthermore, my sensual nature makes me susceptible to that facile music, lazy, amorous, lascivious, and passionate all at the same time. I am German by conviction, in heart and soul, but sometimes I am led astray into bad artistic fashions. And I secretly confess to you that I find endless delight in them.

In short, I love Italian music the way one loves a courtesan, but she must be charming! After citing two thirds of *Norma*, four pieces from *I Puritani*, and three from *Sonnambula*, two acts of *Rigoletto*, one act of *Trovatore*, and almost half of *Traviata*, add *Don Pasquale* and you can throw away the rest. As for Rossini, he has his *Guillaume Tell* — his sun; and *Comte Ory*, the *Barbier*, one act of *Otello* — his satellites; for these he can be forgiven that terrible *Semiramide* and all his other sins.

---

2 In 1866 Paul Lacombe, a twenty-eight-year-old composer, began taking a correspondence course in composition from the twenty-eight-year-old Bizet, which continued until Bizet's death.

I wished to make this little confession to you so that my advice may have the proper import. Like you, I place Beethoven above the greatest and most celebrated. I think the Choral Symphony is the apex of our art. *Dante, Michelangelo, Shakespeare, Homer, Beethoven, Moses!* Neither Mozart with his divine sense of form, nor Weber with his powerful, colossal originality, nor Meyerbeer with his striking dramatic genius can, to my mind, contest the palm of the *Titan,* the *Prometheus* of music. He is overwhelming! You see we still understand each other.

Now I come to you and your two pieces:

Trio: Page 1. The beginning is a little dry; your C sharp abandoned by the strings will sound awkward with the C natural on the piano. I advise it this way.

I think this is really what you want.

If you insist on separating the C sharp from the C natural, it would have to be written like this:

but I much prefer the first example. . . .

I have been perfectly sincere about the Trio; I will also be sincere about the Reverie. Well, I don't like it very much. I hope you won't hold it against me. I owe you the truth and I shall tell it to you every time just the same. Some of your things irritate me. In art, no indulgence. I have no detailed criticism of this piece to give you. After pointing out a little reminiscence of the septet from *Les Troyens* [3] on the last page,

---

3 Opera by Berlioz.

I have nothing to say expect about what concerns the work in general. It is slack, dull. The idea is slight. The poetry isn't refined enough to warrant the dreamy tone you adopt. Of course it has a certain languor, a certain charm, but not enough. Obviously it isn't bad, but you should and can do better. Believe me. My judgment will seem severe. Wait awhile. Put it aside and when you look at it again, after having almost forgotten it, you will agree with me. You will find it a sort of soap-bubble. I have always noticed that my least successful compositions are those I cherish most at birth. I distrust those things which smack of improvisation.

Look at Beethoven, take his vaguest, most ethereal works; they are always *deliberate*, always *controlled*. He dreams and yet his idea has body. One can grasp it. Only one man knew how to write quasi-improvised music, or at least seemingly improvised — Chopin. He has a delightful personality, strange, inimitable, he can't be imitated. To sum up, before condemning my opinion of your piece, do me the favour of putting it in a box for two or three months. After that examine it and judge, and you will judge rightly.

I also want to talk to you about your plans for the future. You don't want to consider the theatre? All right, you feel and you know what you should do. But you haven't the right to dismiss the symphony. You must work at the symphony. Take my word for it, you will do it well. Be ambitious and I shall be ambitious for you. I warn you I shall keep after you on this.

I am leaving my letter unsealed. I am going out to dine and then to *Don Carlos*.[4] I'll give you the news.

Two o'clock in the morning

Only two words. I am stunned, exhausted. Verdi is no longer Italian. He wants to do a Wagner. He has thrown out the sauce without saving the roast. It has no head or tail. It has no defects, but also none of his good qualities. He wants to be stylish and succeeds only in being pretentious. It is astonishing — a complete and utter failure. Perhaps the Exposition [5] will prolong the agony, but it's a lost battle. The public, especially, is furious. The artists may perhaps forgive him for an unfortunate attempt, which, nevertheless, is proof of his taste and artistic integrity. But the good public came to be entertained and I fear me they won't bite again. The press will be murderous.

---

4 First performance of Verdi's *Don Carlos* at the Paris Opéra.
5 Paris International Exposition.

Good-bye and believe me, always with the warmest feelings, devotedly and affectionately,

GEORGES BIZET

❀❀❀❀❀❀❀❀❀❀

To *Madame Halévy* [6]

May 29, 1871

Dear Madame Halévy:

Here is the truth. The last cannon-shot was fired yesterday, Sunday, at half past two. The Tuilleries (all the part near the gardens), the façade of the Ministère des Finances, the Conseil d'État, the Cour des Comptes, and, they say, the Caisse de Crédit Municipal, the Préfecture de Police, the greater part of the Palais de Justice, a good part of the Hôtel de Ville, forty or fifty houses — destroyed! Saint-Chapelle saved! All the rest is the invenion of that odious race, the journalists.

The crimes committed are appalling enough. Society is sufficiently justified in taking revenge by applying the laws in their full force, without those boulevard fops thinking it necessary to plunge all the provinces into anxiety. When our troubles are bad enough already, it is wicked to exaggerate them.

Your brother saw the situation clearly three months ago. I was blind and unfortunately, the directors of our national defence were no less blind. There is no more time for recrimination. Our most urgent need is to rid every land of this powerful association of scoundrels. The next concern of our leaders should be not to let themselves be carried away by the Catholic reaction. Let us hope.

Thus far no news of hostages. Has the Archbishop of Paris been shot? Unfortunately, what seems certain is the death of my poor and excellent friend Chaudey, honest and brave republican, shot by those bandits!

Again I've heard, on the best authority, that the rue de la Victoire, rue Lepeletier, rue de Douai, and boulevard Malesherbes (40 and above) have definitely not been touched, and so we were not hit. Melanie and Flore have returned to Passy; they are well. You can feel relieved. As for us, we have nothing to fear since we are *protected* (!) by a German garrison.

---

6 Wife of the composer Fromental Halévy, and Bizet's mother-in-law.

Excuse the disorderliness of this letter, but I wanted to reassure you completely. There has been some burning of oil, but not in the quantities described in the *Gaulois, Journal de Paris*, and the other papers. In short, the intentions were as criminal as possible, but the results, though disastrous, are not irreparable. The Louvre, the Archives, the Registrar's Office, the Registry of National Debt, everything that constitutes the organization of an intelligent and artistic society has been saved.

I won't talk much about Wagner today. How unfair you are! But then, it is the lot of these great geniuses to be misunderstood by their contemporaries. Wagner is no friend of mine and I hold him in slight esteem, but I cannot forget the immense pleasure I owe this original genius. The charm of that music is utterly indescribable. It is voluptuousness, tenderness, love! If I played you some for a week, you would dote on it. The Germans, who, unfortunately, are mighty important to us in music, have grasped the fact that Wagner is one of their most solid pillars. The German nineteenth-century spirit is incarnate in that man. You yourself do not have to be told how much cruelty there is in contempt for a great artist. Luckily for Wagner, he is gifted with such insolent pride that criticism cannot touch his heart — granted he has a heart, which I doubt. I don't go as far as you; I shall not pronounce the name of Beethoven beside Wagner's. Beethoven is not a man, but a god! Like Shakespeare, like Homer, like Michelangelo! But take the most intelligent audience, let them hear the greatest page our art possesses, the Choral Symphony — they will understand nothing, absolutely nothing. The experiment has been tried: they try it over again each year with the same result. Only Beethoven died fifty years ago and it is the fashion to consider this beautiful.

Judge for *yourself*, forgetting everything you've heard people say, forgetting the stupid and nasty articles and the nastiest book written by Wagner, and you will see. It is not the music of the future — which means nothing — but it is, as you so well put it, the music of all times, because it is to be admired. Well, you're not convinced, of course, and you're not the only one. Voltaire did not understand Shakespeare because he was prevented by the *conventions* that he took to be the truth. You are prevented also, and from these last pages you will believe only one thing — that I love you with all my heart.

GEORGES BIZET

Understand that if I thought I was imitating Wagner, despite my admiration, I would never write another note in my life. Imitation is for fools. It is better to write badly like oneself than like others. Besides, the more beautiful the model, the more ridiculous the imitation. There have been imitations of Michelangelo, Shakespeare, and Beethoven. Heaven knows what horror this rage for imitating has afflicted us with.

PIOTR ILYICH TCHAIKOVSKY

Votkinsk, 1840 — St. Petersburg, 1893

✥❧✥❧✥❧✥❧✥

To *Vladimir Stepanovich Shilovsky* [1]

Moscow, July 6, 1877

Volodya:

Your ranks are increasing. I am getting married today. About my future spouse I can only say that she is a respectable girl, very much in love with me, extremely poor, and pretty enough. What will happen in the future, I don't know. You understand from this letter that consequently you are not to expect me. Much as I love Usovo, and pleasant as it would be to see you, after I am married I shall have to live with my wife. But toward the end of summer, if possible, I shall travel somewhere to nurse my catarrh.

I am entering upon matrimony not without trepidation and alarm, but with the complete conviction that it is necessary and better to do this now while some youth still remains than later on.

I spent all of June at Kostya's, where it was very pleasant, and I wrote two whole acts of my new opera, not *Ephraim*, but, imagine, *Yevgeny Onyegin*. A rather daring idea, but I wrote with great satisfaction and enthusiasm.

I came here two days ago and had time to arrange everything for the wedding celebration today. The matter had already been decided at the end of May, but nobody has known anything about it until now. There will be only two witnesses at the wedding, Brother Tolya and Kotek.[2] My bride's surname is Milyukova. We are leaving this evening for St. Petersburg, where I shall have to introduce my wife to Papa.

And now farewell, my soul. I hope that all is well in Usovo and that your health is good. Give my regards to your wife and the

---

1 Former student and close friend of Tchaikovsky.
2 Yosif Kotek (1855–85), violinist.

Count. I am very sorry that I shall not be visiting Usovo, of which I retain the pleasantest memories. Write me at the Conservatory in Moscow, where I shall be in about ten days.[3]

Your

P. TCHAIKOVSKY

❂❁❂❁❂❁❂❁❂

To *Nadezhda Filaretovna von Meck* [4]

Vienna, December 8, 1877

I am still in Vienna. Yesterday I heard that my servant would leave Moscow on Saturday. Though I gave him the most detailed instructions about what to do on the journey, I have no idea how he will manage to cross the frontier since he doesn't know a word of any foreign language. I imagine there will be many tragicomic incidents. Sometimes I think it was not very wise to have sent for a Russian servant. But I don't know what else I could have done since I cannot bear complete solitude. Besides, it will be comforting to my brothers to know that I am not completely alone. Didn't you, too, advise me not to be alone? You even wrote me about it. Despite the coming hour of separation from my brother, I spent the last days very pleasantly. Kotek lives in our hotel. We play 4-hands frequently and talk a great deal about music.

I do not look into the future and flatter myself with the hope that all will be well. Like you, I am superstitious. For a long time I have had a strong feeling that I am under the guardianship of Fate, perhaps, or some other kind spirit who protects me from possible danger or misfortune. There will be many difficult moments, but in the end everything will be all right.

I have seen Wagner's *Walküre*. The performance was excellent. The orchestra was superb, and the best singers did everything within their power — and yet it was tiresome. What a Don Quixote Wagner is! He expends all his energy pursuing the impossible, and if all this time he would only follow the natural bent of his extraordinary gift, he could evoke a whole world of musical beauty. I believe Wagner is, by nature, a symphonist. He is gifted with genius, but he is ruined by his tendencies; his inspiration is paralysed by the theories that he invented himself and that he insists on putting into

---

3 The marriage lasted only a few weeks.
4 An admirer of Tchaikovsky who granted him an annuity for thirteen years.

practice at any cost. In his efforts to achieve *reality, truth,* and *rationalism* in opera, he lets *music* slip quite out of sight, and in his four latest operas [5] it is conspicuous chiefly by its absence. I cannot consider music something that consists of kaleidoscopic, shifting phrases that succeed one another without a break and never come to an end; that is, never give the ear the slightest opportunity to rest upon musical form. Not a single broad, rounded melody, nor one moment of repose for the singer! The singer must always follow the orchestra and be careful not to miss his note, which has no more importance in the score than some note for the fourth horn.

But there is no doubt that Wagner is a magnificent symphonist. I will prove to you by just one example how far the symphonic prevails over the operatic in his operas. You have probably heard his celebrated Ride of the Valkyries. What a great and marvellous picture! We actually seem to see these fierce giants flying on their magic steeds through thunder and lightning. In the concert hall this piece makes an extraordinary impression. On the stage, the view of cardboard rocks, canvas clouds, and the soldiers who run about awkwardly in the background — in short, when you see this very inadequate theatrical heaven, which makes a poor pretence of realizing the infinite realm above, the music loses all power of expression. Here the stage does not enhance the effect, but helps to spoil it. Finally, I cannot understand, and never shall, why the *Nibelungen* should be considered a literary masterpiece. As a national saga, perhaps, but as literature — certainly not!

Wotan, Brünnhilde, Fricka, and the rest are all so impossible, so inhuman, that it is very difficult to feel any sympathy with their destinies. And so little life! For three quarters of an hour Wotan reproaches Brünnhilde for her disobedience. How boring! And with it all there are many fine and beautiful passages of purely symphonic character.

Yesterday Kotek and I looked through a new symphony by Brahms (No. 1, in C minor), a composer whom the Germans exalt to the sky. He has no charm for me. I find him cold and obscure, full or pretensions, and without any real depth. On the whole it seems to me that Germany is deteriorating in music. I think that the French are now coming to the fore. They have many new and fine talents. Recently I heard Delibes's very skilful music — in its own style — for the ballet *Sylvia*. I became acquainted with this music in the pianoforte arrangement some time ago, but the splendid per-

5 *Tristan und Isolde, Siegfried, Die Meistersinger, Götterdämmerung.*

formance of it by the Vienna orchestra quite fascinated me, especially the first part. *Swan Lake* is poor stuff compared with *Sylvia*. Nothing during the last few years has charmed me as much as *Carmen* and Delibes's ballet. Perhaps Russia will have a new word to say and also the rest of Europe. But in Germany there is a marked decline and Wagner is the representative of the period of decadence.

Yours,

P. TCHAIKOVSKY

❦❦❦❦❦❦❦❦

To *Nadezhda Filaretovna von Meck*

San Remo, January 5, 1878

Dear Nadezhda Filaretovna:

Yesterday I was in a state of complete madness. Didn't I say something stupid and rather indelicate in yesterday's letter? If so, for Heaven's sake, pay no attention to it. This is what happened recently: I received an appointment, which seemed rather delicate to me, to the Paris Exposition, with the condition that I go there right away and live there until the end of the Exposition. This drove me into a panic, though, being completely free and independent, I could have refused it; instead I staged a whole drama.

Only today did I come to my senses and realize how stupid my reaction was. I imagined it was my duty to go there, that I should be acting rudely, selfishly, stupidly, if I refused to accept such a flattering position. I felt that my brothers and sisters and you and all the Conservatory people, and all those sympathetic toward me would suddenly begin to hate and despise me for my laziness, faint-heartedness, etc. At last, after a struggle which probably cost a few days of my life, I realized that it would be better to refuse now than after arriving there, and then find myself in a state of complete confusion.

Today I am calm, but I still don't feel quite well. I went to the post office just now and found your letter. I can't tell you how delighted I am. Right now I need some such expression of warm feeling and there is so much of it in your kind letter. I shall answer you in detail.

All the new Petersburg composers are very talented, but they are all filled with the most horrible presumptuousness and a purely amateur conviction of their superiority over all other musicians in the universe. The one exception, recently, is Rimsky-Korsakov.

Like the rest, he is also self-taught, but lately he has undergone a complete change. He is very earnest, honest, and conscientious by nature. As a very young man he fell in with a crowd that first solemnly assured him he was a genius and then proceeded to persuade him that he had no need of study, that academies were destructive to all inspiration and succeeded in drying up creative activity.

At first he believed all this. His earliest compositions manifest striking ability and lack of training in theory. The circle to which he belonged was a mutual admiration society. Each member tried to imitate the work produced by the other members, which they proclaimed to be something quite magnificent. Consequently the whole circle suffered from one-sidedness, lack of individuality, and mannerisms. Rimsky-Korsakov is the only one among them who discovered, five years ago, that the doctrines preached by this circle had no sound foundation, that their mockery of the schools and the classical masters, their denial of authority and the masterpieces, was nothing but ignorance.

I have a letter dating from that time which moved me deeply. Rimsky-Korsakov was overcome by despair when he realized how many unprofitable years he had wasted, and that he was following a road leading nowhere. He began to study with such zeal that academic theory soon became the indispensable atmosphere for him. During one summer he completed innumerable exercises in counterpoint and sixty-four fugues, ten of which he sent me to look over. From contempt for academic training Rimsky-Korsakov suddenly turned to the cult of musical technique. Shortly after, his symphony and his quartet [6] appeared. Both works are full of obscurity and — as you will justly observe — bear the stamp of dry pedantry. At present he seems to be passing through a crisis, and it is hard to predict how it will end. Either he will turn out to be a great master or he will get lost in contrapuntal intricacies.

C. Cui is a gifted amateur. His music is not original, but graceful and elegant; it is too coquettish, too "made-up," one might say. At first it is agreeable, but it soon satiates us. That is because Cui's specialty is not music, but fortification, which keeps him busy giving lectures in the various military schools of St. Petersburg. He himself once told me that he could compose only by picking out his melodies and harmonies at the piano. Whenever he hit upon a pretty idea, he would work it up in detail, and this process was very lengthy, so that his opera *Ratcliffe*, for instance, took him ten years

---

6 Symphony No. 3 in C major; String Quartet in F major, op. 12.

to complete. But, as I said, we cannot deny that he has talent of a sort — and at least taste and fine instincts.

Borodin — age 50 — professor of chemistry at the Academy of Medicine — also has talent, very great talent, which, however, has come to naught for lack of instruction and because blind Fate has led him into the science laboratories instead of a vital musical life. He hasn't as much taste as Cui, and his technique is so poor that he cannot write one measure without assistance.

Mussorgsky, as you so rightly remark, is a lost soul. His gifts are perhaps the most remarkable of all, but his nature is narrow and he has no aspirations toward self-perfection. He has been led astray too easily by the ridiculous theories of his circle and the belief in his own genius. Besides, his nature is not very delicate and he likes what is coarse, rough, and ugly. He is the exact opposite of his friend Cui, who has little depth but who is always correct and refined. Mussorgsky enjoys his lack of polish and even seems proud of his ignorance. He writes just as it comes to him, believing blindly in the infallibility of his genius, though, as a matter of fact, flashes of his highly original talent do come out now and then.

Balakirev is the greatest personality of the whole circle, but he relapsed into silence before accomplishing much. He has a remarkable talent, which various fatal hindrances helped to blot out. After having announced his agnosticism rather widely, he suddenly became "pious." Now he spends all his time in church, he fasts, kisses the relics, and does very little else. Despite his great gifts, he has done a good deal of harm. For instance, it was he who ruined Korsakov's early career by assuring him he had no need to study. He is the inventor of all the theories of this remarkable circle which brings together so many immature, badly developed, or prematurely decaying talents.

These are my frank opinions of these gentlemen. What a sad phenomenon! So many talents from which — except for Rimsky-Korsakov — we can hardly dare to hope for anything serious. But this is always Russia's trouble; vast forces are prevented by the fatal shadow of a Plevna from taking to the open field and fighting as they should. But these vast forces exist. Thus, Mussorgsky, with all his ugliness, speaks a new idiom. It may not be beautiful, but it is new. We can reasonably hope that some day Russia will bring forth a whole school of strong men who will open up new roads in art.

Anyway our roughness is better than that poor, seemingly serious pose of a Brahms. The Germans are hopelessly played out.

But with us there is always the hope that the moral Plevna will fall and that our strength will make itself felt. So far, however, little has been accomplished. The French have made great progress. True, Berlioz has only just begun to be appreciated, ten years after his death, but they have many new talents and they are against routine. In France the struggle against routine is a very difficult matter, for the French are extremely conservative in art. They were the last nation to recognize Beethoven. Even as late as the forties they considered him a *madman* or *eccentric*. The foremost of the French critics, Fétis, bemoaned the fact that Beethoven had committed so many sins against the laws of harmony, and obligingly *corrected* these mistakes twenty-five years later.

Among the modern French composers, Bizet and Delibes are my favourites. I do not know the overture *Patrie* you wrote me about, but I am very familiar with Bizet's opera *Carmen*. The music is not profound, but it is so fascinating in its simplicity, so full of vitality, so sincere, that I have almost learned it by heart from beginning to end. I have already told you what I think of Delibes. In their efforts toward progress the French are not so rash as our younger men; unlike Borodin and Mussorgsky, they do not go beyond the range of possibility. . . .

I am very tired and shall close my letter for today. Farewell, my dear, much beloved Nadezhda Filaretovna. Thank you for your letter.

Yours,

P. Tchaikovsky

❖❄❖❄❖❄❖❄❖

To *Nadezhda Filaretovna von Meck*

Florence, March 1, 1878

Your letter today brought me infinite joy, dearest Nadezhda Filaretovna! I am inexpressibly delighted that you are pleased with the symphony [No. 4] and that while hearing it you felt just as I did when writing it, and that my music found its way to your heart.

You ask whether I had a particular program in mind when I composed this symphony. I generally reply to questions of this sort about my symphonic works: nothing of the sort. Actually it is extremely difficult to answer this question. How can one interpret those vague feelings which course through one during the composition of an instrumental work, without reference to a definite subject? It is a purely lyrical process. A sort of confession of the soul in music; an accumulation of material flowing forth again in notes just as the lyric poet pours himself out in verse. The difference is that music possesses much richer means of expression and it is a more subtle medium for translating the thousand shifting moments of the feelings of the soul.

Generally speaking, the germ of a future composition comes suddenly and unexpectedly. When the soil is fertile — that is, if the inclination for the work is present — it takes root with amazing force and rapidity, shooting up through the earth and putting forth branches, leaves, and finally flowers. I cannot describe the creative process in any other way than by means of this simile. The great difficulty is that the seed must appear when conditions are favourable; the rest happens by itself.

It would be useless to attempt to put into words the sense of incomparable bliss that comes over me when a new idea awakens in me and begins to assume definite shape. I forget everything and behave like a madman. Everything inside me starts trembling and quivering; hardly have I begun the sketch before one thought pursues the next. In the middle of this magic process it frequently happens that some external interruption awakens me from my hypnotic state. The bell rings, my servant comes in, the clock strikes, reminding me that I must take care of some business. Such interruptions are really dreadful. Sometimes they cut off the thread of inspiration for a considerable length of time so that I have to seek it again, often in vain.

In such cases cool headwork and technical knowledge have to come to my assistance. Even in the works of the great masters we find moments when the organic sequence stops and we can observe a seam where the parts of the whole are pasted together artificially. But this cannot be helped. If that condition of mind and soul which we call *inspiration* were to last a long time without interruption, no artist could possibly survive it. The strings would break and the instrument would be shattered into fragments. It is necessary for the principal ideas and general outline of a work to come without racking one's brains, as the result of that supernatural and inexplicable force we call inspiration.

But I have wandered from the point without replying to your question. *Our* symphony [7] does have a program; that is, its content

---

7 Tchaikovsky met Madame von Meck while at work on his Fourth Symphony, which he dedicated to her.

can be expressed in words and I shall tell you — and you alone — the meaning of the entire work and its individual movements. Of course I can do so only in regard to its general outlines.

The introduction is the kernel, the leading idea of the entire work:

Fate, that inexorable force which holds back our aspirations toward the goal of happiness; it watches jealously lest our peace and happiness might be complete and cloudless; like the sword of Damocles, this force hangs perpetually over our heads and it continually embitters our hearts. It is inevitable and unconquerable. The only course is to submit and lament, inwardly.

The feeling of hopeless despair grows stronger and more poignant. Isn't it better to turn away from reality and lose oneself in dreams?

Oh joy! A sweet, tender dream enfolds me. A bright and serene presence leads me on.

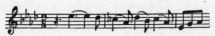

How lovely! Now the first theme of the Allegro is very remote. Deeper and deeper the soul sinks into dreams. Everything that was dark and dismal is forgotten. Here is happiness! It is but a dream. Fate roughly awakens us.

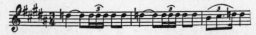

And thus life is only a constant alternation between grim truth and fleeting dreams of joy. There is no refuge. The waves drive us hither and thither until the sea swallows us up. That, approximately, is the program of the first movement.

The second movement expresses another phase of loneliness. Now it is the sadness stealing over us at evening when we sit alone indoors, tired of work, while the book we picked up for relaxation has slipped from our fingers, unnoticed. A long procession of old memories streams by. How sad to realize how much is *past and gone!* But these recollections of youth are sweet. We regret the past though we have neither the courage nor the desire to begin a new life. We are weary of life. We should like to rest for a while and look back, remembering many things. There were times when young blood coursed through our veins and life gave us all we asked. There were also moments of sorrow and irreparable loss. All this has receded so far into the past. How sad, but sweet, to lose ourselves in this!

In the third movement no definite feelings are expressed. In this there are only capricious arabesques, intangible things that come into a man's head when he has been drinking wine and his nerves are rather disturbed. His mood is neither happy nor sad. He thinks of nothing in particular. His fancy freely follows its flight and it draws the strangest patterns. Suddenly memory recalls the picture of tipsy peasants and a street song. From afar we hear the sounds of a military band. These are the confused images that course through our brains as we fall asleep. They have no relation to reality, but are queer and wild and bizarre.

The fourth movement. If you find no reason for happiness in yourself, look at others. Go among the people and observe how they enjoy life and give themselves up entirely to merry-making. A rustic holiday is portrayed. Hardly have we had time to forget ourselves in the spectacle of other people's happiness when indefatigable Fate reminds us once more of its presence. Others pay no attention to us. They do not spare us a glance nor bother to notice that we are sad and lonely. How merry, how joyful they all are! All their feelings are so light, so simple. Now, would you still say that all the world is immersed in sorrow? Happiness does exist, simple and unspoiled. Take joy in the joy of others. That makes life tolerable.

I can tell you no more about the symphony, dear friend. Of course my description is not very clear nor satisfactory. But herein lies the peculiarity of instrumental music: we cannot analyze it. As Heine said, "Where words leave off, music begins."

It is getting late. I won't tell you anything about Florence in this letter except one thing — I shall always have a pleasant memory of this place. The end of next week, around the 24th, I plan to go to Switzerland, where I expect to spend the whole of March very quietly, composing in various small forms. So when you receive this letter my address will be again: Clarens, Canton de Vaud, Villa

Richelieu. My dear, I thank you for today's letter. Thus far, not one word from my Moscow friends. I'll write you about their opinions in detail. Last night I went to a public theatre and laughed a good deal. The Italians have a coarse sense of humour, devoid of refinement and elegance, but extremely captivating.

[PIOTR ILYICH TCHAIKOVSKY]

PS. Just as I was putting this letter in the envelope, I began reading it over and I had misgivings about the confused and incomplete program I am sending you. This is the first time in my life I have tried to put my musical ideas and forms into words and phrases. I haven't been very successful. I was horribly out of sorts all the time I was working on this symphony last winter, and it is a true echo of my state of mind at the time. But only an echo. How could one possibly reproduce this in clear and precise language? I don't know. I have already forgotten a good deal. Only the general impression of my passionate and sorrowful experiences has remained. I am very, very anxious to know what my friends in Moscow will have to say about this work.

⚬ᛇ⚬ᛇ⚬ᛇ⚬ᛇ⚬ᛇ⚬ᛇ⚬

To *Nadezhda Filaretovna von Meck*

Clarens, March 28, 1878

My dear Friend:

Do not be surprised at my starting all my letters with news about the weather. How could one not talk about it when for almost three weeks we have been living in the hope of good weather and thus far haven't had any. There were only two good days. Today again, as keeps happening lately, it is cold, grey, damp, and sad. I am beginning to be irritated and indignant.

Yesterday I received your letter with the news of Rubinstein's concert. I am so pleased that you liked my concerto.[8] I knew from the first that Nikolay Grigoryevich [9] would play it splendidly. The work was originally intended for him and I took his tremendous virtuosity into consideration. I was so glad to learn from your letter that you follow every new musical event attentively. Hardly does a new concerto by Max Bruch appear but you know all about it. I do not know it yet, nor the Goldmark concerto you mention. I

---

8 Piano Concerto No. 1, in B-flat minor, op. 23, composed in 1875.
9 N. G. Rubinstein, brother of Anton Rubinstein; pianist and composer.

know only one of his orchestral works, the Overture to *Sakuntala*, and a quartet. Both of these are clever and agreeable. Goldmark is one of the few German composers who have some originality and freshness of invention.

Why don't you like Mozart? In this our opinions differ, dear friend. I not only like Mozart, I worship him. To me the most beautiful opera ever written is *Don Giovanni*. You, who have such fine taste in music, must surely love this pure and ideal artist.

It is true that Mozart used his gift too generously and often wrote without inspiration because he was compelled to do so by poverty. But read his biography by Otto Jahn and you will see he could not help it. Even Bach and Beethoven have left a considerable number of inferior works, not worthy of being mentioned in the same breath as their masterpieces. Occasionally Fate compelled them to lower their art to the level of a handicraft. But think of Mozart's operas, of two or three of his symphonies, his Requiem, the six quartets dedicated to Haydn, and the G-minor String Quintet. Do you feel no charm in these works?

True, Mozart reaches neither the depths nor the heights of Beethoven; his range is not so wide. And since in life, too, he remained a careless child to the end of his days, his music does not have that subjectively tragic quality which is expressed so powerfully in Beethoven. But this did not prevent him from creating an objectively tragic type, the most superb and wonderful human presentation ever depicted in music. I mean Donna Anna in *Don Giovanni*. Oh, how difficult it is to make anyone see and feel in music what we see and feel ourselves! I am quite incapable of describing to you what I felt on hearing *Don Giovanni*, especially the scene where the noble figure of the beautiful, proud, revengeful woman appears on the stage. Nothing in any opera has ever impressed me so deeply. Afterwards, when Donna Anna recognizes in Don Giovanni the man who has wounded her pride and killed her father, and her anger bursts out like a rushing torrent in that magnificent recitative, and that aria later on, when every note of the orchestra seems to speak of her wrath and pride and actually quiver with horror — I could cry out and weep from the overpowering strain on the emotions. And her lament over her father's body, the duet with Don Ottavio where she swears vengeance, her arioso in the great sextet in the churchyard — these are incomparable, superb operatic scenes!

I love the music of *Don Giovanni* so much that even as I write you, I could shed tears of agitation and emotion. In his chamber music Mozart fascinates me by his purity and distinction of style and his exquisite handling of the parts. Here, too, there are things that bring tears to our eyes. I shall mention only the adagio of the G-minor String Quintet. No one else has ever known how to interpret so beautifully and exquisitely in music the feeling of resignation and inconsolable sorrow. Every time Laub [10] played the adagio I had to hide in the farthest corner of the concert-room so that others would not see how much this music affected me.

I could go on speaking interminably about that radiant genius whom I worship. Though I am used to considerable variety of taste in music, and though I certainly appreciate freedom from authority, I must confess, my dear, that I should like very much to convert you to Mozart. I know that would be difficult. I have known some other people who also understood and loved music very much but did not recognize Mozart. I have tried in vain to open up to them the beauty in his music, but never have I wished to convert anyone into a Mozart-admirer so much as I now want to convert you.

Frequently chance circumstances influence our musical preferences. The music of *Don Giovanni* was the first music to produce an overwhelming effect on me and it aroused in me a holy ecstasy that bore fruit later on. Through it I entered the realm of artistic beauty where only the greatest geniuses dwell. Until that time I had known only Italian opera. Mozart is responsible for my having dedicated my life to music. He gave the first impetus to my musical strength; he made me love music more than anything else in the world. That may have great significance in my exclusive love of Mozart and I cannot require everyone I love to feel the same way toward him. But if I can somehow help change your opinion of him, I shall be very happy. I should be delighted if some day, for example, after listening to the Adagio in the G minor, you would write me that you were moved.

Now I must ask your forgiveness for speaking at such length about Mozart. But how could I not want my dear, best, incomparable friend to worship the one I worship over all musicians? How could I not try to make you feel moved and carried away by that music which makes me tremble with indescribable bliss?

I sleep much better now though I am not quite well yet. The heart disturbances are not serious, one of the symptoms of nervousness. When it becomes unbearable, I apply cold compresses to my

---

10 Ferdinand Laub (1832–75), violin virtuoso.

heart and they finally quiet me down. I shall start the cold-water treatment in Moscow. Here it is tied up with too many difficulties.

I finished the concerto [11] today. All I have to do is copy it, play it several times (with Kotek, who is still here), and do the instrumentation. Tomorrow I'll start copying it and clean up the details. The news that you go to concerts often cheers me up; it means you are well. Give Milochka a thousand greetings. Be well, my dear.

Yours with endless love,
P. TCHAIKOVSKY

To *Nadezhda Filaretovna von Meck*

Kamenka, July 6, 1878

Your letter has come, dear N. F., and I hasten to reply. You want to know my methods of composing? That is a rather difficult question, my friend, because the circumstances under which compositions are born vary a great deal. But I shall try to describe to you in a general way how I work, and to explain the process of composition I must first divide my compositions into two categories:

1. Those written on my own initiative, through sudden inclination and urgent inner necessity.
2. Those inspired by external means such as the request of a friend, or publisher, or commissions; for example, my Cantata written for the Polytechnic Exposition, or the *Slavic March*, written for a Red Cross concert.

I hasten to explain that, as shown by experience, the value of a work does not depend upon which category it belongs to. Frequently a composition that was artificially engendered turns out quite successfully, while pieces invented wholly through my own inspiration are sometimes less successful for various incidental reasons. The circumstances surrounding the composer at the time of composition, upon which his state of mind depends, are very important. The artist must have tranquillity when he is creating. In this sense, creative activity is always objective, even musical creativity, and those who think that the artist can use his talent to relieve himself of specific feelings of the moment are mistaken. The sad or happy emotions he expresses are always and invariably retrospective. With no particular reason for rejoicing, I can experience a happy creative mood, and on the other hand, in the happiest circum-

---

[11] Violin Concerto, op. 35.

stances I might write music filled with darkness and despair. In short, the artist lives a double life, an everyday, human one, and an artistic one, and these two lives do not always coincide. Anyway I repeat that to compose, the important thing is to rid oneself of the troubles of everyday existence and to surrender oneself unconditionally to the artistic life. But I am digressing and I must return to my classification.

For compositions belonging to the first or inspired-from-within category, not even the smallest effort of will is necessary. It is enough to submit to one's inner voice, and if the everyday life does not rise up to crush the artistic life, work proceeds with the most wonderful ease. One forgets everything, the spirit trembles with sweet excitement, and before one has time to follow the swift flight to its end, time has gone by unperceived. There is something somnambulistic in this state — "*on ne s'entend pas vivre.*" It is impossible to explain these moments. Whatever emerges from the pen at such times, or merely remains in the head, is always of value and, unless interrupted from without, will be the artist's best work. It is unfortunate that outside interruptions are absolutely unavoidable. One must go to work, one is summoned to dinner, a letter comes, and so on. That is why compositions in which musical beauty is evenly balanced throughout are rare. That explains why there are seams, ends hanging out, unevenness, irrelevance.

For commissioned work one sometimes has to create one's own inspiration. Very often one must first overcome laziness and lack of inclination. Then there are various impediments. Sometimes victory comes easily, sometimes inspiration entirely escapes me. But I believe it is the duty of an artist never to submit, for laziness is a strong human trait, and nothing is more harmful to an artist than to let laziness get the better of him. One cannot afford to sit and wait for inspiration; she is a guest who does not visit the lazy but comes to those who call her. Perhaps there is good reason for the charge that Russia lacks creative activity and that the Russian is terribly lazy. He loves to procrastinate; he has natural talent, but also natural lack of self-discipline. One must acquire this; one must conquer oneself and not lapse into dilettantism, which affected even so powerful a talent as Glinka. Endowed with great original powers of creation, he lived to a ripe old age and yet wrote amazing little. Read his memoirs and you'll see that he composed like a dilettante, at his leisure, when the mood came. We are proud of Glinka, yet we must admit that he did not fulfil the task his genius set before him.

Both his operas, despite wonderful and quite original beauty, suffer from striking inequality of style. Pure and gracious loveliness is followed by childish naïveté and insipidity. What would have happened had Glinka been born in some other stratum of society, if he had lived under different conditions and had worked as an artist who, recognizing his strength, felt it his duty to perfect his talent to the utmost, instead of writing music like a dilettante because he had nothing else to do?

I have explained that I write through inclination, stimulated by a higher, unanalysed power of inspiration that either appears or does not appear when summoned, and in the latter case my work is not warmed by real feeling. I hope you will not suspect me of self-praise, my friend, when I tell you that my appeal to inspiration is never in vain. I can only say that this power, which I have called a capricious guest, long ago became so accustomed to me that we live inseparably and she leaves me only when she feels herself superfluous because my everyday human life has temporarily intruded.

But the cloud always disappears and she comes again. So I could say that in my normal state of mind I write music always, anywhere, at every moment of the day. Sometimes I curiously watch that busy flow of creation which, quite by itself, apart from the conversation I may be having at the moment or the people I am with, keeps functioning in that compartment of my brain which is dedicated to music. Sometimes it is the elaboration, the melodic detail of a little work I have planned before; at other times a completely new, original musical idea appears and I try to retain it in my memory. Where it comes from is a mystery.

I shall now sketch for you the actual process of composition — but let me postpone it until after dinner. *Au revoir*. If you only knew how difficult it is to write to you about this subject, but how agreeable!

Two o'clock

I write my sketches on any piece of paper at hand, a scrap of notepaper sometimes, and I write in very abbreviated form. The melody never enters my head without its accompanying harmony. In general, these two elements of music, together with the rhythm, cannot be conceived separately; each melodic idea carries its own inevitable harmony and rhythm. When the harmony is very complicated, I have to indicate the voice parts in the sketch. If the harmony is simple, I often jot down the bass or write out a figured bass, and at times I don't even need that, because it remains in my head.

About the instrumentation — if one is composing for orchestra, the musical idea carries with it the suitable instrument for its expression. But one often changes the orchestration later on. One can never write the words after the music because it is the text that calls forth the appropriate setting. Of course one can adapt words to a little melody, but such a procedure is impossible for a serious composition. Thus the rumour you mention about *Life for the Czar* is false.[12] You cannot write a symphony and then find a program for it, because here again each episode of a chosen program evokes its own musical illustration.

The preliminary sketch of a work is very pleasant to do. Sometimes it offers almost inexpressible delight, but it also means nervous excitement and anxiety. I sleep badly and often completely forget about eating. The actual execution of the project is done very calmly and quietly. To orchestrate a work that is already ripe, it having been worked out in one's mind to the last detail, is very enjoyable. But one cannot say the same about writing piano pieces, songs, or little things in general. These are annoying; right now I am occupied with this sort of thing.

You ask whether I limit myself to established forms. Yes and no. Some compositions imply the use of traditional forms, like the symphony, but only as concerns their general features — the order of the various movements. There can be considerable freedom in handling the details if the development of ideas requires it. For instance, the first movement of *our* symphony [No. 4] is written in a very informal style. The second theme, which properly ought to be in the major, is in a rather remote minor key. In the recapitulation the second theme is entirely omitted, etc. Also in the finale there are many deviations from traditional form. In vocal music where everything depends on the text, and in fantasies (like *The Storm* and *Francesca*), the form is quite free.

You ask about melodies constructed on the notes of the harmony. I assure you, and could prove it by many examples, that this is quite possible and one can develop millions of new and beautiful melodic combinations by means of rhythm and transposition of these notes. But this would apply only to homophonic music. In polyphonic music such a method of creating melodies would interfere with the independence of the parts. In Beethoven, Weber, Mendelssohn, Schumann, and especially Wagner we frequently find

---

12 Actually Glinka first wrote a good deal of the music of this opera before the libretto was completed, and the text was then accommodated to the music.

melodies consisting of the notes of the common chord; a talented musician will always be able to invent a new and interesting fanfare. Do you recall the lovely Sword motif in the *Nibelungen*?

I am very fond of a melody by Verdi (a very gifted man):

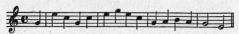

How glorious and fresh is the principal theme of the first movement of Rubinstein's "Ocean" Symphony:

If I racked my brains a bit, I would find innumerable examples that support my assertion. Talent is the sole secret. It knows no limitations and it creates the most beautiful music out of nothing. Could anything be more trivial than the following melody? Beethoven, Seventh Symphony:

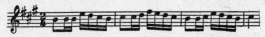

or Glinka, *Jota aragonesa*:

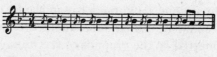

And yet what magnificent musical structures Beethoven and Glinka built on these themes! . . .

[PIOTR ILYICH TCHAIKOVSKY]

❊❊❊❊❊❊❊❊

To the Grand Duke *Constantine Constantinovich*

Frolovskoe, October 3, 1888

. . . Fet [13] is quite right in asserting that everything that does not add something to the principal idea should be put aside even though it is lovely and melodious. But from this we should not deduce that only what is concise can be highly artistic, and therefore,

---

13 Afansi Afansievich Fet (1820–92), poet.

in my opinion, Fet's rule that a perfect lyric must not exceed a certain limit is completely wrong. Everything depends on the nature of the leading idea and the poet who expresses it.

Of two equally inspired poets or composers, one because of his artistic temperament will manifest greater breadth of treatment, more complexity in developing his leading ideas, and more inclination for varied and prolix elaboration, while the other will express himself concisely. Everything that is good but superfluous we call *remplissage*. Do we find such *remplissage* in Beethoven's works? I think we most decidedly do not. On the contrary, it is astonishing how well balanced, significant, and forceful this giant of musicians always remains, and how well he understands the art of curbing his vast inspiration, never losing sight of balanced and traditional form.

Even in his last quartets, which were long regarded as the productions of an insane and deaf man, there seems to be some *remplissage* until we have studied them thoroughly. Ask someone who knows them very well, a member of a quartet who plays them frequently, whether there is anything superfluous in the C-sharp minor Quartet. Unless he is an old-fashioned musician, brought up on Haydn, he would be horrified at the idea of abbreviating or cutting any part of it.

But in speaking of Beethoven I was not merely thinking of his latest period. Can anyone show me a bar in the "Eroica," which is very long, that could be called superfluous, or any portion that could really be omitted on the grounds of *remplissage*? Thus everything that is long is not *too long*; many words do not necessarily mean empty verbiage, and conciseness is not, as Fet maintains, the essential condition of beautiful form. The same Beethoven who in the first movement of the "Eroica" created a superb edifice — an endless series of varied and ever new architectonic beauties — from such a simple and ostensibly poor subject, now and then knows how to surprise us with tight and compact forms. Your Highness, do you recall the Andante of the Pianoforte Concerto in B flat? I know nothing more inspired than this short movement; I turn pale and cold whenever I hear it.

Of course the classical beauty of Beethoven's predecessors and their knowledge of keeping within bounds are of the greatest value. However, it must be admitted that Haydn had no occasion to restrict himself, for he did not have any inexhaustible wealth of material at his command. As for Mozart, if he had lived another twenty years and had seen the beginning of our century, he certainly would have tried to express his lavish inspiration in forms less strictly classical than those with which he had to be content.

While defending Beethoven from the charge of long-windedness, I confess that music after Beethoven offers many examples of prolixity carried so far that it becomes mere *remplissage*. That great musician, who expresses himself with such majesty, breadth, force, and even brusqueness, has much in common with Michelangelo. Just as the Abbé Bernini flooded Rome with his statues, trying to imitate the style of Michelangelo, though not possessing his genius, and making a caricature of what is really powerful in his model, so Beethoven's musical style has been imitated again and again.

In reality, isn't Brahms a caricature of Beethoven? Isn't this pretension to profundity and power detestable? The content poured into the Beethoven mould is not really of value. Even in Wagner's case (he certainly has genius), whenever he oversteps the limits, it is the spirit of Beethoven that prompts him.

As regards your humble servant, all my life I have suffered from the realization of my inability to grasp form in general. I have fought against this innate weakness, not — I am proud to say — without good results, but I shall go to my grave without having produced anything with really perfect form. There is frequently *remplissage* in my works; an experienced eye can detect the stitches in my seams, but I cannot help it. About *Manfred*, I can tell you without trying to pose as being modest that this is a repulsive work, and I hate it, except for the first movement. By the way, I must tell Your Highness that, with my publisher's consent, I intend shortly to destroy the three remaining movements, which are quite poor musically, and the finale especially is deadly, and then turn this long-winded symphony into a symphonic poem. In that case I am sure that the public would like my *Manfred*, and that is the way it should be. I enjoyed writing the first movement, while the others were the result of strenuous effort, in consequence of which — as I recall — I felt quite ill for a time. I could not think of being offended at what Your Highness says about *Manfred*. You are quite right and even too indulgent.

I beg Your Highness's pardon for the sloppiness of this letter. I wanted it to go today and the mail will be collected in a moment.

[PIOTR ILYICH TCHAIKOVSKY]

EMMANUEL CHABRIER

Ambert, 1841 — *Paris*, 1894

❀❀❀❀❀❀❀

To *Édouard Moullé*

Granada, November 4, 1882

"Too many flowers," Granier used to say, in I don't know what, and I, in turn, might say: too many marvels! We are satiated, drunk with masterpieces. Yes, my dear friend, this certainly is a magnificent country! The cathedrals of Burgos, of Ávila, of Toledo and Seville, the Madrid museum, the Cartuja de Miraflores, gleaming Cádiz and radiant Málaga, the Alhambra, the Generalif, the Sierra Nevada — Córdoba, which we are going to see in a few days, then Murcia, then Valencia, and Elche surrounded by palm trees, and Barcelona and Saragossa.

We shall have seen everything, gone everywhere, and in a month we shall have to bid farewell to the Spanish girls, for I tell you only this much, they have made a hit, the little devils! I haven't seen one really homely woman since arriving in Andalusia. I won't talk about their feet, the smallest I've ever seen; their hands are darling, first-rate, and their arms have the most exquisite shape. I'm talking only about what shows, but they show it to great advantage; then their curls and ringlets and the way they wear their hair, the usual fan, the flower in the chignon, and the comb sticking out on one side, the flowered crepe-de-Chine shawl tied around the waist and the long fringe hanging down, the bare arm, the eyelashes so long they could curl them, the dead white skin or orange colour, depending on their race — all this laughing, gesticulating, dancing, drinking, and not caring a damn about Montceau-les-Mines. That is Andalusia.

Every night, with Alice,[1] we make the rounds of the café-concerts where they sing the *malagueñas*, the *soledas*, the *zapatéados*

---

1 Chabrier's wife.

and the *peteneras;* then the dances, which are positively Arabian, that sums it up. If you could see them wriggling their rear ends, twisting and squirming, I don't think you'd care to leave. At Málaga the thing got so strong I had to get my wife out of there, it wasn't even funny. It can't be written down, but I'll remember and tell you about it.

I don't have to tell you that I've observed an enormous number of things: the tango, a kind of dance where the woman imitates the pitching of ships with her behind, that is the only one in 2 time; all the rest are ¾ (Seville) or ⅜ (Málaga and Cádiz). In the north it is different, there they have a very strange kind of ⅝. The ¾ of the tango is always in the habanera style. This is the picture: one or two women dance, two fellows strum any old thing on a couple of old guitars, and five or six women howl, in the queerest voice, triplets impossible to write down since they change the tune every second, and they yell, I say, little bits of tunes like this:

with syllables, words, grace notes; they clap their hands and beat groups of eighth notes accenting the third and sixth, yelling: "*Anda! Anda! la salud! eso es la Mariquita! gracia, nacionidad! Baïla, la chiquilla! Anda! Anda! Consuelo! Olé! la lola! olé, la Carmen! que gracia que elegancia!*" All this to get the young woman to dance, it's too wonderful, it makes you dizzy!

The *sevillana* is different; it is ¾ in this sort of style (with castanets):

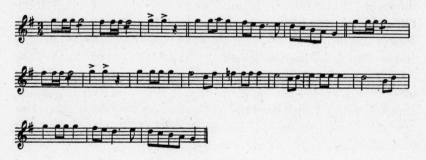

or else:

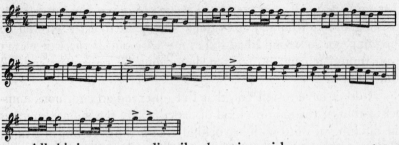

All this is so extraordinarily charming with two grace notes, a pair of castanets, and a guitar. The *malagueñas* cannot be written down; it is a melisma, but with a definite form, and always ends on the dominant. The guitar provides a ⅜, and the old codger (when there is one) is always seated beside the guitarist; he holds a cane between his legs and beats out the ⅜ on this rhythm:

It is always syncopated, by instinct the women themselves syncopate the measures in a thousand ways, and during the dance their feet tap out an unheard-of number of rhythms; their heels tap things like this:

all this with the heel, it is rhythm and dance. The tunes the guitar scratches out are no good, anyway you can't hear them with those shouts of "*Anda! Olé! la chiquilla! que gracia! que elegancia! Anda! Olé! Ole! la chiquirritita,*" and the more they shout, the more the dancer laughs, and all her teeth show, and she throws herself around and is crazy with her whole body.

If you want to hear about a bull-fight — we have five of them on our conscience — let me know ahead, general delivery, Valencia (Spain), where I shall have the pleasure of hearing from you.

Alice's best regards to Madame Moullé and to your wife, a kiss for Albertito, and *besitos au chiquirritito.*

EMMANUEL

To *Costallat*

[1886]

Why doesn't C. talk to me about that quadrille? I'm astonished you don't like it. Well, it probably means that nothing good can be done with it, for I defy anyone, I don't care who he is, to do a better one, especially for dancing. If I had played it for you myself, you would have liked it better. For that matter, show it to the professionals and see what they say.

But it's obvious that I'm old-hat for these young masters — super-old-hat. Lalo too. Even Franck. I go further. I think that at bottom Wagner strikes them as threadbare. As for me, my first concern is to do what I please and above all try to disengage my personality. Secondly I try to be not the least bit crappy. *They all write the same music.* It could be signed by this one or that one; it doesn't make any difference, it all comes from the same studio. It is music that tries to do everything and does nothing. And with ideas like that you can easily be surpassed in ten years. Next it will be Bruno's[2] and Marty's[3] turn to be old-hat; don't worry — somewhere young brains are certainly at work making them old-hat.

In the meantime the *Oberon* opening chorus in F, which I heard a Boulogne municipal band do yesterday, more or less well, is simple and naïve and eternal. They never will make that old-hat. On the whole it is the *form* of the opera libretto that is outdated. Since Meyerbeer we always use the same libretto. It's irritating, you want something else. On the other hand, a musical conversation that goes on during four acts, the sort of thing they're rooting for nowadays, results in desperate monotony. You have three characters; each one has a characteristic motif — March! With three motifs developed symphonically you have to write your work. That's what they want. I don't care, I can do it. In this way a work certainly gains in *unity*, it is an entity, but it is detrimental to variety, rhythm, and a thousand forms which this sublime art can assume, and which we do without so benevolently.

Did Berlioz, a Frenchman above all (he wasn't old-hat in his time), put variety, colour, rhythm, into *La Damnation, Roméo*, and *L'Enfance du Christ*? But they lack unity, people say. I answer, shit! If in order to be *one*, I am fated to be boring, I prefer to be 2,

2 Alfred Bruneau (1857–1934).
3 Georges Marty (1860–1908).

3, 4, 10, 20, — in short, I prefer to have ten colours on my palette and to break up all the tones. And to do that I don't necessarily want to do over and over again the everlasting (1) act for the exposition, (2) act with silly women and vocal exercises by the queen, (3) act with a ballet and the interminable finale that reshuffles the cards, (4) the indispensable love duet, (5) the drunken orgy at twenty minutes before midnight, firing of muskets, Jews' cauldron, death of the leading characters.

On the pretext of unity — I almost said uniformity, there are in Wagner (and he is more capable than Father Bruno) some quarter-hours of music or *absolute recitation* during which every sincere person who is not a fetishist and has an open mind must find each minute as long as a century. I could prove this with the score in my hand, if anyone wanted me to. But they don't give a good God-damn!

These are the *rivets*, just as in the old regime, which are used to reach more interesting passages, sometimes. Me, I want it to be beautiful *everywhere*, and the beautiful has a thousand and one forms. If I can handle only pearl-grey or canary-yellow and their nuances, I am not satisfied, and in the catalogue of the *Bon Marché* there are three hundred shades of nothing but pearl-grey. A little red, for Heaven's sake! To hell with the *gniou-gniou*! Never the same shade! Variety, form, life above all, and *simplicity* if possible, and that's the hardest thing.

What can I do to bamboozle the gallery? There is your enemy. Yes, the gallery falls for it, of course, but only once the same way; you don't catch them twice. But of course everyone knows that these people are very skilful; that's taken for granted. Only nobody asks them to show it. The first movement of the E-flat Symphony [4] is very skilful too; it lasts twenty minutes, but would you ever guess it? Shit!

Do you want to know something? *They don't believe in their own music.* They think it's *put together well*, modern, but they are the first to be bored stiff by it. But of course they have to do it that way or pay the penalty of being pretentious, like that damned Weber or that old dolt of a Father Beethoven!

Hypothesis: if one of them could, oh so reluctantly, write a *Freischütz* Overture some fine morning, *he wouldn't dare show it.* The fact is it's lousy with melody. Damned if I know where Weber's mind was that day. What's good about it? I can hear the *Oberon*

---

4 Beethoven's "Eroica."

Overture twenty times in succession; I couldn't listen twice to the "*Bénédiction des poignards*"; [5] and I've had my fill of one as much as the other.

Speaking of masterpieces, let's talk about the song from *Le Roi*, "*Cher pays*," [6] which a cellist performed this morning (rather amateurishly, too amateurishly, alas) in the guise of an offertory for the nine o'clock Mass. I played the organ (600 francs, imitation old oak, from Alexander's).

I know *The Tempest* by heart. There are some good things in it, but Blau is right in wanting some development of the love part, otherwise Papa Prospero would get tiresome. As for the so-called *drama*, where is it? Is it really dramatic — all that conspiring by those old fogies, Alonso, Antonio, Gonzalo, Stephano, and those two bums, Caliban and Interpocula [7] and Enculo? Could you care less about anything than their peregrinations across that island?

So we have to bolster up the interest on that side. But there is (1) the idyll of Ferdinand and Miranda, first appearance, (2) the whole wedding part with the spirits, etc. for the fourth act, (3) even a comical section with all the drunks. Is that enough to write an opera about? Let's see. The first scene on the sea — it's stupid, it's the Overture to *Der fliegende Holländer* and it isn't by me, alas! It's terrible to do it over again. The *thunderstorms* and the *shipwrecks*, brrr! After Beethoven and Wagner, brrr again. We shall wait and see.

Anyway, end of August I'll drop in on Godinet even if I am satisfied with *The Tempest*. From now until then I shall continue reading Quinet's *Merlin* (a masterpiece) and I'm going to make some cuts in the rest of the second act of *Le Roi*. Burani hasn't sent me the couplets for the first act, he'll hold me up. Here's to all of you and thanks for the word, etc., etc.

Your

EMMANUEL

---

5 From Meyerbeer's *Les Huguenots*.
6 From his opera, *Le Roi malgré lui*, first performance, May 1887.
7 Apparently an error.

ANTONÍN DVOŘÁK

Nelahozeves (Mühlhausen), 1841 — *Prague*, 1904

❧❧❧❧❧❧❧❧❧

To *Emil Kozánek*

Spillville, Iowa,
September 15, 1893

My dear Friend:

I was very glad to receive your last letter dated August 26. Thank you very much. Since you also want a letter from Spillville, you shall have one, because tomorrow, the 16th, we are leaving via Chicago and Niagara Falls for New York, where my work [1] starts on September 21.

These three months we spent at Spillville will remain a very dear memory to us for the rest of our lives. We loved it here and were very happy although the long heat, which lasted for three months, bothered us a good deal. Still there was the compensation of living among our own people, Czech compatriots, which pleased us enormously.

Spillville is a completely Czech settlement, founded by a Bavarian named Spielman, who christened the place Spillville. He died four years ago, and in the morning when I go to church, I pass by his grave and all sorts of queer ideas go through my head when I see it and other graves of Czech countrymen who sleep their eternal sleep here. Some came here around forty years ago, mostly from the regions of Písek, Tabor, and Budějovice. They were all miserably poor, and after much strain and hardship they eventually became rich and are now enjoying life. I liked being among these people and they liked me too, especially the old folk, who were so pleased when I played for them in church *God before Thy Greatness* or *We Greet Thee a Thousand Times.* . . .

It is very strange here. Few people and so much empty space. One farmer lives 4 miles from the next one, especially on the prairies, which I call "the Sahara" because there is nothing but grass fields and that's all you see. You never meet a soul and you live in woods

---

1 He was director of the National Conservatory of Music.

and meadows where there are innumerable herds of cattle grazing in the wide fields. To milk them the men have to go right into the woods or meadows where the cows graze. Everything here seems very wild and sometimes even rather sad, and one could get quite desperate, but getting used to it overcomes these feelings. I could go on talking to you this way and what curious things you would hear about this America! But now something different.

Not long ago we went as far as Nebraska, to the town of Omaha, where there also are many Czechs. I went there to see Mr. Rosewater, a Czech from Bukovany, who, though a Jew, is a very nice gentleman. He is a personal friend of Harrison and Cleveland and many outstanding political men. He got rich here and his journal, the *Omaha Bee*, has had the greatest influence in the state. On the whole he is the most honoured and respected person here. We stayed at his home for three days. In the evening the Czechs came to play a serenade for me, and as we were leaving, an American band arrived and played several pieces for me. There was even a banquet and we felt very gay and I enjoyed it a great deal.

Omaha is 400 miles from here, and from there we went to see — guess whom — the minister Rynda. . . . Mr. Rynda is a charming man and an excellent minister and just the right kind for America. He promised to come and see his mother next year in Kojetín and then we shall all be together.

I, too, hope very much to see Bohemia again; whether or not my contract is extended, I simply must see Bohemia again. I hear that our papers say I intend to remain here. Oh, never! I am, thank God, having a good time; I am in good health and working hard, and I know that if I had not seen America I never should have written my new symphony or my string quartet or my quintet [2] the way I did. You will hear about them later, after the New York performances. Simrock wrote to me and bought everything I had. I hope that by spring you at home will hear all about these — the *dumky*, overtures, symphony, quartet, quintet, rondo, etc. I shall probably have the *Te Deum* and *The American Flag* published by Novello. Now I am very enthusiastic about composing *Záhoř's Lair*.[3] If only I can succeed in making it as good as Erben's work, everything will be all right.

With warmest greetings to all of you,

A. DVOŘÁK

---

[2] Symphony in E minor, *From the New World*, op. 95; Quartet in F, op. 96; Quintet in E flat, op. 97.

[3] Ballad by Karel Jaromír Erben.

EDVARD GRIEG

Bergen, 1843 — Bergen, 1907

❦❦❦❦❦❦❦❦❦

To *Edouard Colonne* [1]

Aulestad, September 12, 1899

Dear Master:

While thanking you very much for your kind invitation, I regret to say that after the issue of the Dreyfus trial I cannot make up my mind, at this moment, to come to France. Like all who are not French (*tout l'étranger*) I am indignant at the contempt for justice shown in your country, and therefore unable to enter into relations with the French public. Pardon me if I cannot feel differently, and I beg you to try to understand me. My wife and I send you our best remembrance.

[EDVARD GRIEG]

❦❦❦❦❦❦❦❦❦

To *Edouard Colonne*

October 4, 1899

My dear Master:

Allow me to thank you for the charming and noble manner in which you referred to my answer to your kind invitation, and I beg you to be so good as to hear me a few moments more concerning the affair.

The French translator of my answer to you asked my permission to print it in the *Frankfurter Zeitung*. In the indignation of the moment (it was just after the verdict in the trial at Rennes) I consented. There is only one point of view from which I regret this: namely, the thought of having possibly hurt your feelings in neg-

---

1 Director of the Colonne Concerts, Paris.

lecting first to get your consent, which would deeply mortify me. But I hope you can readily understand the situation. In writing my answer I was in the country, in the hospitable home of the poet Björnson, whose family, like my wife and myself, are Dreyfusards. In this way the whole thing followed naturally. I remember having asked the German translator, who was present: "Do you believe, really, that any good will result from the printing of the letter?" and that he and others answered: "Yes, undoubtedly!"

I wish I could show you all the abominable letters I receive daily from your country. To me they are solely tokens of a bad conscience, and additional proofs of the innocence of the unhappy Dreyfus. Yesterday I received from M. Henri Rochefort his "noble" journal, the *Intransigeant*, addressed to the " Jewish musical composer, Ed. Grieg." There! I am proud of it! "Hurrah for Mendelssohn!" One of the letters from Paris threatens *"de me recevoir dans votre ville par coups de pied dans la partie la moins noble de mon individu"* if I dare to come there. However, I believe that the easily aroused passion of the French nation will soon be replaced by a saner attitude, resembling the rights of mankind proclaimed by the *République française* in 1789. I hope, primarily for France, but also for my own sake, that I may be able once more to see your beautiful country.

[EDVARD GRIEG]

To *Henry T. Finck*

Christiania, December 21, 1900

If I had a catalogue of my books, your volume on song-writers would be marked with two stars.[2] Higher praise I could not utter. And yet: everything in this world has its faults. I confess that your judgment of Brahms was a great disappointment to me. That you, with your great, wide horizon, have failed to discover the real Brahms is really quite too extraordinary and shows how the most many-sided men have their limitations. For me there is no doubt concerning Brahms. A landscape, torn by mists and clouds, in which I can see ruins of old churches, as well as of Greek temples — that is Brahms. The necessity of placing him by the side of Bach and Beethoven is as incomprehensible to me as the attempt to reduce

2 *Songs and Song Writers.*

him *ad absurdum.* The great must be great, and a comparison with other great ones must always be unsatisfactory.

That you have not only sympathy with my art, but a deep comprehension of it, is a real boon for my heart. Believe me, I have hitherto nearly always fared badly with the so-called critics. Where there was sympathy there was no comprehension, and for so-called comprehension without sympathy I do not give a penny. As for America, I doubt if I shall ever see it. But I hope you will soon come to Norway so we can shake hands.

For reviews of your book in the local papers I regret that no copies can be obtained here. Allow me to suggest that a copy be sent to our leading liberal paper, *Verdens Gang* (*Course of the World*), of which the editor is Mr. O. Thomassen.

[EDVARD GRIEG]

To *Mrs. Edward MacDowell*

Christiania, December 14, 1905

Dear Madam:

The news of MacDowell's serious illness has deeply affected me. Permit me therefore to express to you my own and my wife's sincerest sympathy for you. I am a great admirer of Mac-Dowell's Muse, and would regard it as a severe blow if his best creative period should be so hastily broken off.[3] From all that I hear of your husband, his qualities as a man are as remarkable as his qualities as an artist. He is a complete Personality, with an unusually sympathetic and sensitive nervous system. Such a temperament gives one the capacity not only for moods of the highest transport, but for an unspeakable sorrow tenfold more profound. This is the unsolvable riddle. An artist so ideally endowed as MacDowell must ask himself: Why have I received from nature this delicately strung lyre, if I were better off without it? So unmerciful is Life that every artist must ask himself this question. The only consolation is: Work — yes, even the severest labours. . . .

But: the artist is an optimist. Otherwise he would be no artist. He believes and hopes in the triumph of the good and the beautiful. He trusts in his lucky star till his last breath. And you, the wife of a highly gifted artist, will not and must not lose hope! In similar cases,

---

3 A few months later MacDowell had to abandon all his musical activities.

happily, one often witnesses a seemingly inexplicable recovery. If it can give MacDowell a moment's cheer, say to him that he has in distant Norway a warm and understanding friend who feels for him and wishes from his heart that for him, as for you, better times may soon come.

With best greetings to you both,

Your respectful
EDVARD GRIEG

NIKOLAY ANDREYEVICH RIMSKY–KORSAKOV

Tikhvin, 1844 — St. Petersburg, 1908

◈╼◈╼◈╼◈╼◈╼◈

To *Vladimir Vasilyevich Stasov*

Riva, Lake Garda, Austria
July 5, 1906

Dearest and most excellent
Vladimir Vasilyevich:

   100000000000000000000000000000000 thanks for looking through *Sadko* and all the trouble you had putting the translation in order. Thank you for removing the platter from the sturgeon (very tasty, by the way) and producing the fish itself in fine shape. I was very much amused.

  I am glad you are hearing Chaliapin, whom you like so much, but he does not have a suitable ensemble in the Summer Opera Company. When *Die Meistersinger* was produced in Vienna, as I wrote you, there was no Chaliapin, but they had an ensemble that made me both happy and envious. If only once I could hear one of my operatic works done by such an ensemble! That the orchestra was good was not surprising, but it was amazing that everything that took place on the stage was so well planned and integrated that it seemed like the easiest job in the world. Actually it is extremely difficult and complicated and requires constant attention.

  Once more I repeat that *Die Meistersinger von Nürnberg* is a great work, not because of its length and continuity, but because of its significance. The scene during which Beckmesser sings his stupid serenade while Hans Sachs knocks and disturbs him, and the people who have been awakened come out and then the fight that follows and nobody understands anybody else, and the night watchman arrives, and after his invocation in F major, blazes out in G flat — it's absolutely incomparable!

  And to realize that it was composed at the beginning of the

[280]

sixties — almost forty-five years ago! In addition to this scene there is so much superb material in the work! The faults in *Die Meister-singer* are its excessive length and too much repetition of practically identical music.

Be well and scribble a note to me some time. Nadezhda Nikola-yevna sends her regards. Your

N. R-Korsakov

PS. Ah! What goes on in Russia! But it makes one happy rather than sad.

VINCENT D'INDY

Paris, 1851 — Paris, 1931

❖❖❖❖❖❖❖❖❖

To *Charles Martin Loeffler*

[*Paris*] December 15, 1915

My dear Friend:

Before writing to you I waited for a personal note of thanks from the presidents of the two charity committees to which I donated your generous gift — as regards the 530 francs:

260 francs for the *Mutilés* (President: Maurice Barrès)

270 francs for the *Orphelins* (President: Duchesse d'Uzés)

I was obliged to wait until several days ago for the acknowledgments, which accounts for my delay as well as the fact that I returned to Paris only very recently. Thank you also *on my part* for your mark of sympathy for those among us who need help.

Now, at last, the U. S. has decided to act and join in against the attacks of the Boches, those filthy soldiers who are not worthy of wearing the uniform because they are the accomplices of ordinary criminals. This decision has had the best result in Europe and we are very grateful to you.

As for us, we are doing nicely. Our soldiers have the certainty of knowing that though the Germans may try, they will never be able to break us down, while we shall take all the time we wish for retrenchments. The quality of their troops at present is extremely mediocre while the morale and the physical strength of our soldiers is increasing a great deal; they know that the command only has to will it to break through the German front. But since they are powerful, chiefly because of their machinery, such an effort would cost us dearly in human lives. The attempts made in September proved it then and the command prefers to wait (time is fighting on our side) until the effective forces deteriorate even more, and are so reduced everywhere that on certain fronts 300 men can be replaced by 2 machine-guns. Once this result has been attained, victory will be neither difficult nor far off. You realize that among us absolute confidence in victory prevails everywhere (the extraordinary success of our loan subscription proves it) and not only in the higher circles but especially among the people.

My son, who is a *capitaine de chasseurs*, had five days' leave this summer. He arrived here full of enthusiasm and told me that this enthusiasm on the part of the officers is not even comparable to that of the men; the ordinary soldiers are certain of the incontestable superiority of our army over the German army and they always remain in the best spirits in the assurance of success. You cannot mention peace to them. Anyone who even pronounces the word *armistice* would not be treated very gently by the *chasseurs du 18ᵉ*. And all our soldiers are like that.

Thus far I have not had to mourn any losses in my own family, but I now have a son and seventeen nephews in the combat lines, only 10 among them wounded (one has an amputated leg). As for my artistic family, I have had many losses, musicians of much value, 3 charming little violinists killed in the retreat at Charleroi, and since then 8 other pupils from classes at the Schola also killed, a dozen wounded, and 11 prisoners in Germany. . . . The Schola is doing better and better and is overflowing with pupils because of the refugees from the north, who no longer have the conservatories of Lille, Brussels, and Liége; naturally there is a majority of women, but many of the classes are completely full.

As for the rest, I consider this war extremely beneficial since it has forced from the depths of our hearts our old French qualities of clarity, logic, integrity, and uprightness, which, particularly during the last twenty years, since the Dreyfus affair (in this now can be clearly seen the hand of the German Emperor toward the destruction of our general staff and our intelligence service, which bothered him) have been hidden under a layer of German influence. All these [qualities] have now come to the surface again, breaking through the layer, and I believe that artistic progress will take the road of simplicity and beauty instead of seeking the *small* and the *rare* as in recent years, at least I hope so with all my heart.

But it's time for me to put an end to this excessive chatter; I am enclosing herewith the letter of Barrès thanking you and the photograph of the Duchesse d'Uzés that she gave me to send you. Believe always, my dear Loeffler, in the most sincere affection of your old friend,

VINCENT D'INDY

To *Daniel Gregory Mason*

Paris, January 30, 1930

I am altogether ashamed not to have given you a sign of life for such a long time, but I am more and more overwhelmed with the most diverse occupations: journeys to direct provincial concerts, my *eight* courses a week at the Schola, examinations, my classes at the Conservatoire, and, above all, books that editors have asked me for and that take all my available time. However, I have found some free moments to read your book *The Dilemma of American Music,* and I want to thank you with all my heart for the way you have treated me — myself and my works.

I have written in this recent period many new chamber-music works; I find that this genre is by far the most attractive and the most intimate; it is there that the heart of the artist can best express itself and talk with other hearts and tell them its sufferings and its joys. Nowadays everybody orchestrates well; there is no use making orchestral pieces, as there is a whole nursery of orchestrators both skilful and — amusing, so far as the sonorities employed are concerned, while few are able to make chamber music, a genre that requires a particular way of writing, very strict and intimate. I have therefore abounded in this type these last years: a Quintet with piano, a Concerto for flute, cello, piano, and string orchestra, a Suite for quartet and harp, a Sextet for strings, a Trio with piano, and finally a String Quartet of which the *première* will take place at once. All this has given me much joy.

Thank you for the details you give me about your young composers; I hope for them that they will not give themselves to the utopias of atonality and polytonality which adroit time-servers, without any knowledge or talent, have made the fashion with us, and I wish them good careers.

But I shall have to stop and only have time, my dear Mason, to send you my most cordial regards.

Vincent d'Indy

ERNEST CHAUSSON

Paris, 1855 — Limay, 1899

❖❖❖❖❖❖❖❖

To *Paul Poujaud*

[Poitu] 1886

Dear Friend:

It's true that I've barely mentioned Poitu. That's because I hardly ever think of the scenery now. I get irritated by this
everlasting swooning before one tree, or two trees which form a
cluster, or three trees which seem like the beginning of a forest. It
isn't that I'm losing any of my taste for nature, but in it I seek for
something other than the object in itself. If I were a painter and
painted landscapes, I might think differently. Since I am not, and
since I don't even do water-colours any more, I admire especially
those things which arouse ideas in me. I hardly tell this to anyone
but you, for I know you won't accuse me of being utilitarian. I have
always been convinced that beauty has no other reason for existence
than itself. But how many things are not beautiful except for the
way we see them! That means that in the whole earth there isn't
a single little corner where we can't find something lovely from
some point of view or other.

I haven't written you about the country because I have looked
at it very little, while admiring and *feeling* it a great deal. I should
feel obligated to it, for it has just given me an idea that I have been
searching for, in a vague sort of way, for a long time. You know
how much I dislike descriptive music. At the same time I feel incapable of writing pure music as did Bach and Haydn. So I had to
find something else. I have found it. Now I only have to see whether
I have in myself the power to express what I feel. As long as I do
nothing but think about it, I am full of confidence; once I pick up
my pen, I feel like a little boy.

However, I've started. Next fall I shall show you a symphonic
poem that is a mere attempt in this direction. It has progressed quite

[285]

far already and the sketch would be finished now if I hadn't had to stop for about eighteen days because of some idiotic little practical difficulty. I still have to find about thirty measures to reach the end, which I think I'll write quite rapidly. I can't seem to find a title I like. At the moment I call it *Dans le bois*,[1] but I'd like to find something better — especially since this doesn't at all give the effect of what I want to express, and so perhaps it would be better not to give it a title.

Think of the *Fontaines aux lianes* by Leconte de Lisle. Take away the exotic side (Indian efflorescence) and the semi-dramatic side (the dead man with his eyes wide open) and you'll get an approximate idea of the symphonic poem I have in mind. I don't know whether I'm expressing myself clearly and if you understand me. I should like to make up a *poem* in my head, myself, and then give only a general impression of it to the public. Above all, I want to be completely musical, so that the audience that doesn't entirely follow me will be sufficiently satisfied with the musical side. There is no description, no story, nothing but sensation. I am thinking of writing four or five symphonic poems of this sort at my leisure, among which there will be *La Nuit*, which I'm definitely not working on this summer. I am already planning a *Printemps* (Botticelli) and a *Chant de la terre*. Don't talk about this to anyone, and write me what you think.

About poor *Roi Arthus*,[2] Boucher has completely worn me out about it and there seemed to be so many difficulties involved that for a while I was very discouraged. I am taking it up again now. Despite everything they say about it, *I like it*, as our good Franck would say. When will it be finished? Will it ever be finished? You're right, one must always have something ready. I am sure that an opera-theatre will be started and that I'll even have a chance of being accepted. But I feel instinctively that I will finish my opera the day after it goes bankrupt.

Anyway, what difference does it make? Isn't the main thing to do what one feels, as best one can, without worrying about a more or less hypothetical performance? Just as I was writing the last sentence, a stern voice that often speaks in me reminded me that I am deluding myself, and that after coming here I felt completely discouraged, and that a performance now and then is necessary to raise the morale of composers of little faith.

---

1 Completed under the title *Solitude dans les bois*, and later destroyed.

2 Opera based on a libretto by Chausson; first performed at Karlsruhe, 1900.

You see I'm working, my dear friend, at least mentally. Add *Joconde*, which I've been thinking about a bit, and a new opera that Lerolle has been pestering me about — I just don't want to get swallowed up without having written even one page which appeals to the heart.

I pity you for being busy with requests and petitions. But, in a way, it is very healthy to have an occupation which rests the mind. Spinoza used to make glasses.

Lerolle is working. He enjoys the country. He won't go to Bayreuth since I'm not going, and both of us regret it. When do you expect to leave? I shall return most likely during the first half of August and I won't leave the Paris region any more.

Good-bye. This really is a long letter and it answers your questions. I got *Joconde* from Boucher. He tells me he's going to read you his *Hercule* and that you are a pearl among listeners.

Warmest regards, I'd like to see you soon.

Your friend,
Ernest Chausson

SERGEY IVANOVICH TANEYEV

Vladimir Government, 1856 — Moscow, 1915

꘎꘎꘎꘎꘎꘎꘎꘎꘎

To *Piotr Ilyich Tchaikovsky*

March 30, 1878

. . . The first movement of your Fourth Symphony is too long in proportion to the others. It seems to me like a symphonic poem to which three other movements have been added accidentally. The trumpet fanfare in the introduction, which is repeated in other sections, the frequent changes of tempo in the secondary themes — all this makes me think that you are describing a program here. Otherwise I like the movement. But the rhythm ♪♪♫ is used too much and it gets boring.

The Andante is charming (I don't particularly care for the middle theme). The Scherzo is exquisite and sounds wonderful. I cannot bear the trio; it sounds like a ballet piece. Nikolay Grigoryevich [1] likes the finale best, but I do not quite agree with him. Since I know the way you transcribed the *Zhuravl* and what you can do with a Russian theme, the variations on *Vo pole bereza stoyala* seem rather unimportant and uninteresting.

I think the symphony has one weakness to which I shall never become reconciled. In each movement there are phrases that sound like ballet music: the middle section of the Andante, the trio of the Scherzo, and a sort of march in the Finale. When I hear the symphony my inner eye involuntarily sees Madame Soleshchanskaya, [2] which disturbs me and spoils my pleasure at the many beautiful things in the work.

I have given you my frank opinion. Perhaps I have expressed it a little too freely, but don't be hurt. It isn't surprising that I don't like the symphony. If you had not sent me *Yevgeny Onyegin* at the

---

1 N. G. Rubinstein, brother of Anton Rubinstein and a leading figure in Russian music at that time.

2 A ballerina.

[288]

same time, perhaps I should have been satisfied with it. It's your own fault for having composed such an opera, after which everything must seem less interesting than it really is. *Onyegin* has given me much pleasure and I've spent many enjoyable moments examining the score and I am unable to find any fault in it. A splendid opera! And still you say you want to give up composition. You have never done so well. Be happy at having achieved such perfection, and profit by it.

[SERGEY IVANOVICH TANEYEV]

GIACOMO PUCCINI

Lucca, 1858 — *Brussels*, 1924

❧❦❧❦❧❦❧❦❧❦

To *Tito Ricordi*

New York, February 18 [1907]

Dear Tito:

Butterfly went very well as far as the press and public were concerned, *but not so far as to please me*. It was a performance without poetry. Farrar is not too satisfactory. She sings out of tune, forces her voice, and it does not *carry* well in the large space of the theatre. I had to struggle to obtain two full-dress rehearsals, including the general! Nobody knew anything. Dufrich had not taken the trouble to study the *mise en scène*, because the composer was there. Vigna did his best but he can't control the orchestra. As long as he had me at his elbow things went very well, but whenever I left the field there were disasters.

However, it went well, on the whole, and the press is unanimous in its praise. This is the first day that I have been able to write after six days of influenza which *m'a tué*. I am sailing on the 26th in the *Kronprinz*. I wanted to go to Niagara, but now I have neither the desire nor the time to go.

Now there is the question of *Conchita*. I am still terribly doubtful about the subject. When I think of the novel [1] I have no doubt, but when I think of the libretto I have many. Its structure and its dangerous and far from clear psychology frighten me.

Conchita never succeeds in standing out with the clear picture that she makes in Pierre Louÿs's story.

The development lacks colour, and is frightfully difficult and dangerous to represent musically, with the variety that is necessary in the theatre. The first and second scenes are all right, but the scene at the window in the dance-café and the last scene are both, in my opinion, unsatisfactory. Let us ponder it well, because I shall never

---

1 *La Femme et le pantin* by Pierre Louÿs.

be able to set to work on a subject if I am not fully convinced about it first — for my own sake and for yours. Are you, with your discernment in matters theatrical, convinced of it?

Examine this *boat* all over and see if you find any leaks. I can see them. And what am I to do? The world is expecting an opera from me, and it is high time it was ready. We've had enough now of *Bohème*, *Butterfly*, and Co.! Even I am sick of them! But I really am greatly worried! I am tormented not for myself alone, but for you, for Signor Giulio, and for the house of Ricordi, to whom I wish to give an opera that is sure to be good.

Here too I have been on the lookout for subjects, but there is nothing possible, or, rather, complete enough. I have found good ideas in Belasco, but nothing definite, solid, or complete.

The "West" attracts me as a background, but in all the plays I have seen I have found only some scenes here and there that are good. There is never a clear, simple line of development; just a hodge-podge and sometimes in very bad taste and very *vieux jeu*.

I have written all this by way of preparing you, that you may not suffer an unpleasant surprise when I expose my doubts about *Conchita*.

You will say, of course: "Why did you ever fasten on to the subject then?" My dear fellow, I have been torturing my brains and my spirit for three years to find a place to lay my four notes, and have fastened with feline hunger on the subject that has impressed me more than any other. The book is beautiful — but the libretto, or rather the theatrical lay-out, is imperfect, because I realize that it is *impossible* to reproduce for the stage the speech and action of the original.

The scene of the naked dance must be disguised. The virginity question, which is the crux of the book, *cannot* be made clear in a *spoken* version of the story.

I am afraid of the last scene, which, if it is not exceptionally realistic, is only an ordinary duet. And this scene is perilous and, in the form in which I have imagined it, will not be accepted by the public. In short, I assure you that my life is not all roses, and this state of mental excitement is making my existence nervous and my humour most melancholy.

Before I leave, I am to have an interview with Belasco, but I do not expect much from it. Long, too, whom I met in Philadelphia the other night at the second performance of *Butterfly*, wishes to suggest a subject to me. I am going to see a powerful drama of Belasco's called *The Music Master*, and another by Hauptmann of which I have heard good reports. Then I have finished and I shall see you soon again in Milan.

I do need a rest! After Paris, New York — I've had enough of it!

Kindest regards to you and your father.

[GIACOMO PUCCINI]

❈❂❈❂❈❂❈❂❈

To *Giuseppe Adami* [2]

[1920]

Dear Adamino:

If I touch the piano my hands get covered with dust. My desk is piled up with letters — there isn't a trace of music. Music? Useless if I have no libretto. I have the great weakness of being able to write only when my puppet executioners are moving on the scene. If only I could be a purely symphonic writer! I should then at least cheat time — and my public. But that was not for *me*. I was born so many years ago — oh, so many, too many, almost a century — and Almighty God touched me with His little finger and said: "Write for the theatre — mind, only for the theatre." And I have obeyed the supreme command. Had He marked me out for some other task, perhaps I should not be, as now, without material.

Oh you, who say you are working while you are really doing something quite different — films, plays, poetry, articles — and never think, as you ought to think, of one who has the earth under his feet and yet feels the ground receding from him every hour and every day as if a landslip would swallow him up! I get such nice encouraging letters, but if, instead of these, one act were to arrive of our glittering Princess, don't you think it would be better? You would give me back my calm and my confidence, and the dust would not settle on my piano any more, so much banging would I do, and my desk would have its brave array of scoring sheets again. Oh, you of the city, think to more purpose of one who is waiting in the country! I need not only the first act, but the third also, since then Act II would be finished. And *La Rondine*? When are you bringing it to me? It is urgent because it has forty theatres waiting.

Affectionate regards to you and Renato.

[GIACOMO PUCCINI]

---

2 Librettist for Puccini's *La Rondine*, and with Renato Simoni for *Turandot*.

GUSTAV MAHLER

Kalischt (Bohemia), 1860 — Vienna, 1911

❋❋❋❋❋❋❋❋❋

To *Josef Steiner* [1]

[*Tétény, Hungary*] June 17, 1879

Dear Steiner:

Do not be angry at me for not having replied sooner. Everything is so desolate around me and the twigs of a hard, dried-out existence snap in back of me. Much has happened within me since I stopped writing. But I cannot tell it to you. Only this much, I am a changed man — whether a better one, I don't know. In any case not a happier one. The most ardent, vital joy and the most consuming longing for death — both reign by turn in my heart, often changing with the hour. One thing I know — I cannot go on this way! If the horrible pressure of our modern hypocrisy and deceit has driven me to the point of self-degradation, if the indestructible bond with the relationships of art and life could put loathing into my heart for everything that was holy to me, art, love, religion, is there any other way out but self-destruction? Forcibly I tear the bonds that chain me to the vile, nauseous quagmire of existence. With the strength of despair I cling to my sole comforter — sorrow.

Now the sun smiles at me and the ice is gone from my heart. I see the blue heavens again and the swaying flowers, and my scorn dissolves into tears of love. And I *must* love it, this world, with its fraud and frivolity, and with eternal laughter. Oh, that a god might tear the veil from my eyes, so that my clear glance could penetrate to the very core of the earth! Oh, I should like to gaze upon this earth in its nakedness, without decoration, without ornament, as it lies unfolded before its Creator. Then I would come before its Genius: "Now I know you, liar! You have not fooled me with your dissembling, you have not blinded me with your brilliance. Behold

---

1 Childhood friend of Mahler's.

a man who has been tantalized by the glittering game of your du-
plicity, who has suffered the most fearful blows of your scorn, but
who stands upright, strong! May anguish find you wherever you
hide! From the valley of humanity may this sound up to you on
your cold lonely heights. Can you hear the unutterable lamentation
that, down below, has been heaping up through the ages into mountains? And on their peaks you reign and laugh! How will you answer before the Avenger if even once you cannot expiate the grief
of one single anguished soul!"

June 18

Yesterday I was too disturbed and exhausted to write further.
My wild excited mood of yesterday has now given way to a calmer
one. I am like someone who, after long anger, feels tears of relief in
his eyes. Dear Steiner! You wish to know what I have been doing
here all this time. A few words suffice. I have eaten and drunk, slept
and awakened, cried and laughed. I have stood on the hills where
the breath of God drifts. I have been on the heath and in a dream
the tinkling cow-bells sang for me. But I have not escaped my destiny; doubt follows me on every path. I cannot feel truly joyful
about anything and tears accompany my most blissful smiles.

I am living here on a meadow in Hungary with a family who
engaged me for the summer. I have to teach the boys piano and now
and then put the family in a musical frame of mind. Like a fly in a
spider web I sit here and writhe. But the slave does his duty.

Still, when I go out in the evening and climb a linden tree
which stands there alone, and I look out on the world from my
friendly tree-top, before my eyes the Danube winds its old accustomed way and its ripples reflect the glow of the setting sun. Behind
me in the town I hear the evening bells peal and they waft over to
me a loving breath of air and the tree boughs sway in the wind and
rock me to sleep like the Erlking's daughter, and the leaves and
blossoms of my darling tenderly caress my cheek. Everywhere tranquillity! The most blessed tranquillity! Only from afar comes the
melancholy croaking of the toad sitting sadly in the reeds.

Then like shadows of long past happiness, pale figures of my
life appear and once more the song of yearning sounds in my ears.
Again together we wander over familiar fields. And there stands the
organ-grinder holding his hat in his withered hand. And in those
sounds, so out of tune, I hear the greeting of Ernst von Schwaben [2]

2 *Ernst von Schwaben*, early opera by Mahler with libretto by Steiner.

and then he himself appears and holds out his arms to me, and as I look at him, it is my poor brother.[3] Veils descend. The pictures and sounds grow dim.

From the grey sea emerge two friendly names — Morawan,[4] Ronow. And I see gardens filled with friendly people and a tree on which is engraved the name Pauline. A blue-eyed maiden curtsies and smiles and brings me a cluster of grapes. My cheeks redden again at the recollection. I see those eyes which once made me a thief — and again everything disappears. Nothing! Now there rises up the fateful umbrella; from its ribs and entrails I hear prophetic voices predicting misfortune for me like a Roman augur. Suddenly a table rises up from the ground and a spectral form completely clothed in blue clouds is seated at it. It is Melion,[5] who is celebrating in song the Holy Spirit, and he offers incense to it with real *Dreikönig*. We sit there like two sacristans officiating for the first time at a holy Mass.

Behind us a hobgoblin hovers sneeringly; he is dressed in playing-cards and his face is that of Buxbaum. In a fearful voice he calls to us in the melody of the *Bertinischen Etüden:* "Humble yourselves! This glory, too, will disappear!" A stream of clouds from Melion enfolds the scene, and the clouds grow thicker and thicker. Suddenly the head of an angel shines forth, like the face of the Raphael Madonna; beneath her stands Ahasuerus with his burden and he wishes to come up to her, into the holy, redeeming realm, but the angel laughs and disappears and he stares after her with immeasurable grief. He takes up his staff and goes on, dry-eyed, eternal, undying!

Oh, my beloved earth, when, oh when, will you take the forsaken one to your breast! Behold! Mankind has cast him out and he flees from her cold bosom, from her heartlessness, to you, to you. Oh, take to you the lonely one, the restless one, all-eternal Mother!

June 19

Dear Steiner:

Now already on the third day I return to bid you a joyful farewell. It is the story of my life that is sketched in these pages. Strange fate which casts me about on the waves of my long-

---

3 His brother Ernst, who died five years before this letter was written, at the age of thirteen.

4 Near Čáslav, Bohemia where Mahler vacationed during 1875–6.

5 An acquaintance of Mahler's at the Iglau Gymnasium.

ing, now into a storm, now drifting toward the shining sunlight. Only I fear that some time I may be dashed to pieces on a crag; my keel has touched it so often.

It is six o'clock in the morning. I have been out in the pasture and I sat with Farkas, the shepherd, and listened to the sound of his shawm. Ah, how sad it sounded, and yet filled with such ardent rapture, the folk tune that he played! The flowers growing at his feet trembled beneath his dreamy dark eyes, and his brown hair fluttered about his sunburnt cheeks. Oh, Steiner! I have already seen the dew on the grass and you are still asleep in your bed. I am so peacefully happy now. This calm steals into my heart like the spring sun on winter fields. Will there be spring in my heart?

And now let us take leave of each other, faithful friend. Write soon, very soon, for I am so completely alone. I have neither people nor books. Fare thee well.

Your
GUSTAV MAHLER

☙☙☙☙☙☙☙

To *Arthur Seidl* [6]

Hamburg, February 17, 1897

My esteemed Friend:

Your kind and thoughtful letter gave me much pleasure and stimulated me a great deal. It is typical of you to have given me, in a certain sense, some insight into myself. You described my aims quite strikingly in contrast to those of Strauss, and you are quite right in that "my music finally arrives at a program as the last, ideal elucidation, whereas in Strauss the program is set forth as though it were a given task." I believe that in this you have touched on one of the great enigmas of our age, and at the same time you have expressed that *aut . . . aut*.

When I conceive a large musical creation, I invariably reach the point where I must introduce the "word" as the bearer of my musical idea. It must have happened similarly in the case of Beethoven and his Ninth Symphony, only the times then could not yet offer him the appropriate materials. For, basically, the Schiller poem was unable to formulate what was unheard, what lay in his thoughts.

---

6 Critic and writer on music.

I recall that R. Wagner expresses this very frankly somewhere or other. It happened that in the case of the last movement of my Second Symphony I really looked through all of world literature up to the Bible in order to find the liberating word, and finally I was compelled myself to bestow words on my feelings and thoughts.

The way in which I received the inspiration for this is deeply characteristic of the essence of artistic creation. For a long time I had been thinking of introducing the chorus in the last movement and only my concern that it might be taken for a superficial imitation of Beethoven made me procrastinate again and again. About this time Bülow died, and I was present at his funeral. The mood in which I sat there, thinking of the departed, was precisely in the spirit of the work I had been carrying around within myself at that time. The chorus in front of the organ intoned the Klopstock chorale *"Auferstehn!"* Like a flash of lightning it struck me, and everything became clear and articulate in my mind. The creator had been awaiting this flash, that is "the holy conception."

Then I only had to create in sounds what I had *experienced*. And still, if I had not already been carrying this work inside of me, how could I have experienced this? Even though thousands were sitting with me in church at the moment! That is the way it always happens with me: *only when I experience* do I "compose" — only when I compose do I experience. I know you will understand without my having to elaborate further.

The nature of a musician can hardly be expressed in words. It is much easier to say in what ways he *differs* from others. But as for what he is, perhaps he least of all should be allowed to elucidate this question. It is the same with his goals. He changes them, like a sleep-walker, to — he does not know what road he is taking (perhaps along dizzy precipices), but he goes toward the distant light whether it be an eternally shining star or an enticing will-o'-the-wisp!

I was much pleased with what you said about the "productive" critic. I have felt this for a long time in everything I've heard or seen of yours. Fortunate the artist who is associated with such a "critic"! I must consider your having met me an uncommon piece of good luck. I hope you won't regard this as flattery or repayment. The fact that you won't be present in Berlin is a drop of wormwood in my cup of joy; a cup of joy, I say, since I am still a newcomer among "those who have been played." You can't imagine what mental agony I suffer when I put score after score in my box without anyone having noticed my works (despite spasmodic efforts on my part).

I will never forget Strauss, because he gave me the impetus for this in such a really generous spirit. Anyway, no one can ever accuse me of regarding myself as a "competitor" (as unfortunately so often happens now). I repeat to you that I cannot regard two such people as an example of "subtraction." Aside from the fact that I might well be a monster just looking on, if Strauss' successes had not cleared a path for my works, I think it my greatest pleasure to have found such a comrade and fellow artist among my contemporaries.

Somewhere Schopenhauer uses the image of two miners who are buried in two opposite sides of a shaft and later meet each other in a subterranean passage. This story strikingly illustrates my relation to Strauss. How lonely I should feel and how hopeless my struggles would seem if I could not look ahead to a future triumph from such "signs and wonders"! When you describe the two of us (in such flattering fashion for me) as the "opposite poles of the new magnetic axis," you express a viewpoint that I myself have been secretly approaching for a long time. If you saw the scores I have begun since my Second Symphony, you would realize how much intuition your opinions reveal.

Forgive my hastiness. I am writing this in a great hurry, half-way through preparations for a trip of several weeks which will take me to Moscow, St. Petersburg, Munich, Budapest, etc. My anxiety at not being able to answer your precious letters for several weeks necessitates this all too hasty scrawl.

In closing, my deepest thanks for your touching solicitude in collecting the Dresden opinions on my visit. I can say nothing definite now about Vienna and its conductor crisis. *Between us*, the crisis cannot be settled until the fall, and there no longer seems to be any choice between Mottl [7] and my humble self. Frankly speaking, I don't know whether I want this position, which might estrange me from my own aims. However, I am a total fatalist about this and won't think about it any more but will let it come to me.

My most cordial regards, and again thank you, not for what you've done for me, but for what you are — I consider this a gift for my life and works.

In sincere friendship,

Your devoted
GUSTAV MAHLER

7 Felix Mottl (1856-1911), conductor. Mahler was appointed conductor of the Vienna *Hofoper* that year.

To *Julius Buths* [8]

Vienna, March 25, 1903

Esteemed Friend:

I agree with all your suggestions and beg you to do as you please in each case. Accordingly, the main pause in the concert would occur between the fourth and fifth movements. I am quite astonished at your sensitivity in having recognized the natural break in the work. I have been of this opinion for a long time, and it has always been reconfirmed in every performance I have conducted.

Nevertheless, there must also be a long, complete rest after the first movement since the second movement is not in the nature of a *contrasting* section but sounds completely incongruous after the first. This is my fault and it isn't lack of understanding on the part of the audience. Perhaps you have already felt this after playing the two movements in immediate succession. The Andante is composed as a sort of intermezzo (like an echo of long past days from the life of him whom we carried to the grave in the first movement — "while the sun still smiled at him").

While the first, third, fourth, and fifth movements are related in theme and mood content, the second is independent, and in a sense interrupts the stern, relentless course of events. Perhaps this is a defect in the structure, but my intentions should be clear to you from the above indications.

It is very important to interpret the beginning of the fifth movement as related to the first movement and the long rest after the first will help make it clear to the audience.

May I tell you about an experiment with the *a cappella* chorus in the last movement? Up to now I have observed that it is impossible to avoid an intolerable disturbance when the chorus rises just before its entrance as it usually does. Attention is strained to the utmost by the trumpet fanfares and then the mysterious sound of human voices (they should enter *ppp* as if from a very great distance) is supposed to produce an astonishing effect. I advise you to have the chorus (which has been seated up to this point) remain seated and rise only for the E-flat major section: *"Mit Flügeln, die ich mir errungen"* (basses). This has always created an astonishing

8 Director of the Düsseldorf Conservatory. Mahler's directions refer to a performance of his Second Symphony.

effect. It is also important to have a very careful arrangement of the horns and trumpets in the *Grosse Appell*. Horns and kettle-drums should be placed together, and whenever possible the trumpets opposite them, but the former should sound as if they were widely separated from each other. The flutes and bass clarinets are so well trained and perform their functions so well in the orchestra that they hardly need the conductor any more, so you won't have to beat time during the entire passage.

I suggest that you have a separate rehearsal for this passage. I consider it the most difficult in the entire work. The two solo voices: *"O Schmerz, du Alldurchdringer — O Tod, du Allbezwinger"* must stand out strongly above the orchestra and it requires the greatest discretion not to cover up the singers.

As I had anticipated, I regret very much that I shall not be able to be with you on April 2. Accept, from this distance, my very best wishes and deepest gratitude for your trouble and your verdict, which pleased and elated me enormously. These days I shall be thinking of you often.

Your very devoted
GUSTAV MAHLER

○)○)○)○)○)○)○

To *Bruno Walter*

[Summer] 1906

Dear Friend:

Many thanks for your letter. The remark of Wagner you cite is quite clear to me and I do not know what error you discern. One must not throw out the baby with the bath. Of course no one would deny that our music involves the "purely human" (everything belonging to it and therefore also the "contemplative"). Just as in all art, this is purely dependent on the means of expression, and so on. If one wishes to make music, one should not paint or write poetry or desire to describe anything. But what one makes music out of is still the whole — that is the feeling, thinking, breathing, suffering human being. There would be no objection to a "program" (though this may not be exactly the highest step on the ladder) provided that it is a *musician* who is expressing himself in it and not a writer, philosopher, or painter (all of these being contained in the musician).

In a word: those who have no genius should stay away and those who have should not be discouraged by anything. All this rumination about these matters strikes me like this: someone has created a child and then starts breaking his head about whether it is really a child, and whether it was conceived with the right intentions, and so on. He simply loved and was *able to. Basta!* If one cannot love and is *unable to*, then there is no child. Also *basta!* And if one loves and is *able to*, then there is a child. Again *basta!* My Sixth [Symphony] is finished. I think I was *able to*. A thousand times *basta!* With warmest regards,

Your old
MAHLER

❁❁❁❁❁❁❁❁

To his wife

Berlin, January 1907

My dear, good Almschili:

Yesterday afternoon I went to see Strauss. She met me at the door with pst! pst! Richard is sleeping, pulled me into her (very slovenly) boudoir, where her old mama was sitting over some mess (not coffee) and filled me full of nonsensical chatter about various financial and sexual occurrences of the last two years, in the meantime asking hastily about a thousand and one things without waiting for a reply, would not let me go under any circumstances, told me that yesterday morning Richard had had a very exhausting rehearsal in Leipzig, then returned to Berlin and conducted *Götterdämmerung* in the evening, and this afternoon, worn to a frazzle, he had gone to sleep, and she was carefully guarding his sleep. I was dumbfounded.

Suddenly she burst out: "Now we have to wake up the rascal!" Without my being able to prevent it, she pulled me with both her fists into his room and yelled at him in a very loud voice: "Get up, Gustav is here!" (For an hour I was Gustav—then suddenly Herr Direktor again.) Strauss got up, smiled patiently, and then we went back to a very animated discussion of all that sheer bilge. Later we had tea and they brought me back to my hotel in their automobile, after arranging for me to take lunch with them at noon Saturday.

There I found two tickets for parquet seats in the first row for

Salome and I took Berliner along. The performance was excellent in every respect — orchestrally, vocally, and scenically it was pure Kitsch and Stoll,[9] and again it made an extraordinary impression on me. It is an extremely clever, very powerful piece, which certainly belongs among the most significant of our time! Beneath a heap of rubbish an infernal fire lives and burns in it — not just fireworks.

That's the way it is with Strauss's whole personality and it's difficult to separate the wheat from the chaff. But I had felt tremendous respect for the whole manifestation and this was confirmed again. I was tremendously pleased. I go the whole hog on that. Yesterday Blech conducted — excellently. Saturday Strauss is conducting and I am going again. Destinn was magnificent; the Jochanaan (Berger) very fine. The others, so-so. The orchestra, really superb.

This afternoon I am going to Frau Wolff's with Berliner. I promise you, darling, that I won't fall in love. The young girl you dreamed of does not exist. Anyway, today I dreamed of you. You were wearing your hair the way you did as a girl and I liked you so much. Almschili, wear your hair the way you used to then. I like it better than the present Jewish way.

At twelve o'clock I have a rehearsal with the lady singer. I'm afraid I've caught a chill. For the last three days I've been sleeping until ten o'clock and another hour in the afternoon. It makes me feel very good and apparently this idleness is very good for me. I kiss you, dear heart. Why do you write nothing about the children?

Your old
GUSTL

❖❖❖❖❖❖❖❖❖

To *Willem Mengelberg*

New York, February 1908

Dear old Friend:

Very shortly you will receive (I hope) a proposal from Boston inviting you to assume the direction of the (magnificent) orchestra as successor to Muck.[10] Yesterday I talked to Schelling about this and he told me you were not much inclined to accept the position. Since I can easily imagine your reasons, perhaps

---

9 Mahler's stage managers at the Vienna Opera.
10 Karl Muck, conductor of the Boston Symphony Orchestra, 1906–8 and 1912–18.

it would not be amiss for me to give you a few details so that when you make your decision you won't be too prejudiced and will have a clearer idea of the situation.

The position in Boston is the finest conceivable for a musician. The *first* and *foremost* of the entire continent. An orchestra of the *first rank*, unlimited authority, a social position that the musician in Europe can never achieve. A public so appreciative and eager to learn that Europeans can't even conceive of it. After your experiences in New York you are in no position to form any opinions on this subject. Here in New York the theatre is the main attraction and the concert is the affair of only a small minority.

In addition you should also seriously consider the salary. If they approach you, ask for $20,000 (around 50,000 gulden or even a little more). You can manage quite beautifully on $6,000 to $8,000 and put the rest aside. I would accept the position unconditionally in your place because the most important thing for the artist is the instrument he has and the echo his art awakens. Please let me know immediately what you think about this and whether I should pursue the matter further for you. I'm going to see Higgins[11] around the end of March (up to now I've only been corresponding with him) and at that time I could arrange everything for you, which is difficult to do in writing. It would be glorious for me to have you close by. Indeed I, too, will also spend next year in America. I am quite enraptured with the country though the artistic satisfactions of the Metropolitan are only rather so-so. I am in a great hurry and want this to reach you soon. Please answer immediately, even if in brief.[12]

Greetings to your dear wife and our friends in Amsterdam and best regards from your old friend,

GUSTAV MAHLER

---

11 Henry Lee Higginson, founder of the Boston Symphony Orchestra.
12 The position was filled by Max Fiedler.

CHARLES MARTIN LOEFFLER

Mulhouse, Alsace, 1861 — Medfield, Mass., 1935

❀❀❀❀❀❀❀

To *Elise Fay* [1]

[*Washington, D.C.*] [May 3] 1888

My dearly beloved Elise,

Don't think I would have waited so long to write but I haven't been feeling at all well — since the afternoon I left, my digestion has been very unsettled. I would eat and then feel ill and that's how it was each day. Today I am feeling better and I assure you that the weather here is lovely enough to cure a dying man.

Since my childhood I've had an absolute preference for southern countries and I can't help regretting that Boston does not have the same longitude as Washington. The cherry trees and apple trees and lilacs — all these summer flowers are in blossom and with this a kind sun and a sapphire sky. Besides all this a lovely city with the finest buildings in the country — wide vistas full of trees — the thousands of Negroes here are far more interesting and picturesque than those in New England. Sitting here outside the hotel in a warm and pleasant country, reading a book by Dostoievsky — I have the most curious and uneasy sensation — one of those ironies of chance — my heart is filled with sadness and pity for the suffering of a martyr in an opposite place while my body experiences perfect well-being.

Our concerts [2] have not been a great success financially and they have given up the idea of a second one at Baltimore on Saturday — so instead of arriving in Boston on Monday we shall be there by Sunday which pleases us all a great deal. I spent a very nice day in Philadelphia, and except for my being indisposed, it would have

---

1 His future wife.

2 Loeffler was a violinist in the Boston Symphony Orchestra, which was then on tour.

[304]

been perfect. Mlle. E. sang my songs exquisitely and she gave me some good advice — in the afternoon I went for a walk with Ingersoll in the zoo — the monkeys catching their fleas was enough to make you die laughing. Our concert at Concord was not a great success because afterwards we had only $25 left which means a profit of $18.

I'd like very much to go see *Henriette* with you Monday evening if *you* want to. I assure you there isn't anyone happier than I am to return to Boston and gradually begin taking a *rest* — I need it so much for I am completely exhausted. I bought you a little gift, a remembrance, it's a —— and a little —— —— for your sister, — well you'll see. You can bother your heads about it but you won't know. I embrace you with all my heart, darling, and I hope you are well, and also Temple and Thérèse. Always your

LOEFFLER

To *Mrs. Grace M. Schirmer*

Medfield, Mass.,
January 17, 1907

Dear Mrs. Schirmer,

I am glad to hear of your interest in Gregorian Chant. I do not know how fine a choirmaster the Paulist Fathers have — but probably a very efficient man. The great trouble is that there are so many views and opinions on the subject. For instance, I thoroughly dislike the treatment of the harmonization for organ of the chants, which Giulio Bas, organist of the Sistine Chapel in Rome, publishes. Then there is the Benedictine Dom Pothier who is at present printing the chants, having been appointed by the Pope for this task. His antagonists claim, that he *alters* sometimes the chants — using his taste as a criterion — 130 instances are mentioned by them.

Then there is Dom Mocquereau (both of these monks are real experts in the matter); he has done little however to bring light to us musicians. These men lose themselves in polemics. Then there are the Niedermeyer suggestions about the harmonizing of the organ! This latter seems to me very dry. One of the charms of the Chant is its unexpectedness in regard to rhythm: *eigentlich ritmuslosigkeit.* . . . D'Indy is a very fine connoisseur of all matters pertaining to Gregorian music — yet his harmonization seems to me also questionable — at least, at present it seems so. Still I consider him very much until further developments.

The truth (after everything has been said) is that Gregorian Chant ought to have neither organ accompaniment nor harmonies put under it anyhow. The Solesmes Monks sing *Unisono* without harmonization. When I see you I shall talk this over with you. My [choir-] boys are all having such severe colds, that to hear them sing now, makes you think of young crows cawing after they leave their nest. They are taking hold however of some new and difficult things quite well. Some of the better ones I hope that you will listen to some day with interest. I am thinking in particular of a *Resurrexi* in the IV Mode in which there is a great deal of chanting to a very few words. Two little fellows in the middle of the chant intone

This is really very moving and for unknown reasons! It is so simple — the children are not artists — they are in fact poor singers, and although they all know what the Latin words mean, they do . . . not try . . . to put a deep meaning into their music, and still it is affecting! What is it, do you think? It must be the true, sincere ring of the faithful soul that conceived the words and music which speaks so forcibly and convincing[ly] to us. Well, enough of that now. I am happy that you are interested in this sort of art.

How will the German Dr. affect you and Mr. Schirmer next Tuesday? [3] Please tell me all about it after the première. I hope to hear it later too; then I shall probably enjoy my staying with you much more than the opera. I have misgivings! Dr. Heitzel played to me some of the important scenes. They may be theatrically effective — beautiful they are not. Adieu, dear Mrs. Schirmer, for today. A line from you will be welcome to yours devotedly

CH. M. LOEFFLER

---

3 The first American performance of Richard Strauss's *Salome* at the Metropolitan Opera House, January 27, 1907.

EDWARD MACDOWELL

New York City, 1861 — New York City, 1908

◕❭◐❭◕❭◐❭◕❭◐❭◕

To *Mary M. Shaw*

New York, April 24, 1897

My dear Madam,

  Many thanks for your kind note. The compliment you propose to pay me is appreciated, I assure you. It is impossible for me however to make any suggestions for your programme for two reasons. First the choice of selections, I think, would have to rest entirely according on the means at your disposal (I mean of course executive ability) and on the other hand I must tell you frankly that after careful consideration I have come to the conclusion that concerts composed entirely of American music are not advisable for many reasons. To name a few — I think the massing together of work by Americans affords no means of estimating their merits, except by comparison. This I think is a pity, for while it may mean the elevation of one man's work, it just as inevitably means also the disparagement of another American's work — Americans should not strive with one another for ascendancy. Far better would be the comparison of American with foreign art. This gives us a standard for criticism and does no harm.

  Another reason for my opinion is, that to classify music according to nationalities is to narrow its scope. In spite of Mr. Dvořák's desire to clothe American music in Negro costume I hold that such foreign artificiality should have no place in our art if it is ever to be worthy of our free country. American concerts provoke comparisons and should by any means this not be the case — they give rise to the equally unpleasant "mutual admiration" which has done as much harm to our art as the first. Pray pardon my frankness. I trust it will not prevent your recognizing the sincerity of my appreciation. Believe me, Yours faithfully,

E. MacDowell

To *Felix Mottl*

[*New York City*, February 13, 1904]

I see by the morning papers a so-called American Composers' Concert advertized for tomorrow evening at the Opera House.

I have for years taken a strong stand against such affairs, and though I have not seen the program, fearing there may be something of mine in it,[1] I write to protest earnestly and strongly against this lumping together of American composers. Unless we are worthy of being put on programs with other composers, to stand or fall, leave us alone.

By giving such a concert, you tacitly admit that we are too inferior to stand comparison with composers of Europe. If my name is on the program, and it is too late to have new ones made, I beg you to have a line put through the number, crossing it off the programs. If necessary, I will pay the expense of having this done.

Hoping this may not be necessary, and that my name has not been added to the list of American composers whose works you have selected,

Believe me,

Very truly yours,
EDWARD MACDOWELL

---

1 MacDowell's Suite for Orchestra, op. 42, was included in the program along with works by Rubin Goldmark, Horatio Parker, Henry Hadley, and George Chadwick.

FREDERICK DELIUS

Bradford, 1862 — Grez-sur-Loing, 1934

⊖⊕⊖⊕⊖⊕⊖⊕⊖⊕⊖

To *Ethel Smyth* [1]

Grez-sur-Loing,
March 15, 1909

Dear Miss Smyth,

Firstly let me tell you how delighted I am that your opera [2] will be brought out in June and that Beecham will bring it out. You will only understand Beecham entirely when he has brought one of your own works out. Then you will realise how deep the man goes into your work and how he personifies himself with it. Of course I shall do my utmost to be present. . . .

You must have misunderstood me about German music. I am a great admirer of the great German composers. I protest only against the school which imitates them and would palm its imitations off as the real thing — the so-called classical direction. The Russians and French have tried to break away, and partly the Norwegians — Grieg. The English and Americans, however, go on stolidly creating dead works.

The French, although perhaps not great composers, know that their force lies in charm and grace, and the light touch in the orchestra. The Russians also try to give that strange mixture of the Orient and Occident; the half-barbaric — the peculiar mixture of Wagner and the "Danse du Ventre." Grieg has given us charming and poetical music based on the Folk Song, the English nothing. They go on conscientiously working on foreign models and on Biblical subjects, and indeed the public is *abruti* to that degree that they will listen with respect and awe to any twaddle having Jesus or the Virgin Mary as a subject. And when it is more than usually dry and long they call it "noble and severe."

---

1 English composer (1858–1944).
2 *The Wreckers*, performed at His Majesty's Theatre in London later in the year.

[309]

Handel is the creator of this public and of the "genre ennuy-eux," which is still the bane of music in England, and every conductor in England flatters that public except Beecham. I believe there is lots of talent in England and that it will gradually become more daring and independent, but there is as yet very little to encourage it.

I consider Percy Grainger the most gifted of all the young composers I have met, and he is again Australian. Have you met him? He does quite remarkable things and is most refreshing. I shall be in London for June 7th (*A Mass of Life*) [3] and hope to see something of you. . . .

I am extremely glad to hear you like Beecham and hope you will be able to get him subscribers for his concerts. He deserves the support of all the best London musical people. We ought all to write and push in one direction in order to form a new public and create a new musical centre.

Very sincerely yours,
FREDERICK DELIUS

3 By Delius, 1905.

CLAUDE DEBUSSY

Saint-Germain-en-Laye, 1862 — Paris, 1918

❂❂❂❂❂❂❂❂❂

To *E. Baron*

[*Rome*] February 9, 1887

My dear Friend:

Now it's my turn to ask you not to accuse me of indifference because I took so long to answer your letter, especially since it contained unpleasant news. I pity you with all my heart and silently pray that you will be relieved. My own excuse is my *envoi*,[1] which bothers me a great deal and makes me lead a life compared to which prisoners are well off.

I took it into my head to write a work with a special colour which was to communicate the greatest possible number of sensations. The title is *Printemps* [2] — not spring taken in the descriptive sense, but from the human point of view. I should like to express the slow and painful genesis of beings and things in nature, then their gradual unfolding, culminating in a burst of joy at rebirth into a new life — something of that sort.

All this, of course, without a program, since I have the greatest contempt for music that has to follow a bit of literature which they've been careful to hand you when you come in. Well, you must realize how much evocative power this music requires and I don't know whether I shall be able to carry out this project perfectly.

Your letter mentions the need of taking yourself to a city of "eternal spring." Don't come to Rome. Right now this city, hitherto known for its sunshine, seems like Moscow, completely covered with snow and cold enough to turn you into ice. The Romans don't understand it at all; they always wear their coats too short and find it very hard to put on real overcoats. All this [snow] gives the ruins

---

1 As a Prix de Rome scholar, Debussy had to compose an annual *Envoi de Rome*.
2 His *envoi* for that year, for orchestra and chorus; first performance, 1913.

a very lovely colour, making them look clean and adding a little originality to their cold, correct lines. It's a thousand times better than the usual pipe-clay colours and the stupefying blue sky.

I readily accept your proposal of sending me *Francillon* and I'd like you also to include *La Revue indépendante* and *Paysages de femmes* by J. Ajalbert, published by Vesnier. Hope my letter will find you completely recovered, and please believe me, affectionately,

A. DEBUSSY

◊)◊)◊)◊)◊)◊)◊)◊)◊

To *Ernest Chausson*

[Paris] September 6, 1893

Dear Friend:

I've tried in vain, I can't succeed in brightening up the sadness of my landscape — sometimes my days are as dark and gloomy and silent as those of an Edgar Allan Poe hero, and thus my romantic soul like a ballad by Chopin! Too many memories fill my solitude, but I can't throw them away, well, one must live and wait. It remains to be seen whether I haven't got a wrong number for the bus of Happiness, though I'd be quite content with standing-room! (Excuse this cheap philosophy!)

Now the hour of my thirty-first year has struck and I still am not very sure of my æsthetic and there are still things I do not know! (how to write masterpieces, for example, and then how to be very serious, among other things having the weakness of caring too much about my life and never seeing its realities until they become insurmountable). Perhaps I'm more to be pitied than condemned; anyway, while writing you, I'm counting on your forgiveness and patience.

I had a visit from Henri de Régnier, who shows great liking for you — it's somewhat like speaking of hemp in the house of one who has been hanged! Also, to make things worse, I made myself as charming as possible and played *L'Après-midi d'un faune*, which he found as hot as a furnace and he praised the shivering in it! (Make what you can of this.) On the other hand, when he talks poetry, he is extremely interesting and shows very refined sensibility.

While he was speaking to me about certain words in the French language whose gold had become tarnished through too much use by the *hoi polloi*, I thought to myself that the same thing was true of certain chords whose sound had become commonplace in music for export; this reflection is not strikingly novel unless I add that at the same time they have lost their symbolic quality. Really, music should have been a hermetic science, protected by texts so long and difficult to interpret that they surely would have discouraged the herd of people who use it as casually as they do a handkerchief! Moreover, instead of trying to extend art further among the people, I propose the establishment of a "Society of Esoteric Music " and you'll see that neither M. Helmann nor M. de Bonnières will belong. While I am writing to you, the girl at the piano below me is sawing out some music in D which is really fearful! Alas, it's living proof that I'm right.

And you, my dear friend, are you working hard, are you feeling content? Haven't you any more pretty little children who create an uproar like 500,000 claps of thunder! Have you definitely decided to let that poor Genièvre [3] die! The last thing you showed me led me to expect very lovely music from you — I'm waiting with great confidence. Me, I'm working like mad, but is it my misanthropic existence — anyway I'm not pleased with what I'm doing. I wish you were here for a while. I'm afraid of working in a vacuum and it begins to seem like youthful barbarism, which, in any case, I can't resist.

Your poor Claude Achille is waiting like another Sister Anne for your return, which will fill his heart with joy. I embrace you affectionately.

CLAUDE DEBUSSY

Latest News

I've just finished the last *Proses lyriques*,[4] dedicated to H. Lerolle, first to give me pleasure and not to end a friendship.

Received a letter from V. d'Indy, very friendly, containing enough praise to make the lilies blush which lie sleeping between the fingers of *La Damoiselle élue*.[5]

C. A. Debussy is completing a scene from *Pelléas et Mélisande*, "*Une fontaine dans le Parc*" (Act IV, Scene iv), for which he would like to have the advice of E. Chausson. I wonder if there isn't any way of organizing some special pleasure trains between Paris and Royan for this event, whose general interest requires no further explanation.

3 Heroine of Chausson's opera *Le Roi Arthus*.
4 Songs.
5 Lyric poem for orchestra and women's voices (1887).

To *Jacques Durand*

Pourville, September 3, 1907

Dear Friend,

Now you see that hidden beneath the appearance of a recently discovered mummy, this M. Sonzogno has the soul of a discerning dilettante. Have you considered what the word *éclat* could mean in connection with *Pelléas*? Does he intend to introduce a few voice exercises into it?

Well, I am satisfied and congratulate you on your fine success.[6] When you ask me when I plan to return, you make me feel very impatient. But you know that our house is being painted, and according to news from Paris, it won't be ready for ten days or two weeks. It is very cold here and I have more or less recovered.

The *Images* will be ready if I can manage to finish the "*Rondes*"[7] the way I'd like. The music of this work has a special incorporeal quality all its own and consequently it can't be handled like a robust symphony, which marches along on its four feet (sometimes three, but it marches just the same). Further, I am more and more convinced that music, by its very nature, is something that cannot be poured into a rigid and traditional form. It is colours and time, in rhythm. The rest is a joke invented by those unfeeling imbeciles who place the blame on the masters, who, in general, wrote almost nothing but period music. Bach alone had an idea of the truth. In any case, music is a very young art, in method as well as in "knowledge."

I hope to be in Paris around the 15th. If you want to send me *Pelléas* in English, I shall be very glad to see it.

My affectionate greetings to your father.

Your devoted friend,
CLAUDE DEBUSSY

---

6 Durand had arranged for a performance of *Pelléas et Mélisande* in Italy.
7 "*Rondes de printemps*" from *Images* (3rd set), completed 1909.

To *Jacques Durand*

Paris, March 1908

Dear Jacques:

There is a letter for you at the Hôtel Gonnet that contains some news in very minute detail. Do get it, since I am incapable of repeating it and you may be rather amused. Don't blame the sea too much for irritating your nerves; you can really believe that it is completely involuntary, and if her caresses are rough, at least they are sincere.

As for the "Parisian whirl," I have very little to do with it, if you don't mind. I find our age so singularly unattractive because of all the uproar over nothing. We are wrong to make fun of the Americans, for we ourselves cultivate a kind of artistic bluff that one of these days will come home to roost, and it will be rather disagreeable for French vanity.

The *Images* will not be completely finished when you return, but I hope to play you a large part of it. I am trying to do "something different" — in a way, *realities* — what the idiots call "impressionism," a term used as badly as possible, particularly by the art critics, who don't hesitate to wrap up Turner in it — the finest creator of the mysterious there is in art.

From the tone of this letter don't think I've become a pessimist. I have a horror of that mental attitude. Only now and then people disgust me and I have to cry out to someone who won't consider it a disease. My wife and I send all good wishes for your trip, and for your return, and I remain your faithful friend,

CLAUDE DEBUSSY

❀❀❀❀❀❀❀

To *Jacques Durand*

Pourville, August 5, 1915

Dear Jacques:

It's because people have the unfortunate privilege of not being able to regulate their "thinking-machine" the way they would like that you are not happy, despite the charms of Bel-Ebat. As for me, despite the sea, the garden, and Mon Coin, I suffer from the terrible uncertainty of this war. Sometimes I do not even dare pick up the paper, which knows nothing and keeps speculating according to its particular slant, to hold the reader's interest. Otherwise I should relapse into the state I was in at Paris, and I want to work, not so much for myself, but to give proof, no matter how small, that if there were thirty million Boches, they would not be able to destroy French thought, even though they tried to brutalize it before completely destroying it.

I am thinking of the youth of France, so crassly mowed down by these dealers in *Kultur*, through whom we have for ever lost the renown they would have brought our heritage. As for the Russians, people seem to forget that they have been our worst enemies, and quite plainly they are starting up again with the Germans — who haven't yet burned Moscow. And now people are talking about a Japanese intervention. Why not the inhabitants of Mars while they're about it?

All this only makes the Boches feel more arrogant, and they don't need to, damn it all. And what a frightful business of straightening out accounts afterwards! Why all these guests invited to eat a cake that hasn't been baked yet? La Fontaine wrote a nice fable on this theme, but that was when France had enough good sense for all of Europe.

You will receive, perhaps even before this letter, the *Sonate pour violoncelle et piano*. It isn't up to me to pass on its excellence, but I like its proportions and almost classical form, in the good sense of the word. You will also find what should replace, in the *2nd Caprice*, the original bars:

(left hand 1st part)

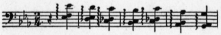

and continues up to the return of the motif in augmentation:

(a device that comes to us from the old masters, as you know, long before the "school" of the fugue).

My concern about the proportions accounts for this change; besides it has become lighter and the atmosphere has been cleared of that sickening haze which the Luther chorale spread through it, or rather what it represents, for it is really very lovely.

I'm resuming work on the proofs of the Chopin *Polonaises*, after which I beg you to excuse me, but the Muse whom you think dwells in me at this moment is a person whose fidelity I've learned not to trust, and I'd rather hold on to her than run after her.

That, my dear Jacques, is what is going on in my "thinker," not to mention the *Études* [8] on which I'm working. With all my heart I wish you not a more tranquil, but a more hopeful stay at Bel-Ebat. We send our regards, and I am, as always, your devoted

C. D.

---

8 *Douze Études*, for piano.

HORATIO PARKER

Auburndale, Mass., 1863 — Cedarhurst, N. Y., 1919

❋❂❋❂❋❂❋❂❋❂❋

To *Douglas Moore* [1]

Bluehill, Mass., July 1, 1917

My dear Douglas,

We shall miss you greatly but hope to see you sometimes and to see your work as well.

Thank you for Francis Thompson. I suspect him of ability to fill a large vacant space in me when I shall get at him really. So far I have just lapped a little at the cream of the verse and find it sympathetic, satisfying, good work.

Thank you still more for your kind letter. I think we have an atmosphere of honesty about our musical doings, however imperfect they may be and I love to hear you say it has been helpful. Your problem now is to get things out of yourself rather than out of others or out of atmosphere. It can be done better with the head than the fingers which are for recording purposes rather than for producing. I think you have much feeling and much talent for music making, and, if you are a little backward in the technique of expression, that gives you a concrete point of attack for your work. Don't let a week go by without some definite progress. *Vita brevis!* Get a professional attitude and keep it. Make something worth printing and have it published *on its merits*. That will encourage you largely and legitimately. You are a bit inclined to confound solemnity and seriousness. Things can be cheerful and serious too. But all this is words and no substitute for music.

I hope sincerely that you will find your métier and your true direction before long and that you will make long strides. Forgive me for being so darned didactic, it is the evil habit of many years. I would far rather be personal but you are caught in the cogs of my

---

1 Moore had studied with Parker at Yale and was now leaving for Paris to study with d'Indy.

educational machinery such as it is and I have difficulty in detaching you so soon.

You have always given us much pleasure and have always been very welcome. Be sure that your welcome will not grow cool and claim it whenever you can.

We all join in sending you our love and every good wish.

Sincerely yours,
HORATIO PARKER

RICHARD STRAUSS

Munich, 1864 —

❖❖❖❖❖❖❖❖

To *Hugo von Hofmannsthal* [1]

December 15, 1913

The highly talented musician Wolf-Ferrari, in conjunction with the equally highly talented librettist Herr Batka, has written an opera called *Der Liebhaber als Arzt,* taken from Molière's *Le Médecin malgré lui.* This opera was produced in Dresden a few days ago, with our *Ariadne* [2] costumes, and had an overwhelming success — the press welcomed it as "*the* long-expected musical comedy of our time"! How many comic operas in the last five years have been welcomed as "*the* musical comedy of our time" — with the one exception of the *Rosenkavalier,* which was given here three days ago for the eighty-ninth time, and not a seat to be had in the house!

In a Dresden paper I read that the Wolf-Ferrari-cum-Batka work is the real "renaissance of Molière" through the medium of music — a thing that I, thanks to your "clumsiness," was unable to achieve in *Ariadne!* The fellow has evidently heard something about Nietzsche's *The Birth of Tragedy from the Spirit of Music* and now he will have Molière born again through Wolf-Ferrari. My dear friend, must we take all this nonsense lying down? Ought one not rather to protest in some form or other? Or must I go on waiting patiently till people come to see for themselves how carefully and conscientiously you have pondered over the subject before carrying it through — with what nicety we have selected every-

---

1 Poet and dramatist (1874–1929). His collaboration with Strauss produced *Elektra* (1909), *Der Rosenkavalier* (1911), *Ariadne auf Naxos* (1912), *Die Frau ohne Schatten* (1919), *Die Ægyptische Helena* (1928), and *Arabella* (1933).

2 *Ariadne auf Naxos,* incidental music to Molière's *Le Bourgeois Gentilhomme,* produced at Stuttgart, October 25, 1912; rewritten as an opera and performed in Vienna, November 1916.

thing from Molière's play that lends itself to music, how our comedy gradually brings us into the very heart of music and leads us on to heights of which no reincarnation of Molière could have any conception! Is it not enough to make one swear when one reads how the public was vastly entertained for a whole evening by the ravishing musical comedy of MM. Wolf-Ferrari and Batka, while in the case of our short abridgment of Molière — in which you have left really nothing that is not amusing and characteristic — the same public was so bored to death that it could not even wait for the opera?

Must we put up with this sort of thing for ever? Have you no one among your friends who could say a few plain far-reaching words that might quash once for all this legend of "the tedious *Bourgeois*"? This story, which has spread all over the world, gaining, as it goes, by elaboration and innuendo, sprang from the trifling fact that at the original production in Stuttgart, in consequence of two intermissions of fifty minutes each (for which the royal visitors were to blame), the public was made to wait three hours before the eagerly expected opera of the composer Strauss began — and their impatience was put down to their boredom at Molière and Hofmannsthal's comedy.

And not a single one of the scribblers has taken the trouble to examine for himself this catch-phrase about the "dreary, unending play of Molière" that in Stuttgart lasted, with intermission, for three hours — although now, whenever it is given, it plays just one hour.

During our Strauss week the good Princess Marie von Meiningen was here on a visit and heard all my operas (with the exception of *Salome*) for the first time. After reading the text of the *Rosenkavalier* she wrote me saying she found it tedious; after the performance on Friday she confessed to me that, to her astonishment, she now found the text enchanting! This lady had the courage and the decency to revise, after the performance, the judgment she had previously given — which of the critics would do as much? I should like to see what these people would say if they had to criticize the book, say, of the *Meistersinger* or *Parsifal* without knowing it was by Richard Wagner; I wager ninety per cent would declare it unspeakably tedious, and quite unsuitable for composition.

After all, we must recognize the value of the sort of work we have done in *Ariadne*, and I will allow no one to belittle it; for this reason I am opposed to any revision, or separation of the opera from the comedy. Negotiations are now in progress for the production of *Ariadne* (in English) in America next year, just as we wrote it, and in a small theatre.

Once more I ask you, have you no one who can secure a wider publicity for the work by some weighty and influential utterance about it — the style of the whole and the value of Molière's share in it? The perpetual nonsense one has to listen to on this subject gets on my nerves after a time. I shall get Dr. Bie to come out this afternoon before the performance and talk this matter over with him, for if one allows wrong impressions to go too long uncorrected, they end by being taken for the truth.

STRAUSS

To *Hugo von Hofmannsthal*

Garmisch, October 8, 1914

. . . It was a great relief to me to hear ten days ago from Baron Franckenstein that you were no longer in the field, but had been given some other post. I think you will be rather pleased when I tell you that my sketch for the first four tableaux in Act II [3] is already finished, as well as the scene for the Empress. . . . It is all very rich in contrasts. As for the text, it is absolutely brilliant, and marvellously easy to compose — its terse and pregnant style is a continual stimulus. My dear Da Ponte, this is certainly your masterpiece!

Except for the splendid deeds of our army, the news is gloomy enough — our only refuge is in hard work; otherwise one would fret oneself to death over the stupidity of our diplomacy and our press, the Kaiser's apologetic telegram to President Wilson, and all the indignities one has to swallow. And how they are treating the artists! The Kaiser cuts down the salaries at the Hoftheater, the Duchess of Meiningen turns her orchestra into the street — Reinhardt is playing Shakespeare — at Frankfurt they are giving *Carmen, Mignon, Tales of Hoffmann*. How can one ever hope to understand the German people, that blend of stupidity and genius, heroism and servility? What is the feeling in Vienna? One hears so many accounts that one knows not what to think. Of course we shall win

---

3 *Die Frau ohne Schatten* (1919).

— and when we have won, heaven only knows whether they won't mess everything up again! . . . If I succeed in getting Act II finished in October, I shall put the whole thing aside till Easter, and then start again with fresh energy for the finish. In the winter I mean to score my *Alpine Symphony*.

STRAUSS

JEAN SIBELIUS

Hämeenlinna, Finland, 1865 —

◦)◦◦)◦◦)◦◦)◦◦)◦

To an unnamed recipient

May 20, 1918

. . . as if I were preparing to quit this life and in descending into my grave shot an eagle on the wing — sighted well and skilfully without a thought of what was in store.

My new works — partly sketched and planned.

The Vth symphony in a new form — practically composed anew — I work at daily. Movement I entirely new, movement II reminiscent of the old, movement III reminiscent of the end of the I movement of the old. Movement IV the old motifs, but stronger in revision. The whole, if I may say so, a vital climax to the end. Triumphal.

The VIth symphony is wild and impassioned in character. Sombre, with pastoral contrasts. Probably in 4 movements, with the end rising to a sombre roaring of the orchestra, in which the main theme is drowned.

The VIIth symphony. Joy of life and vitality, with appassionato passages. In 3 movements — the last a "Hellenic rondo."

All this with due reservation. . . . It looks as if I were to come out with all these three symphonies at the same time.

As usual, the sculptural more prominent in my music. Hence this hammering on the ethical line that takes hold of me entirely and on which I must concentrate and hold out. . . .

With regard to symphonies VI and VII the plans may possibly be altered according to the development of the musical ideas. As usual, I am a slave to my themes and submit to their demands.

By all this I see how my innermost self has changed since the days of the IVth symphony. And these symphonies of mine are more in the nature of professions of faith than my other works.

[JEAN SIBELIUS]

To *Rosa Newmarch*

March 10, 1930

You cannot imagine what a great joy came over me on receiving your letter. I felt as though I had retrieved something infinitely precious.

I was very much interested to hear that Basil Cameron had conducted my music so well. He came here to see me and we talked of England.

I still go on composing, but I feel very much alone. There is so much in the music of the present day that I cannot accept. For example, that one should be able to make for oneself an ideal by reflection (a reflected ideal). Also it seems to me that modern music does not progress, that it marks time without getting a step farther. It is the urgent need for progress that is lacking when the architectural form is neglected.

"Little" Katarina has been married several years to a judge, named Elves, and has two children — a daughter and a son. Our fourth daughter is also married, so only the youngest remains at home. She is studying "applied art" in Helsingfors.

My wife was delighted to receive your greetings, and sends you her kindest remembrances. I have a great wish to come to England to see you again. I am afraid it will not come off this spring, but during the summer perhaps I might manage to meet you in Karlsbad. It would be a great, great pleasure to continue our interesting talks of old.

With all my heart,

Your grateful,
JEAN SIBELIUS

VASILY SERGEYEVICH KALINNIKOV

Government of Orlov, 1866 — Yalta, 1901

❁⟊❁⟊❁⟊❁⟊❁⟊❁

To *Alexandre Tichonovitch Gretchaninoff*

Yalta, July 19, 1900

Dear Alexandre Tichonovitch:

My recent letters dealing with music in general and your music to *Snyegurochka* in particular have apparently disturbed you a little. But you must not think that "I imagine the music of *Snyegurochka* incredibly bad." How could I, since I do not know your music, and what's more — I am certain you won't compose it badly, but that your music will run true to form and be beautiful? I merely was and still am against the *kind of composing* that places our beloved art of music in a third-rate position — almost like putting it on a par with the properties. That's the way Alekseyev's plan for the music to *Snyegurochka* strikes me.

Moreover you write that you are trying to make everything "just like in a village" and that the orchestra will consist of five pieces. I cannot conceive of anything "just like in a village" being good. In a village everything is usually very nasty, and our village has no conception of any orchestra, even if it's only five pieces.

Folk music, it seems to me, is beautiful only when it is idealized (but in folk style, of course). Think how disgustingly village peasant women sing what are really often beautiful songs. Remember those wild screams and roars which accompany the best of melodies and the untrained voices that howl them. Such singing might perhaps please Lev Tolstoy, but he can't lay down the law for us. Imagine making everything on the stage "just like in a village!" No, you won't do it, and if you have tried, it was perhaps only because of Alekseyev, who is also probably under Tolstoy's influence. Such unrestrained realism in art, in music especially, I do not like and do not recognize. It lowers the art, pulling it down from those lofty regions where the human soul dwells to the level of physiological necessities, gymnastics, massage, etc.

You say that "music in drama always impresses me very strongly." That is not quite clear to me. What music do you mean? Name one play with music in which the music makes an impression. I have never seen or heard such a play. I have only seen some Ukrainian plays, but I have already written you what I think of them. And I do not think that plays with music can be developed in the future; I think even less of the future of opera, though at present it has engulfed music. It seems to me that mixing drama with music is impossible in any form, especially in opera. In that respect Wagner squandered his genius and only demonstrated to artists of word and sound that fusion of these two arts is an absurdity. I think I have expressed myself this way to you before and I know you do not agree.

And now for your wily question: "How can the Art Theatre stage *Snyegurochka*?" [1] You say that "most of the play is acted in the midst of various old Slavic rituals with music and dancing." I could simply say I don't know — it isn't my intention to solve the problems of the Art Theatre or to further their plans. Besides, you must agree that the question itself is of secondary importance, what and how to do it, and so on. However, I shall reply so that you won't reproach me for not carrying my argument to its logical conclusion. That is: the Art Theatre has no business staging *Snyegurochka* as long as they want it to be "just like in a village." *Snyegurochka* is a highly artistic, idealized national work of Ostrovsky and, in my opinion, it will lose all meaning in all its aspects, particularly the musical one, if it is presented "just like in a village."

Dear friend, you must understand that while I cling to my opinion on this matter, I do not wish to impose it on you. If only you would free yourself of outside influences and see my point (though I think you do not wish to see it), I shall be glad if it will help you to see the other side of the question. Again I repeat that I may be wrong. But prove to me how and why I am wrong.

Very cordially,

Yours,

V. S. KALINNIKOV

---

1 The Moscow Art Theatre performed this several months later.

GRANVILLE BANTOCK

London, 1868 —

❂❂❂❂❂❂❂❂❂❂

To his son *Raymond*

Buxton, May 12, 1926

My dear old Boy,

Your letter of April 6th I found awaiting me on my return home from Ireland last Saturday, by the last and only Mail boat that was run during the week. We were all glad to hear of your safe return to Japan after your adventurous wanderings, and we are already beginning to count the months that are to pass before your return home.

I left home at *9 a.m.*, and after changing trains at Derby, and again at Miller's Dale, and then getting a lift in a car to Buxton, arrived here at 3 p.m., to learn that the General Strike has petered out and been called off. There was no other course possible. The Trades Union Council never expected such an effective resistance. The country has been solid behind Baldwin and the Government kept cool and took effective measures to guard against panic and to protect the people. It was good to see the University students driving the omnibus and motor lorries with a bobby on every bus, and in Bham alone over 20,000 men were enrolled as special constables. Angus joined up and went on duty, while Ham was taken on by the Midland Railway at Saltley to get up steam and fire the engines ready for journeys. He was lodged in their barracks under police protection. Beyond wrecking the Flying Scotsman Express, the strikers were able to do nothing, and had they tried rioting, I fancy they would have got much the worst of it. So much for the strike, which might have become a Revolution but for the firmness of Baldwin.

I am glad to hear that you enjoyed Sean O'Casey's play *Juno and the Paycock*. I have seen it acted 5 or 6 times, and enjoy it more each time. When in Dublin last week, I saw O'Casey's new play *The Plough and the Stars* at the Abbey Theatre, and met all the

[328]

players in the Green Room, with Yeats and Lennox Robinson. It is a play dealing with the Irish Rebellion, and is a splendid piece of realism, though hardly equal to *Juno* in greatness. On the Monday night previous, Mrs. Despurd, Maud Gonne, Mrs. Sheffington and other irreconcilables stood outside the Abbey Theatre, and let off some stink-bombs inside as a protest on behalf of the Irish martyrs. They were promptly locked up by the Free State Government. I saw AE twice, and had tea with him at his home on Sunday. We went over his play of *Deirdre*, which I shall tackle as a Folk Opera, as soon as I have scored *The Song of Songs*. He was much interested to hear about you, and has given me another picture. The *Feis* was a great success as you will gather from the copies of *The Irish Times* which I sent to you from Dublin. This week, I am adjudicating at the Buxton Festival for the 4th time — on Thursday, Friday and Saturday, and will spend Sunday with some friends at Alderley Edge, where I am adjudicating next year. These Festivals are a god-send, and I shall be away now each week-end until July. . . .

Sybil Thorndike has asked me to write the music for her production of *Macbeth* at Xmas, and I am very tempted to see what I can do. The play is my favourite, and I have an idea of using only brass instruments with Oboes and Bassoons (no strings at all) to express the savage barbarism that might shock the nerves of the stolid B. P. I am going to talk the matter over with her and her husband, Lewis Casson, when I am next in London or when they are in N. Wales for their holiday in the summer. Your time-table of work amazes me, and I wonder how you succeed in getting so much done. Now that your play is finished, you will be able to get some articles or stories written, which I hope may bring you in something.

I am much looking forward to reading your review of Claudel's *Tête d'Or*. It will be a very valuable experience for you, if you can return by Siberia, and visit Tashkent, Samarkand and other Russian centres en route, especially if you can get introductions from the Russian Consul at Tokyo or Soviet representatives at Vladivostok and Harbin, where you seem to have made several good friends.

Well, I must get to work. Your new photo snapshot was very welcome. You are looking very well and younger.

Much love, dear boy, from

Your ever affectionate
DADDY

ALBERT ROUSSEL

Tourcoing, 1869 — Royan, 1937

❁❁❁❁❁❁

To *L. Dunton Green* [1]

[1928]

Forgive me if I reply somewhat briefly to the interesting inquiry to which you open the pages of the *Chesterian*. I returned to Paris only two days ago and my study is crowded with overdue correspondence and proofs awaiting revision. . . .

You ask me what I think about musical inspiration and the manner in which it reveals itself during the composition of a long work. What is by common consent called musical inspiration is, if I am not mistaken, the artist's faculty of conceiving and clearly expressing ideas that should be admirable both for quality and for copiousness. It presupposes the perfect function of a musically organized, sensitive, and imaginative brain, and the possession of a technique that enables the composer to solve the problems that will necessarily confront him. That he should be able to keep this faculty intact in the course of a composition on a large scale does not strike me as at all mysterious. It is probably that, once he has written down the last note of his score, he will feel the need of a period of rest before he undertakes a new work; this applies to every profession demanding a high cerebral tension.

You tell me that the author of the book on psychology and music [2] wonders whether in the process of creation the composer is influenced more by sentiments of a general nature which he could describe or by purely musical motives. In my view that depends largely on the character of the work. If it is a question of a symphonic work devoid of a program or commentary, there is no general feeling that could be defined and the composer is concerned

---

1 In reply to a question concerning the nature of musical inspiration for publication in the *Chesterian*.

2 Frank Howes: *The Borderland of Music and Psychology.*

only with the interplay of sound-combinations, the infinite variety of which offers his imagination unlimited scope. It is possible that such music may suggest to certain hearers feelings that the composer himself did not experience in the least, but this is one of the inevitable consequences of the undefined character of the musical language.

In the case of a descriptive or dramatic work, on the other hand, an element foreign to music directs the composer's thought toward some quite definite object and he is caught up in an atmosphere where musical ideas present themselves in certain particular forms. Themes, harmony, rhythm, and orchestral colour are all influenced by it. Although of little account in the case of a certain type of symphonic poem without a detailed program, this foreign element may become predominant in program music and in music drama; but whatever its importance, it would be wrong to suppose that the musician remains absorbed in the contemplation of the object of his attention during the whole course of composition of a long work. He will come to a point where his mind will find itself turned in a direction he will follow almost unconsciously and without effort, and he will then be free to bring his whole intellectual power to bear upon the musical aspect of his work.

Needless to say, this is merely a personal view. What is true of one composer cannot be applied to another and I have no doubt that you will gather in some vastly divergent opinions on the subject. A long dissertation might be written on such a subject and I am a little afraid on rereading what I have said, lest it should be wanting in interest. If I nevertheless send you these few lines it is because I wish to show you how anxious I am not to leave your request unanswered.

[ALBERT ROUSSEL]

ALEXANDER SCRIABIN

Moscow, 1872 — Moscow, 1915

❉❉❉❉❉❉

To *Nicholas F. Findeizen*

Lausanne, December 26, 1907

Dear Nikolay Feodorovich:

First, many thanks for the speed with which you responded to my request. In turn, I am very glad to be able to help you by giving you some details about myself and I shall answer all your questions in order. I shall send you the text of the *Poem of Ecstasy* in a few days. It was published in Geneva in brochure and has not yet appeared for sale.

I first met Belyayev [1] in 1892 and Mitrofan Petrovich at once showed the most touching friendliness and fatherly solicitude for me. I made my first concert tour with him (for the purpose of introducing my compositions to the public), and this journey brought us even closer together. My memories of Belyayev are very dear to me and his loss was a great blow.

The results of my first trip abroad were splendid. Success everywhere, and better than good reviews in the papers. In Paris I had the greatest success.

I became a professor at the Moscow Conservatory after a great deal of vacillation, for purely material reasons, since at that time I had no inclination for pedagogical activity and my health was none too good. I left the Conservatory in order to devote myself exclusively to my aims, which I am incapable of describing in a few words. I can only say, in so far as the content is concerned, that the *Poem of Ecstasy* offers a small hint of what I wish my principal work to be. Its text requires commentaries, which I may perhaps publish separately.

I have preferred to live abroad because life in Russia, and espe-

---

1 Founder of a music-publishing firm and a series of concerts devoted exclusively to Russian music.

cially Moscow, with our inability to become oriented into this age, did not permit me to put into practice the discipline that is essential to the fulfilment of my task.

I brought back with me an excellent impression of America! In my judgment, the customary opinions about that country are frequently immature and prejudiced. The Americans are not at all dull and artistically untalented, as is generally believed.

Concerning the poems, many of them have a specific psychological content, but not all of them require programs. The Fourth Sonata has a text which has not been published; it was written after the music and in accordance with it. It happened that the Third Symphony was performed in St. Petersburg without any program. In Paris a brief text was included in the program.

I think that is all. Permit me to express my thanks for your interest in my work, and with very best wishes,

Most sincerely,
A. SCRIABIN

MAX REGER

Brand (Bavaria), 1873 — Leipzig, 1916

⊕⧓⊕⧓⊕⧓⊕⧓⊕⧓⊕

To *Adalbert Lindner*

Wiesbaden, June 6, 1891

Cavalleria Rusticana! It has been performed here three times and has been a great success, of course. But believe me, it will not have a long run and the second opera will not materialize. We'll see whether I'm right. It is a tragic operetta, very humdrum and even more pompous.

I don't think that the more intelligent audience will be fooled very long. Really, in our Wagner-impregnated atmosphere with chromatics and enharmonics for oxygen, it isn't surprising that suddenly a piece with melody (though its melodious character may be somewhat questionable) should take hold — only to disappear again soon. Believe me, this success has come too early to last. Don't think my opinion is due to jealousy or envy. For all I care, people can write as many operas as they like.

What sort of opera shall we have after Wagner? Are we going to have more Wagners? Or shall we revert to the principles of Weber? When will there come an Alexander to boldly cut these Gordian knots? A merging of Wagner and Gluck is the only ideal the new opera can have.

It seems to me that in music today we have to enter a new era. The signs of the dawn are increasing. For the Liszt-Berlioz program, and all the later ones such as Richard Strauss, Nicodé, and others, are basically on the wrong track. Music should not (as is true of program music) require any intermediary to be generally understood. Music, in and by itself, should generate a flow of pure emotion without the least tinge of extraneous rationalization.

But enough of this æsthetic speculation. I seldom make such statements openly; at most, I discuss these things with Riemann.[1]

---

1 Hugo Riemann (1849–1919), music historian.

When they have company, as they did the other Sunday, we retire to his study and smoke and chat informally about this and that (while the other gentlemen are busy entertaining the ladies).

You say that my sonata [2] moves along completely original lines. I am glad to have in you at least one devotee of the sonata. But you have no idea what it really sounds like, because first you would have to have strings, and secondly a Guarnerius with tremendous volume. The Adagio is in the Beethoven style.

[MAX REGER]

ഠ⊹ഠ⊹ഠ⊹ഠ⊹ഠ⊹ഠ⊹ഠ

To *Ferruccio Busoni* [3]

Wiesbaden, May 11, 1895

Please forgive me for not answering your kind letter before this. I rather envy your taking a summer vacation right now and wish I could do the same. But I'll have to endure it here until the middle of August giving lessons, mostly to people completely lacking in talent, and for a pittance, at that. And what would I do during four weeks of vacation? I wouldn't do anything in my native haunts but compose, anyway. At present I am working on a piano concerto (dedicated to Eugen d'Albert) — may I dedicate my second piano concerto to you? Variations on a Beethoven theme for large orchestra will follow.

The curse of teaching is that if you take it seriously, you run up against all sorts of difficulties and unpleasantness, and if you take it lightly, the students don't learn anything. I'm very pleased with your kind offer to send me some of your works, and also some criticism of my works in another letter. Unfortunately, here in Wiesbaden there is no opportunity for making innovations; everything is as dead musically as you can possibly imagine. Yes, I don't think I should find the right soil for myself in Leipzig. As long as Leipzig continues to be under the influence of the guiding star Reinecke, it will offer very little stimulus to a "modern musician." And the thought of once more entering the conservatory as a student goes against my grain.

For three years I have deliberately refrained from composing any larger works in order to arrive at more inner artistic clarity and

2 Sonata in D minor for piano and violin, op. 1.
3 Composer and pianist (1866–1924).

to avoid falling into those partly unjustifiable exaggerations which exist in my earliest works. But, God, I'm only twenty-two years old and still have time enough to relearn. Of "direction" I have none, I take whatever is good as it comes. And I intensely dislike all musical partisanship — such as Brahms versus Wagner. I also consider it an utterly mistaken notion on the part of our music journals to be eternally preoccupied with Wagner. After all, by the grace of God, every artist knows that Wagner is just what he is — why then continually persist in publishing Wagner articles?

The younger generation in particular should be brought back again and again to the original source of musical creation and divine art — Johann Sebastian Bach — and first of all, people should know what Bach really signifies. It's too bad that Franz Liszt did such a bad job on his transcriptions of Bach's organ pieces — they're nothing but hackwork. And how will the youth of today, permeated with *Tannhäuser* and *Tristan*, ever reach a proper understanding of Bach? Bach must be played academically, that is the battle cry of the learned professors. Pardon my frankness, but every now and then I fly into a rage when I see how music is being written.

Astound the musical world again with your new works and, believe me, there is scarcely another musician who will gladly recognize the creations of a real contemporary composer with less envy and more admiration than yours cordially and very respectfully,

MAX REGER

◆)◆)◆)◆)◆)◆)◆)◆

To *Adolf Wach*

Meiningen, December 5, 1914

Your Excellency:

There are certain gentlemen on the board of directors of the Gewandhaus who look forward with mixed feelings to every performance of my new works. They consider me the reddest of anarchists. Who knows what revolutionary and extravagant ideas they attribute to me — as droll an irony of world history and the history of music as one could imagine!

I can say with good conscience that of all living composers I am probably the one who is in closest touch with the great masters of our rich past. I have never concealed these views and only recently, in a long conversation with Richard Strauss I explained them to him so fully that he finally had to admit I was right. As a result of that conversation Strauss and I, who up to now have been on very bad terms, are now very friendly. Strauss is really a great musician with tremendous ability, and at last he understands me! Two days ago I received a letter from him in which he writes about a certain matter and says: "I don't have a light hand and no such reliable and ready composing technique as you have; your inexhaustible fertility arouses my astonishment and admiration." But, as I said before, it is a rare joke in the history of music that I should be known as a bloodthirsty anarchist.

I am taking the liberty of sending Your Excellency my latest composition,[4] which has just appeared; anyone who can find revolutionary tendencies in this is beyond hope. But in spite of that, I know that if today I "begged" to have this piece performed in the Gewandhaus, there would be no dearth of male Cassandras who, wailing and weeping, would claim that if something like this were performed, sacred traditions would be turned to dust and ashes. If only the good people would finally get at least a faint idea of the force with which I bravely turn against all the perverted rubbish of Wagneritis and Straussomania! But therefore I am an outlaw, and all those who have inherited good taste as their birthright shudder and cover their heads at the sight of my infamy.

[MAX REGER]

---

4 *Variationen und Fuge über ein Thema von Mozart,* op. 132.

SERGEI RACHMANINOFF

Oneg, Novgorod, 1873 — Los Angeles, 1943

❀❀❀❀❀❀❀❀❀

To *Marietta Shaginyan* [1]

May 8, 1912

In addition to my children, music, and flowers, I love you, too, dear Re, and your letters. I love you because you are clever, interesting, and because you don't run to extremes (one of the qualities necessary to please me) and I love your letters because they are full of faith, hope, and love for me — balm for my wounds!

Though I am still full of timidity and uncertainty, your description of me is wonderfully appropriate — you know me well. How is that? I can't help wondering. In future whenever I discuss myself I shall boldly refer to you and make marginal notes from your letters — your authority is beyond question. Just one thing isn't good. I'm not completely convinced that your portrait of me resembles the original like two drops of water. You seek in me what does not exist and you want me to be something I shall never be. I regret that my "criminal internal timidity" is apparent — and I agree with you that "my defeat at the hands of philistinism" seems to be imminent. This is all true! And it's also true that I don't believe in myself. Dear Re, teach me to believe in myself! At least half as much as you believe in me! If ever I believed in myself, it was long ago — very long ago — in my youth. (By the way, at that time I was "long-haired" — a type undoubtedly more acceptable to you than . . . whom neither you nor I like and toward whom you wrongly accuse me of partiality.)

It is not without significance that in the past twenty years my only doctors have been the hypnotist, Dal', and my two cousins (one of whom I married ten years ago and I love her dearly — please add her to your list). All these people, or rather doctors, taught me

1 Poet, born 1888. She first made Rachmaninoff's acquaintance through correspondence.

that I must take courage and have faith. At times I have been successful. But my illness is here to stay and it gets worse with the years. It won't be surprising if some day I decide to stop composing and become a bona fide pianist, or a conductor, or a landowner, or a taxi-driver. . . .

Yesterday it struck me that what you would like me to be you already have completely, right before you, in someone else — Medtner.[2] You describe him as acutely as you do me, and you wish to implant in me what is innate in him. It is significant that you devote half of every letter to him. You really want to see me with him, in his circle, that "holy place" where they argue, defend, confess, and repudiate. Shall I then not be among the "youth of today, dextrously spinning verse which, alas, is infinitely far from poetry"? Surely they are "the long-haired ones"! It is good, though, that the central figure, the pivot, was rightly chosen. Actually Medtner himself is not "long-haired" as you would like to see me. And I am not prejudiced against him. On the contrary, I like and respect him very much. To be honest (as, by the way, I always am with you), I consider him the most talented of all contemporary composers. Both as musician and as man he is one of those rare persons who inspire more admiration the closer you get to them. Few men are so constituted and I give him my blessing!

But that's Medtner: young, healthy, cheerful, strong, and armed — a lyre in his hand. And here am I, spiritually sick, dear Re, and unarmed — already rather old. If my fate holds anything good, the good is not present now. As for Medtner's circle, let's drop the subject. I am afraid of them all ("criminal timidity and cowardice"). To all this "sediment of authentic art" I prefer your letters. . . . Why do I write this to you, dear Re? "Alone with my soul" — I am dissatisfied with this letter.

In conclusion I shall write a few words about something different. Always paying close attention to your letters and demands, I write "drowsy from the spring evening." Probably the "drowsy evening" is responsible for this impossible letter, which I beg you to forget soon. The windows are closed. It is cold, dear Re. However, in accordance with your instructions, the lamp is burning on the table. Because of the cold, those beetles you love, but which I hate and fear, have not yet been born, thank God! My windows are covered with big wooden shutters which are closed with iron bolts. In the evening and at night I feel more at peace. But even then

---

2 Nicolas Raslovich Medtner (born 1879).

I feel that "criminal timidity and cowardice." I am afraid of everything — mice, rats, beetles, oxen, murderers. I am frightened when a strong wind blows and howls in the chimney, when I hear the raindrops on the windowpane; I am afraid of the darkness, etc. I don't like old attics and I'm even willing to admit there are goblins around (you also are interested in this). Otherwise it would be hard to understand why I am frightened even in the daytime alone in the house at Ivanovka, an ancient estate belonging to my wife. I consider it my own, my very own; I lived there for twenty-three years. Yes, long ago when I was young there my work proceeded smoothly. . . . But that's an old song.

What else can I tell you? Better nothing. Good night, dear Re. Keep well and try to cure me too. I probably won't write you again very soon.

S. R.

ARNOLD SCHÖNBERG

Vienna, 1874 —

☙❧❙❧❙❧❙❧❙❧❙❧❙❧☙

To *Nicolas Slonimsky*

Hollywood, California
June 3, 1937

Dear Mr. Slonimsky:
   The "Method of composing with twelve
tones" had many "first steps" (*Vorversuche*). The first step happened about December 1914 or at the beginning of 1915 when I
sketched a symphony, the last part of which became later the
Jakobsleiter, but which never has been continued. The Scherzo of
this symphony was based on a theme consisting of the twelve tones.
But this was only one of the themes. I was still far away from the
idea to use such a basic theme as a unifying means for a whole
work.

  After that I was always occupied with the aim to base the
structure of my music *consciously* on a unifying idea, which produced not only all the other ideas but regulated also their accompaniment and the chords, the "harmonies." There were many attempts to achieve that. But very little of it was finished or published.

  As an example of such attempts I may mention the piano
pieces op. 23. Here I arrived at a technique which I called (for myself) "composing with tones," a very vague term, but it meant
something to me. Namely: in contrast to the ordinary way of using
a motive, I used it already almost in the manner of a "basic set of
twelve tones," I built other motives and themes from it, and also
accompaniments and other chords — but the theme did not consist of twelve tones. Another example of this kind of aim for unity
is my *Serenade*. In this work you can find many examples of this
kind. But the best one is the *Variationen*, the third movement. The
theme consists of a succession of fourteen tones, but only eleven
different ones, and these fourteen tones are permanently used in

the whole movement. With lesser strictness still I use the tones of the first two measures in *Tanzscene*.

The fourth movement, *Sonett*, is a "real composition with twelve tones." The technique is here relatively primitive, because it was one of the first works written strictly in harmony with this method, though it was not the very first — there were some movements of the Suite for piano which I composed in the fall of 1921. Here I became suddenly conscious of the real meaning of my aim: unity and regularity, which unconsciously had led me this way.

As you see, it was neither a straight way nor was it caused by mannerism, as it often happens with revolutions in art. I personally hate to be called a revolutionist, which I am not. What I did was neither revolution nor anarchy. I possessed from my very first start a thoroughly developed sense of form and a strong aversion for exaggeration. There is no falling into order, because there was never disorder. There is no falling at all, but on the contrary, there is an ascending to higher and better order.

ARNOLD SCHOENBERG

GUSTAV HOLST

Cheltenham, 1874 — London, 1934

To *William Gillies Whittaker*

[1921]

. . . I'm greatly averse to fixed principles in art and I like everything — form, melody, harmony etc. — to grow out of the original inspiration which latter is one of the mysteries and therefore quite unfit for polite conversation!

I think a good rule is — "never compose anything unless the not composing of it becomes a positive nuisance to you."

I find that *unconsciously* I have been drawn for years towards discovering the (or *a*) musical idiom of the English language.

Never having managed to learn a foreign language, songs had always meant to me a peg of words on which to hang a tune. The great awakening came on hearing the recitatives in Purcell's *Dido*.

Can you or anyone tell me

1) how he managed *straight away* to write the only musical idiom of the English language we have yet had?

2) why he — who developed in every other way in music — never even repeated this idiom (or hardly ever), but contented himself with more and more conventional *recit. secco* in pure Italian style?

Well, I didn't get very far in *Sita*[1] I fear. But in the *Vedas*[2] matters improved, and in the *Cloud Messenger*[3] and *Savitri*,[4] especially the latter, the words and music really grew together. Since then I've managed now and then to do the same thing with other

---

1 Opera in three acts with libretto by Holst (1906).
2 *Choral Hymns from the "Rig Veda"* for chorus and orchestra (1910).
3 Ode based on a Sanskrit poem of Kalidasa, for chorus and orchestra (1910).
4 Chamber opera in one act with libretto by Holst (1908).

people's words, especially in the violin songs. (*My Leman* [5] is a good instance of a tune at one with the words.)

But in all this there is no conscious principle, no "ideal," no axe to grind.

And I may do something quite different tomorrow.

[GUSTAV HOLST]

---

[5] No. 4 of *4 Songs for Voice and Violin*, op. 35, 1916.

CHARLES IVES

Danbury, Conn., 1874 —

❂❂❂❂❂❂❂❂❂❂

To *Lehman Engel*

May 18, 1937

Dear Mr. Engel:

Many thanks for your letter telling us of the Madrigal concert last week.[1] The news that the *67th Psalm* was so warmly received by the audience and critics was much appreciated — but it was something of a surprise to me as it brought back the memory of the trouble it made, and the scowls it brought from some of the pews (but not from the pulpit) — about forty years ago because of its two-key tonality basis. But evidently in music, custom, habit and easy ear-leaning, static rules based on even vibratory sounds are having less to say — at least not the whole say — today.

Your remark "the lazy ear has been an enemy to musical progress" is well taken. Yes, and it has been a help in keeping it not always, but too often, from stronger ways and bigger fields and higher mountains. You ask if there are any objections to having the record of the *67th Psalm* made. No, there are none, we are very glad to have it made.

I am afraid some of the manuscripts of some of the other early chorales are not legible and rather difficult to read. The *Harvest Home* pieces — for chorus, organ and some brass, etc. used to go well sometimes after some rehearsal trouble — they are a kind of outdoor music and have something in common with the trees, rocks, and men of the mountains in days before machinery.

Probably the old ladies (male and female) would not — but there are some men who would like to hear some of the choruses with orchestra today especially those about the world problems of

---

1 Engel was director of the Madrigal Singers.

the people, etc. sounding up over the stone walls, and "west moun-tain."

The one called *An Election* (in the original score) was called *Down with the Politicians, Up with the People.* I think you have a copy of this score, if not, would be glad to send one on and with it the Unison Universal Chorale *Majority — Thanksgiving and Forefathers Day.* The last movement of the Symphony *Holidays* — "Our exiled fathers crossed the sea; for freedom of body and soul."

These are about things that are not discussed enough by the people in this world today. I feel strongly that the great fundamentals should be more discussed in all public meetings, and also in meetings of schools and colleges, not only the students but also the faculty should get down to more thinking and action about the great problems which concern all countries and all people in the world today, and not let the politicians do it all and have the whole say.

I have often been told that it is not the function of music (or a concert) to concern itself with matters like these. But I do not by any means agree. I think that it is *one* of the things that music can do, if it happens to want to, if it comes naturally, and is not the result of superimposition — I have had some fights about this.

Now I will stop and let you finish your symphony. Again many thanks for the fine work you and your singers are doing.

With best wishes, in which Mrs. Ives joins, I am,

Sincerely yours,
CHARLES E. IVES

PS. At the end of the *Election*, published as an arrangement (for voice and piano) is a footnote, referring to a suggested Twentieth Amendment that the people may have more of a direct say in the important public matters which concern us all. Will send a copy to you.

MAURICE RAVEL

Ciboure, 1875 — Paris, 1937

To the *Committee of the National League*
for the Protection of French Music

War zone [*France*], June 7, 1916

Gentlemen:

A compulsory rest at last enables me to reply to the notice and by-laws of the League for the Protection of French Music which reached me after a long delay. Please excuse me for not having written sooner; my constant changes and unsettled existence have left me scarcely any leisure until now.

Forgive me for not being able to adhere to your statutes; a careful study of them and your notice has made this impossible. Naturally I have nothing but praise for your *"idée fixe* of the nation's triumph," which has never left me since the outbreak of hostilities. Consequently I fully approve the "necessity for action" that gave birth to the National League for the Protection of French Music. This necessity for action has been so strong in me that it made me leave civilian life although nothing compelled me to do so.

But I cannot agree with you when you pose the principle that "the role of musical art is economic and social." I have never thought of music or the other arts in that light. I shall be glad to let you have the "motion pictures," "phonograph records," and "song-writers." All these have only remote relationships with musical art. You may even have those "Viennese operettas," though they may be more musical and more artistic than similar products of our own. That, like all the rest, would belong rather to the economic domain. But I do not believe that in order to "safeguard our national artistic heritage it would be necessary to prohibit the public performance in France of contemporary German and Austrian works which are not in the public domain."

If "there can be no question of our and the younger generation

[347]

renouncing the classics which constitute the immortal monuments of humanity," there should be even less question of "setting aside for a long time" those interesting works which may, in their turn, become monuments, and from which we can derive useful instruction in the meantime.

It would even be dangerous for French composers systematically to ignore the productions of their foreign colleagues and thus form a sort of national coterie; our national art, so rich at present, would soon deteriorate and lock itself up within commonplace formulas. I care little whether Monsieur Schönberg, for instance, is an Austrian. He is none the less a musican of great value whose extremely interesting researches have had a happy influence on certain Allied composers, and even on us. I am delighted that Monsieur Bartók and Monsieur Kodály and their disciples are Hungarian and show this in their pieces with so much zest.

In Germany, apart from Monsieur Richard Strauss, we see almost nothing but second-rate composers, and it would be easy to find their equal without going beyond our frontiers. But it is possible that there may be some young artists soon whom we should find fairly interesting.

Moreover, I do not think it necessary that French music predominate completely in this country or that it be propagated in other countries, whatever its value.

You see, gentlemen, that my opinion on many points is sufficiently different from yours not to permit me the honour of being included among you. Nevertheless, I hope to continue to "appear as a Frenchman" and to "count myself among those who would like to remember."

Believe me, gentlemen, very sincerely yours,

MAURICE RAVEL

ERNEST BLOCH

Geneva, 1880 —

✪❧✪❧✪❧✪❧✪❧✪

To *Nicolas Slonimsky*

Mill Valley, California
December 31, 1928

Dear Sir:

It seems as if a century has passed since our too hasty en-
counter at Monsieur Kefer's and in a little restaurant in Rochester —
but it was in 1925! So many things have happened in my life since
then — mostly three years of illness and terrible suffering. But none
of that can obliterate a most vivid and pleasant recollection. If my
memory is good — though I'm very indulgent toward those who
forget, and they are very numerous in our fragile and superficial
existence; life has taught me much about this as it has so many other
things. So you can imagine how surprised and delighted and touched
I was by the splendid study you devoted to me in the *Boston Evening Transcript*.[1] Boas Piller had the happy thought of including
it among a batch of clippings. I happened to glance at the others and
seeing what they were — having preserved a delicate sense of smell
— I threw them in the wastebasket without reading them. But the
sight of your name attracted my curiosity. And right I was! I cannot tell you how impressed and delighted I was by your fidelity to
common memories and the astonishing comprehension your article
reveals. At first I was thunderstruck by your managing in so little
time — for you had hardly seen me — to get such a clear and correct
idea of what, essentially, I represent as a man and as an interpreter of
life. That shows unusual perspicacity. I imagine it is my work, especially, that enlightened you. And that, too, gives me great happiness
for, I ask you, *how many are there* who can read and understand?

Biblical times have not changed: "They have eyes and see not,

---

1 December 27, 1929.

they have ears and hear not," and I add: "They have *brains* and do not think, *hearts* and do not feel!" Yet the truth is so plain, only a hand's grasp away. But we have obliterated Life! After demolishing God, to put man in His place, today we are destroying the *man* to substitute instead the *machine!* Machines for killing, machines for walking, machines for thinking — the newspapers, the movies — machines for healing — the X-rays and ultra-violet rays instead of a *true* diagnosis! And even music, forgetting its biological origins, the *voice* and the *larynx*, tries to turn itself into a machine for machines! What a superb claim to fame this new fetish is (with so many others) — the big B. (Business) and the big S.'s (Science, Stocks, Sports!!!). And all this in the name of *Progress!* Whose progress? Of playthings we don't know how to use, certainly, but of *Man?*

Among all these blind and deaf people you have preserved your intelligence and your Freedom. Because, dear sir, slavery of thought has never been worse than it is today. And we have no right to it. The epochs of great crystallized belief, of common faith and integral unity, are manifested in life and art by a *Style*. Intransigence of opinion could be justified. Thus the Greeks, the Egyptians, the Middle Ages, the Renaissance. Thus Voltaire and even Schopenhauer — whose classic tastes excluded a Shakespeare for the first and Gothic Art for both! But it seems to me that in a spineless age such as ours, where everything is left open to question, where the old values are crumbling and new ones do not yet exist, except *maybe* in Russia, the great *privilege*, whether one likes it or not, is to be *eclectic* — for better or worse — but this fact must be accepted.

The way you brought out this point in relief in your study has consoled me for the immeasurable stupidity of the masses surrounding us who call themselves intellectuals. I thought: here at last is a *young* man who is also free and independent and who can see, understand, and has the *courage* of his opinion. It's so rare, so rare! And it also means a little hope, I assure you, for among the young people and even my students I have *few* friends. I am rather exacting. I know it. I have never been able to become part of a clique and they don't forgive you for that! In this respect I am self-sufficient and I think that a group really conceals weakness.

Yet all my being, as you have pointed out so magnificently, is impregnated above all with humanity and love for humanity, despite all the suffering and bitterness I have been burdened with for thirty-five years. "He who sees farthest has the most faith!" But to preserve this faith, it is necessary once in a while to feel a mind and heart vibrating in sympathy with one's own. 1 out of 10,000! Often not even that — but it's enough. For you know very well that honours, success, and the whole publicity racket have no effect on me, no value for me. If you really understand my terrible isolation among the artists of our time — I say "artists," but should more correctly say "musicians," for I correspond with artists, thinkers, like R. Rolland, Havelock Ellis, Dr. Brocq, etc. — you will understand what your study means to me and why I had to try to tell you.

What a shame that Boston is so far from San Francisco! But I see that distance doesn't matter much to you — another reason for my gratitude. You would give me great pleasure if you told me a little about what you are doing yourself, and what is happening to you aside from the great step forward you have made as a psychologist. And I hope you will understand that this wish, I assure you, is expressed not out of "curiosity" but of sympathy.

I've been able to escape from the city — I *detest* the city more and more, although the one in which I am living at present is the finest on the continent. I have stolen a bit of life, eight days of peace, and then — work. After tomorrow I take up the yoke again. My address is: 1000 Union Street, San Francisco, California. I hope to have news of you soon. Thanks once more and with my most cordial regards,

ERNEST BLOCH

❉❁❉❁❉❁❉❁❉

To his daughter, *Suzanne*

Oswego, Oregon, July 24, 1940

My dear Suzanne:

I arrived here five days ago, after a fine and leisurely trip as you will have learned from my cards. After Crater Lake, which is *superb*, I spent two or three days at Diamond Lake, also magnificent, and Mother and I may perhaps go there for several weeks — then to another enchanting spot, Suttle Lake, and via McKenzie Pass to the incredible Lava Beds — Eugene and Oregon.

This trip has done me more good than anything else. I made a complete recovery en route, regaining my energies and some weight

(I had lost 10 pounds in 15 days). And most important — I managed to forget a little the nightmare of the recent news and developments, which had completely crushed and overwhelmed me. . . . A more general view of things, more cosmic and historical — frightful as things are — has gradually taken the place of the atrocious vision of the present. . . . The spiritual values and the progressive but slow advance of humanity cannot be destroyed even if current developments were to obliterate them. . . . Alas for those who live in these times, especially the victims! I am thinking of them all, my family in Geneva, my friends everywhere. You have to read their letters between the lines; the major part is censored. One understands that it is horrible and that the papers here don't give us even a hundredth part of it.

On arrival, I found your good letter of the 8th, and shortly after, your letter of the 19th arrived. Both of them are so consoling, so full of health and harmony, with the comforting view of your life, of this beautiful country, of Paul's work and yours, of Matthew, who seems to have such a delicate, dreamy nature and is certainly very gifted in music. I, too, suffer from being so far from you and from not being able to follow the development of my little friend, but the main thing is that he is coming along so well.

While I am writing you, Jodi woke up and he is making up a long conservation out of his head — it's priceless! Marianne has gone to lunch with some unexpected visitors at Oswego. Ivan was supposed to have left for Washington yesterday, by plane. (I live across from them with some neighbours who put a room at my disposal.) I have developed my films and am gradually getting round to a large correspondence which has been waiting for me. I also read your letters to the family, and really, all of them breathe forth such a healthy, normal atmosphere, it rejoices me. Thank you also for your good wishes. Yes, sixty years old! That's the way the wheel turns, for all of us, and for the world.

In this quiet spot I hope to take up my work again, which was interrupted at the "Eroica" and the comparative studies. That in itself helps maintain one's equilibrium. The first part had been finished — 40 pages! I had started the second, an enormous task, but passionately interesting . . . one redoes, backwards, all the work of Beethoven and one follows his mind and his heart — one goes into ecstasies over his superb *technique* (despite Nadia Boulanger), and the infallible *logic* that guides him. I have discovered (after 45 years of study) a thousand details that had escaped me up to now

. . . it is a whole world — and the *step* between the Second Symphony and this one is the greatest a composer has ever taken! The orchestration, too, is a miracle of sobriety, invention, imagination, and *mastery*. From the standpoint of *rhythm* it is incomparable! Frequently there are seven or eight sketches for a passage or even more (Nottebohm does not give them all). I have copied all of them in different colors of ink above the *final version;* beneath is the final version on two, three, or four lines, depending on the case, and below that the tonal and rhythmic analysis — the punctuation. This comparative study is extraordinary, a lesson every hour, in each measure! You can sometimes see in it, after the most unbelievable groping, the development of all of Beethoven's thinking.

I had also begun, I believe I told you, a new quartet. I had to interrupt it when I could no longer live in music during the disasters in Europe — the collapse of all those values which constituted my life, our lives. But the first part (*lente*) is finished, and I believe it is something completely "new." There is no thematic development, no tonal restrictions, no *repetition* of motifs — and still the "story" unfolds with absolute logic and *organic continuity*. Why? I don't know. I do not know any literary work that even comes close to it. If I can succeed in writing the whole quartet this way, it will be extraordinary, a complete regeneration of my style — (though it's pure Bloch). With this I stop.

Today I developed five films; moments like these are "holiday feasts" greeted with a hearty appetite.

Have a nice vacation, don't work too hard, take care of yourself, and store up some air and sunshine and energy for the winter. You are right. One must ignore the musical world so far as possible. It is only, alas, that one knows what *real* music is, detached from all the vanity and irrelevancy that have nothing to do with ART itself. It's probably the same way in everything. On the trip I ran into several people here and there who were very intelligent and cordial and they bore witness of the finest side of America, far from these radios and newspapers.

Regards to Paul, I kiss you and the baby, with all my heart,

ERNEST

ALFREDO CASELLA

Turin, 1883 —

❊❉❊❉❊❉❊❉❊

To *Isidor Philipp*

Rome, October 22, 1941

My dear Friend:

Hardly a day passes without me and Yvonne talking at least once about our dear, good Philipp, who is so far from us in person but so close to us in spirit. I read your long article in one of the recent issues of *Musical America* and found it very interesting.

Our life goes on as well as possible during these terrible times. Fortunately, up to now, Rome has been lucky enough not to feel the destruction of war — and the thought that there still exists a city in the world that is capable of escaping these crimes of brute strength comforts us a great deal.

I am overloaded with work. The symphony I wrote for Chicago last year has been a great success and this year it has already had twenty performances in Europe, half of which I conducted myself. I am still working on a *Divertimento* for orchestra (for the centenary of the Vienna Philharmonic) based on themes of Paganini, which will be very entertaining. And I'm still working on a new edition of the Mozart sonatas and fantasies for piano (for Ricordi).

In addition I have undertaken an enormous task that I've wanted to start on for years and years; a complete analysis of the six hundred Scarlatti sonatas in order to classify them according to chronological order. If this is successful, as I hope, I think the government will bring out a new complete edition to replace the defective one by Longo. When I tell you that the government has commissioned me to do an opera (I've chosen Shakespeare's *Coriolanus* for a subject), you will see that I don't have time to be bored. Not only that, but God has given me the rare privilege of maintaining

[354]

intact my spiritual strength for work — the only way of avoiding the horrible reality that surrounds on all sides.

Aside from all this, my family's health is good. Yvonne has had news of her family and is calmer now. The little one is a big girl (thirteen!) and is developing very well. She has remarkable inclination for dancing and music. We shall see.

You no doubt have learned that I have touched up the Beethoven sonatas with the help of the original manuscripts, and the revision has been further improved.

Send me some news, you will make me very happy. I think you have found, in the midst of your American friends, that calm and serenity which you would look for in vain in Europe today.

Yvonne sends her love. I beg you to write and not to forget us.

Your faithful

CASELLA

Is it true that Paderewski had completed his great Chopin edition before he died? Will it come out soon?

LOUIS GRUENBERG

Brest-Litovsk, 1883 —

☰☰☰☰☰☰☰☰

To *Claire Reis* [1]

Vienna, April 15, 1927

My dear Claire:

Your letter has just arrived — and I can fully appreciate and sympathize with your desire to be relieved from the very necessary, but very exhausing technical activities of the League. And it seems to me from here, that the business end ought to have been put long ago (I believe I advocated something of the sort years ago) into the hands of some capable person, who would merely execute the decisions of the board, and who would have no other authority. *The position should be put on a salary basis — so that we would have the authority to discharge.* If a well-known manager is considered, care should be taken to receive personal, individual attention — (It occurs to me at this moment, that when the now very dead American Music Guild decided to do this very thing and put matters into the hands of a professional manageress — it never received such miserable management ever before or ever afterwards.)

As to better programs — No organization can guarantee good works — it can only give *adequate representations.* Good compositions lie outside of the realm of even composers — and they occur like all miracles — miraculously. So don't worry over matters you cannot change — we are doing our best with the material the living composers offer us — that *must* suffice.

Regarding the proposed experiment of offering a program of early music contrasted with works of today — I can only say, that we should place in the hands of our friends, the critics, a very valuable weapon with which they would surely avail themselves of, to attack the very foundations of our society. As much as I would love to hear Monteverdi *anywhere,* I don't believe the programs of the

1 Executive chairman of the League of Composers.

League should show the names of other than *living* composers. For that purpose we originally conceived our idea —

As to the proposed amalgamation of all modern music societies into one — *which one* — ours? Artistic amalgamation is always a sign of defeat. Does the League need it? I think not — I hope not. As to your idea of publication — and how to choose the work to be published — I shall go more into this detail when matters have progressed further than the present moment. Birchard and I have met here, and I have found him sympathetic — possibly because we have as yet had no business connections.

I hope you are coming over, and that I shall be able to meet you. I know as yet nothing of what I shall do this summer, but I have a vague hope, fear and desire, to be in New York next November.

Best wishes to you and yours,
LOUIS

ARNOLD BAX

London, 1883 —

❀❀❀❀❀❀❀❀

To *L. Dunton Green* [1]

[1928]

The smug cliché has it that Genius consists of an infinite capacity for taking pains. I myself think it probable that all that remains really vital in the work of artists throughout the ages, has been given to the so-called "Creator," with little or no conscious mental effort on his part.

The hour or moment of inspiration conditions a total quiescence of that creaking engine, "the brain," — a state of mind comparable to that of the religious ecstatic.

It may be true, that "one must have chaos in the heart if one could give truth to a dancing Star," but no star was born of the struggling intellect.

I should say that a Genius may be described as a man possessed of unusually vigorous physical and nervous vitality and awareness of the actualities of the external world, plus an infinite receptivity and sensitivity to those super personal — and other — world ideas capable of being moulded in the crucible of art. Every human being must have occasionally known these moments of fiery enlightenment, but perhaps the only difference between the normal man and the Genius (or even the highly talented) is that the latter experience them in greater numbers and with more intensity.

I believe too, that these visitations are dependent upon nothing but chance.

Every artist must remember mornings when all the conditions seemed favourable — a mood unharrassed by any particular worry, and lit by a fire and excitement that promised to be pregnant with creative force. And yet nothing has come, perhaps because the

---

1 In reply to a question concerning the nature of musical inspiration, for publication in the *Chesterian.*

flame was merely cerebral, or because the man's being was preoccupied with some transitory enthusiasm underived from basic emotional life.

We all waste a certain amount of time in the attempt to express states of feeling the depths of which we are temperamentally incapable of plumbing.

On another occasion, when the psychic environment would seem to be more than usually unpromising — it may be in an hour of disenchantment or vexation — the vision may suddenly become blessedly clear, possibly through the lack of self-consciousness, or because the various conflicting emotional agents cancel one another out, and leave room for the entering of the radiant guest.

But a subject so obscure as this could scarcely be treated adequately in many volumes let alone in few sentences.

All that can be said with certainty is that the truly inspired artist does not possess a gift, but is possessed by it as by a demon.

[ARNOLD BAX]

EDGARD VARÈSE

Paris, 1885 —

❂❂❂❂❂❂❂❂❂

To *José Rodriguez*

Paris, March 1, 1933

Dear Mr. Rodriguez,

I read with great pleasure your article, *The Old Lady Gets Three Shots in the Arm* in Bob Wagner's Script, which Nicolas Slonimsky sent me. Your praise of such colleagues as Ives and Harris gives me a rare satisfaction. That is the kind of appreciation needed to make the American public realize that American music must speak its own language, and not be the result of a certain mummified European formula.

It is disheartening to see the young school here in France becoming zealously academic. The neo-classical ideal does not certainly make for creative effort. It is lassitude constructing a theory by which to excuse itself and this theory has become the fashion. It is perhaps normal at a time of world-wide hesitancy to wish to escape into the categorical past, but life with its exigencies goes on and in the end will sweep away all that is static, all that does not move with the rhythm of life itself. But it is really too bad that American critics and public should so often judge American music by the standards of what is nothing more than a fashion. And I see no reason for young American composers coming to study over here if it is only to take back a lot of old-maidish mannerisms as so many of them have done. You will, of course, understand that I do not speak of those who come to study with masters such as Schoenberg, etc.

As for your "prime donne" conductors — the public must be made to resent conductors who use music to serve their own ends. What we need is more writers like you and conductors like Slonimsky to proclaim Freedom of speech for music.

V.

SERGEY PROKOFIEV

Sonzowka (Ekaterinoslav), 1891 —

✿✦✿✦✿✦✿✦✿

To *Paul Bowles*

La Naze, Seine-et-Oise,
August 27, 1930

Dear Mr. Bowles:

It isn't that your Minuet is old-fashioned, but it is written in a rather uninteresting way. This is why: it consists of 24 measures, then three closing chords, but in these 24 measures there are only 5 measures of music (1–4, and 9). The rest is nothing but repetition of these five measures.

Now suppose I were to compose a symphony lasting 24 minutes in which there were only 5 minutes of music, and the remainder nothing but repetition of the preceding part. How boring!

You will say that the reason this happened was that you haven't learned how to compose, and that you sent me the manuscript to find out whether it was worth the trouble of learning. Well, my friend, I can't judge a composer on the basis of 5 measures, and no composer has ever sent me 5 measures for me to give my opinion of his music.

Very sincerely yours,
SERGEY PROKOFIEV

JOHN DONALD ROBB

Minneapolis, Minn., 1892 —

◖◗◖◗◖◗◖◗◖◗◖◗◖◗

To *Frank Colapinto* [1]

New York City, January 27, 1944

Dear Mr. Colapinto:

I am happy to send you my thoughts on the two questions which you have submitted to me as follows:

1. What should post-war music be like?

In answering this question let me state my feeling that the music which followed the last war *followed* the spirit of the times. It was full of harshness, bitterness, novelty. The world was seeking salvation in something new. "Try anything!" was the watchword and we saw a generation of disillusioned experimenters frantically seeking happiness in developing new material things, in new social experiments. Music followed the trend. It did *not* lead. Hence we had an almost psychopathic emphasis on novelty (which was unfortunately confused with originality) and the slightest similarity between a new work and the work of any previous composer or even the use of any traditional approach was condemned by all those whose voices reached farthest. The result — composers have been composing for composers, critics and conductors and the public has reacted by demanding less of this "modern" music in our concert halls or by turning to popular music — a field in which oddly enough conservatism has prevailed. I do not speak here of orchestration — a field in which the jazz boys have experimented more boldly than the composers of serious music.

In considering what music should be like after this war I want to say that disillusionment was natural. What was not natural was the result. A serious approach to the problem would have studied the past, holding fast to those things which are good in our tradition and seeking merely to supplant what was bad with something

---

1 Librarian of the National Orchestral Association.

new and better. Instead the prevailing sentiment was revolutionary, "Let us destroy all loyalty to tradition and start with totally new 'inventions' like the twelve tone technique" said the spokesmen.

Well, it didn't work. The public would not come along. A revolution had failed. The mind could not create great music without the heart.

Now — after this war composers must stop *following* trends like a group of political opportunists. They must lead people to faith in mankind and in a good future. They must first of all reaffirm their faith in the great traditions of the past thus again reaching a common meeting place with the public. Let the originality of the composer assert itself in a language which can reach out to all men here and now — and not merely to a hypothetical generation yet to be born. Frankly, I think I see that the tide has already set that way. — Just as our cynical college men of five years ago have found a new loyalty to their country which swept away their corroding sophistries, so our composers are beginning to have the courage again to write in a manner that sounds like music even to the uninitiate.

2. Who among the living lead to light and in what works?

Stravinsky — *Fire Bird* — . Even this great genius has apparently become ashamed of the traditional elements upon which he built such great works as this.

Hindemith — *Mathis der Maler, Kleine Kammermusik, Viola Sonata, Acht Stücke* for Strings.

Prokofieff — Classical Symphony. In a sense he has been truer to himself than any other great composer.

Shostakovich — First Symphony. Here is a man of very uneven performance. Of late he betrays great faults — even so a great figure.

Now for the Americans —

Deems Taylor — He has created some fine music like the music for the play *Casanova* — and his *Looking-Glass Suite*.

Aaron Copland — One of the obscuranti he still does produce things like *Billy the Kid* in which he actually lets you recognize American folk tunes.

Douglas Moore — His *Village Music* is I think a really fine work.

The list is long but here are the names of some a part of whose music is I think on the right track. By this I mean that I have felt a whole-hearted response to some part of what they have done —

Americans   Walter Helfer — *Hunter College March* and *Water Idyll*.

Ross Lee Finney — *March*.

Ulric Cole — *Divertimento* for 2 pianos and strings.

Robert Sanders — Setting of the song, *Old Paint*.

Poulenc — *Les Biches*

Tansman — *Triptyque for Strings*.

Americans   Anis Fuleihan — Concerto for violin and piano.

Ernest Gold — Concerto — a bit Gershwinesque but what of it? It's *music*. I heard this at one of your rehearsals.

Jean Francoix — Concertino.

I have gone way out on a limb for you. I haven't mentioned many of those who are played most. Omission of some of these may be due to a mere failure to remember them while writing this letter. But in general I feel that our most sincere creators are being neglected — even today — for the more influential members of the group whose work rests entirely upon revolutionary intellectualism.

Sincerely yours,

J. D. ROBB

DOUGLAS MOORE

Cutchogue, N. Y., 1893 —

❖❖❖❖❖❖❖❖❖

To *Rose Resnick* [1]

New York, February 4, 1941

Dear Miss Resnick:

I put aside your request of last fall because I was appalled at the scope of it. Now that you limit it to a quotation from my own compositions let me say first of all that humor in music is one of the last things that audiences look for. It may be the sparkling musical wit of such men as Haydn, Mozart, and Prokofieff, or it may derive from humorous titles such as those employed by Satie. In these cases the fun is often literary rather than musical. Musical fun is concerned with music alone and represents the witty manipulation of ideas.

I have tried several experiments in my own works, notably in the *Pageant of P. T. Barnum* in the section dealing with General and Mrs. Tom Thumb. The humor consists of a shrill military music alternating with a sour mincing waltz which seems to work very well as an interpretation of the literary idea. I have noticed that when the orchestra percussion section uses a cap pistol as directed to open the music, the fun is always more evident to the audience. They seem to need obvious effects of this kind in order to be sure that the composer means to be funny. Oftentimes they think that the music is just bad. I was less successful in attempting to interpret the spiritual nature of Babbitt in an overture. Apparently the kind of character drawing which can be done in a novel is too subtle to be appreciated by audiences. I have since rechristened the piece *Overture on an American Tune*, so that it may stand or fall on its musical merits, without depending too much on the program. With best regards and very best wishes for the success of your thesis, I am,

Yours sincerely,

Douglas Moore

---

1 Student who was preparing a thesis on "Humor in Music."

To *Carl E. Lindstrom* [2]

New York, January 17, 1942

Dear Mr. Lindstrom,

Thank you for sending me your interesting article about my lecture at Hartford. I didn't realize that what I was saying was to be subject to review but appreciate the attention you paid to it.

I would agree with you entirely in what you say about Americanism in music. American flavor must come from within and must be the spontaneous expression of a personality. No superficial adornments, such as folk songs and stage trimmings, will give this. However, for a stage work, I see no objection to an American composer choosing a colorful American story and my criticism of some of the Metropolitan's productions of native opera was of an attitude that formerly prevailed when composers felt that they had to deal with opera subjects in the stuffy tradition of the past.

Above all I think that American composers should avoid being self-consciously nationalistic but keep their ears and eyes open for the flavor of American life which is going on around us. If the American composer is drawn today toward American material, it may very well be because it is a part of his background and he understands it, as Thomas Benton and Vachel Lindsay understand the Middle West. In the old days our American musicians were trained abroad, came back with all sorts of European prejudices, and were inclined to think that American source material was somehow inferior and to be avoided by the artist.

Yours sincerely,
DOUGLAS MOORE

---

2 A newspaper critic in Hartford, Connecticut, who had objected to some remarks by Moore on the subject of "Americanism in music as being contrary to the accepted point of view that music is truly an international art."

WALTER PISTON

Rockland, Maine, 1894 —

❧❧❧❧❧❧❧❧❧

To *Arthur V. Berger*

Cambridge, Mass., August 2, 1943

I have already sent the only two pictures I could dig up. . . . Add to the list of works — *Sinfonietta*, 1941; *Chromatic Study on the Name of Bach* (for organ), 1939; *Quintet for flute and string quartet*, 1942; *Passacaglia for piano*, 1943; *Prelude and Allegro for Organ and String Orchestra*, 1943.

The Suite from *The Incredible Flutist* [1] was played this July 4th at an official concert in Moscow, along with Roy's [2] *Johnny Comes Marching Home.*

We are carrying on at Harvard with still a sufficient number of students in music courses, counting Radcliffe, with a three term year (July, November, March).

As a composer, I had a slump for the first year of the war, feeling that writing music was about the most futile occupation. What got me out of it chiefly was getting letters from men in the armed forces who said they hoped I was keeping on composing because that was one of the things they were out there for. I have now completely recovered a sense that it is important and that I am meant to do that job (along with other things like teaching and civilian defense). I am now on my second symphony, commissioned by the Ditson Fund in Columbia University. With best wishes,

Yours sincerely,
WALTER PISTON

---

1 Ballet (1938).
2 Roy Harris.

ROBERT RUSSELL BENNETT

Kansas City, Mo., 1894 —

☙❧❧❧❧❧❧❧❧

To the *National Orchestral Association*

New York City, January 21, 1943

Gentlemen:

Your unsigned letter requesting biographical data and information on *Hollywood* is at hand.

Answering your second question first: *Hollywood* was commissioned by the League of Composers in 1936. Its first performance under Dr. Frank Black was under the sponsorship of the League, and one of its subsequent performances was at an earlier anniversary of the League.

The piece is a large introduction and scherzo, written in Hollywood, and designed to show impressions of the place not always seen or considered in the popular appraisal. I had a little schedule before me as I wrote:

HOLLYWOOD

As the world sees its — Girls, Glitter, Goofiness
As it sees itself — Divans, Divorces, Deviltry
As I see it — Mountains, Motors, Morality.

The profounder moments are based on the solemn hills and the religious temples; the gay parts have the songs of those wonderful mocking-birds, the headlong dash of irresponsible chauffeurs, the shine of white markets and drive-ins; the sarcastic parts are devoted to my idea of moving picture studios — their profane treatment of sublime thoughts — and to the smiling banality and friendly "insouciance" of the whole fantastic place.

I was born in Kansas City in 1894, studied composition with Carl Busch and Nadia Boulanger, married in 1919 in New York, have one daughter who is in Hollywood now, — and died when I saw you forgot to sign your letter.

Yours sincerely,
ROBERT RUSSELL BENNETT

MARIO CASTELNUOVO–TEDESCO

Florence, 1895 —

To *Aldo Bruzzichelli*

Beverly Hills, California,
October 18, 1941

My dear Aldino,

      I have lost count a bit (in consulting that prophetic little book of mine, I see that I haven't written to you in ten days); but you have lost count even more than I, because if I am not mistaken, your last letter was dated September 27, and you still owe me replies to two of mine (of September 30 and October 7). But I do not write to recriminate. Today I am in good spirits! And I want to write a good letter to you, as I used to do in the pleasant days of the past, when we still had hopes and illusions (or rather I had, for I do not wish to assume responsibility for others than myself).

      Well, today I finished *King John.* (I have not actually finished writing; four pages of the score are lacking; these I shall put on paper between tonight and tomorrow, but they are already "ripe" in my mind.) And, unfortunately, because I cannot let you hear it for the present, I shall have to tell you a bit about it. I believe, however, that I told you some time ago how Barbirolli during this past winter had requested me to write an overture for the centenary of the New York Philharmonic. I had no inclination at all to write a "Festive overture" (or an "Academic" in the Brahmsian sense); I wanted to continue working on my cycle of Shakespearian overtures, but simultaneously to do something related to the "times" and to present conditions. By accident, in rereading *King John* (in fact, while reading it for the first time), one of the lesser known and less beautiful tragedies by Shakespeare, I found, at the very end, the following verses (which might sooner have been written by Churchill than by Shakespeare!):

This England never did, nor never shall,
Lie at the proud foot of a conqueror,
But when it first did help to wound itself.
Now these her princes are come home again,
Come the three corners of the world in arms,
And we shall shock them. Nought shall make us rue,
If England to itself do rest but true.

And these seemed to me perfectly adaptable to the "event." I spoke to Barbirolli about them and he was enthusiastic about the idea, and I started to work with no less enthusiasm. From the beginning I had a very clear conception of what I wanted to do; I wanted to write an extremely virile, logical, solid and concise overture; with a single germ of rhythm which would give birth to both the principal themes (the second more "pathetic," in memory of the "Green Island"); and to move on, inexorably, to the very end with this martial and warlike rhythm, in order to give an impression of firm will, of determined resistance, almost of stubbornness! And the themes came to my mind immediately (as is customary with me), "by illumination." In other words, nothing remained but — to write the music!

But my enthusiasm passed away quickly, after I had written about a third of it (part I, the so-called exposition of themes, about twenty pages of score); it was not that the music already written displeased me, or that I regretted having started the project; actually, I did not have the strength to go ahead! I felt both physically and morally depressed (and for a while it grew continually worse — now a course of injections has put me back on my feet, at least physically). Even though Barbirolli spent the summer here, I did not become more alive — I felt so mortified and vile because of my inaction; I even thought (although I did not want to confess this to myself) of "renouncing" the whole thing (like that Pope whom Dante mentions! — "*colui che fece il gran rifiuto.*" Who was it? Celestine I, it seems to me); and that would have been a shame — to renounce the Philharmonic, to give up the opportunity, rare during these times, one that might not again present itself.

At any rate, things were at this point when, two weeks ago, Barbirolli wrote asking to see me, me and the overture, before his departure for New York. Well, I took the bull by the horns and accepted the appointment, and in ten days had written thirty more pages of score! So when I went to see Barbirolli on Monday, I was able to show him more than three quarters of the work (it still lacked the ending, but this, in the logical construction that is mine, was in a certain sense "inevitable." At any rate, he was able to get a very clear impression of the character of the piece at that stage). Barbirolli (I shall whisper it into your ear) was full of admiration, for "the happiness of the initial idea, for the sureness and logic of construction." Anyway, he was most encouraging!

I finished the missing section during these last days (after the visit); and as a result I am exhausted! It was a strenuous effort to write all those pages of score, using India ink (so that it can be blue-printed) and a fine, fine pen — at times it seemed to me that I was a Persian miniaturist (or who was it of whom Dante speaks? Ode-risi da Gubbio, I think — and where was he? perhaps in hell! However, he belongs to posterity!). And now I must tell you (disregarding the perhaps unnecessary and excessive eulogies of Barbirolli) what I think of my piece. It is not the favorite among my Overtures, because I generally feel more at home in music of a contemplative or fantastic character; I prefer, among my latest, the overture of *The Dream* and it is understood that I prefer *Aucassin et Nicolette* (which I replayed a few nights ago, and which always remains by far my best work). *King John* as a type is above all closest to *Julius Cæsar* and (at the end) to the *Merchant*. I have the vague suspicion (I confess it) that it has a flavour of Tchaikovsky! (A composer whom I have always detested!) Be that as it may, it has certain characteristics of Tchaikovsky (actually those which have made him famous), a great deal of constructive certainty, a large amount of melodic fluidity, and, above all, a solid and at the same time malleable instrumentation. It is (this I can tell you, without false modesty) an excellent score! — especially in its last pages, where I have "measured out" (in the dispositions and colourings) with infinite patience, in order to obtain a continuous crescendo until the very end; and think, during the last fifteen pages practically everyone plays continuously — but they go higher and higher, until, with the last chords, when the trumpets and violins are almost — strangled, a tempest from the tympani breaks loose — a *solo*, apocalyptical and thunderous. All in all, I am content — content to have imposed this discipline and this effort upon myself, content to have broken (at least so far as I am concerned) that run of bad luck which for some time has weighed upon my work.

And now, dear Aldino, nothing remains for you but to hear the music. And I am sorry that we cannot hear it together. But you will hear it before I do. Barbirolli will play it at two concerts on Saturday and Sunday, the 21st and 22nd of March,[1] with the charming idea (since the Sunday concert is broadcast by radio) that I also may be able to hear it (because the Minister of Finance doesn't allow me to visit New York for the occasion, despite the fact that Clara and I want so much to feel a bit of New York cold again, and to see you all); so we shall hear it from our modest home radio on the 22nd (which is Clara's birthday, by the way). But you should go on Saturday night, if you can, and then send me a night-letter if you have the money; if not, write me a letter next day!

Dear Aldino, if you see Carlo and Oscar, have them read this letter also, for perhaps it will be of interest since a bit of it is also for them, and it is one of those letters which one does not write twice —but, naturally, among my friends, it is your due. I embrace you, and Anja also, with much love,

Your
MARIO

---

1 The first performance was, instead, on March 15.

ERNST LÉVY

Basel, 1895 —

❀❀❀❀❀❀❀❀

To *Barnett Byman*

[February 18, 1945]

Dear Mr. Byman:

       I guess the two letters I corrected in the enclosed sheet are printing errors — or are they not? Anyway, make sure. Of course Rabbi Perilman's desire as to the translation must be complied with; I wholly agree with you.

       I have not yet received the 25 circulars, but I am sure they will arrive to-morrow Monday. Thank you very much.

       Now that question of writing something in lieu of an interview embarrasses me very much. Here are a few lines that you may use and "cook up" however you wish — consider them as "raw material" to be processed by your expert pen!

       I believe that art in general, and music in particular, is not a mere amusement, a mere ornament of life. The series of world catastrophes in which we are involved are the outcome of an evolution that has begun at the end of the Middle Ages with an ever increasing development of the intellectual side of our nature. To-day humanity, with its armies of specialists who, as Nicholas Murray Butler puts it, are people who "know more and more about less and less," resembles a huge ant-hill. Only, the ant state is held together by natural instinct. Humanity has no such instinct. She has to rely on her consciousness of spiritual principles, which alone can guarantee the awareness of *values* without which the intellect and its inventions will run amok. There is no need to explain what that means — we are unfortunately experiencing it. We are witnessing the terrible revenge of the *affective* side of our nature, whose integration into our daily life has hardly been attempted. Sentiment, feelings, ideals — all that has been relegated to small corners of our civilization, as a matter of concert-halls, museums, Sunday-religion. Our inner life has been thrown off balance, and let's not forget that it is our inner life that fashions the outer world.

To a humanity looking for elements of hope, music ought to be an important matter. We may even say that man will begin to recover the moment he takes art as seriously as physics, chemistry, or money. There is no other human activity that asks for such a harmonious cooperation of "intellect" and "soul" as artistic creation and, especially, music (I do not say this only because I am a musician! I have very good reasons to say so!). Music is human. Music is also extra-human inasmuch as it is a mirror of universal laws. To destructive analysis music opposes synthesis. To the uniformization of science, which reduces qualities to quantities, music opposes a hierarchy of values. *Our mechanized minds need to be musicalized.* We have developed only half of man's possibilities, or rather, have developed that half completely out of proportion to the other half. We have deified the intellect, we have separated it completely from the other side of human nature. We must seek a synthesis. Music as an art and as a science can do it. This is not a petty problem. It is *the* problem of our time.

I hope that'll do!

Let me know if you want more, or if that isn't what you want. Glad to help as much as I can!

Very sincerely yours,
E. L.

HOWARD HANSON

Wahoo, Nebraska, 1896 —

❁❁❁❁❁❁❁❁

To the Music Editor of *The New York Times*

Rochester, N. Y., July 29, 1935

To the Music Editor:

The Eastman School of Music has this year completed the first ten years of its American Composers' project, and some of the results of the experiment may be of interest to your readers. You will recall, I am sure, the origin of the plan. There was at that time no place in the United States where a young composer, without an already established reputation, could send his works with any assurance that they might receive a hearing. The established orchestras could hardly be expected to turn their regular series of concerts into a laboratory, and though there had been some "reading rehearsals" carried on previously, these had been only sporadic.

The first practical discussion of the idea took place, as you will recall, at a luncheon at the Hotel Roosevelt which was attended by a number of distinguished musicians and critics. Acting on Mr. George Eastman's behalf and with the enthusiastic support of President Rush Rhees of the University of Rochester, I journeyed to New York and explained to the group what we hoped to do in Rochester. An interesting discussion followed, giving rise to many helpful suggestions. It was determined to follow certain definite policies: first, that the choice of works should not be confined to any one "school," but should be as catholic as possible, with every effort made to discover and perform new works which had not yet received performances; second, that the works should not be "read," but should be carefully rehearsed and performed before an audience; third, that the concerts be free to the public to eliminate any "box-office" influence in the experiment.

[375]

It would be presumptuous of me to take the time of your readers in detailing the many steps in the working out of the experiment. We made, undoubtedly, many mistakes and attempted to profit by them. We made also many changes designed for the purpose of increasing the efficacy of the experiment. The concerts were held first in the Eastman Theatre, then moved to the smaller Kilbourn Hall for a more intimate atmosphere and then moved back again to the large theatre when the size of the audience overwhelmed the small hall.

The need for such a laboratory was immediately apparent. From the very beginning the office was flooded with orchestral manuscripts of every possible size and quality, none of which had ever been translated into sound. The number of concerts has been increased from one a year to four or five, with an entire festival of American music added, and still it is possible to perform but a small percentage of the scores submitted. (This in spite of the fact that we have in the past ten years performed about the same number of American works as the Boston Symphony has played in its long history, and it has played a great many!)

In the early days of the experiment almost all of the works played were from the pens of young, and in many cases unknown, composers. Later, however, well-known composers began to signify their desire to have their works performed on these programs, and the plan was expanded to include scores by many distinguished names in American composition.

At this time a new and very interesting factor entered the scene — the audience. Rochester showed a decided interest in the experiment. As one composer remarked, "They suffer, but they keep coming!" And they did keep coming, and in increasing numbers, until at certain of the more popular performances the audience crowded the Eastman Theatre and it was necessary to ask for additional traffic police to handle the crowds!

The reactions of this audience were in themselves as interesting as the works performed. This audience was not a formal symphony audience, though it numbered hundreds of regular symphony-goers. It was an intensely interested, curious and eager audience, positive and unfailing in its reactions. Its opinions were its own. They had to be, for there was no "Bach," "Beethoven" or "Brahms" on the right-hand side of the program to indicate whether or not the music was "good" music. I publicly disclaimed responsibility, telling the audience that some of the numbers which we played I cordially disliked, though I would do my best to keep the audience from discovering which they were!

And their judgment seemed to me, in the great majority of cases, to be critically sound, giving me new confidence in a natural audience reaction if that reaction is in fact "natural" and uninfluenced. A work which meandered through yards of score-paper without, as they expressed it, "getting anywhere" received scant applause. They showed admiration for a good tune, for infectious rhythm and for musical vitality, and a work such as Randall Thompson's Second Symphony (first produced at these concerts and later performed by the New York Philharmonic under Bruno Walter), which has all three of these qualities, earned their immediate affection and had to be repeated at later concerts.

I have been often asked whether a distinctly American idiom was developing in these concerts. I have never known exactly what "American music" was except in its simplest definition — viz., music written by Americans; but I must admit that the Thompson work, together with others such as Burrill Phillips' *Selections from McGuffey's Readers*, have something about them that smells American and which is quickly perceived by the audience. I don't know exactly what it is. Perhaps it is partly rhythmic, partly a homely sentimental quality of melody and mood, and probably it is something much less tangible. Whatever it is, it is certainly there, and those who insist on a typically "American" idiom can rest content. They are going to get it.

Another point should be mentioned — the enormous orchestral technique of these young composers. Anyone who says that the young American cannot write for orchestra simply doesn't know his American scores. The weakest point, I believe, lies generally in the matter of form; that is, form taken in its broadest sense. With the ultimate relaxing of all formal restrictions there is a tendency for the young composer to spread himself over a large canvas with not always a keen enough sense of architectural necessities.

Statistics are dull things, but this report to you would not be complete without noting the fact that we have performed over 200 works during the past ten years at the concerts and festivals more than half of which were given their first performance. In addition, student composition has been so stimulated that it has been necessary to give two orchestral concerts a year in addition to and outside of the American series. Seventy-five of these student orchestral works have been given, many of which compare favorably in quality with the works performed on the regular series. Which leads me to reiterate again my belief that composition is like farming; the more you cultivate the soil the better crops you grow!

I appreciate, Sir, the constant interest that you have taken in our experiment and your consistent helpfulness.

HOWARD HANSON

VIRGIL THOMSON

Kansas City, 1896 —

❖❱❁❰❁❱❁❰❁❱❁❰❁❱❁❰❁❖

To *Aaron Copland*

Paris, March 20, 1939

Dear Aaron:

I imagine you are as vague about news of me as I am about what you are up to. Besides which I have never thanked you for *The Second Hurricane* [1] and for the book.[2] I now do so. And very sincerely indeed. The *Hurricane* in score is as satisfactory as it was in performance. It is a very beautiful work, a very rich work, touching, exciting, gay, and a real music-pleasure. The book I read through twice and I still find it a bore. Marian writes me it sells swell and that is a good thing of course. Not that the book doesn't contain a hundred wise remarks about music. But it also contains a lot of stuff that I don't believe and that I am not at all convinced you believe.

Supposing you do believe that analytic listening is advantageous for the musical layman, it is still quite possible and not at all rare to believe the contrary. It even remains to be proved that analytic listening is possible even. God knows professional musicians find it difficult enough. I suspect that persons of weak auditive memory do just as well to let themselves follow the emotional line of a piece, which they can do easily, and which they certainly can't do very well while trying to analyze a piece tonally. In any case, I find it a bit high-handed to assume the whole psychology.

I find similarly unproved assumptions in the musical form chapters. I do not believe, for instance, that the loose and varied sonata-form practised by the great Viennese has very much relation to the modern French reconstructed form that d'Indy made up for pedagogical purposes. The first kind, even in its final Mahlerian

1 Play-opera for high-school performance (1937).
2 *What to Listen for in Music* (1939).

decay, retained a spontaneity, a Viennese *désinvolture*, that enabled it to be written consecutively, and most certainly it was practically always written consecutively, Beethoven's note-books being pre-compositional reflections, like anybody else's note-books.

The modern French version, on the other hand, is really written as you describe, that is to say, pieced together like a picture-puzzle. That there is a cardinal difference between the two is proved by the fact that the French synthetic version has never been able to be reintroduced into Vienna successfully. The Viennese thing is dynamic, even as late as Strauss and Schoenberg. The French thing is static, like nearly all French musical conceptions. The compositional procedure in the two cases is hence quite different. I don't say you should discuss such controversial matter in an elementary text-book, but I don't think you are quite justified in discussing the sonata-form as if it were one thing instead of two and as if no controversy existed about it. You know privately that it is the most controversial matter in all music, has been so since Beethoven. I find it a little dull of you and a little unctuous to smooth all that over with what I consider falsehoods.

That static-dynamic business you never go into either. You even describe rhythm as if it were a static pattern. Prosodic metre *is* static mostly. But what about muscular impulsions? Dance-music and the ballet are nothing but, rhythmically. The Viennese sonata-form (and this is known historically, is in the books) is a superimposing of this dynamic, muscular dance-rhythm on to the static French overture, the fluid Italian song-style being the combining agent.

I'm not trying to rewrite your book for you. I'm just complaining that you didn't think it up for yourself. Almost any music-teacher could have written it. Maybe not quite so smooth and high-toned. Certainly not nearly so clear and authoritative as when you give your own answers to things. But that is far from always. Enough of that.

What the hell has happened to our music-printing business? Not a word, a catalog, a copy of anything have I had. The last letter I had from Lehman was in September and he was about to publish my *Christmas Pieces*. Please write or ask him to do something about it all and if anything has been published, why can't I have a catalog or even a complimentary copy. After all, my name is (or was) on the incorporation-papers.

Also what has happened to the American Composers' Alliance?

My only reports from them are periodic blurbs of an advertising nature. Has any work been done? I called at the small-rights society here and had a very pleasant conversation with the president. He knew all about us, approved, told me how they collected everything here and gave me lots of historical literature and all the rule-books. I also learn privately that the administration is not so pretty as it looks on paper. There are universal complaints about the slowness of payment and high-handed distribution and all the other same complaints as about ASCAP.

As you know, there is a world congress on the subject of musical performing-rights fees to be held in London in May. If I have time and any money extra I shall go, though both are doubtful. Is our gang up to anything at all? *Time* magazine is probably publishing a reportage on the subject of royalties at the time of the London conference. There is a magazine published in Berne called *Les Droits d'Auteurs* that is worth looking at.

Lincoln writes *Billy the Kid* is a success and I am happy. Charlie Ford saw somebody who had seen *Five Kings* and said that was OK too.

Please write me of ACA and of the Arrow Music Press. Also thank Edwin for his part in the *dedicace* of *Second Hurricane*. I shall write him later.

My book[3] gets toward being finished. I like it better than yours. I only hope it sells as well.

Devotedly,
Virgil

---

3 *The State of Music* (1939).

HENRY COWELL

Menlo Park, California, 1897 —

❖❖❖❖❖❖❖❖

To *Olive Cowell*

New York City, June 1, 1932

Dear Olive:

Enclosed are the New School report and a program with a note on the rhythmicon.

My part in its invention was to invent the idea that such a rhythmic instrument was a necessity to further rhythmic development, which had more or less reached the limit of performance by hand, and needed the application of mechanical aid. That which the instrument was to accomplish, what rhythms it should do, and the pitch it should have, and the relation between the pitch and rhythm, are my ideas. I also conceived that the principle of broken-up light, playing on a photoelectric cell, would be the best means of making it practical. With this idea, I went to Theremin, who did the rest. He invented the method by which the light could be cut, did the electrical calculations, and built the instrument.

The purpose of the instrument is twofold: to make possible the production of rhythm and related tone beyond the point where they could be produced before now by any known means; and to be used, first, for making rhythmical melody and harmony for use in musical composition, and, second, for the carrying on of numerous scientific physical and psychological experiments with rhythm.

Love,

HENRY

To *Olive Cowell*

San Francisco, March, 1936

Dear Olive,

My recital at Schaeffer's Studio, Friday the 20th. The Creative Music class begins there the following Friday. You ask for a statement about what creative music is, as a study, and why.

It consists of the study of the *organization* of the materials of sound, such as rhythm, melody, and of the general form to contain them. Mistakes usually made in this definition: it is not the study of instrument-making. It is not an attempt to stimulate the student into writing down any sort of music that happens to come into his mind. (The latter two have no organization.)

The value of such a study is general, not limited to music specialists, and it is of value as an approach to music, even more than as a study to follow previous instrumental study. If the student learns to perceive how to organize sounds, and to hear how sound is organized in the works of others, he will have the musical advantage of being able to appreciate the form and content of any music he hears, no matter of what style, and he is very apt to take an interest in learning how to perform music on an instrument, and to read notes. From the physiological standpoint, he will then have the advantage that his aural sense will be trained and aural stimuli marshalled into order.

Mistakes usually made by those who teach what is called creative music in the schools today: Teachers practically compose (instead of the student composing) by (1) setting the number of measures to be filled; (2) insisting that the melodies fall about a chord, and giving the chord in advance; (3) instructing the student in "active tone tendencies" in such a way that every tone written has a preconceived obligation; (4) insisting on confining to three or more simple rhythms, which are given in advance. Or else the teacher places no curb on the student but insists on "inspiration" alone. The result lacks organization.

The method I recommend: Induce the student to compose a very short fragment of melody, then get the student to consider every possible variant of his own melody (inverted, retrograde, etc.). Let the student hum (or play, if he can), to try out how the melody and each variant will sound on every degree of every familiar scale. After he has this knowledge of his own theme, he will usually be able to organize a longer melodic line from the materials first developed. Further studies include a consideration of different ways of accenting the notes of the theme, how to vary the note-lengths, how to build from two or more contrasting themes, how to plan complete forms.

The advantage of this method is that the completed works have organization, economy of materials and form, yet the student has developed these things for himself, instead of their being laid out by a teacher. I hope this is what you want. Love,

HENRY

Have a good time in the south.

ROY HARRIS

Lincoln County, Oklahoma, 1898 —

❖❭❂❭❂❭❂❭❂❭❂❭❂

To *Nicolas Slonimsky*

[*Colorado Springs*]
January 10, 1944

Dear Nicolai:

As Composer-in-Residence to Colorado College, I am pleased to advise you that our administration has seen the light ahead of current trends in education. The decision in regard to me as Composer-in-Residence is somewhat as follows: I shall be allowed to be a composer through the winter months and teach only in the summer school. Of course, I shall also do some radio broadcasting in the winter time for the college, but you will be interested to know that the theory upon which this unprecedented decision was acted upon by the academic machinery, is somewhat like this:

1. That the educational process is a three-fold one.
   A. Materials to be learned
   B. Students desiring to learn those materials
   C. A faculty capable of teaching them to the students
2. Therefore, that the creator of materials is an organic part of the educational process and has importance as either student body or faculty, and
3. Therefore, the composer-in-residence should be supported by an educational institution to create materials suitable to the educational process, not only locally but to the national scene.

Therefore, I am composer-in-residence to the national scene by courtesy of Colorado College. This is quite extraordinary foresight — something which all institutions of higher learning will be getting around to with the creative arts as they have already accepted with the research sciences.

You will be interested to know that consequently I am not a part of the Music Department at all in the winter time, but I am a little special department of my own, known as "Composer-in-Residence." I think you will also be interested to know that I am only a month away from finishing the Sixth and that I will be seeing you at the end of March or the first of April.

Koussevitzky is to produce the Sixth over the Blue Network. It is being performed in honor of Lincoln, on the anniversary of the date of his death — April 15th.

I have been writing a great deal of music for military bands of this region, and have had several nation-wide hookups with military bands over the NBC system out of Denver.

Johana joins me in sending our best regards to you and Dorothy and Electra.

Cordially,
ROY HARRIS

✦)✦)✦)✦)✦)✦)✦

To *Ruth Bracher:*

[*Colorado Springs*]
March 15, 1945

Dear Bracher:
In regard to the hearing and publishing and general dissemination of your friends' "popular" songs, I am afraid that my advice will be somewhat cynical. The process is something like this:

First, a word about the songs themselves. As you know, they seem to be practically all the same songs. The melodies are composed of little diatonic sequences, the harmonic textures are all grouped in very much the same root relationships, with a special emphasis on altered dominants. They all contain exactly the same number of measures in verse and chorus. You could make a machine to turn out popular songs mechanically at a nickel apiece. Let's say three different types of "hot" I Love You, three different types of "blue" I Love You, and maybe a couple of nonsense songs. Of course, I am not telling you anything that you don't know. I merely preface my remarks with these comments for the simple reason that since this is the case, every little town in the United States has someone who writes these songs, and New York is bulging with these compositions, and so is Hollywood. They are as stereotyped as our patent breakfast foods and women's hair-do's.

Consequently the marketing of these wares has become a very

eral that seemed unoriginal to you. Vecchi, of course, did tell a story in a series of choruses.[2] I knew that and I deliberately imitated him; — not in respect to texture (as some imitate Bach or Weber), nor subject matter (as some imitate 18th century opera) nor handling of voices (as some imitate Strawinsky), but simply in the way of telling a story through the medium of an unaccompanied chorus of mixed voices. My choruses were sacred and Vecchi's were secular, though that difference alone would not suffice to claim "originality" for them. Or did you, ——, perhaps not know the madrigal sequences of Vecchi and therefore not have them in mind? If not, what did you have in mind and ought not your reviews to give some clue to that?

The truth is, a critic can't sling the word "original" around without doing a lot of thinking about it and then, preferably, giving his readers the benefit of his cogitations. It is a *crux criticorum* of the first magnitude and merits straight thinking — if any aspect of criticism does.

Equally difficult and important was the æsthetic principle touched on by one of the N. Y. scriveners. I simply do not believe that a work can reveal "technical mastery" and not be good. My definition of technique includes making a work good. Either it did *not* reveal technical mastery or it *was* good. I am ready to refute its "technical mastery" and I am willing to agree that it was not wholly good. The fuzzy thinking that makes a reviewer link "technical mastery" with anything *short* of goodness is regrettable. Nor do I see much to commend in a writer who picks countless "flaws" in a work and closes by saying that "the work deserved the enthusiasm which it aroused." Obviously it didn't; the public was duped and the reviewer was under a moral obligation to tell them so!

You understand, I hope, that I am not gored by these destructive criticisms. It is the lack of consistency and sound æsthetic that I find distressing. To ease that distress, — and I know it will be deeply gratifying to you to know it, — the *Christian Science Monitor* came out with an exquisitely appreciative and flattering write-up. . . .

This is much too long a reply to your model of brevity. But I don't want to stop without telling you what I hinted at in the Town Hall, namely: that I enjoyed and admired the Overture to *White Wings* [3] very, very much. It is just the sort of music that it should be and the sort that you should write. I was a little surprised at its short-

2 Orazio Vecchi (1550–1605) wrote a comedy entirely in the form of madrigals entitled *L'Amfiparnasso.*

3 Chamber opera, text by Philip Barry (1935).

ness, but that is perhaps the fault of the title Overture. It is more an Introduction to Act I and if called that (or something similar) would seem just the right length, which it undoubtedly is in its rôle of starting things going. It seemed very well suited to the story, the period and the stage. It all sounded and I congratulate you on the way it was written and the way it was scored. I hope someone will have the sense to put it on. But if not you must go right ahead anyhow and count it not a bean. Excelsior!

We hear you are moving back to N. Y. but otherwise have no knowledge of your plans. I'm sorry the day and a half we spent in N. Y. was so crowded that we only caught a glimpse of you. We must meet and go over the ground.

Affectionately,
RANDALL

⊙⊱⊙⊱⊙⊱⊙⊱⊙⊱⊙⊰⊙

To Mr. and Mrs. *Douglas Moore*

Encampment, Wyoming
July 22, 1940

Dear Emily and Doug,

If I was one day late in visiting you, it was as nothing compared to the time I have taken to send you formal thanks for a lovely visit. Without that all-too-brief interlude I doubt whether I'd have pulled through the past month. I felt sorry for Douglas, with a movie score to write under such pressure, and no sooner did I get back to Phila. than a similar pressure descended on me. Thank heavens for the breather with you two.

First Wallenstein rang up and wanted an orchestral score for *Americana*. Then Koussevitzky sent word he'd like a choral piece for the opening exercises of the Berkshire Music Center. *Americana* ran to 65 pages of scoring. Then I saw Margaret and three of the children off for Wyoming, went home and began the choral piece. It had to be of a kind that would fit a Solemn Occasion, and that could be performed after one rehearsal on the first day of the school. I enclose a copy of what I turned out.

On July 5, I turned the piece over to the lithographer and left for a long weekend at the Reiners' in Westport. I then returned to Bryn Mawr long enough to close the house and get Varney and head for the Berkshires. There I gave 5 lectures and fell swooning onto the train for the West!

The Music Center is truly marvelous — a wonderful set up in heavenly country and such a fine group of students and teachers. I was there the first week but already the place had such spirit and atmosphere. Most congenial, and stimulating to a degree. My *Alleluia* had been sung to perfection at the opening exercises, so my entrance into the place two days later was not so awkward as it might have been. I went to several of the Institute ("professional" students) Orchestra rehearsals, which gave its first concert on Friday night of the first week, opening (if you please) with a certain E minor Symph. led by Leonard Bernstein, student from C.I.M.[4] I confess I enjoyed this privilege because it was really a fine performance. Most of all I relished watching Koussevitzky sit directly behind the student conductors at all rehearsals, criticizing them at every turn. He has proved himself a fine teacher and — still more surprising — a most skillful administrator of the school. His outlook is very broad and he seeks at every turn to do equal justice to the professional and non-professional students. There is no doubt in my mind that he has come out with a permanent institution of the greatest value and importance. It preserves the best in Mr. Surette's Summer School, with an added *plus* of a fine performing group, the presence of members of the B.S.O. and facilities of all kinds — little operas, masques, plays, large choral works, and a situation that is simply beautiful. You must go up, and so must the Giddings.

Enough. How did the movie music turn out? It certainly began very promisingly. I long to hear about the orchestration of it and all attending circumstances — the performance and the visit from the Brants, the opening of the show and all. Do let me hear.

A-Bar-A is just what we all hoped it would be. I began relaxing at once and am still at it. The children ride every day and swim and go on picnics and listen to cow boy songs and wrangle the horses at 5:30 a.m. Margaret is having the first complete vacation in yrs, and you might say the same of me. I actually have ridden once myself and shall hope to get good enough at it to tag along with the young. We are counting the days till the Bronsons arrive and only wish you were going to be here too.

It occurs to me that Jim Giddings might like to see my *Alleluia*, so I'm enclosing also a copy for him. Will you give it to him with my compliments? I've already sent it to E.C.S. in hopes it will be published by fall, but one never knows.

---

4 Curtis Institute of Music.

We hope your summer proves happy and productive, with no more incursions of plagues or nuisances of any kind. Margaret sends her love with mine and I send you my most affectionate thanks for a heartwarming visit. By now, hearing from me will enjoy an element of surprise which I rely on heavily to obscure my sinful procrastination.

Yrs devotedly,
RANDALL

CARLOS CHÁVEZ

Mexico D. F., 1899 —

❀❀❀❀❀❀❀❀

To *Aaron Copland*

Mexico D.F., December 1, 1934

My dear Aaron:

Here is the program of our last concert. I hope you will agree with the way your work was placed between the Stravinsky suite and *H.P.*[1] The performance was accurate and "simple"; we had 10 rehearsals and it was worked out with the utmost of interest and energy; the orchestra men were at first sceptical but by the third rehearsal or so they had a more genuine and growing interest.

I was amazed to see this, as it seldom happens with your works and mine. This last concert was the best of the entire season; it was warm and enthusiastic. It is impossible to tell you in a few words how much I enjoy the *Little Symphony*.[2] I have already begun to write an essay on it which I intend to send to Minna Lederman for *Modern Music*.

The dialectic of this music, that is to say, its movement, the way each and every note comes out from the other as the *only* natural and logically possible one, is simply unprecedented in the whole history of music. The work as a whole, I mean to say in its entirety, is an organism, a body in which every piece works by itself 100% but whose mutual selection is such, that no one part could possibly work and exist without the other. There has been much talk about music in which everything is essential, nothing superfluous, but, as far as I know, *the talk* about such music exists, yes, but not the music itself. The *Little Symphony* is the first realization of this I know of, and yet the human content, the inner expression is

---

1 Ballet by Chávez.
2 *Short Symphony* by Copland (1933).

purely emotional. It is precisely that tremendous human impulse which made possible such realization.

What I understand by "modern music" or "contemporary music" is merely *our music;* all the rest belongs to historical periods, no matter how close or dear these historical periods may be to us. . . . Let me tell you what I thought when I got the *Little Symphony* — well, here is the real thing, here is our music, here is my music, the music of my time, of my taste, of my culture, here it is, a simple and natural fact to myself, as everything belonging to oneself is simple and natural.

I am sending you the piano score of *Llamadas;* that is already out; also the completely recorded *H.P.* — seven single records — good for any standard machine; a complete collection of programs and a book *Instrumental Precortesiano* containing the research work that we have carried out in the Conservatory in that direction. I have just written a piece for piano and violin and soon will have a copy for you.

I wish to go on writing to you about a thousand things but I'd better send you this and not wait. You know how deeply related to you I feel. I do not have to tell you how proud I feel to see my name on the first page of the *Little Symphony*!

CARLOS

GEORGE ANTHEIL

Trenton, New Jersey, 1900 —

❂❂❂❂❂❂❂❂

To *Hans Heinsheimer*

Hollywood, California
February 16, 1945

Dear Hans,
When, in my letter of yesterday, I spoke about Bruckner, Sibelius, Shostakovich, I meant that in my estimation these
three men more than any other continued the line of the great symphony; and that whatever else may be said against them, they always
shot at the stars and attempted to progress music beyond the point
beyond that which the last had taken it.

To illustrate: a great many people today write things they
call "symphonies" — a title which, incidentally, one can prefix to
almost anything with a sonata-allegro first movement, and of sufficiently imposing length. I suppose that, from the classic or text-
book point of view, they are symhonies, at least in part. It is not
too difficult to learn how to write pieces in the classic sonata-allegro
form and tack three or four like and contrasting pieces thereupon,
and call it a symphony. The *Symphonie Classique* of Prokofieff is
such a work, as strict in form as early Mozart.

But these symphonies — and there are a great many of them
today particularly — are not really symphonies, but caricatures of
the symphonies of other days; this is the reason — they have simply
adopted the old "classique" symphonic form, giving it no new important alteration, no new progression, no new advancement. Prokofieff, at least, was frank in his caricature — and bright too — but
the others are heavy, plodding, anxious to write something that can
be called a "symphony" in order to enhance their reputations, rami-
fied if need be with the most flatulent nationalism either in theme or
philosophy. In other words, they do not do the thing which every
new symphony writer of every new age is supposed to do, and al-

[395]

ways has done, and that is to take the symphony at the point which one's predecessor has broken off, and continue — as Beethoven did with Mozart, and continued to do from the First Symphony to the Ninth; as Bruckner did with Beethoven; as Sibelius and Vaughn Williams did with Bruckner (or at least tried with best and most sincere will) and as Shostakovich takes up after Sibelius and Bruckner.

I maintain that, today, one cannot go back and write a symphony in the form of the Beethoven First, after Beethoven had written eight other mighty symphonies, each progressing the form further and further into the future. Yes, if one wishes to label it as a caricature, or a *tour de force*, as does Prokofieff, but not otherwise. All this brings forth an unpleasant truth about present day music — the boys are primarily stylists, occupied not with discovering great new truths or significances about music, but with fabricating a style so substantially theirs that any old ancient scaffolding will do to exhibit it to the world. Their motto: "you can look at any five measures of my music and tell that it is mine!" I wonder what Beethoven would think. . . .

Sincerely,
GEORGE ANTHEIL

ERNST KRENEK

Vienna, 1900 —

❧❧❧❧❧❧❧❧

To *George Perle*

Poughkeepsie, N. Y., March 13, 1940

Dear Mr. Perle,

       I read your paper [1] with keen interest, and I think it is a very clear and logical presentation of the result of your studies. As far as immanent criticism goes, the main points I should like to raise are the use of the term *"twelve tone scale"* and of the terms "mode" and "scale" in general.

       For the sake of clarity in the discussion underway, I would strongly suggest using the term "twelve tone scale" for nothing but the chromatic scale, or not use it at all. The reason for this suggestion is that the term "twelve-tone scale" has been so preposterously misused by incompetent scribblers that it seems no longer capable of any intelligent meaning. (Another question of terminology is whether "row" or "series" is more adequate for describing what we mean by that; you know that I have been repeatedly advised to use the term "series" rather than "row" since the latter is said to mean in English, any linear arrangement showing recurrent regularities in the order of its elements — which certainly is not a characteristic of our "tone successions." I am not good enough at English to decide this problem, but it would be wise to unify the terminology in this regard.)

       As to the term "mode," you endow it with a quite new and unusual significance. Your definition of "modal forms" on p. 1 has certainly nothing to do with the usual connotation of "mode" in the sense, for example, of the medieval Church modes, which were hardly more than scales. In my opinion, the difference between a mode and a scale, in the historical sense, consists in that the mode

---

1 "The Twelve-Tone Modal System," *Music Review* (Cambridge, England), November 1941.

is a linear arrangement of the tones used in certain music according to their pitch, while the scale (as major and minor scale) is an arrangement of the same nature, but representing certain harmonic relationships between the chords built on the various steps of that scale. Hence, there is no difference in the *nature* of these phenomena, the difference only shows up when their significance for the development of music is considered. (As a matter of fact, some of the medieval modes are practically identical with later scales.) [2]

What you understand by a mode goes even farther than the concept of "functional modes" in Hill.[3] The functional mode of R. S. Hill is supposed to show the harmonic relationship of tonality clearer than the merely statistical arrangement of the original scale, but Hill does not by any means go so far as to contend that such a mode would "provide the only sound-relationships that may be utilized at a given time," as you put it in your definition.

This brings me to a more substantial comment on your paper. I realize that the above definition is actually the core of your theory. Your contention is obviously that the present stage of composition needs regulations to the effect that only certain sound-relationships may be utilized, and you try to support this thesis quite skillfully with several arguments. I am, however, not absolutely sure that the problem of the present practice of the twelve tone technique is to be found in that direction. Speaking very concretely from the standpoint of the every day experience of a twelve tone composer, the predicament is exactly this: working along the lines of the "classical" [4] technique, we find ourselves every now and then embarrassed by the necessity of locating remaining tones of the series, even when we would not "feel like that." The meaning of this plight is simply

---

2 "In the light of historical studies carried out in the meantime, I would today [March 1942] express myself somewhat differently. I am now of the opinion that the old modes, at least at the time of their origin, were common denominators of certain melodic prototypes; that the material of the modes finally was arranged, according to pitch, in modal scales; that two of them, the Ionian and the Aeolian modes, survived under the name of major and minor (modes) in the modern system of tonality. Thus, I would now abandon the methodological discrimination of mode and scale as given in the text, but maintain that the medieval modes are generated by melodic considerations, while the modern (major and minor) modes demonstrate harmonic relationships." E. K.

3 Richard S. Hill: "Schoenberg's Tone-Rows and the Tonal System of the Future," *Musical Quarterly*, January 1936.

4 "Those ways of applying the twelve tone technique in which the identity of the original twelve tone series remains unaltered." E. K.

that the series pattern suited us well in the beginning of a certain musical complex, but that our "intuition" took us, during the process of composing, some other way.

To put it even more exactly, our creative mind was not able to embrace at once a concrete musical figure containing three or four complete series-forms, the choice of which was suggested by our primary inspiration. There are several ways out of this situation: either we could train our mind to think more and more faithfully in terms of twelve tone patterns (I do not know whether that is possible); or we should abstain from "inspirations" which require more series forms than we can easily survey at once (an unalluring limitation of our imagination); or we can try to get along without the series. This latter alternative seems not only cowardly and retrogressive — it also does not work as soon as we want to stick to what we recognize as the main virtue of the technique: density, compactness, interdependence, etc.

When I, at least, made some experiments of this sort, I felt very soon I might as well write down and systematize the required patterns since I wanted to use them as strictly as possible. This of course does not mean anything else than ruefully coming back to the "classical" twelve tone technique. The only imaginative way out of the dilemma seems to be a freer treatment of the series as I indicated in my book,[5] and practised in my *Symphonic Piece*.[6] (By the way, in the opera which I am sketching now, I have not felt thus far any necessity to deviate in principle from the "classical technique.")

As to your mentioning the "prejudices" of some atonalists against the facts presented in the overtone series, I do not feel guilty of such prejudices. I am only of the well-grounded opinion, that these facts have very little influence on the problems involved in composition. Your derivation of the diatonic seven tone mode from the overtone series is just as arbitrary as any other explanation along these lines. You have to assume a "primitive five tone scale," the "addition" of two tones, a "place of honor" given to the tonic, and so on. If all that is true (and I think it is, in some way or other), what then is the use of the overtones? Moreover, if there really were such an immediate "natural" connection between the overtones and the major scale, it is hardly conceivable why the major scale was not historically the primary phenomenon and why it is not used by all

5 *Music Here and Now* (1939).
6 *Symphonic Piece* for string orchestra, op. 86.

primitive peoples which, after all, have the same ability to perceive overtones as we apparently have. (I, of course do not think that we have any such ability.)

Looking forward to a continuation of our important discussion, I am very cordially yours,

ERNST KRENEK

AARON COPLAND

Brooklyn, N. Y., 1900 —

❀❀❀❀❀❀❀❀

To *Nicolas Slonimsky*

[1927]

Dear Kolya,

You're a darling to have sent all those delightful write-ups.[1] After reading them I went to the mirror to see if I could recognize myself.

How flattering it was to read that the "Listener" can understand Strauss, Debussy, Stravinsky — but not poor me. How instructive to learn that there is "no rhythm in this so-called concerto." And how badly I felt for Mrs. Gardner of Bridgeport when I thought how badly *she* must have felt when she discovered her mistake in the title. Only one thing got my nanny — how dare H. T. P. talk of *reducing* me to my level, when I am waiting to be *raised* to my level. And all that really worries me is whether or not the Maestro will ever again have sufficient courage to perform me anywhere. . . .

When the Concerto is played again ("O horrid thought!") we must see if we can't get the police to raid the concert hall to give a little added interest to this "horrible" experiment.

Till soon
AARON

---

1 "Letters from readers of various Boston papers following the *première* of the jazzy Piano Concerto performed by the Boston Symphony Orchestra under Serge Koussevitzky with the composer as soloist." A. C.

[401]

To *Arthur V. Berger* [2]

Lavinia, Minnesota
August 6, 1934

Dear Arthur:

Duly flattered at your starting your "series" with the *Piano Variations*. What are you planning to take up — why can't we use one of the series in *Modern Music*?

The Variations were written during 1930, though I had the initial germ as early as 1928. In January of 1930 I took a house in Bedford, New York, and lived there until July. I remember working very concentratedly on them during those six months. There was more work in Yaddo during August–November 2 of that year. I played the work for the first time in New York at a League Sunday afternoon concert in January 1931. (It has never been performed in Berlin.) Martha Graham heard it at that concert. While it's true that I did not play from notes at that concert and even did not have it written down in a *definitive* version (i.e. in ink), what I played was essentially the present printed version with two exceptions: the dynamics were less varied, and one of the variations near the end was recast into a somewhat different form — also to vary the dynamic scheme. (Virgil Thomson still thinks I play it too "hard"!) That first version was written down — Martha Graham uses it for her Dithyrambic.

The second American performance was at the first Yaddo Festival. (There had been one in England in December, 1931.) At Yaddo, for the first time I had the impression that the audience was "getting it."

I think it important in connection with the Variations that you point out that, as happens with so much American music, it has been heard only by the "inner circle." It has never been performed in New York in the ordinary musical channels and has never been written about (or heard, to my knowledge) by any of those first-line music critics who never tire of generalizing about "our American music."

Glad to hear you were satisfied with Yaddo and that Yaddo was satisfied with you.

Always,
AARON

---

2 Reply to a request for some notes on Copland's Piano Variations.

To *Arthur V. Berger*

Hollywood, April 10, 1943

Dear Arthur:

The other night, while walking down Hollywood Blvd., I happened on a copy of the *Partisan Review*.[3] Imagine my surprise when I came upon your piece on the *Piano Sonata*. I wonder what made you not tell me about it — just neglect? or was it "fright" at my reaction? Anyhow it was lots of fun to be surprised like that. Subsequently Victor wrote me that you had mentioned it to him.

I don't know what others will think, but I liked it. My one objection is that it came to a rather sudden end, just as things were getting along. Were you cramped for space? It gives that impression.

There are a few things that I'd like to comment upon. One is the meaning of my articles and "pronunciamentos." When I call for a "style that satisfies both us and them," I am mostly trying to goad composers on toward what I think is a healthy direction. I am emphatically *not* laying out an *a priori* plan for my own future compositions. I reserve the right always to practise not what I preach, but what the muse dictates.

I think also that for the sake of drawing sharp distinctions you rather overdo the dichotomy between my "severe" and "simple" styles. The inference is that only the severe style is really serious. I don't believe that. What I was trying for in the simpler works was only partly a larger audience; they also gave me a chance to try for a home-spun musical idiom, similar to what I was trying for in a more hectic fashion in the earlier jazz works. In other words, it was not only musical functionalism that was in question, but also musical language. I like to think that in *Billy* and *Our Town*, and somewhat in *Lincoln*, I have touched off for myself and others a kind of musical naturalness that we have badly needed — along with "great" works.

The reference to David's and Harold's [4] building up the "thinned out musical substance" needs to be expanded to be clear. I didn't understand it myself. But I'm sure they were pleased with the plug!

Did Victor tell you Stravinsky had me and Antheil to dinner?

---

3 March 1943.

4 David Diamond and Harold Shapero.

(After reading Kazin's book [5] I've come to the conclusion that Stravinsky is the Henry James of composers. Same "exile" psychology, same exquisite perfection, same hold on certain temperaments, same lack of immediacy of contact with the world around him.) He was extremely cordial with us. We played S.'s Symphony from off-the-air records. I don't think he's in a very good period. He copies himself unashamedly, and therefore one rarely comes upon a really fresh page — for him, I mean. I know this is blasphemy in the Berger household, but there it is — so make the most of it.

Love to Esther,
AARON

---

5 Alfred Kazin: *On Native Grounds* (1942).

DMITRI SHOSTAKOVICH

St. Petersburg, 1906 —

❋❋❋❋❋❋❋❋❋

To *The New Masses*

Leningrad, [October 1941]

On the morning of June 22 I volunteered for service at the front. I received a reply: "You'll be called when required." So I went back to my duties at the Leningrad Conservatory. We attended classes by members of the graduating class, gave an evaluation of their performances, and signed their diplomas. This year many gifted pianists, violinists, and singers graduated from the Leningrad Conservatory.

I joined the Conservatory Fire-Fighting Brigade. We were housed in barracks and it was here that I began work on my Seventh Symphony. Later I was asked to become musical director of the Popular Guard Theatre. Soon this theatre became the centre of Leningrad's leading playwrights, poets, and writers. We produced several interesting works, one of them an operetta on how Ribbentrop gathered his celebrated conference of diplomats shortly after the outbreak of the war. One after the other groups of actors from our theatre left for the front. And when some of them returned they brought with them the splendid fighting spirit of our army. I visited front-line units on two occasions and witnessed numerous instances of the courage that typifies our people. Simple people, men you meet every day, turned out to be real heroes.

Take, for example, Danya Shafran, member of the Popular Guard, who saw some very heavy fighting and showed distinguished valour. One of my pupils, Fleischman, who has just finished his first one-act opera, was always very modest and inconspicuous in the Conservatory. But now in these trying days he proved worthy of his country. And my Seventh Symphony (I am working on it now) will tell of these so-called simple people.

The first part of the symphony tells of the happy, peaceful

[405]

life of a people confident in themselves and in their future. It is a simple life, such as was enjoyed by thousands of Leningrad's Popular Guards, by the whole city and the whole country before the war broke out. Then comes the war. I have made no attempt at naturalistic interpretation of the war by imitating booms of cannon, shell explosions, etc. I tried to give an emotional image of the war. The reprise is a memorial march, or more correctly a requiem for the war's victims. Plain people pay tribute to the memory of their heroes. The requiem is followed by an even more tragic theme. I don't know how to describe it. Perhaps it is the tears of a mother or even that feeling which comes when sorrow is so great that there are no more tears. These two lyrical fragments form the conclusion of the first part of the symphony. The closing chords resemble the din of distant battle, a reminder that the war continues.

While I was working on this music, Leningrad was converted into an impregnable fortress. Fresh Popular Guard detachments were constantly being formed. The entire population learned the art of warfare and it seemed that war had replaced all other affairs. I found, however, that that was not so, for one of my friends told me that all tickets for the Philharmonic concerts had been sold out. Indeed at all these concerts I found the audience in high spirits and keenly responsive to our performance. My excitement at these concerts was something new, for I came to understand that music, like every art, is a genuine requirement of man.

My work on the symphony continued at a rapid pace. I finished the second and third parts in a surprisingly short space of time. Generally speaking, I do not hurry with my work, but on this symphony I worked with a speed that I myself couldn't understand. When I am through with it, I shall have to start from the beginning, of course, for it still requires much polishing and work over details. But as I was writing the score, I didn't think of this aspect. The second and third parts of the symphony aren't closely bound to the main theme. They serve as a lyrical relief. The second part of the symphony is a lyrical scherzo. The third part, adagio, is the dramatic centre of the symphony.

It is with a feeling of admiration and pride that I watch the heroic deeds of Leningrad's people. Despite frequent air-raid alarms, everyone goes about his work with precision and efficiency. People are calm and life continues normally. Factories and offices successfully cope with the rush orders. Theatres are as active as ever and give the people that spiritual encouragement which helps them in their work at the front or rear. Everyone shares the common cause and strives for a common aim. Wives and mothers don't complain. They show every concern for the menfolk at the front and they themselves help to guard the city and fight fires. Even the children are doing their bit to help strengthen Leningrad's defences.

I have still to write the finale of the symphony, but its general outlines are already clear to me. I could describe it with one word — victory. This finale is devoted to a happy life in the future after the enemy is crushed. Never have I dedicated any of my works. But this symphony, if my work meets with success, I intend to dedicate to Leningrad. Every note in it, everything I have put into it, is linked up with my native city, with these historic days of its defence against the fascist barbarians.

DMITRI SHOSTAKOVICH

PAUL CRESTON

New York City, 1906 —

❂❂❂❂❂❂❂❂❂

To *Denton Rossel*

February 28, 1945

Dear Mr. Rossel:

 In my own development as composer I have followed the evolutionary principle of "from the simple to the complex"; that is, from short pieces to larger works, from solo music to chamber music to orchestral music. My first orchestral work is Opus 16 (*Threnody*) and my first Symphony, Opus 20.

 I have always considered the practice of four-part vocal harmony as a specialization rather than a general training in harmony. If you think that four-part vocal harmony is the only or best method of learning harmony, I suggest you study Ernest Fowles' book, *Ear, Eye and Hand in Harmony Study* for a more practical course.

 This judgment applies also to the practice of writing in the styles of different composers. It is no more essential to write quartets *à la* Haydn, Mozart or Beethoven to learn the structure of a string quartet than it is to learn to drive a Model T Ford in order to drive a 1942 Buick. In this respect, an analytical rather than an imitative procedure is valuable. But whatever creativity is attempted in any particular branch should stem from an original, personal, intuitive and sincere motivation.

 To enlarge on this thesis: I have studied the harmony of all the great composers but I have never written any exercises emulating their harmonies. I have studied counterpoint from Palestrina to Hindemith, but I have not tried my hand at duplicating their practices. These studies have been from a purely historical and analytical approach. I believe the chronological method has also been taught in story writing. But even in this field, I cannot see the value of practising an old idiom for the purpose of learning the idiom of today.

[408]

It would be as if learning to write Chaucerian English would help our self-expression at the present time.

In the matter of Form: it is more important to understand the principles of form (unity, coherence, balance) and the devices (repetition, imitation, variation, etc.) rather than the form-types (rondo, sonata, passacaglia, etc.). Practice in the various forms: binary, ternary, theme and variations, etc., is quite helpful so long as it is not pure imitation but an effort to instill a personal element or effect some variation in it. Compare, for example, the ternary form of a Minuet (Haydn or Mozart) with the use of that form by Chopin in some of his Nocturnes and Etudes, and you will see what I mean. The chapter on Musical Structure in Aaron Copland's book *What to Listen for in Music* is probably the clearest and most concise presentation of this subject I have read.

I think your method of learning orchestration [1] is not quite genuine. It is a method of *transcribing* for orchestra rather than *composing* orchestral works. Rimsky-Korsakov's axiom "to orchestrate is to create" is unquestionably true. Of the many books on orchestration which I have studied only two are essential: 1) *Orchestration* by Cecil Forsyth (for knowledge of instrumental techniques, though there are a number of errors) and 2) *Principles of Orchestration* by Rimsky-Korsakov (a bible to many composers and the fruit of actual experience rather than academic theory). But what is even more important than books is the constant practice of listening to orchestral music with score in hand and the deepest concentration on the tone-color of the various instruments and combinations of instruments. I cannot suggest any text-book on orchestral exercises as I have never used any.

The best way to learn to orchestrate is to write orchestral pieces, after, of course, one has learned the range, technique and characteristics of each instrument, and the tonal color and balance of the various combinations of instruments. When I say orchestral pieces I do not mean full compositions, but short (eight or ten measures) passages. For example, one exercise could be an eight-bar phrase for solo Oboe with Strings; another could be a chorale for Brass choir; another for Woodwinds with the melody in the flute, or clarinet or bassoon, or oboe. Eventually you should work on passages for full orchestra.

---

1 "Mr. Rossel's method is: to orchestrate, for example, a Brahms symphony from the piano version — and then compare the result with the original." P. C.

I hope this letter has been of some help to you. I know I could
do much better, in the same period of time necessary in writing this,
in a personal talk.

With best wishes for your success, believe me

Sincerely yours

[PAUL CRESTON]

WILLIAM SCHUMAN

New York City, 1910 —

❖❖❖❖❖❖❖❖

To *Robert Beckhard*

Bronxville, New York,
March 21, 1942

Dear Mr. Beckhard:

Thank you for your note telling me that Victor will release the *American Festival Overture* next month. This is the first I've heard of it. Your publication, *Houston Record Society* sounds like a fine idea and I'm very happy to write a few words about the piece in question.

The Overture was written for the special concerts of American music given by the B.S.O. under Koussevitzky in 1939, the first performance of this work being given on October 6th. I can recall how very exciting it was for all of us that the orchestra was going to devote two entire programs to the works of our own boys. This thought was very much in mind when I started working on the piece. I kept thinking of it in terms of a kind of pep talk. "Here it is at last — come and get it — "

The opening paragraph of the program notes I prepared for the concert might interest you: "The first three notes of this piece will be recognized by some listeners as the 'call to play' of boyhood days. In New York City it is yelled on the syllables 'WEE-Awk-Eee' to get the gang together for a game or a festive occasion of some sort. This call very naturally suggested itself for a piece of music being composed for a very festive occasion. From this it should not be inferred that the Overture is program music. In fact, the idea for the music came to mind before the origin of the theme was recalled. The development of this bit of 'folk material,' then, is along purely musical lines."

Let me wish you the greatest success with your publication.

[411]

Your society is another proof of the importance of music on records and another bit of evidence that the music of America doesn't take place exclusively in Carnegie Hall. More power to you.

Sincerely,
WILLIAM SCHUMAN

DAVID DIAMOND

Rochester, N. Y., 1915 —

❖❖❖❖❖❖❖❖❖❖

To *Charles Naginsky* [1]

New York, February 14, 1938

Dear Charles,

       Please come Friday and bring your suite with you. We shall have a good time going over the orchestration. Don't worry; it will sound full and the texture will remain delicate. Orchestration, after all, is a personal gift. You get exactly what you put into it. When you say you'd like to be able to orchestrate like a professional Hollywood arranger, you make me laugh good and loud. With all Hollywood's ability to get every orchestral choir sounding like the Empire State Building looks, you will still find only formulated orchestral technique. There is not one Hollywood orchestrator who had the good taste to keep his orchestration clean, free from excess padding. How I wish I could afford to send the leading ones out there copies of Stravinsky's latest works. One day I hope Aaron goes out there and shows them up brown. In France, how effective the scores by men like Auric, Tansman, Milhaud and Honegger are. But then Hollywood is not Joinville.

       I am sorry to have found you so depressed the last time we had dinner together. I know we ought, all of us, to be retrospective about our life. But listen, Charles, we are, you and I, only beginning. We haven't the right to get depressed about the musical set-up. I do as well as I can, write my music and hope. Resentment is OK; especially resenting injustice. But let us, for heaven's sake, be careful. Let's really tread the "fantastic" lightly! Remember, the field of action is actually very narrow. We'll go on wanting to be happy and successful and nothing will be able to stop us; it is man's natural propensity to want to be somebody. We'll be accused of being vain, over-indulgent, impractical. But our work will be done. Even our most tawdry pleasures will bear fruit. I like going to the —— Bar,

---

1 Composer (1909–40).

accepting the fleeting adventures there because I have confidence in the people willing to share those adventures with me. I believe in the solidarity of loneliness. We are, you know, a Miss Lonelyhearts Club. Still, we are humorous about it. But if we get tragic about it, as you did the other night, and begin accusing no one of understanding, you'll get nowhere fast. Be patient, Charles. Gird yourself, be generous with your heart, work like a beast of burden. R.'s talk about "delivering the goods" is fine. Once you begin delivering, no matter how long it takes for people to purchase the product, you'll find yourself a happier person.

If I have anything to be grateful for, it is knowing that at the age of twenty-three, I have several large works to my credit, most of them unusually gifted and full of promise. What more can I ask for now? By hook or crook I'll hold onto this apartment if I have to beg, borrow, or steal. You are welcome to it too. Any time. The WPA red-tape is not getting any simpler though H. A. has written somebody in Washington about S.   Chalmers Clifton was kind, and as I told you, gave me the loan of fifty dollars to hold through. But it doesn't bring me any nearer to a job as a composer. My soda-jerking stops in three weeks; the Irish kid comes back from National Guard. What then? I'll simply hope the Guggenheim people find me worthy of a fellowship. If not, I shall take your advice and apply to Mrs. Ames at Yaddo. I'll be glad if you write her a word in my behalf. I've never met her. I hope for the *Prix* for you. I'm sure you'll have the score ready in time. R.'s word will count much, he is so highly respected. Don't be too unhapy about your work with him. He is very heavy, I know; but you come away with much after it is all over. Don't let his yawning upset you. It doesn't necessarily mean he is bored. Maybe there is something in the gland theory. Just don't feel you have to write music like his. He wouldn't expect you to.

How I wish R. would not feel bitterly towards me. One day, perhaps, he'll see my decision to study with B. was for the best. When the most critical decisions face us, how aggravating our insouciance can be! Be full of courage, Charles. I have a feeling the *Prix* will be yours. Think, if we both get our wishes, we might meet at Paris, have an *Oxygenée* together at the Dome or the Flore, go to see Fernandel and Rosay in the movies — but —

See you Friday, then, unless you call to the contrary.

Best ever,
DAVID

To an unnamed recipient

Paris, January 12, 1939

Dear Mr. R.,

      I want to thank you for your very interesting and stimulating letter; also, for the wonderful dinner and good talk the other night. I want very much to know you better, so do hurry your trip to Hungary and come back to Paris as soon as you can. I shall certainly not leave here before February or March. In any case, not before I've finished the entire orchestration of the *Cello Concerto.*

      You ask me to write you about my work. I hardly know what to tell you outside of what you already know. I always find it difficult to discuss my music in analytical terms. Surely, if I submit the scores to you for your proposed article, you'd have a more practical approach to work from. A composer when he explains, runs the inevitable risk of being a fool, a fantastically conceited egotist, or, he finds himself involved in a series of definitions which eventually becomes a dispute about names. He is bound to use terms which, quite clear though they may seem to him, nevertheless produce a kind of mist that obscures the boundaries of his art and gives rise to strident polemics out of which come more vague terms served up with a kind of intellectual froth.

      Some composers adore this sort of thing; I resent it and would much rather talk about what gives the Paris sky its particular hue at sundown or why American tourists make such god-damn fools of themselves in Paris. I have a feeling that the composer who goes about knowing his craft most completely is the one who troubles himself least with technical analysis, unless, of course, he is giving lessons to his pupils. The Musical Art is an instinctive one; it was never meant to be analyzed for exploitation purposes. The intellectual approach to music, no matter how well modified for the layman who wants to know, I suspect will produce a serious and rather destructive reactionary element in America's musical smugdom. It is producing a mass of windbags who can go on for hours about the whole tone scale which even Schönberg and his disciples cannot give intellectual or aural clarity to. Music really should not be excused in the guise of reason. Too many people today are trying to justify the precision with which organized musical sound is produced rather than the energy with which it is manipulated.

You mention the music of Arnold Schönberg. I have studied all the works available. One sees the details too clearly to the detriment of the whole. All the febrile brilliance is a kind of irritating flood-light that makes us blink when suddenly turned upon us. The style is subtle and profound but quite still-born, dry, and fatigued. I know that Schönberg is a mature, serious, and penetrating musical mind, but his method of analyzing the infinite number of convolutions of his craft is not half as gratifying to the heart as, say, the works of Stravinsky or Copland: the former's moving *Perséphone* [2] or the latter's *Statements* and *Ode*.[3] The works of both these men can, if necessary, be analyzed from the air, so to speak. Stravinsky's is an extraordinary technique. His splendid equilibrium secures a perfection of formal procedure. His marvelous spirit and feeling for transvaluation encourages the manner of distributing material based on solidly fortified principles found in the modification of tradition. The perfection which exists in each new work he writes stems from a necessity for absolute order within the musical form. His particular kind of musical discipline is wonderfully creative; it has helped him solve the riddle of lucid thinking within the most extremely compressed musical thought. His art is that mysterious harmony between sensuality, sensitiveness and intelligence. His latest works are of a glowing purity and make few concessions to the vulgar-hearted. His is music of the longer time; it does not deal with fleeting hours.

I could continue this way but I feel myself running out on ideas because I'm trying to avoid shop terms. It all boils down to what I professed in the beginning: the solitary mysteries of the composer's musical alchemy are not to be tampered with. I feel we can have a much more satisfying talk when you return. Please make it soon. Thank you, really, for your good and encouraging words about my *Cello Concerto* and *Psalm*. I am pleased that you were impressed with the *Heroic Piece*. I thought Scherchen did a splendid job all around. Wasn't Copland's *Music for Radio* a love? I hope you succeed in meeting Bartók. I understand he teaches at the well known Conservatory there, in Budapest. Please do study his *Music for Strings, Percussion and Celesta* carefully. I have enormous faith in this remarkable work. And don't lose my score; it is all marked up for some future use.

---

2 Melodrama on André Gide's poem (1933).
3 *Statements* for orchestra (1935); *Symphonic Ode* (1929).

With my warmest regards and thanks. Please come back soon. Don't get too fascinated by those attractive Hungarian girls and glittering night spots. I like you too.

Sincerely,
DAVID DIAMOND

SOURCES

1. ADAMI, GIUSEPPE: *Letters of Giacomo Puccini*, translated by Ena Makin. London: George G. Harrap & Co.; Philadelphia: J. B. Lippincott Co.; 1931.

2. ALTMANN, WILHELM: *Letters of Richard Wagner*, translated by M. M. Bozman. London: J. & M. Dent & Sons; 1927. New York: E. P. Dutton & Co.; 1927.

3. ANDERSON, EMILY: *The Letters of Mozart and His Family*. London: Macmillan and Co.; 1938.

4. AUER, MAX: *A. Bruckner: Gesammelte Briefe*. Regensburg: Gustav Bosse Verlag; 1924.

5. BELLINI, VINCENZO: *Lettere Inedite*. Milan: Ricordi; 1884.

6. BIZET, GEORGES: *Lettres à un ami*. Paris: Calmann-Lévy; 1909.

7. BURNEY, CHARLES: *A Letter from the Late Signor Tartini to Signora Maddalena Lombardini*. London; 1779; reprinted, London: Wm. Reeves; 1913.

8. DESAYMARD, JOSEPH: *Chabrier d'après ses lettres*. Paris: Fernand Roches; 1934.

9. DEUTSCH, OTTO ERICH: *Franz Schubert's Letters and Other Writings*, translated by Venetia Savile. London: Faber & Gwyer; 1928. New York: Alfred A. Knopf; 1928.

10. DIANIN, S.: *Pis'ma A. P. Borodina*. Moscow: State Musical Publications; 1936.

11. DUNSTAN, H. M.: *The Life and Letters of Berlioz*. London: Remington & Co.; 1882.

12. DURAND, JACQUES: *Lettres de Claude Debussy à son éditeur*. Paris: A. Durand et Fils; 1927.

13. EKMAN, KARL: *Jean Sibelius, His Life and Personality*, translated by Edward Birse. London: Alan Wilmer; 1936. New York: Alfred A. Knopf; 1938.

14. ENGLAND, PAUL: *Correspondence between Richard Strauss and Hugo von Hofmannsthal*. New York: Alfred A. Knopf; 1927.

15. FINCK, HENRY T.: *Grieg and His Music*. New York: John Lane Co.; 1909.

16. FOERSTER-NIETZSCHE, ELIZABETH: *The Nietzsche-Wagner*

Correspondence, translated by Caroline V. Kerr. London: Gerald Duckworth & Co.; 1921. New York: Boni & Liveright; 1921.

17. GANDERAX, LOUIS: *Lettres de Georges Bizet*. Paris: Calmann-Lévy; 1907.

18. GILMAN, LAWRENCE: *Edward MacDowell*. New York: John Lane Co.; 1908.

19. GOUNOD, CHARLES: *Autobiographical Reminiscences*, translated by W. Hely Hutchinson. London: William Heinemann; 1896.

20. HASE-KOEHLER, ELSE VON: *Max Reger, Briefe eines deutschen Meisters*. Leipzig: Koehler & Amelang; 1928.

21. HENSCHEL, GEORGE: *Personal Recollections of Johannes Brahms*. Boston: Richard G. Badger; 1907.

22. HERBERT, MAY: *Early Letters of Robert Schumann*. London: George Bell & Sons; 1888.

23. HOLST, IMOGEN: *Gustav Holst*. London: Oxford University Press; 1938.

24. IMBERT, HUGUES: *Lettres inédites de G. Bizet*. Paris: Librairie Fischbacher; 1894.

25. LaMARA [IDA MARIA LIPSIUS]: *Briefe hervorragender Zeitgenossen an Franz Liszt*. Leipzig: Breitkopf & Härtel, 1895–1904.

26. LaMARA [IDA MARIA LIPSIUS]: *Letters of Franz Liszt*, translated by Constance Bache. London: H. Grevel & Co.; 1894.

27. LaMARA [IDA MARIA LIPSIUS]: *Musikerbriefe aus fünf Jahrhunderten*. Leipzig: Breitkopf & Härtel [c. 1890].

28. LITZMANN, BERTHOLD: *Letters of Clara Schumann and Johannes Brahms*. London: Edward Arnold & Co.; New York: Longmans, Green & Co.; 1927.

29. MAHLER, ALMA MARIA: *Gustav Mahler Briefe*. Berlin: Paul Zsolnay Verlag; 1924.

30. MAHLER, ALMA MARIA: *Gustav Mahler, Erinnerungen und Briefe*. Amsterdam: Allert De Lange; 1940.

31. MARTINI, P. GIAMBATTISTA: *Carteggio Inedito*. Bologna: Nicola Zanchielli; 1888.

32. MASON, DANIEL GREGORY: *Music in My Time*. New York: The Macmillan Co.; 1938.

33. MAZZATINTI, G., and MANIS, F. E G.: *Lettere di G. Rossini.* Florence: G. Barbèra; 1902.

34. MENDELSSOHN-BARTHOLDY, PAUL and CARL: *Letters of Felix Mendelssohn Bartholdy*, translated by Lady Wallace. London: Longman, Green, Longman, Roberts & Green; 1864.

35. MUSSORGSKY, M. P.: *Letters to Golenishchev-Kutuzov.* Leningrad-Moscow: State Musical Publications; 1939.

36. MÜLLER, ERICH H.: *Heinrich Schütz, Gesammelte Briefe und Schriften.* Regensburg: Gustav Bosse Verlag; 1931.

37. MÜLLER, ERICH H.: *J. S. Bach, Gesammelte Briefe.* Regensburg: Gustav Bosse Verlag [1938].

38. MÜLLER, ERICH H.: *The Letters and Writings of George Frideric Handel.* London: Cassell & Co.; 1935.

39. NEWMARCH, ROSA: *Jean Sibelius.* Boston: C. C. Birchard & Co.; 1939.

40. NOHL, LUDWIG: *Letters of Distinguished Musicians*, translated by Lady Wallace. London: Longmans, Green and Co.; 1867.

41. OLLIVIER, DANIEL: *Correspondance de Liszt et de Madame d'Agoult.* Paris: Bernard Grasset; 1933.

42. OPIEŃSKI, HENRYK: *Listy Fryderyka Chopina.* Warsaw; 1937.

43. OREL, ALFRED: *Wiener Musikerbriefe aus Zwei Jahrhunderten.* Vienna: A. Harleben Verlag; 1925.

44. PINCHERLE, MARC: *Musiciens peints par eux-mêmes.* Paris; 1939.

45. PRELINGER, FRITZ: *Beethoven Sämtliche Briefe.* Vienna: C. W. Stern; 1907–10.

46. PROD'HOMME, J.-G.: *Écrits de musiciens.* Paris: Mercure de France, 1912.

47. PROMBAUM, SOPHIE: *Richard Wagner and the Seamstress.* New York: Frederick Ungar; 1941.

48. PRUNIÈRES, HENRY: *Monteverdi, His Life and Work.* New York: E. P. Dutton & Co.; 1926.

49. RADICIOTTI, GIUSEPPE: *Lettere Inedite di Celebri Musicisti.* Milan: G. Ricordi; 1892.

50. REESE, GUSTAVE: *A Birthday Offering to Carl Engel.* New York: G. Schirmer; 1943.

51. SCHMID, ERNST FRITZ: *Carl Philipp Emanuel Bach und seine Kammermusik*. Kassel: Bärenreiter Verlag; 1931.

52. SCHÜNEMANN, GEORG: *Friederich Bachs Briefwechsel mit Gerstenberg*. Bach Jahrbuch, 13. Jahrgang. Leipzig: Neuen Bachgesellschaft; 1916.

53. SELDEN-GOTH, G.: *Felix Mendelssohn Letters*. New York: Pantheon Books; 1945.

54. SERAUKY, WALTER: *Samuel Scheidt in seinen Briefen*. Halle: Gebauer-Schwetschke Verlag; 1937.

55. SLONIMSKY, NICOLAS: *Music since 1900*. New York: W. W. Norton & Co.; 1937.

56. SMYTH, ETHEL: *Beecham and Pharaoh*. London: Chapman & Hall; 1935.

57. STORCK, KARL: *The Letters of Robert Schumann*, translated by Hannah Bryant. London: John Murray; 1907.

58. TCHAIKOVSKY, MODEST: *Zhizn Petra Ilyicha Tchaikovskovo*. Moscow: Jurgenson; 1900, 1901, 1902.

59. TEIGE, KAREL: *Dopisy Smetanovy*. Prague: Urbanek; 1896.

60. TERRY, CHARLES SANFORD: *John Christian Bach*. London: Oxford University Press; 1929.

61. THAYER, ALEXANDER WHEELOCK: *The Life of Ludwig van Beethoven*, edited and revised by Henry Edward Krehbiel. New York: The Beethoven Association; 1921.

62. TIERSOT, JULIEN, *Lettres de musiciens*. Turin: Bocca; 1924.

63. WASIELWSKI, JOSEPH W. VON: *Life of Robert Schumann*, translated by A. L. Alger. Boston: Oliver Ditson Co.; 1871.

64. WERFEL, FRANZ, and STEFAN, PAUL: *Verdi, the Man in His Letters*, translated by Edward Downes. New York: L. B. Fischer; 1942.

65. ZHDANOV, V. A., and ZHEGIN, N. T.: *Perepiska s N. F. von Mekk*. Leningrad: Akademiya; 1934–6.

PERIODICALS, NEWSPAPERS, AND PAMPHLETS

66. *Christian Science Monitor*, January 18, 1919. Boston: The Christian Science Publishing Society.

67. *Hudební Revue*, Vol. III. Prague: Hudební Matice Umelecké Besedy; 1910.

68. *Monthly Musical Record*, August 1, 1902. London: Augener & Co., Vol. XXXII, no. 380.

69. *New Masses*, Vol. XLI, no. 4 (October 28, 1941). New York.

70. *New York Times*, August 11, 1935.

71. *Novyi Mir*, 1943, No. 4. Moscow: State Publishers.

72. *On Inspiration*, from the *Chesterian*. London: J. & W. Chester [1928].

73. *Revue des deux mondes*, April 1, 1936, Année 106. Paris.

74. *Revue musicale*, Numéro Spécial "Ernest Chausson," December 1, 1925. Paris.

75. *Revue musicale*, Numéro Spécial "Hommage à Maurice Ravel," December 1938. Paris.

76. *Rivista Musicale Italiana*, Vol. XII. Turin: Bocca; 1905.

77. *Rivista Musicale Italiana*, Vol. XX. Turin: Bocca; 1913.

78. *Rivista Musicale Italiana*, Vol. XXI. Turin: Bocca; 1914.

79. *Russkaya Mysl*, September 1910. Moscow.

80. *Zeitschrift der Internationalen Musikgesellschaft*, 3. Jahrgang. Leipzig: Breitkopf & Härtel; 1901–2.

AUTOGRAPHS

81. Archives of the Bakhrushin State Museum of Theatre in Moscow.

82. Library of Congress Music Division: Collection of Autographs.

83. National Orchestral Association files.

84. Private collection.

INDEX

[i]

A NOTE ON THE TYPE IN WHICH THIS BOOK IS SET

This book was set on the Linotype in Janson, a recutting made direct from the type cast from matrices (now in possession of the Stempel foundry, Frankfurt am Main) made by Anton Janson some time between 1660 and 1687.

Of Janson's origin nothing is known. He may have been a relative of Justus Janson, a printer of Danish birth who practised in Leipzig from 1614 to 1635. Some time between 1657 and 1668 Anton Janson, a punch-cutter and type-founder, bought from the Leipzig printer Johann Erich Hahn the type-foundry which had formerly been a part of the printing house of M. Friedrich Lankisch. Janson's types were first shown in a specimen sheet issued at Leipzig about 1675. Janson's successor, and perhaps his son-in-law, Johann Karl Edling, issued a specimen sheet of Janson types in 1689. His heirs sold the Janson matrices in Holland to Wolffgang Dietrich Erhardt.

Composed, printed, and bound by The Plimpton Press, Norwood, Massachusetts. The typographic and binding designs are by W. A. Dwiggins.